The Reformatic

Philip Pilkington

The Reformation in Economics

A Deconstruction and Reconstruction of Economic Theory

palgrave
macmillan

Philip Pilkington
GMO LLC
London, United Kingdom

ISBN 978-3-319-40756-2 ISBN 978-3-319-40757-9 (eBook)
DOI 10.1007/978-3-319-40757-9

Library of Congress Control Number: 2016953821

Printed on acid-free paper

This Palgrave Macmillan imprint is published by Springer Nature
The registered company is Springer International Publishing AG
The registered company address is: Gewerbestrasse 11, 6330 Cham, Switzerland

To the students who know in their hearts that something is rotten. For when pupils grow wiser than teachers the light of knowledge grows dim and the acidic mists of ignorance corrode all that is good and true.

Foreword

In this lucid, extremely lively book Philip Pilkington offers a radical critique of economics from within the profession. He does not hesitate to pulverise the great panjandrums of the discipline like Paul Samuelson, chief architect of the neoclassical synthesis of Keynesian and pre-Keynesian economics. He reserves special scorn for the Nobel Laureateocracy, which closes the profession to heterodoxy. His heroes are John Maynard Keynes, Hyman Minsky, George Shackle, Nicholas Kaldor, Mikhail Kalecki, Wynne Godley and George Soros, who, in their different ways, have opened up new paths of thought.

Philip Pikington's starting point is that economics is a 'contested subject firmly grounded in the humanities and should be taught as such'. This is in contrast to the usual division between politics and economics, in which politics is viewed as necessarily contested, whereas economics, being a science, leads to a 'shared consensus'. Pilkington has great fun demolishing economics' scientific claims, without denying that it can be useful in many contexts. In principle, economics should be as 'open' as any of the other humanities. But it retreats to closure via mathematics. The author emphasises the lure of mathematicisation, especially for 'men in lab coats'. Mathematics is a way of shutting down free enquiry, because the truth is contained in the mathematical model. The most famous of economists' constructs—Homo Economicus—is necessary to make mathematical models tractable. Pilkington quotes Robert Lucas: 'the game [is] to get logically consistent mathematical systems of various degrees of complexity'. Whether or how they relate to the real world is secondary.

Pilkington attributes economics' dogmatic turn to the marginal revolution of the late nineteenth century, which sought to build the world in its image of perfect efficiency. It assumed that people have 'static preferences which they order in line with their marginal utility'. This ignores the heterogeneity of behaviour grounded in contexts, reflexivity and uncertainty—in short, the fact that humans, by acting, make economies what they are. By ignoring these things marginalism became a 'convenient fantasy'. But worse, by assuming that all agents are clones of a single utility maximising agent (the Representative Agent construct of contemporary rational expectations theory), marginalism is inherently totalitarian. It is ideological, not in the sense of being Left or Right, but in treating the economy as a machine whose parts can be perfectly known.

So how, then, can economics be 'opened out'? The author's main proposal is to start with the macro-economy, not the micro-economy. The latter starts from the individual. This is, in principle, liberating, but marginalism sees individuals 'as robotic calculators that act exactly as the economics models and equations tell them how to act'. Paradoxically—and this will be a paradox for many readers—macro-economics is much more open, and therefore neutral, about the desirable type of society because it makes no assumptions about individual behaviour. It classifies people into very large groups, which are treated for analytical purposes as homogeneous, and studies the relationships between them. It does not assume or prescribe behaviour, but investigates the stability properties of the system as a whole, as revealed by the movement of aggregate quantities and relationships. This, of course, was in the pre-marginalist tradition of Ricardo and Marx, who studied the growth and decay of economies in terms of the class divisions between workers, capitalists and landlords and the forces determining the allocation of national income to wages, profits and rent. The assertion that there are no political implications in starting from the collective rather than the individual can, of course, be debated.

This is the main plot; but the book surveys the whole field of economics, and readers should not miss the sparkling discussion of Money and Prices in Chap. 6.

Pilkington's attempt to recast economics is underpinned by his understanding of the fundamental uncertainty which humans face in making their choices, the respect they are owed as they struggle to make the best they can of the situations in which they find themselves, and the need for a becoming modesty by economists as they themselves try to make sense of the human predicament. 'Everything we study as economists is ultimately the result of people making decisions in the face of an uncertain future'.

Robert Skidelsky
19 August 2016

Contents

List of Figures

List of Tables

CHAPTER 1

Introduction

For this prolepsis of being equal to God had blazed a trail for all philosophical knowledge and legislative justice. This forceful seizing was the first lie of the first attempt to displace our senses from simplicity in words, and to oversalt the peace of God on earth to the debauched taste of reason.

—*Johann Georg Hamann*

This is a book about economics. But it is also a book about human limitations and the difficulty of gaining true insight into the world around us. There is, in truth, no way of separating these two things from one other. To try to discuss economics without understanding the difficulty of applying it to the real world is to consign oneself to dealing with pure makings of our own imaginations. Much of economics at the time of writing is of this sort, although it is unclear such modes of thought should be called 'economics' and whether future generations will see them as such. There is every chance that the backward-looking eye of posterity will see much of what today's economic departments produce in the same way as we now see phrenology: a highly technical, but ultimately ridiculous pseudoscience constructed rather unconsciously to serve the political needs of the era. In the era when men claiming to be scientists felt the skull for bumps and used this to determine a man's character and his disposition, the political discourse of the day needed a justification for the racial superiority of the white man; today our present political discourse needs a Panglossian doctrine that promotes general ignorance, a technocratic language that

W.P. Pilkington, *The Reformation in Economics*,
DOI 10.1007/978-3-319-40757-9_1

can be deployed to cover up certain political aspects of governance and tells us that so long as we trust in those in charge everything will work itself out in the long-run.

But the personal motivations of the individual economist today is not primarily political—although it may well be secondarily political, whether that politics turns right or left—the primary motivation of the individual economist today is in search to answers to questions that they can barely formulate. These men and women, perhaps more than any other, are chasing a shadow that has been taunting mankind since the early days of the Enlightenment. This is the shadow of the *mathesis universalis*, the Universal Science expressed in the abstract language of mathematics. In this case, they aim at a Universal Science of Man. They want to capture Man's essence and understand what he will do today, tomorrow and the day after that. To some of us more humble beings that fell once upon a time onto this strange path, this may seem altogether too much to ask of our capacities for knowledge. And this book is undoubtedly written for them. But it is worth empathising to some extent with what these men and women seek in their daily activities. Is it a noble cause, this Universal Science of Man? Some might say that if it were not so fanciful, it might be. Others might say that it has roots in extreme totalitarian thinking and were it ever taken truly seriously, it would lead to a tyranny with those who espouse it conveniently at the helm. These are moral and political questions that will not be explored in too much detail in the present book.

What we seek to do here is more humble again. There is a sense today, nearly six years after an economic catastrophe that few still understand and only a few saw coming, that there is something rotten in economics. Something stinks and people are less inclined than ever to trust the funny little man standing next to the blackboard with his equations and his seemingly otherworldly answers to every social and economic problem that one can imagine. This is a healthy feeling and we as a society should promote and embrace it. A similar movement began over half a millennia ago questioning the men of mystery who dictated how people should live their lives from ivory towers; it was called the Reformation and it changed the world. But this book is not an updated version of Martin Luther's *Ninety-Five Theses.* We are not so much interested in the practices of the economists themselves, as to whether they engage in simony, in nepotism and—could it ever be thought?—the sale of indulgences to those countries that had or were in the process of committing grave sins. Rather, we are interested in how we gotten to where we are and how we can fix it.

The roots of the problems with contemporary economics run very deep indeed. In order to comprehend them, we must run the gamut from political motivations to questions of philosophy and methodology to the foundations of the underlying structure itself. When these roots have been exposed, we can then begin the process of digging them up so we can plant a new tree. In doing this, we do not hope to provide all the answers but merely a firm grounding, a shrub that can, given time, grow into something far more robust. Some of the material in this book is new but much of it has been excavated from the best work done in economics over the past two centuries, much of which was buried deep in the crevices where academic libraries keep the books marked 'Withdrawn'. Before we begin our journey, let us first briefly discuss some questions that the reader might have before proceeding.

Down with Mathematics?

The reader of this book will likely have flipped through the pages and seen something that may well have put them off reading it, namely, equations, dreaded equations. There are not many in what follows but there are certainly a handful. If you are one of those people whose eyes glaze over when they see linear algebra, who find that mathematics is not generally conducive to understanding the social world, then I would implore you: *please read on*. You are, in a sense, the perfect reader. Economics needs more people who distrust mathematics when applying thought to the social and economic world, not less. Indeed, as will be argued in a moment, the major problems with economics today arose out the mathematisation of the discipline, especially as it proceeded after the Second World War. Mathematics became to economics what Latin was to the stagnant priest-caste that Luther and other reformers attacked during the Reformation: a means not to clarify, but to obscure through intellectual intimidation. It ensured that the common man could not read the Bible and had to consult the priest and, perhaps, pay him alms.

So, why are there dreaded equations in what follows? Because—and I plead with the sceptical reader to give me the benefit of the doubt here—mathematics can, in certain very limited circumstance, be an opportune way of focusing the debate. It can give us a rather clear and precise conception of what we are talking about. Some aspects—by no means all aspects—of macroeconomics are quantifiable. Investments, profits, the interest rate—we can look the statistics for these things up and use this information to promote economic understanding. That these are quantifiable also means that, to a limited extent, we can conceive of them in mathematical form. It cannot be stressed enough, however, the limited extent to which this is the case. There are always, as we shall see in this book, non-quantifiable elements that play absolutely key roles in how the economy works. We can only utilise mathematics productively and to some very limited extent if we keep this in the forefront of our minds. In what follows, I have tried my best to do this.

In addition to this, I have written the chapters that do have equations in such a way that I believe they can be understood by those who do not want to bother with the mathematics. In the section of his *General Theory* which had extensive mathematics, Keynes wrote in a footnote (much to the chagrin of certain other people in the profession at the time): 'Those who (rightly) dislike algebra will lose little by omitting the first part of this chapter' (Keynes 1936a, b, Chapter 20). We are here trying to do something similar. The mathematics is there if the reader cares to understand it. But it is secondary to the argument which is purely textual. And if your eyes glaze over when you encounter the equations, fear not because so long as you have understood the text (and perhaps a few simple numerical examples provided), you will lose little.

The mathematisation of the discipline was perhaps the crucial turning point when economics began to become something entirely other to the study of the actual economy. It started in the late nineteenth century, but at that time many of those who pioneered the approach became ever more distrustful of doing so. They began to think that it would only lead to obscurity of argument and an inability to communicate properly either with other people or with the real world. Formulae would become synonymous with truth and the interrelation between ideas would become foggy and unclear. A false sense of clarity in the form of pristine equations would be substituted for clarity of thought. Alfred Marshall, a pioneer of mathematics in economics who nevertheless always hid it in footnotes, wrote of his distress in his later years in a letter to his friend.

> [I had] a growing feeling in the later years of my work at the subject that a good mathematical theorem dealing with economic hypotheses was very unlikely to be good economics: and I went more and more on the rules—(1) Use mathematics as a shorthand language, rather than an engine of

> inquiry. (2) Keep to them till you have done. (3) Translate into English. (4) Then illustrate by examples that are important in real life. (5) Burn the mathematics. (6) If you can't succeed in (4), burn (3). This last I did often. (Pigou ed. 1966 [1906], pp. 427–428)

The controversy around mathematics appears to have broken out in full force surrounding the issue of econometric estimation in the late 1930s and early 1940s. Econometric estimation, for those who do not know, is the practice of putting economic theories into mathematical form and then using them to make predictions based on available statistics. We will discuss this at some length in Chap. 10, but for the moment we should say that it is a desperately silly practice. Those who championed the econometric and mathematical approach were men whose names are not known today by anyone who is not deeply interested in the field. They were men like Jan Tinbergen, Oskar Lange, Jacob Marschak and Ragnar Frisch (Louçã 2007). Most of these men were social engineers of one form or another; all of them left-wing and some of them communist. The mood of the time, one reflected in the tendency to try to model the economy itself, was that society and the economy should be planned by men in lab coats. By this they often meant not simply broad government intervention but something more like micro-management of the institutions that people inhabit day-to-day from the top down. Despite the fact that many mathematical economic models today seem outwardly to be concerned with 'free markets', they all share this streak, especially in how they conceive that people (should?) act.

Most of the economists at the time were vehemently opposed to this. This was not a particularly left-wing or right-wing issue. On the left, John Maynard Keynes was horrified by what he was seeing develop, while, on the right, Friedrich von Hayek was warning that this was not the way forward. But it was probably Keynes who was the most coherent belligerent of the new approach. This is because before he began to write books on economics, Keynes had worked on the philosophy of probability theory, and probability theory was becoming a key component of the new mathematical approach (Keynes 1921). Keynes' extensive investigations into probability theory allowed him to perceive to what extent mathematical formalism could be applied for understanding society and the economy. He found that it was extremely limited in its ability to illuminate social problems. Keynes was not against statistics or anything like that—he was an early champion and expert—but he was very, very cautious about people who claimed that just because economics produces statistics these can be used in the same as numerical observations from experiments were used in the hard sciences. He was also keenly aware that certain tendencies towards mathematisation lead to a fogging of the mind. In a more diplomatic letter to one of the new mathematical economists (Keynes, as we shall see in later chapters, could be scathing about these new approaches), he wrote:

> Mathematical economics is such risky stuff as compared with nonmathematical economics, because one is deprived of one's intuition on the one hand, yet there are all kinds of unexpressed unavowed assumptions on the other. Thus I never put much trust in it unless it falls in with my own intuitions; and I am therefore grateful for an author who makes it easier for me to apply this check without too much hard work. (Keynes cited in Louçã 2007, p. 186)

This book is written in the spirit of Keynes. There is no inherent problem with jotting down a formula or an equation if this helps us clarify matters. But this must always be kept firmly in perspective, and these should never be relied upon as a crutch; indeed, it would be preferable for the reader to skip the equations than to take them up as something to lean their entire weight on. It is for this reason that much of the first half of the book is implicitly or explicitly about how we think about the economy and to what extent certain tools that work in other sciences work or do not work in economics.

Mathematics, like the high Latin of Luther's time, is a language. It is a language that facilitates greater precision in some instances and greater obscurity in others. For most issues economic, it promotes obscurity. When a language is used to obscure, it is used as a weapon by those who speak it to repress the voices of those who do not. A good deal of the history of the relationship between mathematics and the other social sciences in the latter half of the twentieth century can be read under this light. If there is anything that this book seeks to do, it is to help people realise that this is not what economics need be or should be. Frankly, we need more of those who speak the languages of the humanities—of philosophy, sociology and psychology—than we do people who speak the language of the engineers but lack the pragmatic spirit of the engineer who can see clearly that his methods cannot be deployed to understand those around him.

Before we proceed, a quick note on two of the formal expressions used in this book. The great Polish economist Michał Kalecki once said that economics was the 'science of confusing stocks and flows'. If he were alive during our time—the economic Dark Ages—he might have gone on to say that it was also the 'science of confusing identities and causal arguments'. This has a lot to do with the nature of the mathematical formalism that economists use. You see, there are two types of mathematical expressions in economics. One expression are what we call 'identities', while the other are what we call 'causal arguments'. An identity is a tautology that is true by definition. It is like an accounting norm. We use these a lot in macroeconomics. For example, the calculation of GDP is an accounting norm. Once we agree on what make up its components, there is no real debate about what the GDP figure for any given year is. Thus the GDP accounting norm is an identity. Think of it this way: if I hand you $100 and you perform work for me, my spending is equal, *by identity*, to your income. I spend $100 and you receive $100 in income. There is really no debate to be had here. When we equalise something in the form of an identity—that is, something true *by definition*—we will use the mathematical identity sign: ≡. As the reader can see, it is sort of like an equals sign but with an extra bar. So, in the example where I spend $100 and you receive it as income:

My Spending ? Your Income

Causal arguments are entirely different. They imply that one side of a given equation is determining the other side of the equation in some sort of causal manner. These are not true by definition but are rather hypotheses we form about reality. If I say that the interest rate offered by the bank will determine (or 'cause') the amount of money that you save at that bank, then I am making a causal argument, one. that is not true by definition and depends if your behaviour responds to the interest rate offered by the bank. These sorts of arguments are the ones we debate in economics and we will denote them in this book by the standard equals sign: =. So, in the case of our example above:

Bank Interest Rate = Your Savings *at* the Bank

Note that we also try to keep the 'variable' that causes the behaviour on the left-hand side. So, we read the equation from left-to-right. In the case of the above, we read: 'The bank interest rate causes you to save at the bank.'

These may seem like very simple issues, but they account for a lot of confusion in economics debates. Most economists are not properly trained to think about the difference between these in any meaningful way and this gives rise to a lot of needless confusion and sloppy thinking. Again, the profession has a tendency not to understand, in a shockingly large number of cases, what their mathematics actually purports to say. This has been noted in the past by many prominent economists like Joan Robinson, John Eatwell (Eatwell and Robinson 1973, pp. 216–217) and G.L.S. Shackle (1965, pp. 8–9). But contemporary economics has yet to reform itself in the teaching of many of these very basic aspects of the discipline. This accounts for much confusion, especially surrounding policy debate.

Did Keynes *Really* Say That?

The reader will perhaps already have noticed that this book will contain a lot of historical contextualisation. Indeed some chapters, like Chap. 3, will be predominantly concerned with this. This is first and foremost to give the reader a sense of what has gone wrong in economics and why it has gone wrong. Those who do not know history will only end up repeating it. This is one key reason why we must be clear about what forces were pushing towards the contemporary style of economics and what forces were pushing against. Without understanding this, we will be lost. Another reason we do this is because, frankly, those who have been buried six feet deep by the mainstream of the profession today sometimes had some wonderful insights. The plurality of thought that existed in economics from roughly the turn of the twentieth century to the 1960s was impressive and rather beautiful to behold. Reading books from that era not only give the reader a vision of what economics had been and what it could potentially be again but also opens doors to so many novel ways of thinking about things.

Today the manner in which the mainstream represses these insights is by claiming that 'True Science' proceeds through the diffusion of semi-anonymous, formalised ideas and that anything else is only so much religious exegesis.[1] To an outsider looking in this can quickly strike one as a tactical manoeuvre: a conscious decision to repress insights from the past that might undermine what has been taught today. While this may be the functional result of the repression, it is not the cause of it. Rather, many in the profession are too busy learning about and applying the latest mathematical gadgets to what they already know. New ideas are not really valued highly today in the profession; rather, what interests those who inhabit it is new ways of applying the old ideas. The more technically intimidating these are the better because this assures the profession that they are in a perpetual process of 'catching up' with other sciences.

But this is not the nature of the ideas or the material we deal with in economics. Because these ideas deal with humans engaged in decision-making, they must be treated for more like the material we deal with in other social sciences like psychology, sociology and philosophy. In these social sciences, it is well established that keen insights can be picked up in the work of previous thinkers. It is also keenly emphasised that different thinkers have different approaches to different problems and that these are not necessarily mutually exclusive. Thus, a person specialising in Kant and a person specialising in Hume can still argue today over whose ideas are superior, but, so long as we have no dog in the fight, we can see that what is really at issue here are two entirely different ways of looking at the world. What way we choose to look at the world is a personal matter, and, in relation to economics, the work of the past can inspire us in how we think. The effective book burning that has been undertaken by many within the profession today is one of the most vulgar intellectual activities on this side of the Dark Ages. The reason that we seek in this book to get a fairly firm grasp of who thought what and where ideas came from is that we are trying to push a more pluralist, humanist, Renaissance approach to the study of economics. At the time of writing, it is a dead discipline—cold, unable to move, lifeless—but it can be reinvigorated and made to flourish if people treat it as it should be treated.

Finally, there is the problem of cultic hero worship. This is another accusation that the mainstream throw at those who wish to have a diverse, historically informed discipline. When we point out that they are bastardising ideas by misinterpreting them and tearing them out of the context that they were originally cast within, we are accused of being in some sort of cult. 'Oh, so we should believe that Keynes was correct in his interpretation of "animal spirits" and that my approach is wrong', the besmirched mainstream economist will say on cue to criticisms of poor scholarship. 'But that is just an argument from authority. You say that we should believe that because Keynes said it. That is ridiculous.' It is true that we should never take what any given writer said as Pure Truth, but that does not mean that we should read a book and not understand what that writer means. In a sense, the latter is almost worse. Most of the criticisms based on poor scholarship have two targets. The first is to set the historical record straight. The second is to bring to the table certain important debates that were never truly resolved but that the mainstream of the profession acts as if they were.

Nevertheless, if you take the approach that the present author is taking, there will be good guys and bad guys. This is inevitable in trying to argue that something has gone terribly wrong with economics. What is more much of what could have been a more promising direction for economics is today associated for many people with the name John Maynard Keynes. This is because, if you examine the work of Keynes in any detail, he really did have a new conception for how economics should be done: conceptually, methodologically and technically. This new conception was not always clearly stated and it was not always internally consistent, but the bones of it were there. Of course, being people who care about the history of ideas, we will all suspect that Keynes did not lack predecessors, and some people who came after him made important contributions that were entirely absent in his work. All this is true. But, nevertheless, the man has become a sort of rallying point around which people who are interested in reforming economics gather.

There is an element of the need for a strong identity here. When you are entirely marginalised within your own profession, it can get rather lonely, and to be able to look to a figure in the past that the mainstream of the discipline pay lip service to as the most important economist of the twentieth century without understanding is something of a comfort. Perhaps this is a weakness of the critics but I would prefer to see it as a source of strength. There is always a danger that it can tip into cultic worship and that should be resolutely avoided. If anyone makes an argument not because of the quality of the arguments but because it can be found on page X of the *General Theory*—there are a few who do this, but they are very few indeed—they should be distrusted. If they, however, are making the argument because it is a good argument and are simply trying to give it historical context, this should be applauded for its consistency of scholarship, not subjected to derision for being some sort of religious devotion.

Towards a Reformation

Moving forward, how can a reformation of economics be carried out? Certainly, it will not be the result of one man, living or dead. Still less will it be the result of one book. But the forces do seem to be aligning today. Students are becoming increasingly aware that what is being taught to them in the classrooms is suspect. More than that: it is boring and unengaging. Those who are drawn to mainstream academic economics are typically not the type of people, frankly, who I would want working as economists (there are many exceptions to this rule, of course, but the truth must here be told).

The reformation will begin, it seems to me, as a renaissance. It will begin with people who distrust what the authorities of the educational system are teaching and who instead seek out learning on their own. They might be able to navigate the mainstream curriculum with some degree of irony to get their credentials. But their thoughts will be formed from outside of the academic institutions. There is a grand tradition of this, of course. Such people will be following in the footsteps of Da Vinci and Descartes and of the men who, spurned by useless doctors in the Middle Ages, worked hard to give us modern medicine.

The political institutions will change faster than the academic institutions in this regard. Fewer and fewer people in positions of power will believe in the old fairy tales. Rather, they will seek out new ways of looking at the world that actually prove to them useful and cogent. This is already taking place to an enormous degree at the time of writing. The internet is opening the way for this massively. The old factions are still with us at the time of writing, inhabiting some dark (and some not so dark) corners of the net, but they are stuck in an echo chamber of their own making. Students seem to be more interested in other avenues of pursuit and they are using the internet to form communities and study groups. What more than this can we say except that by the time we know that the reformation has taken place, it will have already have passed. So, the best thing to do is to focus on the here and now.

Note

1. This argument appears to have been generated by the current gatekeeper of the status quo, Paul Krugman (see Krugman 2012). The irony being, of course, that Krugman has readily admitted elsewhere

that much of his own work is based on ideas he had read in older books. This leads to many questions about how what might be called 'intellectual property' functions in the profession today.

References

Eatwell, J., & Robinson, J. (1973). *An introduction to modern economics*. UK: McGraw-Hill.

Keynes, J. M. (1921). *A treatise on probability*. USA: BN Publishing.

Keynes, J. M. (1936a). *The general theory of employment, money and interest*. http://www.marxists.org/reference/subject/economics/keynes/general-theory/

Keynes, J. M. (1936b). *Preface to the German edition of the general theory of employment, money and interest*. http://gutenberg.net.au/ebooks03/0300071h/printall.html

Krugman, P. (2012, March 27). Minsky and methodology. *The Conscience of a Liberal*. http://krugman.blogs.nytimes.com/2012/03/27/minksy-and-methodology-wonkish/

Louçã, F. (2007). *The years of high econometrics: A short history of the generation that reinvented economics*. USA: Routledge.

Pigou, A. C. (1966). *Memorials of Alfred Marshall*. USA: A. M. Kelley.

Shackle, G. L. S. (1965). *A scheme of economic theory*. UK: Cambridge University Press.

PART I

Ideology and Methodology

CHAPTER 2

Economics: Ideology or Rationalistic Inquiry?

They don't realize that we are bringing them the plague.

—Sigmund Freud to Carl Jung as the two men arrived in the USA.

Every age has its ideology and every political system its dogma. These ideologies and dogmas are systems of symbols that are endowed by those who uphold them with a mystique or aura of power. This mystique is drawn, during any particular period in history, from whatever field the educated public assume to have a monopoly on Truth. For centuries this field of Truth was religion; today it is increasingly so science. In saying this we are not equating religion and science. These are two entirely different systems of symbols which enquire into entirely different spheres of human existence—religion enquires into the otherworldly and what might be called the spiritual, while science enquires (most of the time) into the worldly and what might be called the physical. Rather, we are making the case that elements taken from either can be used to bolster an ideology. Elements from either can be turned into self-justifying tautological modes of reasoning the function of which is to put people firmly in their place, to tell them to shut up and to do what they are told. What results may superficially seem like religion or like science but is in fact no such thing. Ideologies properly understood, no matter how seemingly different the particular sources they draw upon, have more in common with each other than they do with their sources of authority.

W.P. Pilkington, *The Reformation in Economics*,
DOI 10.1007/978-3-319-40757-9_2

The object of inquiry of science is, broadly speaking, to form an understanding of what we might provisionally call the physical world. Ideology, on the other hand, does not really have an object of inquiry. The true goal of ideology is to channel and canalise thinking, to dictate what can and what cannot be said about how we live our lives at any given moment in time. This is how ideology overlaps with politics. Every good politician has some sort of story that he or she is telling his or her constituents about why things are the way they are and why we should be moving society in the direction that they dictate. When ideology enters politics, it typically does so in a most watered-down form. But there must always be a source, a fountainhead of learning from which the sound bites of the politician emerge. It is from this fountainhead that ideology exists in its most concentrated and powerful form and it is at this point in the ideological food chain that the limitations we place upon how we think exert the most of their power.

Against Change

The peculiar thing about ideologies is that they cannot, by the definition we here give them, point in the direction of change. Ideologies cannot militate for change because they are all about ordering and structuring how we think. To open the door to change would be to interfere with the tidy structure of thinking that the ideology seeks to impose. A political ideology may well vie against a rival political ideology for power—and in that sense it may try to produce an historical shift in the relative power balance between political ideologies—but it will not, by its very nature, seek out change in any meaningful sense. Rather, it will try to bend the historical winds to its own peculiar political whims. This is why, as we shall soon see, ideologies that have very similar, if not identical, foundations and structures can be used to justify political discourses that are the polar opposite of each other.

In a sense the message behind ideology as such is something akin to 'do not think'. An ideology seeks to provide the answers in such a way that there is no longer any point in asking questions. An ideologue, in a very real sense, is someone who seems to have all the answers but who does not appear to be very good at asking questions. Again, this puts the ideologue on a very different footing to the scientist, the philosopher or even the theologian. These people live to ask questions, to probe their fields of inquiry and to never let down their guard against the fact that we probably do not have all the answers. Ideologues may appear to ask questions, but they do so in such a way that presupposes the answers. Ideology poses questions in such a way that the answers flow naturally from the premises of the question. The manner in which ideology operates is rather similar to the pollster who biases their questionnaire by structuring the questions in such a way that they elicit a pre-determined answer. If a mother is asked by a pollster 'would you or would you not like for your child to receive excellent public education if we consider that the countries with the best public education systems have the highest scoring children?', she is likely, at that moment in time, to favour public education unless she has very strong views to the contrary. Likewise, ideology calls forth the answers to the questions it allows to be asked, more often than not, without the ideologue even realising it.

If people cannot ask questions, then change cannot take place. A regime that has all the answers can be imposed—and, indeed, if such a regime is thought to exist what on earth would be the point of questioning it? Questions that require answers can always be imposed from within the regime. The opposite of ideology then is inquiry proper. Inquiry proper is not driven by a desire to uphold the status quo but rather to pry away at it and see if it holds firm. Inquiry asks about the modes of thought themselves and tries to see whether they are operating in such a manner as to ensure a certain functionality in the way we live our lives. Are these modes of thought functioning to tie us down and hold us in place or are they helping us to move into the future? When they are doing the former, surely some sort of shaking up is required by those who can see that doctrines preaching Absolute Truth probably contain no inherent truth at all.

The first and foremost goal of an ideology is to provide a cover for what is really going on. History is nothing if not a series of events and ideologies try to capture these events in their totalising net. No contingency should be allowed to escape; every event must be firmly tied down and branded with the insignia of the ideology in question. Such a process distorts history in a very peculiar manner. It deprives it of its complexity and its lived reality and closes down discussion as to its meaning. When Orwell wrote of Winston Smith throwing offensive events down the memory hole in *1984*, he was really engaged in constructing a metaphor as to how ideology functions. But ideology is not a bureaucrat tossing newspaper articles into an incinerator. Rather, it is a mode of thinking that encourages people to screen their lived experiences and their memories and have them fit into a pre-established mould. In that sense, ideology is far more powerful than any particular bureaucrat covering up for a given government's excesses.

The key manner in which ideologies tie down history is to assume that it is deterministic. That is, to assume that it is subject to some Law or series of Laws. The ambiguity of the word 'law' becomes immediately obvious here. Is a law something that society imposes upon itself to promote order or is it something that is objectively true in the sense that the law of gravity is objectively true? Ideology is where these two distinct meanings of the term 'law' blend into one another. An ideology claims that history has objective laws akin to the law of gravitation, but in practice what it seeks to do is hand down laws as a King would to his subjects. Ideology says 'we must do this because it is inevitable', but what it means is 'we must do this because I say that we must do this'. The fact is, and this will be much explored in the following pages, that history is not subject to laws in the gravitational sense. Rather, it is a series of events upon which we must impose interpretations and which we must act in the face of. History is a process of change that human beings must navigate by coherently formulating their goals and trying to figure out the best way to achieve these. When ideology rules the day, people can no longer ask themselves what they want to achieve and are instead lured into a slumber and forced to dream dreams of being mere puppets of pre-determined processes that play out behind their backs. In this sense ideology seeks to take away from people the power to make their own decisions and formulate their own desires in a wholly free manner. If freedom of thought means anything, it is the freedom to think outside of ideological constraints.

Is Economics an Ideology?

Since its inception economics has, more often than not, been deployed as an ideology rather than as a mode on inquiry. This is rather unfortunate because it need not be an ideology at all but it would seem that the nature of the material that it deals with gives to economics a terrible tendency to degenerate into ideology. Economics deals very directly with how we should structure one of the most important sectors of our societies, namely, the sector of our societies that deals with production, consumption and distribution. Historically this has been tied up with all sorts of political questions and so economics has a tendency to fall quite regularly into ideology—whether that ideology be left-wing or right-wing is a secondary concern. But this need not be so. There is much in economics, properly conceived, that allows us to think quite freely. If we shun the idea that history is a deterministic process that plays out behind our backs, there is much of interest that economics has to offer. But this initial assumption, this assumption that history is not playing out according to some fixed Law or Laws, is key to ensuring that economics does not degenerate into ideology.

At the time of writing, economics has become more ideological than it has ever been in the past. Today it seeks nothing but to shut down questions and tell people to shut up. Even the manner in which it is taught has a certain greyness about it that reminds one of the authoritarian structures of a mid-century boy's boarding school. The problem sets that students are forced to work through, complete with silly puzzles about utility-maximising agents, have an aura of brainwashing to them: a sense of schoolmasterly disciplining of the mind for the sake of disciplining the mind. It is almost as if the student is being coerced into identifying with the utility-maximising agent within the puzzle and then working out what they *should* do given a certain set of choices. Such exercises cannot be anything but exercises in ideological training. The mystique generated by clothing them in mathematics gives them an authority that the student is cajoled into trusting. But at base they are simple ideological stories about how 'rational'—read: 'well-behaved' in the moral sense of the term—people *should* behave in any given situation. This becomes particularly obvious to anyone who has ever witnessed an instructor chastise him or herself for not living up the 'rational' ideal when they are questioned as to whether this is how they themselves behave. 'Alas!' says the devotee, 'This is not how I behave in my day-to-day life! If only I could be more rational! If only I were not a Fallen Being!' The religious-like tones of penance are rather striking indeed. In psychological terms, the student is required to substitute the utility-maximising agent fantasy into the psychic space where their ego-ideal operates.[1]

The roots of the ideological turn that economics has taken today can be traced back to the late nineteenth century and, not uncoincidentally, to the emergence of the image of the utility-maximising agent who we will deal with in more detail in a later chapter. This late nineteenth-century event is generally known today as the turn towards what we call 'marginalism'. Marginalism derives its name from the fact that it conceives of the economy as a means of allocating scarce resources in such a manner that the 'marginal' use of a given resource—that is, the last unit of this resource 'at the margin'—is used in the most effective manner deemed socially desirable. Marginalism might thus be defined as being the idea of how a society, given a number of scarce resources, might allocate these resources in line with a sort of perfect ideal of efficiency. The reader should note the ideological overtones here immediately: is this perfect society a thought experiment or is it thought to actually exist? We will deal with this in more detail when we come to examine the concept of 'equilibrium' in a later chapter, but for now suffice it to say that the marginalist position is far closer to the idea that this perfect society either exists or will come into being of its own accord than it is that this perfect society is a thought experiment. A thought experiment carries no ideological weight; in order for ideology to function, people must be assured that the ideology in some way mirrors the real world. And that is precisely what marginalism claims under a variety of different guises.

In the late nineteenth century, the marginalists found that if they reduced the world in such a way the thought experiments that they asserted were valid, representations of world could be treated using mathematical methods derived from the physics of the era. They took on these methods—methods which are still taught in the classroom today—in order to lend their ideology a cloak of mystical objectivity borrowed from the physical sciences (Mirowski 1991). People then assumed that because they were using a similar mathematical method to manipulate their variables as physics was using, the truth-value of the content of marginalism was the same as the truth-value of the content of physics. This reasoning, if one can call it such, is a bit like assuming that when a person dresses up like a policeman, they thereby gain the powers of arrest. Just because a discourse wears the same clothes as a sister discourse does not mean that the first discourse thereby gains the truth-value of the second discourse. To think otherwise is ridiculous in the extreme and is based on a most fundamental logical fallacy. But in the world of ideology, the ridiculous is often elevated to the status of the sublime.

We should be clear, however: marginalism was *not* forged as a defence of the status quo. It was an ideology that actively tried to intervene in how we structure our societies. Later on, when society had been reshaped to some extent along marginalist lines, it would become a defence of the status quo. But it did not start out this way. Early marginalists saw themselves as moral liberators. They saw themselves as following a broadly Enlightenment tradition of ever-progressing freedom and rationality. They saw many of the more traditional features of human society that prevailed in the Victorian Era as being components of an outmoded morality that needed to be overcome in order to give way to the liberating, progressive force of free individuals engaged in free exchange in free markets. Marginalism, like Marxism in the late nineteenth and early twentieth centuries, was a constructive project to be realised; it was only after components of the ideology had been firmly integrated into society that it became a defensive ideology that sought to maintain the status quo.

There were critics of this approach from the very beginning. Thorstein Veblen spilled a great deal of ink trying to expose what was going on (Veblen 1898). John Maynard Keynes too, a lifelong opponent of ideology in all its forms whose name will crop up again and again in the pages that follow, recognised that something fishy was going on in the gilded halls of the marginalists. He noted that marginalists like Francis Edgeworth had to treat people like simple atoms that were isolated from one another in order to apply the mathematical metaphors that they derived from physics. Keynes' training in philosophy told him that these were not reasonable hypotheses to make and that for this reason the edifice was likely based on foundations that would not allow it applicability to the study of the real world. He wrote:

> The atomic hypothesis which worked so splendidly in physics breaks down in psychics. We are faced at every turn with the problems of Organic Unity, of Discreteness, of Discontinuity … the whole is not equal to the sum of its parts, comparisons of quantity fail us, small changes produce large effects, the assumptions of a uniform and homogenous continuum are not satisfied. (Keynes quoted in Bateman 1989, p. 65)

Throughout this book we will try to explicate what Keynes meant in this quote. We will try to show what these problems are and the issues that they raise for economics. But for now it is enough to simply note that Keynes, like some other of his contemporaries, saw something rotten at the very core of marginalist theory. But he did not recognise it for what it was. Later in his life he would tease those who upheld these ideas and refer to the conclusions that they drew as 'nonsense', but he never managed to see that such modes of discourse serve an inherent function as ideology. Never did he see that the reason these unrealistic foundations were laid was to borrow authority from disciplines like physics which the educated public, quite rightly, assumed to contain a good deal of truth-value.

It should be clearly understood that marginalism was not and is not an inherently left-wing or right-wing doctrine. Many assume today that because most marginalists have a tendency to believe in some spectral entity called the 'free market' that the doctrine itself is inherently right-wing. In fact, many of its founders were firmly on the left. It became crystal clear in the 1930s that the doctrine was flexible in how it should be interpreted politically when a group of far left-wing marginalists including Oskar Lange, Abba Lerner and the well-known British Marxist economist Maurice Dobb made arguments that the doctrine could be used to build a centrally planned socialist system. In fact, this debate showed that certain aspects of the marginalist doctrine were far more suited to ideas about central planning than they were to ideas of so-called free markets. This is because to this day in the marginalist theoretical framework, prices all have to be set at a given moment in time for the system to function. The socialists reasoned that it was far more reasonable to assume that a central planner should set this system of prices than that society would set this system of prices left to themselves (Kirzner 1988). While the socialists were indeed correct and basically won the debate, this little incident was buried since the political discourse changed after the Second World War and students today are not typically informed that the theories they are learning might be a blueprint for a socialist future rather than a justification for free market capitalism.[2] In addition to this, many of the economists who contributed to the emergence of very heavy formalisation and the pseudo-empirical testing of marginalist theory were socialists—one of them, Jakob Marschak (the 'father of econometrics'), was an ex-Menshevik and thus, presumably, a communist. Many of the early mathematical heavy lifters strongly believed in building a centrally planned economy and thought that their work was a key step forward in doing so (Louçã 2007). If an honest history of the roots of contemporary economics is ever written, it will quickly be seen that the main components of what has come to be mainstream economics today were built by men who were consciously trying to promote large-scale and highly intrusive economic planning and social engineering.

The fact that marginalism generally became associated with right-wing politics in the last quarter of the twentieth century is wholly contingent on the fact that such right-wing politics became dominant. If there were ever a swing in politics back towards central planning as might happen, for instance, if there were a planetary-wide catastrophe, there seems little doubt that the central-planning interpretation of the marginalist ideology would quickly bubble up to the surface once more. The *modus operandi* of ideology at its purest is not, we must repeat, to justify a particular type of politics; rather, it is to justify the status quo. The genius of marginalism is that it can and will justify basically *any* system of economic organisation that expressly seeks to impose on the population some sort of micro-managed 'efficiency' criteria. Marginalism is, at its heart, a doctrine of control. Whether that control comes from the diktats of a central planner or from the 'reforms' of someone championing the so-called free market solution matters very little as all the ideology of marginalism seeks to do is cloak such impositions of power in a discourse of pseudo-scientific legitimacy.

Macroeconomics: A Break with Ideology

As already noted, Keynes was long suspicious of ideologies in all their forms. It was no surprise then that it is his name that is generally associated with the form of economics that sought to break with ideology, namely, macroeconomics. And as we shall try to document in this book: the changes that took place in economics after the Second World War were basically an attempt by the marginalists to domesticate macroeconomics and subordinate it to the ideology of marginalism. What then is the essence of macroeconomics? The term itself describes what the discipline aims at: *makro* is the Greek word for 'large' and so macroeconomics means something like 'large-economics'. This means that we are not dealing with economics on a small scale. We are not talking about the economics of individual behaviour, for example; rather, we are dealing with the economics of large groups. Again, many trace this back to Keynes. G.L.S. Shackle, for example, argued that Keynes' key innovation was in turning attention to the economics of large groups in a most immediate manner. Shackle wrote:

> Keynes's first constructive chapter, following his demolition work in Chapter 2 [of the *General Theory*], is the statement of macro-theory, a construction which treats aggregates as though they were simple variables of uniform composition. He was far from being the inventor of this idea, for the Quantity Theory of Money gathers every kind of object or service under the headings of 'transactions'. In Keynes, however, we have not merely the treating of diverse objects as units in a count, but the combining of many people's diverse feelings, reactions and intentions, or at least their resulting conduct, into a variable standing for the conduct of society, or a large sector of it, as a whole ... The macro-model of the *General Theory* does not emerge gradually as a hard-won solution but is explicitly adopted from the outset as though natural and inevitable. This bold and assured imposition of a method is Keynes's claim to be an innovator in respect of macroeconomics. (Shackle 1967, p. 144)

Shackle's characterisation of macroeconomics is a good one. The idea is to collect people into very large groups which we treat for analytical purposes as homogenous and to then try to understand any underlying relationships that govern their behaviour in relation to one another. If this is the essence of macroeconomic theory, then we can make a strong case that David Ricardo and Karl Marx were working in the same tradition. They too broke the economy down into large aggregates—in their case: social classes—and then explored the underlying relationships that tied the activities of these social classes together. It is better to say that *modern* macroeconomics began with Keynes.

Modern macroeconomics had another core component that was largely buried by the marginalist reaction to it after the Second World War. This was the fact that it was entirely neutral with regard to what sort of society it studied. The great idea behind Keynes' modern macroeconomics was that it could be applied to any sort of social organisation. The same basic principles could be applied to a communist society or to a capitalist one. Provided that the society used some sort of money—or, at least, some sort of credit and debit system—the principles of modern macroeconomics could be applied. Keynes noted this himself in the preface to the German edition of the *General Theory* when he wrote:

> The theory of aggregated production, which is the point of the following book, nevertheless can be much easier adapted to the conditions of a totalitarian state than the theory of production and distribution of a given production put forth under conditions of free competition and a large degree of laissez-faire. This is one of the reasons that justifies the fact that I call my theory a general theory. Since it is based on fewer hypotheses than the orthodox theory, it can accommodate itself all the easier to a wider field of varying conditions. Although I have, after all, worked it out with a view to the conditions prevailing in the Anglo-Saxon countries where a large degree of laissez-faire still prevails, nevertheless it remains applicable to situations in which state management is more pronounced. (Keynes 1936b)

This is to be understood rather differently from the fact that the ideology of marginalism could be applied to either centrally planned or 'free market' forms of economic organisation. While marginalism is politically flexible, it is not ideologically flexible. It seeks to build the world in its image. It has a very specific idea of how people (should?) behave and how resources should be allocated and it chastises any real-world economy or any real-world economic actors for not living up to these ideals. This is how it imposes itself as an ideology. For example, the marginalist theory cannot really be applied in a wartime economy in which the needs of the war machine are sovereign over the consumption desires of individuals. This is what Keynes is referring to above as a 'totalitarian' state as this is how the totalitarian states of that day ran their economies. Marginalism function as the ideology of a totalitarian state but only if it adhered to the ideas put forward in the marginalist doctrines about resource allocation and human behaviour. We have yet to see such a totalitarian state emerge, but if it ever did, one gets the sense that it would be the most intrusive ever conceived as it would have an explicit theory stating that, as we shall see in later chapters, humans behave like calculating passionless robots, and if real human beings failed to live up to this impossible ideal, we can only imagine that some sort of 'rationality police' would be waiting in the wings to bully them in conformity.

Macroeconomics, properly understood, is far more pragmatic. For proper macroeconomists it matters little how people behave or how a society distributes its resources. The key is to study the inherent stability of the system and how it can produce and reproduce itself. In this way it can really be applied to any sort of system. Macroeconomic principles can be applied to any form of social organisation provided that the people within that social organisation use money relations and/or basic systems of accounting (including debt accounting). Thus macroeconomics proper leaves effectively moral problems about how people behave and how resources are best distributed to the judgement of the macroeconomist. In this sense it is an extremely liberating discourse.

Taken together, these are the two core components of modern macroeconomics, namely, (1) the aggregation of various individuals into large wholes that are then studied in an abstract manner and (2) the attempt to come up with a framework that is largely neutral in respect to the type of social organisation that is being studied. By doing economic work in this manner, we can come up with some very broad tools to study economic aggregates that are very largely neutral in respect to their object of study. They merely judge the object of study, not in ideological terms, but rather in a detached manner that attempts to track cause and effect. Again, this threatens the marginalist narrative for two interrelated reasons.

First of all, it gives lie to their idea that social structures in some way conform to 'natural laws' that the marginalists have discovered and that if these 'naturalistic' social structures are disturbed by external interference—that is, by anyone who does not believe in the marginalist ideology—this will inevitably lead to worse outcomes because 'nature' has supposedly been violated. Secondly, the danger appears for marginalists that macroeconomic investigations might reveal that, left to itself, the system can break down due to tendencies towards disintegration and disorganisation that exist deep within it. The fact of the matter is that many of the systems that the marginalists study today *are* inherently unstable and any true study of them from the vantage point of good macroeconomic theory will reveal simple truth this rather quickly. The great macroeconomist Hyman Minsky best crystallised this observation when he remarked that stability within a capitalist system itself gives rise to instability. Such judgements do enormous damage to marginalist theory which effectively seeks to show that the status quo is inherently stable and will tend towards some sort of equilibrium outcome.

Breakout Box: The Power of Aggregation
To get a better idea of how macroeconomic theory examines the interdependence of people on one another by examining them as groups or aggregates, perhaps a few simple examples are in order. Consider a football stadium in which there are 100 seats in rows of 10. The seats are on a raised platform with a slight slope upwards and are running along one edge of the rectangular football pitch. Now imagine that the seats are full and are all taken up by people who are of the same height. We can use this simple example to highlight how the group has more powerful effects on the individual than the individual has on the group. This will show the interdependence of various group members on each other and, ultimately, on the group as a whole and it will also begin to show why the 'atomistic' mode of thought applied in marginalism is an incorrect. Below is a simple diagram of the stadium (Fig. 2.1).

Imagine now that when any one person who is not already in the front row stands up, they can get a better view of the football pitch. We mark the people in the front row with circles to show that unlike everyone else, standing up will not allow them to get a better view. But if the person in front of any other person stands up, the view of the latter person will be blocked and in order to regain their previous view, they too will have to stand up. Now consider the effects that

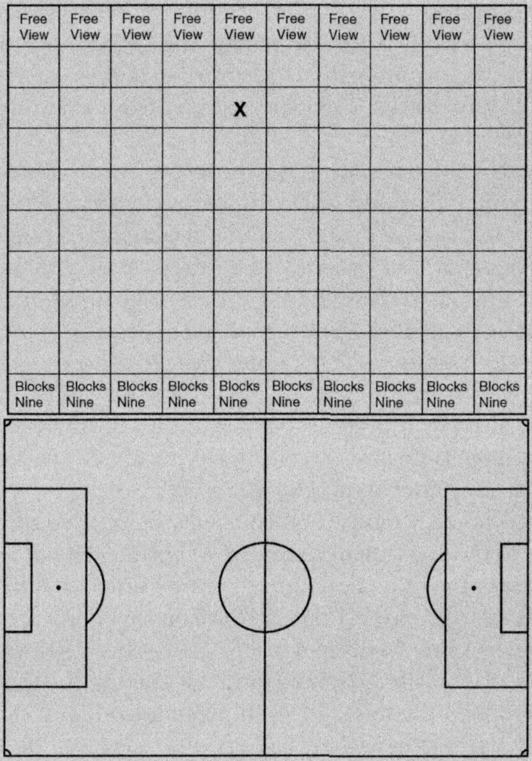

Fig. 2.1 The power of aggregation

each individual can have on the rest of the group. If an individual nearer the back of the rows of seats stands up to get a view, he or she will only cause a few other people to have to stand up. In the case of the individual we have marked with an X for example, their standing up will only lead to two other people having to stand up. The people at the very back of the group can stand up without obstructing the view of anyone else. They can get a better view for free, as it were.

As we move further to the front of the seats, each individual gains more 'power' over others in the group. The individuals in the front row of seats have the most power in this respect. If any of these individuals stand up, they will cause nine other individuals to have to stand up. Indeed, if the front row individuals all colluded with one another, they could cause the entire group to have to stand up. They could thus restrict any other person from standing up to gain a better view.

The point of this exercise is to show a number of things that are important when thinking about macroeconomics. First of all, the key message here is that 'we are all in it together'. Peoples' individual choices have effects on others and so they cannot be taken in isolation. As we aggregate people into different groups—for example, as we did when we assumed that those in the front row might collude to all stand up together—it becomes clear that they can have disproportionate effects on the rest of the group that others cannot have. As we have already said, if all those in the back row were to collude to stand up together, they would have no effect on the rest of the group—although they would all get a better view!

The best-known example of this sort of relationship in macroeconomics is the Keynesian 'paradox of thrift'. The idea behind the paradox of thrift is that all income spent by one individual is another individual's savings. So, if I take $100 from my bank account and go to the shop and buy $100 worth of goods, this $100 then becomes the savings of the shopkeeper (until he spends this and it accrues as someone else's savings). In such a situation if any one individual decides to try to increase their savings, they may well be able to do it. But if all the individuals in the economy try to increase their savings at the same time, then they will not be able to do so. Why? Because if everyone tries to increase their savings, then they will spend less and thus less income will accrue to others that these others can then save.

We find many such relationships in macroeconomics. Joseph Steindl noted one such relationship which he referred to as the 'paradox of debt'. If a small number of firms seek to decrease their debt-to-income ratio, they can spend less money on investment and instead use this money to pay down debt. If, however, a large number of firms try to do this at the same time, they will likely fail. This is because the decrease in investment expenditure will mean that there is less demand for goods and services within the economy as a whole. Thus, although the firms may decrease their debt by paying it down, their income as a whole will also decrease and thus their debt-to-income ratio will increase (O' Hara 1999, p. 831). The fact that in the aggregate their overall debt levels will decrease matters little because their overall income levels will fall and thus, in the aggregate, their debt-to-income ratios will rise because their income will decrease more than their debt.

Keynes saw that such a method of thinking was absolutely essential for the macroeconomic approach to the logic of economic systems. In his *Treatise on Probability*, which founded his basic approach to problems of logic, he spoke again of the problems with applying atomistic reasoning to complex structures like those studied in economics.

> The kind of fundamental assumption about the character of material laws, on which scientists appear commonly to act, seems to me to be [that] the system of the material universe must consist of bodies ... such that each of them exercises its own separate, independent, and invariable effect, a change of the total state being compounded of a number of separate changes each of which is solely due to a separate portion of the preceding state ... Yet there might well be quite different laws for wholes of different degrees of complexity, and laws of connection between complexes which could not be stated in terms of laws connecting individual parts ... If different wholes were subject to different laws qua wholes and not simply on account of and in proportion to the differences of their parts, knowledge of a part could not lead, it would seem, even to presumptive or probable knowledge as to its association with other parts ... These considerations do not show us a way by which we can justify induction ... No one supposes that a good induction can be arrived at merely by counting cases. The business of strengthening the argument chiefly consists in determining whether the alleged association is stable, when accompanying conditions are varied ... In my judgment, the practical usefulness of those modes of inference ... on which the boasted knowledge of modern science depends, can only exist ... if the universe of phenomena does in fact present those peculiar characteristics of atomism and limited variety which appears more and more clearly as the ultimate result to which material science is tending. (Keynes 1921, pp. 249–250)

Since this was written, scientists have become far more concerned with what have come to be known as 'emergent properties'—that is, properties that arise at the level of systems themselves and cannot be accounted for by the collective properties of each of the parts. Many supposed macroeconomists after Keynes, moving as they have in a marginalist direction since the end of the Second World War, have instead chosen to move in the opposite direction of science and have instead focused almost entirely on what they have come to call 'microfoundations' (see: King 2013). We will examine this in more methodological detail in the fourth chapter of this book and try to show that it is an instance where the 'atomic hypothesis' pushes itself to a point where it becomes incoherent and self-destructs, but suffice it to say for now that this is an instance where the marginalists have sought to completely absorb and neutralise the insights of macroeconomics and engulf it in their all-encompassing ideology.

The Potential for Macroeconomics

The potential for macroeconomics is enormous. Understood as a pragmatic discipline that dispassionately and with a minimum of *a priori* assumptions studies how the economy as a whole operates it has great prospects indeed. Purged of silly marginalist assumptions, it can become an extremely useful and practical tool. Not just for policymakers but for those who work in business and finance and, to a large extent, to those who simply want to read the newspaper and understand what is going on in the world around them. Let us try now to sketch out some basic rules for good macroeconomics that will be explored in more detail and put together into the skeleton of a coherent framework in the rest of this book.

We can perhaps summarise the cardinal rule of good macroeconomics in a single sentence: *good macroeconomics does not make strong assumptions about how people behave.* As far as possible, good macroeconomics should avoid altogether trying to describe the behaviour of people in any but the most abstract sense; motivation should be largely a secondary question and should only be raised when it is absolutely necessary. This is because this human behaviour is infinitely complex and is far better left to the psychologists, the anthropologists and the sociologists. What is more, human behaviour is heterogeneous, reflexive and subject to uncertainty. It is heterogeneous in the sense that every human being on the planet has a completely individual set of motivations and set of behaviours designed to take action based on these motivations. It is reflexive in that when academics come to think that they have finally come to understand a given general component of human behaviour, once the public hears of this discovery, they will likely change their behaviour in response to it. And it is subject to uncertainty in that people cannot know the future unless we are willing to leave behind the realm of rational discourse and set down along the path of the study of the paranormal. All of the arguments militate strongly against the fundamental precepts of marginalism without which it cannot exist.

Let us deal with the first of these arguments—that is, that human behaviour is heterogeneous. This basic fact would seem to me to be the most damning charge against marginalist economics in existence. It is more than likely the reason why mainstream economics has tried to insulate itself from other social sciences. The most relevant criticisms in this regard probably come from anthropology and dynamic psychology. Both of these disciplines show just how varied and changeable human motivation is. Anthropology shows us that people behave in different ways due to the cultural structures they live in, while dynamic psychology stresses the fact that peoples' motivations for any given action are due to impulses—mostly unconscious impulses—that have become ingrained in their personality due to past experiences and conflicts. Both disciplines also stress the idea that peoples' behaviours, both at a personal and at a cultural level, change and evolve through time and are in no sense static.

We should be very clear here about what we are saying and what we are not saying. We are not merely saying that every individual has different preferences. This, of course, is the foundation of marginalist theory and we shall examine it in more detail in Chap. 4. Rather, we are calling into question whether people weigh up these preferences in line with some rationalistic, cost–benefit analysis. In the terms of marginalism what we are here criticising is the idea that people have static preferences which they order in line with their marginal utility. Other social sciences that more immediately concern themselves with human behaviour have shown quite clearly that peoples' motivations have nothing to do with fixed preferences and the rational ordering of these preferences. In actual fact, peoples' motivations change almost by the minute.

Motivations are inherently context dependent, and people cannot be thought of as atomistic minds insulated from the outside world or Leibnizian monads closed off, without doors or windows, to everything around them. No other discipline that studies mankind—from psychology to evolutionary biology—would make such extreme claims. Only marginalists seem to get away with it. Nor is this a new criticism. In 1898, Thorstein Veblen noted this when he wrote:

> The hedonistic conception of man [that is, the marginalist conception of man] is that of a lightning calculator of pleasures and pains, who oscillates like a homogeneous globule of desire of happiness under the impulse of stimuli that shift him about the area but leave him intact ... He is an isolated, definitive human datum, in stable equilibrium except for the buffets of the impinging forces that displace him in one direction or another. Self-poised in elemental space, he spins symmetrically about his own spiritual axis until the parallelogram of forces bears down on him, whereupon he follows the line of the resultant (Veblen 1898, pp. 389–90).

Here we see Veblen criticising the inherently deterministic nature of marginalist microeconomics. Marginalism sees human beings as simply fixed bundles of preferences that are ordered in a manner that does not change. As the prices of the various goods in the bundle of preferences change, the human 'calculator', as Veblen calls it, is seen to substitute some goods for others in line with the aforementioned fixed preferences. So, it goes something like: 'I prefer 1 orange to 2 apples, but if the price of apples changes so that I get 3 apples rather than 1 orange I will choose the 3 apples.' This is an entirely absurd conception of human beings. Whether I want apples or oranges is entirely context dependent and is not subject to some sort of rational calculus. The demand for eggs, milk and flour rises on Pancake Tuesday not because the relative price of these goods falls but because peoples' preferences evolve through time—almost minute by minute. Consumers are in a constant state of flux and the same can be said for investors, both those who invest in real goods and services and those in the financial markets.

This is one of the reasons that Keynes and those who followed him away from the marginalist path simply do not deal with human behaviour directly. Rather, we leave that which determines, for example, investment decisions or financial asset-pricing or savings decisions by households up in the air to a very large extent. The only way to answer what is determining these things at any given moment in time is to plug into news, current events and the latest statistics and try as best you can to draw inferences. To try to establish some underlying timeless cause as to what leads to the human behaviour that underlines economic activity is a completely fruitless endeavour, and any theory that brings this to the forefront is bad economics. Those that adhere to such theories will have static, dogmatic views about economic policy and will be extremely bad at actual empirical economic work, which will merely become testing their models against the data in an altogether haphazard and methodologically blind manner (more on this in Chap. 10). If you come to economics looking for Holy Grails and Timeless Truths, you will make a poor economist. What you will end up doing will be ideology plain and simple, no matter how dressed up in the garb of social pseudo-engineering that might be.

Tied to this is the second fundamental defence of macroeconomics against marginalism, namely, that people are inherently reflexive in nature. When people have information about how they are expected to behave, they will change their behaviour in light of this new information. This can run in one of two directions. Some people might sometimes change their behaviour in accordance with how they are expected to behave. If a woman, for example, goes to a fortune teller to get advice on a potential boyfriend that she is unsure about and the fortune teller informs her that their fate is written in the stars and it is a happy one, then the woman might change her behaviour towards the potential boyfriend in light of this new information.[3] Other people might on occasion change their behaviour in opposition to the new information they receive. If, for example, an artist sees in the press that he is expected to come out with more work that closely resembles the work he has done before he might consciously react against this by trying to make his new work as different as possible from that which had come before.

The highly successful financial speculator George Soros has noted this tendency in financial markets and has made a great deal of money by exploiting it. He has even coined a term to describe it; he calls it 'reflexivity'. In his very aptly titled book *The Alchemy of Finance* (did you think that the fortune teller example was arbitrarily selected?), he writes:

> The process is fundamentally different from the processes that are studied by natural science. There, one set of facts follows another without any interference from thoughts or perceptions (although in quantum physics, observation introduces uncertainty). When a situation has thinking participants, the sequence of events does not lead directly from one set of facts to the next; rather, it connects facts to perceptions and perceptions to facts in a shoelace pattern. Thus, the concept of reflexivity yields a 'shoelace' theory of history. (Soros 1987, pp. 42–43)

This is very similar to the manner in which Keynes described, for example, the formation of expectations in the financial markets. He too saw that peoples' opinions had a self-reinforcing and dialectical quality to them in which cause and effect became entirely blurred, and it was not altogether clear who was exerting the influence and who was being influenced. In one of the most elegant and insightful passages in the whole of his *General Theory*, he wrote:

> [P]rofessional investment may be likened to those newspaper competitions in which the competitors have to pick out the six prettiest faces from a hundred photographs, the prize being awarded to the competitor whose choice most nearly corresponds to the average preferences of the competitors as a whole; so that each competitor has to pick, not those faces which he himself finds prettiest, but those which he thinks likeliest to catch the fancy of the other competitors, all of whom are looking at the problem from the same point of view. It is not a case of choosing those which, to the best of one's judgment, are really the prettiest, nor even those which average opinion genuinely thinks the prettiest. We have reached the third degree where we devote our intelligences to anticipating what average opinion expects the average opinion to be. And there are some, I believe, who practise the fourth, fifth and higher degrees. (Keynes 1936a, Chapter 12)

The third reason why macroeconomics should detach itself from supposed individual motivations is that people cannot know the future. This may appear to the reader to be a rather silly point, but at its most elementary level, microeconomic theory assumes that people know the future in some manner or other. At a most basic level, when marginalists discuss an equilibrium that takes place between two or more given economic actors, they are implicitly assuming that the future is known. They are typically assuming that all people involved have knowledge of what the other people are doing and that they all take decisions at a single moment in time while taking this knowledge of each other's actions into account (we will examine this in more detail in Chap. 6). G.L.S. Shackle discusses the unreality of this assumption and how it can be falsified by performing a simple psychological experiment on ourselves in his book *A Scheme of Economic Theory*. He writes:

> In stating the model we explicitly dispensed with the future, saying that our universe of discourse consisted only of immediate acts, and the outcomes of these, so far as relevant for their respective choosers, were unaffected by future acts. Yet in experience the meaning that any act of my own has for me depends on what I assume concerning the future acts of myself, other people

> and nature at large, perhaps to the end of my own lifetime and beyond. It is plain that any full study of the problem of how the necessary knowledge for rational action could conceivably be acquired, would have to consider future acts to be known. And this problem, in our context, has by its nature no solution. For the idea that two or more persons, with rival and conflicting interests, can in general have perfect foresight is self-contradictory, unless we assume complete determinism. But to assume determinism is to abolish choice. (Shackle 1965, p. 14)

As alluded to earlier, the other way of solving this problem is to assume that people have access to paranormal abilities that allow them to gaze into the future. This would allow them to make rational choices with regard to all future choices of other people. Despite being far, far outside the range of acceptable discourse, this still does not address the central paradox that Shackle highlights: namely, if we assume psychic abilities, we also assume that our choices are pre-determined, and if our theory of choice requires this, then it is not a theory of choice at all because there is, by definition of the fact that it is pre-determined, no such thing as free choice (we will explore the question of free will and choice in Appendix A).

The other manner in which marginalist theories attempt to overcome uncertainty in face of the future is with appeal to probabilistic risk. In this framework it is assumed that the future, although it cannot be known, can be predicted on a probabilistic basis. Each event becomes like a coin-toss or a dice-throw. Rational agents can then gaze into the future and map out these potential events. Again, this appears absurd when examined in any detail. What we are effectively saying is that I can assign a numerical probability—whether cardinal or ordinal—to, say, the chances that the world will have another major war by the year 2100 or the chance that we will have landed a man on Mars by the year 2050. Of course, these are such contingent events that I cannot assign any meaningful probability to them at all. Any opinion I express on either matter is completely subjective and giving this opinion a quasi-objective reference point in the form of a probability number is just charlatanism.[4] Besides, the idea that the world we inhabit is one of measurable probabilistic risk is just sneaking in the strong deterministic argument through the back door. Again, we are not truly making a choice in such world at all. Rather, we are being determined by an infinite series of known probability estimates. Rather than our fate being already written in the stars, we have written it ourselves on a blackboard or thumbed it into a calculator (we will explore these issues in more detail in Chap. 10). Once we have done this, we have eliminated choice and thus with it any idea of a theory of choice. Without for now getting into the ancient and interminable philosophical debate about whether humans have free choice or not, they certainly act as if they do and economists often speak as if they build 'theories of choice'. People are forced to act as if they have free choice because of the fact that they face an uncertain future. Any theory that ignores this simple fact of lived human consciousness is not a theory of human motivation but rather a convenient fantasy construction utilised to justify a mode of reasoning with no evidential tie to the real world.

These are the reasons that good macroeconomics avoids making rigid assumptions about peoples' behaviour and they are reasons that will be explored in more detail in the chapters that follow. If we could make such assumptions then we could make exact predictions about the direction of the economy. If we could do that most economists would be very rich men and women indeed because they could use these predictions to speculate on the financial markets. If, for example, they could make exact predictions of inflation two years hence based on a microfounded marginalist model in which an accurate model of human behaviour was set up, they could then make perfectly assured (and thus highly leveraged) financial bets based on this and could reap massive rewards. But the reality of the situation is that economists who use marginalist models are typically poor investors and not well tapped into the real world.[5] Rather, they make proclamations about policy and the state of the economy from a position of dogma. They may be listened to in their journals and by politicians who find their message convenient at any given moment in time, but no one with any skin in the game takes them seriously. This is a key point: the High Theory of contemporary economics is typically shunned by people who make high-stakes investment decisions in the financial markets; rather ironically, contemporary economics does not pass the test of the market that it itself sets up as the key criteria for social usefulness or utility.

Good macroeconomics is the study of aggregates in and of themselves without appealing too much to deterministic 'laws' that characterise the human decisions that underlie these aggregates. In this sense, good macroeconomics is more like an art than a science. Unlike the natural sciences, we cannot rely on much uniform regularity with regard to economic events, just as historians cannot rely on much uniformity with regard to historical matters. Nor can we expect any final answers on any given topic. This is because, whereas in the natural sciences we can formulate an hypothesis and then test it through experimentation with every subsequent experiment diminishing our doubt as to the hypothesis more and more, in economics we are not afforded with the ability to conduct reproducible and repeatable experiments. Nevertheless, there is some logic underlying economic events and trying to discern it is not unlike detective work in the vein of a Sherlock Holmes. Economic events, to paraphrase a famous quote, do not repeat themselves, but they do rhyme. That is what makes macroeconomics interesting and fun. It is a game of logic and wits with the ultimate goal of organising and reorganising society.

And so we are back to where we started. The marginalist mind in the wake of the macroeconomic threat desperately wants economic events to conform to some sort of Natural Law. They especially want this Natural Law to be grounded in the idea of rational human agents freely engaging in some sort of market activity. This allows marginalists to insist on the status quo. 'The economy is a delicate system', they will say, 'and we should not question its functioning. If we disturb it awful things will happen.' Good macroeconomics tells us otherwise. It tells us that, although there are some underlying logical connections within the system that can be explicated and studied, ultimately the economic system is whatever we make it. But good macroeconomics also tells us that we must construct this system within certain limits that are imposed by certain realities. We cannot have our cake and eat it. Too much purchasing power relative to the productive capacity of the economy, for example, will undoubtedly lead to inflation, and if our express goal is to increase purchasing power as best we can while minimising inflation, we cannot ignore this simple point of logic.

That is what good macroeconomics is all about. Its message is: 'There are many different ways—perhaps an infinity of different way—in which we can organise the manner in which we as a society produce and consume. But there are limits to how we can structure this if we have our goals explicitly formulated. There are trade-offs when it comes to social and economic policy and if we ignore them we will find ourselves in a right mess altogether.' One can readily see why the marginalist mind, so steeped in an ideology the function of which is to block change, finds this to be a truly dangerous idea. But it is an idea that is crucial to understand and appreciate if mankind is to realise and actualise its potential in the world.

In this chapter, we have given a brief overview of many of the arguments that follow in this book. We have done this to give the reader a better idea of what macroeconomics is and what it is not and also to understand what it can do and why it threatens the marginalist ideology. In the chapters that follow, we will explore some of these arguments in a more detailed manner and we will also put forward some arguments as to what bad economics is and why it became the way that it is. We will also lay out some basic tools and conceptions that can be used to think about the economy without making absurd and useless assumptions. Much of what follows is not new and the author does not pretend it to be. There is a wealth of interesting literature on economics published over the last two or three centuries. What this book seeks to do is provide both a skeleton of economic theory that the reader can cover with flesh themselves and also provide a contextualisation for economics as it currently stands that will hopefully contribute to the reader's ability to sort the wheat from the chaff. Economics, properly conceived, is a wonderful field of study and extremely socially useful. But those who practise it must constantly be on their guard against it degenerating into ideology. At present, the profession has an enormous apparatus to keep the current ideological state of the discipline afloat—from Nobel Prizes of dubious origins to a system of journals with strict but arbitrary publication rules—but at the time of writing, people are increasingly growing wary of this. In the following chapters, we will try to better understand what all this is about and, perhaps, go some way in trying to provide the basis from which we might change it.

Notes

1. The ego-ideal is generally understood as the inner representation of the self that a person would like to become. For example, a person obsessed with a certain celebrity to the point that they want to become that celebrity is an obvious case of a person who has inserted the image they hold of that celebrity into the psychic space where their ego-ideal operates.
2. The reader might be interested to note that it was out of the socialist calculation debate that the contemporary school of economics generally referred to as 'Austrian economics' was born. The Austrians like Ludwig von Mises and Friedrich von Hayek were horrified that socialists could use marginalist theory to justify and even design a centrally planned system. So they formed a new school of thought that championed the marginalist perspective but evacuated it of its mathematical content. By doing so, they made vague arguments about information processing to justify lack of government

intervention in the economy. The Austrian project was largely a failure. It tried to criticise mathematical marginalism for its mimicry of the mathematical form of the hard sciences but at the very same time used elements taken from the hard sciences (such as what Keynes called the 'atomic hypothesis') as the foundations of their theory. When one surveys the Austrian literature, one gets a sense of methodological opportunism. They criticise mimicry of science when this suits their purpose (which seems wholly political), but then mimic science when this suits their purpose. They talk about uncertainty and lack of information when it buttresses their case for 'free markets' but ignore it when it undermines their case for 'free markets'. It seems to the present writer that Austrian economics in its current form is the degeneration of marginalism from being an ideology to being an apology for a crude political vision.

3. A good psychologist, of course, would try to determine to what extent the fortune teller was simply feeding the woman back what she wanted to hear. That is, to what extent the fortune teller was picking up on discrete signals that the woman was laying down about what her desire in the matter truly was and then reinforcing these desires through a constructive narrative involving constellations and so forth. An even better psychologist would question whether the woman would have taken the fortune teller's advice at all should if the fortune teller had not told her exactly what she wanted to hear. That is, whether the woman was really just seeking out reinforcement and would have continued doing so until she had found it. Human behaviour, I hope the reader appreciates, is a very slippery eel indeed.
4. It should be noted that one stream of probability theory that has become popular with some economists recognises that all probabilities are subjective and not objective. This stream of probability theory is called Bayesianism after the mathematician Thomas Bayes. Some have thought that we might use Bayesian formulae to assess what rational agents might do. This is a complex issue that we will deal with in more detail in a later chapter, but even if we accept the Bayesian framework—this means ignoring the fact that the far future is not subject to probabilistic calculation—this does not solve the problem that we are here dealing with. The reason for this is that the Bayesian framework needs constant 'updating' to achieve more and more accurate probability estimates. But the equilibrium that we are

discussing is one that takes place at a given moment in time and thus there is no room for such updating to occur. Either all the probabilities are known in advance at a given point in time or the system does not function at all. There is no middle ground.

5. A particularly amusing example of this was when two leading Nobel Prize-winning financial economists, Myron Scholes and Robert Merton, were involved in the founding of a hedge fund called Long-Term Capital Management (LTCM) in 1994. Not exactly living up to its name, the fund did not last particularly long at all and caused financial losses that were so large that it had to be bailed out by the Federal Reserve in 2000. In 1997, Scholes and Merton were awarded the Nobel Prize for their derivative pricing theory just a year before LTCM started making losses of $4.8 bn in 1998. The key flaw of this derivative pricing theory was that it made the marginalist assumption that investors could calculate the future in line with known probability estimates (Haug and Taleb 2011, p. 98), something which we have already said to be untenable and which we shall criticise in more detail later in this book.

References

Bateman, B. W. (1989). "Human Logic" and Keynes's economics. *Eastern Economic Journal, 15*(1), 63–67.

Haug, E. G., & Taleb, N. N. (2011). Option traders use (very) sophisticated heuristics, never the black-Scholes-Merton formula. *Journal of Economic Behavior and Organization, 77*(2), 97–106.

Keynes, J. M. (1921). *A treatise on probability.* USA: BN Publishing.

Keynes, J. M. (1936a). *The general theory of employment, money and interest.* http://www.marxists.org/reference/subject/economics/keynes/general-theory/

Keynes, J. M. (1936b). *Preface to the German edition of the general theory of employment, money and interest.* http://gutenberg.net.au/ebooks03/0300071h/printall.html

King, J. E. (2013). *The microfoundations delusion.* Northampton, MA: Edward Elgar.

Kirzner, I. (1988). The economic calculation debate: Lessons for Austrians. *Review of Austrian Economics, 2,* 1–18. http://mises.org/document/437/Economic-Calculation-Debate-Lessons-for-Austrians-The

Louçã, F. (2007). *The years of high econometrics: A short history of the generation that reinvented economics.* USA: Routledge.

Mirowski, P. (1991). *More heat than light: Economics as social physics, physics as nature's economics.* US & UK: Cambridge University Press.

O' Hara, A. P. (Ed.). (1999). *Encyclopaedia of political economy: Volume II.* USA and UK: Routledge.

Shackle, G. L. S. (1965). *A scheme of economic theory.* UK: Cambridge University Press.

Shackle, G. L. S. (1967). *The years of high theory: Invention and tradition in economic thought 1926–1939.* UK: Cambridge University Press.

Soros, G. (1987). *The alchemy of finance: Reading the mind of the market.* USA: John Wiley & Sons.

Veblen, T. (1898). Why is economics not an evolutionary science? *Quarterly Journal of Economics, 12*(4), 373–397.

CHAPTER 3

The Limiting Principle: A Short History of Ideology in Twentieth-Century Economics

> *Too large a proportion of recent 'mathematical' economics are mere concoctions, as imprecise as the initial assumptions they rest on, which allow the author to lose sight of the complexities and interdependencies of the real world in a maze of pretentious and unhelpful symbols.*
>
> —*John Maynard Keynes*

There is a somewhat cheesy film that was released in 1988 called *They Live*. The film did rather well when it hit the box office but soon fell off the top slots. In the subsequent years, however, it gained a cult following. In *They Live*, a group of aliens that mask themselves as humans are engaged in manipulating people and forcing them through subliminal messages to consume, reproduce and generally accept the status quo. But then a drifter finds a box full of sunglasses that allow him to see through the subliminal messages. In a classic scene, the drifter looks out over a typical Los Angeles street scene with numerous billboards advertising various products, but when he puts on his special sunglasses, the glossy, appealing images on the billboards turn into white backgrounds on which is written in large type words such as 'submit', 'obey', 'consume' and 'watch TV'.

Although the film exaggerates the effects of advertising, it does raise an interesting idea, namely, that certain words and symbols in human language act in a manner the basic function of which is to control those who use them or hear them. In contemporary American politics at the time of writing, such words have become known as 'dog whistle' words.

W.P. Pilkington, *The Reformation in Economics*,
DOI 10.1007/978-3-319-40757-9_3

So, the term 'illegal' or 'illegal immigrant' usually refers to people of the Hispanic race, especially those that are viewed as being welfare claimants. These are usually associated with the right-wing of the political spectrum, but you can also find 'dog whistle' words on the left. What is fascinating here is that these words are not used, as we would suppose language to be used, primarily as a means of communication. Rather, they are used to rally the troops, to stir up political feeling amongst people and get them to change their opinions on sometimes unrelated topics.

Something very similar happens in academic discourse, but it operates in a far more subtle way. Although there probably do exist many words in this discourse that aim at rallying the troops, there is a far more insidious creation that the academic community—especially the academic community in North America—foist upon themselves. Let us call this creation the 'limiting principle'. The primary function of the limiting principle is to stifle thought. It is to limit what can and what cannot be thought. If an academic moves too far beyond the realm of acceptable discourse, a dog whistle term is used to rein them in. During the Cold War in North America, the key code word that was used to rein in unacceptable discourse, as we shall see, was 'Marxism' or 'communism'. The trick was to make this code word unacceptable across the spectrum and render suspect anyone who did not accept the basic premise that what it signified at any given moment in time was 'bad'. Thus if I were to say that your work was 'Marxist', this would mean that unless you could then defend yourself against this accusation I would fall under suspicion.

The genius of this is that I am able to put you on the defensive and gain control over the debate. If you say 'Stop talking such nonsense, you do not even know what that word means', you will be immediately rendered suspect. Rather, you have to provide a lengthy response detailing why you are not espousing Marxism or communism. In doing so, you will likely have to alter the way you think more so in line with what I want you to think. Or rather, more accurately, you will have to limit the manner in which you think in such a way that it fits into the frame that I want to keep your thoughts in. You may be able to think somewhat differently in the privacy of your own home. But the thoughts that you will be allowed to articulate will be limited by my interventions. Obviously, the old code words of the Cold War carried with them political overtones. If you were accused of Marxism or communism, you were presumably some sort of traitor to your country. But after the Cold War, a far more insidious code word slipped into the discourse of the limiting principle; this code word is 'postmodernism'. To be postmodern, you are not simply 'unfit' in your political opinions; rather, you are 'unfit' in the manner in which you reason. If I refer to you or your work as displaying aspects of what I define to be postmodernism, then I am implicitly accusing you of rejecting basically all advances in human knowledge that have taken place since the sixteenth or seventeenth century.

Again, there is no defence against this. It is a bit like a bully grabbing your hand, forcing you to hit yourself in the face and taunting you by saying that you should stop hitting yourself. If you say that it is the bully who is, in fact, forcing you to hit yourself he will only derive more power and dominance from the act. Similarly, if you say that the accusation of postmodernism is nonsense because the person making the accusation does not have a well-defined meaning of the term, or if you say that the person making the accusation does not have sufficient grounding in the debates surrounding Enlightenment reason to make prognostications on what 'rationality' means, you will only be rendered all the more suspect. The limiting principle preys on anti-intellectualism which is perhaps why it emerged with such force in North America in the twentieth century. Anyone who says things that sound 'too smart' can quickly be limited in their discourse through the use of whatever code word is active at the time.

In economics, the shock troops of the limiting principle are the more mediocre elements within the profession. These are the people who generally do not fully understand the principles underlying the system of thinking that they espouse. This, at some level, makes them anxious that their ignorance not be exposed and this makes them particularly drawn to the limiting principle. It is an extremely easy way to shut down any criticism, especially if that criticism is about an idea or set of ideas which the person in question claims to uphold but which, at a deep level, they know that they are ignorant of. Often the limiting principle is invoked in economics when you try to go 'behind the mathematics'. The manner in which much contemporary economics is taught is similar to the way that Latin was taught in the past, namely, by rote. The student learns off various formulas while remaining only dimly aware that the truth-value of these formulas is only as good as the assumptions they are built on. If a formula is built on nonsensical or self-contradictory premises, then even if the formula is perfectly coherent on its own terms, it is nevertheless nonsense. If you go 'behind the mathematics' and probe the underlying assumptions, the typical shock troop will get edgy rather quickly and invoke the limiting principle in some form or other.[1]

The Stirrings of Keynesianism in the USA

In what follows in this book, a good deal of what the author claims to be wrong with economics will be contrasted with work that is associated with the name of Keynes. But it is not the writer's intention to paint a picture of a discipline that was completely sick and was then cured of this sickness by a single man in 1936. Keynes made a great many contributions to progressing economics and was probably the most important economist of the twentieth century. But this does not mean that all that is now associated with his name was brought into their world by him personally. For strictly historical reasons that cannot be discussed in this book, many of the problems with the marginalist economics in the twentieth century were tackled in some way or other by Keynes and his work provides as good a starting point as any for trying to clear out all the nonsense from the marginalist framework. That this effort to sanitise the discipline of nonsense is associated with the name of Keynes is, to a very large extent, an historical accident. It is a convention that has become firmly established today, and, although it can sometimes (but more rarely than one might think) degenerate into uncritical cultic worship, I see no problem in provisionally accepting this narrative that has stuck so firmly. When it comes to such conventions, without doubt the best approach is *flectere si nequeo superos, Acheronta movebo*; if we cannot deflect the will of the Heavens, let us instead raise Hell.

In the 1930s, the world was crying out for some new approach to economic explanation. The marginalist theories, which were only just over half a century old at the time, told economists that intractable large-scale unemployment could not exist. After all, markets would always clear; a seller would always find a buyer at a given price; and the labour market was no different. Allow the price of labour—that is, wages—to fall sufficiently and all those who were unemployed would find work. In reality, however, this was not working out. In the 1930s, there seemed to be depression everywhere; everywhere, that is, except the Soviet Union and Nazi Germany where the State was providing people with direct employment. In the face of this, the youth were getting somewhat restless. Many of them were sympathetic that, faced with mass unemployment, the government should do something to help people.

In the UK, something was taking place around Keynes in Cambridge. Not only was he providing a coherent explanation for why this unemployment could take place but he was also, it was said, completely overturning the then dominant economic theory. A few Canadians who had previously been attending American universities made the trip to Cambridge to see what all the fuss was about. Robert Bryce and Lorie Tarshis were those who would then bring the intellectually revolutionary economics of Keynes to the shores of North America. But back in the USA, something altogether different was happening. Those who were observing the economic problems there were already ready and waiting for an alternative. But they were meanwhile becoming ever more steeped in the old marginalist ideas. While the Canadians were having their minds opened to new thoughts in Cambridge, many of the Americans were having their minds closed in university departments like Chicago.

The prime example of this, and the person who would go on to do the most damage to the new economics, was Paul Samuelson. Samuelson was torn between his political belief that the government should do something and his theoretical belief that the labour market should, indeed, adjust to the unemployment. He was a Chicago marginalist to the bone, but he sympathised with the charismatic politics of Roosevelt. In a 1986 interview, he said:

> My friends who were not economists regarded me as very conservative, a person who would debunk schemes for reform and things, because the system would take care of itself, or you would only make things worse. On the other hand I became very enthusiastic for Franklin Roosevelt. It was a little hard to explain how I could rationalize that. (Colander and Landreth 1996, p. 154)

While Samuelson could not seem to rationalise this discrepancy to himself, there is nevertheless a rather simple interpretation: he was enraptured by a charismatic politics that seemed to speak to the times. Reading the entire interview, this is what seems to have motivated Samuelson to create his interpretation of Keynesianism. He never found any actual logical problems with the economics he had been taught at Chicago—he was enamoured with it—but he found that during the 1930s and the 1940s, his politics began to conflict with his economics. So motivated he made a few alterations to the latter. These were, however, alterations that were logically incoherent, but Samuelson glossed over this, quite consciously, because of his political motivations.

He began to interpret Keynes as saying that wages would remain sticky in a recession—they would not adjust downward to make labour cheaper—and this is what accounted for the unemployment. That Keynes had written an entire chapter in his *General Theory* denying this mattered little (Keynes 1936a, Chapter 19),[2] this was the manner in which Samuelson and others would square the political message they liked in Keynes with the theory on which they had been reared on. Samuelson says this quite openly in the interview.

> What I resisted in Keynes the most was the notion that there could be equilibrium unemployment. I'd argue with Bob Bryce and discuss with Leontief, that first chapter [of the *General Theory*] where workers react to an increase in money wages from the way they react to a change in real wages that comes from inflation. The way I finally convinced myself was to just stop worrying about it. I asked myself: why do I want to refuse a paradigm that enables me to understand the Roosevelt upturn from 1933 to 1937? (Colander and Landreth 1996, p. 159)

Frankly, for anyone with a remotely honest scholarly mind, that is a shocking admission. Samuelson had not only interpreted Keynes' economics by reading the first chapter of the book—and, it would seem, ignoring the 19th chapter—but also accepted what he thought to be Keynes' economics based on his own politics. Think about this for a moment. Samuelson had half-understood the book. In his inability to understand it, he had found it to be incoherent. Then he turned around and accepted this incoherent formulation of his own making based on his own personal political inclinations. This is political opportunism at its most nauseating, and the fact that Samuelson would then go on to champion economics as a quite tidy and theoretically precise science is embarrassing in the extreme.[3]

As we shall see, what came to be referred to as Keynesianism in North America was the formalisation of this act of political propaganda. The American Keynesians never saw Keynes as having provided the building blocks for a new approach to economics. Rather, they saw the arguments as a good opportunity to rationalise their political inclinations. Intellectual constructions, as they so often do in the USA, became wholly subordinate to political ideology. Hereafter 'Keynesianism' in America was not a badge that one wore to distinguish one's economic theory. Instead, it became more like an election-day pin worn on one's lapel to signify that believed in a certain form of governance that had emerged with Roosevelt in the 1930s. This has continued on until the present day when the so-called differences between the 'saltwater' and the 'freshwater' schools of economics[4] are mainly based on the politics of the adherents.

Note that by this I do not mean to say anything about party affiliation. Recall that under the conservative presidency of George W. Bush, it was said by Republicans that 'deficits do not matter'. While under the liberal presidency of Bill Clinton, almost every policy was seen through the lens of how it affected the balanced budget. Conversely, during the Obama presidency at the time of writing, most liberals are in favour of Keynesian fiscal stimulus. There is no great consistency here if we simply consider the colour of the flag being waved, and what I mean when I say that the schools of economic thought are tied up with political ideology in the USA has nothing to do with party affiliation. Rather, what I mean is that in the USA, more than anywhere else, technical economic language is used in the place of political argument. How this language is used is an altogether more complex question and would require an entire book in its own right.

We can, however, be quite clear on *why* this language is used: it is because in the USA, there is an underlying discourse of political populism that has been in place since the founding of the country and which has never gone away. It is not surprising that this has never gone away considering that it is written into the language of the US constitution. This populist undercurrent scares the American elite to no end and the vast majority of official politics in that country is a sustained attempt to suppress this undercurrent. The most effective way to do this is to try to recast the frame of debate in pseudo-technical language in order to avoid the uncomfortable possibility that the population might become aware of the actual issues. The development of economics in the post-war years cannot be disentangled from the needs of the American political elite in that era.

The average American intellectual finds it rather easy to stomach the idea that the right-wing might use 'dog whistle' terms to stir the masses against their interests because most American intellectuals are left-leaning. This argument, put forward by the great American cultural historian Thomas Frank (2005), has gained rather a lot of traction on the American left. It is far harder for American intellectuals to recognise that the elite suppress populist sentient through the use of pseudo-technical language and terminology. This is because most of these same liberal intellectuals are the very people who make their living creating and disseminating this pseudo-technical language, as has been well documented by the other great recent American cultural historian Christopher Lasch (1996), and are thus actively employed in these acts of propaganda.

But before we turn to how this act of political propaganda on the part of Samuelson and the other American Keynesians was formalised and sold off by hucksters as science, let us first turn to what happened to the actual economics of Keynes when it briefly reared its head in the USA.

Lorie Tarshis and His 'Marxist' Textbook

By the time the Second World War had ended, there was an appetite for Keynesianism in the USA. Although the term was still taboo amongst the old guard, university students and forward-looking professors were ready to mount the barricades. They had seen the Depression cured by the war and they had also seen that budgets deficits could create economic growth. Perhaps nothing sold the Keynesian policies quite like the war. After all, about half of American GDP was government spending during the war and over half of that was funded by deficits. Factor in the soaring levels of economic growth in those years, it becomes very difficult indeed to counter the basic Keynesian story.

Lorie Tarshis, one of the Canadians who went over to be taught by Keynes at Cambridge, wrote a textbook that he published in 1947 entitled *The Elements of Economics*. Tarshis' textbook was proper Keynes. It was written in the spirit of the idea that economics had to be fundamentally and irrevocably changed. It was not heavy on mathematics, but it was extremely concerned with empirical examples, and theory took a backseat to the real world. What is more, Tarshis was overturning some extremely worn-out aspects of the old theory. In the introduction to the textbook, he writes:

> In keeping with my own preferences, I have tried to avoid introducing concepts which are immeasurable—for example, utility. I have also endeavoured to introduce statistical data where by doing so I could conveniently illustrate how, in my view, economic problems should be treated. (Tarshis 1947, p. X)

Tarshis wanted to throw out the old marginal utility framework and wanted to examine instead statistical data. This was not some Keynes–

Chicago hybrid. This was instead the essence of the Keynesian revolution in thought that was taking place at Cambridge in the 1930s. Tarshis' is not a textbook filled with intellectual puzzles and silly games; it is a textbook filled with practical examples and how to utilise them to undertake functional policy. He was also dismissive of many of the implicit moral arguments in the marginalist framework which we shall discuss later in this book. In this regard, for example, he thought the marginalist theory of distribution lacking and sought to replace it with one in which government policy played an active role in how the social product is shared among various groups in society.

> This book devotes less attention to distribution theory than most books do, chiefly because I am not satisfied that the problems which conventional distribution theory attempts to illuminate can possibly be handled apart from an analysis of the determination of the national income. How, for instance, can an acceptable wage theory be devised which is separated from a theory of employment? It is my sincere belief, however, that what is here said on these matters adds as much to an understanding of distribution as the more ambitious analysis contained in most texts. (Ibid.)

This was set to be a totally different textbook than the one that existed before the war. It was also set to be a totally different textbook to the one that we encounter in most economic classrooms today. There was high demand for it too. Everyone was scrambling to understand this beast called 'Keynesian economics' and so orders rushed in for Tarshis' textbook. In an interview in 1986, he said:

> When the book came out in—probably April of 1947—I kept getting glowing telegrams from the publisher. I thought, "Oh, my God, this is just beyond belief." The publisher was very happy ... I would get letters from my very conservative publisher saying Brown has adopted it, maybe Middlebury adopted it, Yale has adopted it—one place after another had adopted it. Every time I got a letter like this that indicated ten more adoptions or twenty more adoptions, I thought, "Boy, that bank account will be picking up." (Colander and Landreth 1996, p. 68)

But the success was short-lived. During the war, the right-wing in the USA got wind that Keynesianism was a left-wing set of ideas and that it was therefore dangerous. Whether or not Keynesianism is an inherently left-wing set of ideas—I for one do not think that it is—it is not hard to see why the right-wing thought that it might be. As we have seen, many economists in America *were* adopting Keynesianism as a cloak for their politics. They liked what Roosevelt was doing and they wanted to rationalise this with an appeal to an economic doctrine; even if they did not understand the doctrine and found that, in the contorted form in which they espoused it, it was completely incoherent, they nevertheless pushed it as hard as they could. And so the right-wing backlash ensued. One must remember that this is all taking place against the backdrop of McCarthyism. Many of those who supported Roosevelt's New Deal and even some in his administration were under attack by the right for being communists and Marxists. Thus those terms carried a certain weight in those years that they had not carried before and have not carried since. To be labelled a Red was, in some cases, to have one's career destroyed.

A now long-forgotten right-wing ideologue and children's book writer named Rose Wilder Lane started the assault by publishing a review of the textbook claiming that it had Marxist tones in a review of books sympathetic to her cause. This was followed by what appears to have been an organised right-wing campaign against the book wherein various people sent letters to the heads of university departments demanding that the book be removed. The universities were spooked by the backlash and removed the orders that they had placed for the book. The right saw this as an enormous victory. The pundit William F. Buckley Jr. wrote about the book in his account of his years at Yale *God and Man at Yale*. Tarshis' response makes clear the nature of the attacks on his book and his person.[5]

> That bastard Buckley—I get so angry when I think of him, because, you know, he's still parading his objectivity and concern for "moral values", and so on. The amount of distortion is enormous. He would pick a phrase and tack it onto a phrase two pages later, another page later, another page four pages earlier, and make a sentence that I couldn't recognize as anything I'd written—I was only able to see it when I had my book in front of me, and I could see where they came from—and make it seem as though I was no supporter of market capitalism, which I felt I always was. (Ibid.)

As we can see the right-wing had succeeded in using the limiting principle to suppress Tarshis. By the time the bullets had stopped flying, Tarshis was already in the position where he had to defend himself against the accusations of Marxism being hurled at him. But given that he was already on the back foot and the universities had already backed away, he had effectively lost the battle. Being immersed in US culture, the later American Keynesians would recognise that they would have to defend against such attacks in the future. Thus they would adopt a dog whistle of their own. They would become the ones to define what is and what is not science and they would then accuse anyone who disagreed with them of not being scientific. If and when the accusations of Marxism or communism came, they would use the defence of science in their favour to squirm away. The irony, of course, is that while Tarshis came to Keynesianism as an economist interested in ideas and not political ideology, the American Keynesians, as we have seen in the case of Samuelson, actually were using a false interpretation of Keynes to justify their political ideas. Such is the cynical and weary nature of what often passes for intellectual debate in the USA, unfortunately.

Paul Samuelson and His 'Scientific' Textbook

We have seen quite clearly that Samuelson turned to what he thought to be Keynesian economics for explicitly political reasons. Although it is impossible to prove or even properly substantiate a counterfactual, it seems likely that were it not for the political events of the 1930s and 1940s—from Hitler's rise to Roosevelt's reinvigorating fireside chats—Samuelson would have turned out to be a capable and enthusiastic proponent of Chicago school economics. But because of these events, he sought out a new economic framework to rationalise the opinions that he had already formed. He did this by picking up a vulgarised version of Keynes' theory which he derived from the first chapter of the *General Theory* and readily admitted was logically faulty. The next step was to polish this shabby doctrine up, marry it to the previously existing doctrines and veneer over the logical problems with a veneer of science. After this Samuelson would go on to begin to define what is and what is not science in economics; in doing so, he set himself up as the arbiter of what would become economics' new limiting principle.

There is perhaps nothing that fools students and the general public quite like mathematical expression. While it is true that mathematical expression can be used to clarify an argument—we will try to do this later in the book—more often in economics, it is used to obscure. Most of the mathematics deployed in economics is done with the unconscious intention of steamrolling over inconsistencies and nonsense. The more mathematics in an economics book or paper, the higher the likely degree of nonsense and lower the probability that the author is making a valid or even interesting economic argument. Nothing shows this better than the fact that Samuelson, the man who turned economics from a discipline that tinkered with mathematics into a mathematical discipline, himself said of the theory he spent his life expounding: 'The way I finally convinced myself [that the theory I believed in was not deeply flawed] was to just stop worrying about it. I asked myself: why do I want to refuse a paradigm that enables me to understand the Roosevelt upturn from 1933 to 1937?' (Colander and Lamberth 1996, p. 159). Samuelson simply tossed the problems aside, took his own position as Truth based on his political ideology and then went about casting a mathematical fog over the whole edifice. This he would come to call economic science.

Samuelson published his textbook in 1948, and it did not get nearly the same negative response as had Tarshis'. This was because Tarshis' was a readable book that did not hide what it was doing, but Samuelson's was one wrapped in an aura of mathematical mystery that lent it a false air of scientificness. The textbook went through some 14 editions and generated many clones. Basically, every economics textbook written between 1948 and today is a clone, in some sense or other, of Samuelson's. All the problem sets, all the diagrams, all the dubious uses of statistical data to back an obscure argument, all of this can be traced back to Samuelson.

After the books release, Samuelson began to dictate to an eager profession what constituted scientific argument in economics. Naturally, he never said 'arguments which you convince yourself of not because you think them cogent or consistent but rather because they buttress your political ideology', although that would, perhaps, have been more honest. Rather, he went first about banishing any discussion of methodology by disqualifying it as a realm unfit for anyone who aspired to be a scientist. 'Those who can, do science; those who can't prattle about its methodology', he wrote (Samuelson cited in Holcolmbe 2008, p. 61). This was not just about methodology. It went far deeper than that. As we shall see in the next chapter, this was the basic defence deployed whenever any unrealistic aspect of economic theory is challenged, especially by outsiders. It would develop into what is today the limiting principle by which economists insulate themselves from criticisms by accusing their interlocutor of 'postmodernism' or 'not engaging in science'. By defining what was science, Samuelson and his followers were able to roundly dismiss anyone they liked by accusing them of not doing science.[6]

Another key argument that Samuelson put forward as to what constitutes science is that in order to be a science, economics must assume ergodicity (Davidson 1996, p. 479). We will deal with this extensively in a later chapter, but it basically means that the future should, in some way, reflect the past. That is, it basically means that the future is like a kind of mechanism and can be studied using similar techniques to those used in engineering and physics. By allowing this to be a basis for economics to be a science, Samuelson effectively abolished any economic history that was not interpreted along mechanical lines as not constituting economic science. What he was implicitly saying here is that we should view economic history and any others approaches to economics that do not favour looking at the economy as a giant, pre-determined machine as below the sorts of theories that he was espousing in his lectures, books and papers. Given that he had already abolished the discussion of methodology, there was no way that anyone could question these judgements because if they tried to, Samuelson would, presumably, insist that they were doing methodology and that he was only interested in doing what he considered to be science from which he had, as we have seen, excluded methodology. There is a sinister circularity to the arguments put forward by Samuelson and all those economists who followed him which, to this day, encompass the vast majority of the profession. In adopting this sinister circularity, they have become insular and touchy, closed off not just from other disciplines but, to a very large extent, from reality.

It was not so much the substance of Samuelson's approach as it was the style that would infect the discipline in a manner in which it would never recover. In Samuelson's hand, every question became black and white; there was no room for any grey areas. The precision that he thus established was gained only by giving up any subtlety of nuance. In the wrong hands—and there is a good argument to make that Samuelson himself had rather clumsy hands in this regard—this device would quickly degenerate into dogmatic, authoritarian modes of thought. Wade Hands, who has done extensive archival work on Samuelson, summarised the latter's style rather nicely in a 2011 video interview with Perry Mehrling. Hands discusses how he examined Samuelson's letters to try to find how he struggled with various aspects of his theories. How he turned them over in his mind and tried to tarry with the wider issues associated with them. Whereas Hands had found this with many of the other thinkers, he had studied he found none of this with Samuelson.

> Samuelson didn't struggle with these things. His self-persona was of the 'objective scientist' bringing 'science' to bear on the questions he dealt with. He was obviously a Keynesian and had certain preferences but the aspect that I wanted to dig into was not there. You know, how he struggled with these ideas. I've written about Frank Knight in the past and you can read Knight's text and you can see his struggles. He will tell you: "We cannot reconcile these two things" and so on. Samuelson, however, would never do that. His approach was: "Theorem, proof, theorem, proof, theorem, proof" and everything comes out nicely with what you get at the end being what you put in in the beginning. (Hands 2011)

This was, in a very real way, what Samuelson gave to economics. He gave many economists the feeling that they were doing science. He gave them a self-confidence that, if you could lay out a theorem and then supply a proof, then you had reached some higher realm of economic Truth. That Samuelson was later surprised at what the New Classicals and the Rational Expectations theorists were doing, with their highly abstract and other-worldly 'theorem, proof' approach, show that he was either disingenuous or naïve about what he had given the profession. But this is the gift that he gave the profession and, while it stuck in the throats of some, it was eagerly swallowed by others who soon came to see themselves as objective practitioners of a discipline like engineering of physics. The only problem was that the foil in which these people wrapped themselves was paper-thin and any criticism of the formal properties of the discipline had to be met with ruthless repression. Through an informal network of journal referees, invented Nobel Prizes and conferences dissenters and heretics would have their voices silenced lest they threatened the almost hermetic closure that the profession gradually achieved in the latter half of the twentieth century.[7]

But Samuelson's crusade was not quite over yet. In order to gain full control over a discipline, bestow it with arbitrary authority and ensure that awkward questions are not asked, the key thing to do is to expunge the history of what has gone before. Like Winston Smith in Orwell's classic *1984*, Samuelson was to crack open the memory hole and cast all those embarrassing inconsistencies and difficulties. In order to do this, Samuelson proposed that we instead write a 'Whig history' of economic thought where every subsequent development was to be seen as an evolutionary step forward from the previous state of knowledge.[8] In a 1987 address to the *History of Economics Society*, Samuelson said, in his typical lab coat tone:

> When physics is in a vibrant state of progress, a Fermi is contemptuous of any preoccupation with the history of the subject. Thus, after he wrote up his Columbia lectures on thermodynamics for publication, he assigned a junior assistant the chore of filling in a few references. In the time you waste pondering over the paradoxes and foundations of the second law of thermodynamics, Fermi felt you might be discovering a new elementary particle or be theorizing concerning a neutrino that keeps total energy conserved. (Samuelson 1987, p. 51)

But of course economics is not physics. Einstein did not decide to revise the previous physics because he liked the programmes being undertaken by the German government of the day. But we know that Samuelson revised his previous theories in light of the Roosevelt administration's policies of which he was a fan. Despite this rather obvious difference—a difference that Samuelson spent a lifetime repressing through various intellectual means—something deeper was at issue here.

Recall that Samuelson gave this speech in 1987. In 1987, anti-Keynesian economics had reached its nadir and yet Samuelson, purportedly a Keynesian, was insisting at this moment in history that theoretical development only moved forward. Was this an inconsistency on Samuelson's part? It was probably not. When it came right down to it, Samuelson did not care much about Keynesian economics, at least now that the political winds had changed and there was no longer a Roosevelt to be enamoured with. What he did care about was giving the discipline a scientific air of pure objectivity. Whether or not the discipline deserves that air, it is ironic that Samuelson, who was clearly politically opportunistic in his theoretical constructions, was the man who thought that he should be the one to bestow it upon economics.

At the end of the day, one can only conclude that what really motivated Samuelson behind all the inconsistencies and all the politically opportunistic arguments was power and authority. Through the fog of all those inconsistencies, there really only remains one visible constant: the desire that he should be thought an objective scientist in the vein of a Mach or an Einstein. Everything else, it seems, was subordinated to this desire for authority—for the authority of science. But how can we lend such authority to a man who explicitly stated that he supported a theoretical programme, despite the inconsistencies he found with it, because he was enamoured with the politics that he thought it might be used to justify? And let us be clear this is not so much an attack on the person of Samuelson—although what he did to economics and the self-perception of economists was a crime—as it is an attack on the ideas that he disseminated. These are ideas that fog the judgements of economists, allow them to talk rank nonsense and perceive themselves in a manner which is really a well-concealed self-deception.

'Economics' Post-Samuelson

Samuelson's programme—for it was more so a programme then a textbook—was taken on with zeal by most of the profession. Yes, there were dissenters here and there—some of them even quite prominent—but for the most part, the profession became Samuelsonian. This began in the USA. Economics in the UK, Europe and Latin America, still under the influence of Keynes and the earlier methodologies, largely resisted the Samuelsonian thrust for about a generation. But for a wide variety of reasons which have yet to be documented, the teaching of economics seems to have moved more so in line with Samuelson's programme from around the mid- to late 1970s on. Why this occurred, as stated, has not yet been explored, but the primary motivation seems to have been to give the discipline a sheen of scientificness that the other social sciences lacked. Indeed, there was a large-scale political thrust in this direction which included, among other innovations, the invention of a Nobel Prize in Economics of questionable authenticity in 1969. Much of these developments were tied up, it would seem, with the campaign for central bank independence and giving the sense that the profession was a science of the same calibre as physics or chemistry greatly helped these campaigns (Mirowski 2011).

The substantial debates within the profession began to gradually wind down in the 1960s. The pivotal event in this regard was what came to be known as the Cambridge Capital Controversies. These debates were so known because they consisted of participants from Cambridge, UK—including Joan Robinson and Piero Sraffa (the British Keynesians)[9]—pitted against participants from Cambridge, Massachusetts (the American 'Keynesians')—including Samuelson himself and Robert Solow. Without getting too much into depth, the theories had to do with income distribution in capitalist economies. The Americans insisted that market capitalist economies, if they were left to themselves, would result in a homogenous distribution of income. Each factor of production—that is, labour and capital—would receive their 'fair share' in line with what they added to the productive capacity of the economy. The debate quickly became very technical, but at the end of the day, it was generally recognised that, on technical and logical grounds, the British Keynesians won the debate. The end result was that it was pretty much determined that income distribution in a capitalist economies could not be said to be determined by any objective 'market' forces (Harcourt 1972). This led many to conclude what they had long thought, namely, that income distribution is generally the result of political or class forces and that pure economics has rather little to say about this.

The British Keynesians accepted these debates on their own terms. Although they were deeply sceptical of many of the issues surrounding marginalist methodology (Robinson 1953) since the marginalists were unwilling to discuss methodology in depth, they agreed to partake in a debate on purely logical terms. In Samuelson's rather silly characterisation: they agreed to put aside methodology and 'do science'. In doing so, they then won the debate and assumed that this was the end of the marginalist distribution theory which was at the heart of the marginalist economics. But this is not at all what happened. Rather, what happened was that this controversy was gradually buried and forgotten. At first, Samuelson and other economists would still admit that there were serious problems with the distribution theory. In his textbooks, Samuelson would include notes that stated that the distribution theory was still in an unsettled state, but after a few more editions of the book, as the profession gradually began forgetting the incident, he removed these notes (Vienneau 2008). Meanwhile the rest of the profession, barring a few dissenters, simply stopped discussing the debates and later generations would never even be made aware that they took place.

Those involved in the debate on the American side convinced themselves that it was all about politics. Even though they had lost the debate on purely logical terms, they invoked the old limiting principle and chalked the opponents up as 'Marxists'. Thus they implied that because the motivations of those who attacked the distribution theory were 'impure', then the debate was moot and need not further be discussed. Robert Solow in his Nobel Prize lecture told his professional colleagues this in no uncertain terms:

> [In the 1960s] I was already trapped in the famous "Cambridge controversy". I use the word "trapped" because that whole episode now seems to me to have been a waste of time, a playing-out of ideological games in the language of analytical economics. (Solow 1987)

What this incident heralded was the moment when economics became closed to debate. From this point, moving forward economics would hide behind its algebra. This algebra would no longer be 'cracked open' and the concepts the algebra represented would no longer be discussed. Rather, everything would be taken on authority. Theories would be discussed, but the connections between various aspects of the theories would be poorly articulated or understood. What was the relationship between the efficient markets hypothesis in financial theory and the interest rate in macroeconomic theory? No one would say. What implication did the famous 'no trade theory' in finance have on the IS-LM model? Again, silence.

In the confusion, Robert Lucas slipped in his now famous 'critique'. He raised the question of why macroeconomics was not reducible to microeconomics. 'Why', he asked, 'weren't the rational agents of micro theory visible in the great macro constructions?' The answer, of course, was that the macro constructions were incompatible with contemporary micro theory and that people like Samuelson—who had realised this already in the 1930s but veneered over it—had engaged in a shell game when putting together economics after the Second World War (recall that Tarshis said that he had no time for utility-maximisation theory). Lucas then ushered in the era of microfoundations and economics began to completely lose its connection to the real world. Now the game played was to try to get logically consistent mathematical systems of various degrees of complexity. There was no longer a question of what these systems mean in applied terms—methodology had been banished, remember?—and so economists went about their games and turned away from reality.

At this point, we are talking somewhere around the mid-1980s by the time this had truly seeped in, and economics was dead as a doornail. Samuelson had won. His programme had been carried out. No one questioned anything. Everyone just focused on the simplistic logic. 'Theorem, proof, theorem, proof, theorem, proof'. Every graduate student became a little Paul Samuelson. Methodology was ignored. The real world was ignored. Logical debate, beyond a certain point, was ignored. The question of how politics, ideology and economics comingled was ignored. And this is where the new limiting principle came into play. These people, ever more sensitive to interruptions of the real world, came up with the term 'postmodernism' to criticise anyone who questioned what was going on. The irony being, of course, that if the term 'postmodern' means anything, it means the proliferation of meaningless symbols which is exactly what these practitioners of mathematical pseudo-economics do. They proliferate meaningless symbols behind which they stand and pontificate on issues they know literally nothing about.

The older limiting principle had not quite given up the ghost quite yet though. In 2014, students across the world began to protest the state of the discipline they were studying. They felt, rightly, that there existed in the discipline a monoculture and that they were not learning things that would prove useful to them in the real world. They launched a manifesto, a call for the curriculum to be reformed (PCSC 2014). The curriculum, read properly, is a call for a De-Samuelsonisation of the curriculum. They wanted methodology; they wanted history of thought; they wanted a variety of voices producing different cadences rather than a single chorus all singing from the same textbook. John Kay, a popular columnist for the *Financial Times* and a professor at LSE, while agreeing with the students on many issues, nevertheless warned them against listening to certain undesirable groups. He wrote:

> Their demand for more pluralism in the economics curriculum is well made. Yet much of the "heterodox economics" the Manchester students suggest including is flaky, the creation of people with their own political agenda, whether Marxist or neoliberal; or of those who cannot do the mathematics the dominant rational choice paradigm requires. (Kay 2014)

In doing so, Kay combined two key limiting principles in one sentence. He told the world that many of those who disagreed with the dominant economic paradigm were Marxists, and the rest, well they just were not cut out to do the mathematics that 'science' required. Like the drifter in *They Live*, we should put on our sunglasses and read Kay's words again. The pink background of the *Financial Times* on which they were printed fades into whiteness and the small text coagulates into larger font that reads: 'submit', 'obey', 'do your problem set' and 'read your textbook'.

Appendix: Arrogance and Pretentiousness in Economic Punditry

Samuelson's attempt to rewrite economic theory in line with his political affiliations was completely inexcusable and intellectually dishonest. But from time to time, economists find themselves engaged in punditry of a far less toxic nature. For whatever reason, they sometimes find themselves in a position where they make arguments in favour of or against a certain politician or political party. What is so amusing about this is that the discourse quickly defends into farce. It is in these discussions that we realise the true imprecision of economic science—and the silliness, self-importance and chest-puffing with which the economists try to knock one another. The latter is, of course, a function of the former. It is the insecurity about the discipline that generates the clownish overcompensation.

At the time of writing, a heated political battle rages. Bernie Sanders, a socialist senator from Vermont, is fighting the well-known former Secretary of State Hillary Clinton for the Democratic Party nomination. As the polls draw ever closer, the debate becomes ever more heated, with both sides calling to arms as many foot soldiers as they can muster. Gerald Friedman, a Post-Keynesian professor from the University of Massachusetts (UMASS), fired the first shot. His was a positive evaluation of Bernie Sanders' economic proposals (Friedman 2016) warmly entitled 'What Would Sanders Do?' The document itself is not at all awful. It uses simple, well-explained methods in order to derive its estimates. But it is, at the end of the day, a clever piece of public relations; it is, as are all such estimates, political theatre.

To what extent does Friedman, at the time of writing, believe his estimates? I have no idea. But they are unlikely to be in any way accurate. I suspect that Friedman would readily admit that these were vague estimates, as contingent as the assumptions that they rested it—the style of the paper reflects this. He threw down the gauntlet. Let the others say what they will.

The response from the 'establishment' was as humorous as it was pretentious. Some former members of the President's Council of Economic Advisers (CEA) drafted a letter. They indicated that they had all been members of the council under either Bill Clinton or Barack Obama. They then went on to attack the proposal as being filled with 'fantastical claims'. Yes, these advisers were probably Clinton supporters; yes, they were probably threatened by the 'anti-establishment' candidacy of Bernie Sanders as they were such firmly established figures. But there was something deeper at work. The authors of the letter first take a shot at their Republican rivals:

> When Republicans have proposed large tax cuts for the wealthy and asserted that those tax cuts would pay for themselves we have shown that the economic facts do not support these fantastical claims. (D'Andrea Tyson et al. 2016)

'Aha', the reader says to themselves, 'this is just politics! I know this game!' But not so—at least not according to the authors. The authors, like most mainstream economists, take themselves altogether too seriously. They do not see themselves as just one political soldier firing slings and arrows on a larger battlefield. No. They see themselves as defenders of Integrity and Truth. They continue:

> We have applied the same rigor to proposals by Democrats, and worked to ensure that forecasts of the effects of proposed economic policies, from investment in infrastructure, to education and training, to health care reforms, are grounded in economic evidence. Largely as a result of efforts like these, the Democratic party has rightfully earned a reputation for responsibly estimating the effects of economic policies. (Ibid.)

You see, these authors are not simply partisan political economists. No, no, no—they are defenders of 'evidence' and 'rigor'. They even make the grandiose claim that the Democratic Party has 'earned a reputation' for just this (amongst whom?, we might ask—surely not among Republican voters!). They then go on to exclude Friedman from the club. They are the defenders of 'rigor' and 'evidence'—Enlightenment Reason, perhaps?; Friedman is just a sloppy dreamer—a Romantic postmodernist, perhaps?

> We are concerned to see the Sanders campaign citing extreme claims by Gerald Friedman about the effect of Senator Sanders's economic plan—claims that cannot be supported by the economic evidence. (Ibid.)

Ah, there is that elusive 'evidence' again. In fact, Friedman's paper was full of evidence. Probably, this evidence was pulled from the very same data sources as the ex-CEA economists used. It was simply interpreted differently. Rather than recognising that Friedman had a different *interpretation* of the evidence, the CEA economists assured us that he simply had no grasp on the *evidence*. The ex-CEA economists do not even know what they are arguing about. In their self-important delusion, they confuse their interpretation and projection of data with 'evidence'—just as they likely did when they faced off with Republican economists. But it is not evidence. The data is evidence—and *only* the data—everything else is interpretation. At a more fundamental level, the ex-CEA economists seem unable to distinguish between their political biases and what the data can and cannot tell us. This is a distinction that seems to slip away from some people after they have been surrounded by people of like-mind for too long.

An interesting question to ask would be what the actual evidence tells us about the ex-CEA economists. After all, the CEA produces annual forecasts for a variety of variables. Now that time has passed, we have accumulated evidence—*real evidence*—on how robust these forecasts proved to be. Figure 3.1 lays out the CEA forecasts under Bill Clinton and Barack Obama against the actual data.

As we can see, the forecasts consistently missed the mark, often by a very large amount. This is not really the fault of the CEA. Forecasting economic variables like GDP, as we shall explore in more detail later in this book, is basically impossible. But good economists should realise this. They should see such forecasts for what they are: public relations. It is not when economists make overly optimistic forecasts that they should be chastised as much as when they start to think that they can make 'objective' or accurate forecasts at all. It is at this stage that they become deluded, arrogant and pretentious. It is at this stage they start to turn economics from a useful tool into a pseudoscience—and with it themselves from disinterested observers into useful tools.

Samuelson set this trend. He made alterations to the worldviews of a significant numbers of economists—and in doing so rendered these worldviews deeply inconsistent—because of a political love affair with FDR. At the time of writing, economists do this every day. They may not be as inclined to skate over serious logical inconsistencies in their theories to satisfy their political stomach, but they are often encouraged to drop good sense, puff up their chests and declare themselves Kings and Queens of Truth when they undertake what they seem to think of as empirical analyses. Such is a title that every honest economist should strive to reject. By all means make some projections for your favourite politicians. By all means paint the rosiest picture possible. And while you're at it if you actually get an impulse to do something serious maybe help design some policy. But for the love of all things decent, please refrain from donning yourself with the robe of Truth and pontificating about the future as if you had a crystal ball.

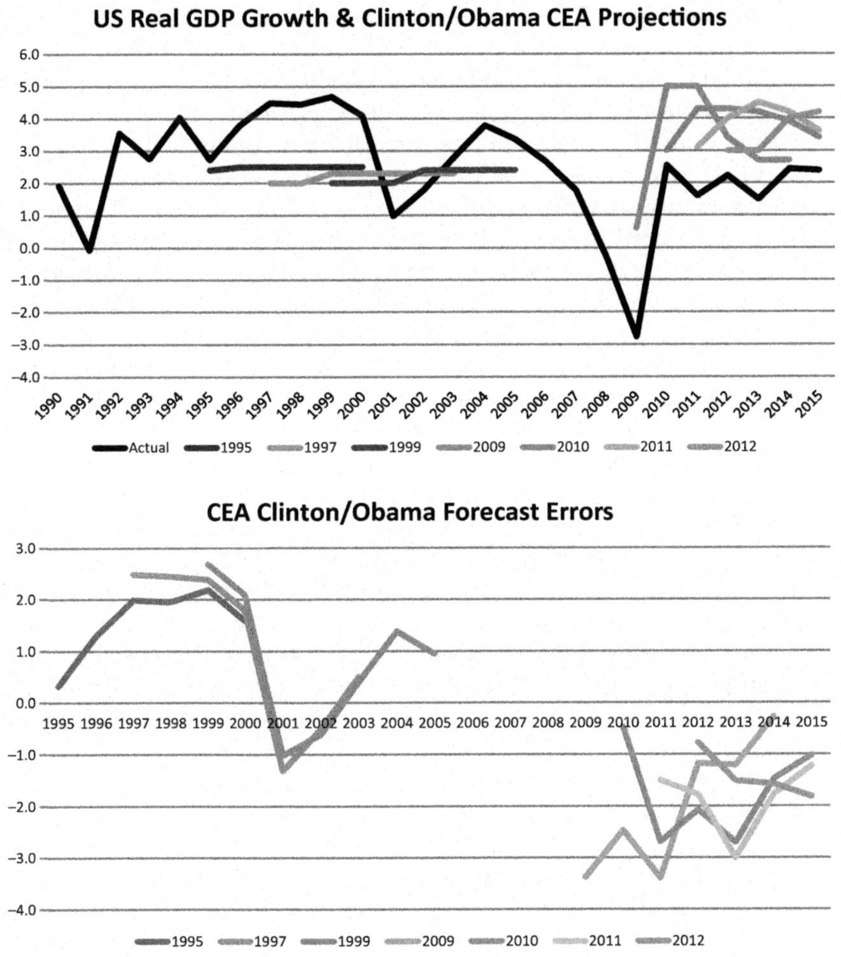

Fig. 3.1 Failed CEA projections

Notes

1. Those with a passing familiarity with the history of mathematics might recognise that I have borrowed the term 'limiting principle' from the outcome of a debate that was started by the Irish philosopher George Berkeley in his 1734 book *The Analyst* written against the foundational principles of the then newly conceived differential

calculus (Berkeley 1734). Berkeley went 'behind' Newton's mathematics to examine the logical and metaphysical foundations of his system of calculus. In doing so, he found the metaphysical foundations to be lacking by the standards which some adherents of the calculus upheld and the logical foundations to be completely inadequate. The logical problems Berkeley highlighted were taken very seriously indeed. Basically the problem was that Newton (and Leibniz) had been unable to formulate a logically coherent limit to the ever smaller quantities that were dealt with in the calculus, and they got around this by engaging in a logical fallacy. It was only in 1966 that a truly coherent foundation was established in the form of a limit principle. The metaphysical issues that Berkeley raised, which are interesting in their own right, are rarely discussed in either philosophical or mathematical circles.

The reason that I take this debate as a point of departure is because it has such bearing on what we are dealing with here. All the key aspects are there: the questioning of the assumptions behind the mathematics; the response in the form of establishing a sort of limit to what can be said; and so on. And before my detractors jump on me with their dog whistles I will state clearly: no, neither Berkeley nor I were or are questioning the usefulness of functionality of the differential calculus. The point is an altogether more subtle one that those whose ears are only attuned to dog whistles will likely never appreciate.

2. 'For the Classical Theory has been accustomed to rest the supposedly self-adjusting character of the economic system on an assumed fluidity of money-wages; and, when there is rigidity, to lay on this rigidity the blame of maladjustment. It is from this type of analysis that I fundamentally differ; or rather from the analysis which seems to lie behind such observations as the above' (Keynes 1936a, Chapter 19).
3. Let us be careful not to fool ourselves into thinking that Samuelson was here playing at being a good empiricist by observing that the economic situation had changed and so theory had to change with it. A devout marginalist could—and, indeed, many did and would—explain the Roosevelt recovery in simple marginalist terms. They would say that wages and prices had bottomed out sufficiently to allow for recovery and that the recovery took place in spite of and not because of Roosevelt's policies (which, incidentally, were not

very 'Keynesian' to begin with). No, Samuelson wanted to believe that the New Deal was working, and he wanted a theory that could buttress this belief. If he had rejected the New Deal, he could have easily provided a cogent marginalist explanation for the Roosevelt recovery. Something altogether different was operating here—something emotional, historically contingent and in no way objective or scientific. Samuelson was, at the end of the day, perfectly willing to forgo logical consistency to uphold his political beliefs.

4. These different schools effectively represent market fundamentalists who believe that the government has a role to play within the economy and market fundamentalists who believe that it has no role to play in the economy (Galbraith 2009).
5. For those unfamiliar with Buckley, he was a clever right-wing rhetorician who regularly debated those he disagreed with. He was well known to simply make things up when it suited his purposes. A nice illustration of this was in a 1972 debate between Buckley and the economist J.K. Galbraith in Cambridge. Buckley cited some economic statistics after which Galbraith asked sarcastically for a source. When Buckley choked up, the audience began to laugh with vague amusement. The debate then continued on. This was a typical Buckley performance. He was generally let away with making stuff up because of his charm. He was not, therefore, interested in serious thought or argument. He was an ideologue all the way, but a clever one who knew how to play the game and get things done.
6. The present author has actually, on one occasion, been accused of not doing science when discussing the philosophy of science! Such accusations make one's head spin! Presumably, the accuser had formed an idea of what he thought to be science in his head without consulting the philosophy of science. Then he used this unformulated definition of science to dismiss doing philosophy of science as 'not science'. A more ready example of how the term 'science' is used in discourse amongst economists to bully, exclude and generate authority is difficult to find.
7. Hands provides an example of how the attitudes towards methodology that Samuelson and others fostered had an impact on his own work. When asked by Mehrling why he has not, until just prior to the interview when he received a grant from INET, been doing his work through grants and has instead been subsidising his work through teaching, he responds:

> If you look at the economists that do that do the history of economic thought or do economic methodology or philosophy of economics in the US you will find a very large fraction at the liberal arts colleges. These disciplines are not mainstream fields that have a lot of respect and so people end up in liberal arts environments in order to do what they do. (Ibid.)

8. For those unfamiliar 'Whig history', which has been completely discredited in contemporary historiography and in other social sciences, together with how it was interpreted by Samuelson and those who followed him, has been aptly summarised by Chick et al. as follows:

> The term 'Whig history' was originally coined by the English historian Herbert Butterfield to refer to what Peter Boettke describe as 'history as written by those perceived to have been the intellectual victors of key debates'. Butterfield's largely successful purpose was to discredit and eliminate the practice, amongst historians, of presenting the past and its ideas as nothing more than an imperfect form of the present. Since then, awareness of the dangers of such reductionism and the necessity of what Bagchi calls a 'contextual' approach to social knowledge has spread through most of the social sciences. In economics alone, the concept of 'Whig-historical analysis' was deemed a positive achievement, thanks to Samuelson's paper, which set out, in characteristically pugnacious terms, the thesis that economists have nothing to learn from past controversies, since their theory at the present moment represents the highest accomplishment attainable, and all previous theories must be an inferior form of the present state of knowledge. (Chick et al. 2014)

9. Sraffa was, of course, actually an Italian. But we will include him in British school.

References

Berkeley, G. (1734). *The analyst; Or, a discourse addressed to the infidel mathematician*. London: J. Tonson. http://www.maths.tcd.ie/pub/HistMath/People/Berkeley/Analyst/Analyst.pdf

Chick, V., Freeman, A., & Kayatekin, S. (2014). Samuelson's ghosts: Whig history and the reinterpretation of economic theory. *Cambridge Journal of Economics, 38*, 519–529.

Colander, D., & Landreth, H. (1996). *The coming of keynesianism to America*. US & UK: Edward Elgar.

D'Andrea Tyson, L., Goolsbee, A., Krueger, A., & Romer, C. (2016). An open letter from past CEA chairs to senator sanders and professor gerald friedman. https://lettertosanders.wordpress.com/2016/02/17/open-letter-to-senator-sanders-and-professor-gerald-friedman-from-past-cea-chairs/

Davidson, P. (1996). Reality and economic theory. *Journal of Post Keynesian Economics, 18*(4), 479–508.

Frank, T. (2005). *What's the matter with Kansas?* (Reprint ed.). USA: Holt McDougal.

Friedman, G. (2016). What would sanders do? Estimating the economic impact of sanders' Programs. *Dollars and Sense*. http://www.dollarsandsense.org/What-would-Sanders-do-013016.pdf

Galbraith, J. (2009). Who are these economists, anyway?. *NEA's Thought & Action Journal of Higher Education*. http://www.veblen-institute.org/Who-Are-These-Economists-Anyway?lang=en

Hands, W. (2011). Paul Samuelson and the neoclassical synthesis. Interview with Perry Mehrling at INET. https://www.youtube.com/watch?v=sjNbMJOYUZI

Harcourt, G. (1972). *Some Cambridge controversies in the theory of capital*. UK: Cambridge University Press.

Holcombe, R. (2008). Pluralism versus heterodoxy in economics and the social sciences. *Journal of Philosophical Economics, 1*(2), 51–72.

Kay, J. (2014, May 20). Angry economics students are naive—and mostly right. *Financial Times*. http://www.ft.com/cms/s/0/23da4f1e-df48-11e3-86a4-00144feabdc0.html#axzz34WpTLd6E

Keynes, J. M. (1936a). *The general theory of employment, money and interest*. http://www.marxists.org/reference/subject/economics/keynes/general-theory/

Lasch, C. (1996). *The revolt of the elites and the betrayal of democracy*. US: W.W. Norton and Company.

Mirowski, P. (2011). Why is there a nobel memorial prize in economics? *INET Blog*. http://ineteconomics.org/blog/inet/philip-mirowski-why-there-nobel-memorial-prize-economics

PCSC. (2014). *The report*. Retrieved from http://www.post-crasheconomics.com/economics-education-and-unlearning/

Robinson, J. (1953). The production function and the theory of capital. *Review of Economic Studies, 21*(2), 81–106.

Samuelson, P. (1987). Out of the closet: A program for the whig history of economic science. *History of Economics Society Bulletin, 9*(1), 51–60.

Solow, R. (1987). Growth theory and after. *Nobel Prize Lecture*. http://www.nobelprize.org/nobel_prizes/economic-sciences/laureates/1987/solow-lecture.html

Tarshis, L. (1947). *The elements of economics: An introduction to the theory of price and employment*. USA: Houghton Mifflin Company.

Vienneau, R. (2008). Some of Samuelson's textbook on reswitching. *Thoughts on Economics Blogspot*. http://robertvienneau.blogspot.co.uk/2008/01/some-of-samuelsons-textbook-on.html

CHAPTER 4

Deconstructing Marginalist Microeconomics

What is the essence of *homo economicus*? *Homo economicus* is a man in search of pleasure. He is a man who knows what he wants and how to get it. There are fixed limits on what *homo economicus* can obtain, but he is a master of getting the best that he can from within these limits. The term was first coined as a criticism. It would seem that when certain people in the nineteenth century read the famous economist and philosopher John Stuart Mill, they did not like what they found. They accused Mill of reducing the human being to nothing but a calculator of his immediate pleasures. They said that Mill had removed anything properly human from Man and replaced him instead with some sort of amoral robot; this robot they called *homo economicus* (Persky 1995).

Mill himself was quite explicit about what he was doing. He claimed that economics—which was then called 'political economy'—was concerned only with certain specific facets of Man's existence. It did not poach on the preserves of other moral disciplines but rather abstracted from them and reasoned as if they did not exist. Mill wrote:

> [Political economy] does not treat of the whole of man's nature as modified by the social state, nor of the whole conduct of man in society. It is concerned with him solely as a being who desires to possess wealth, and who is capable of judging of the comparative efficacy of means for obtaining that end. It predicts only such phenomena of the social state as take place in consequence of the pursuit of wealth. It makes entire abstraction of

W.P. Pilkington, *The Reformation in Economics*,
DOI 10.1007/978-3-319-40757-9_4

> every other human passion or motive; except those which may be regarded as perpetually antagonizing principles to the desire of wealth, namely, aversion to labour, and desire of the present enjoyment of costly indulgences ... Political Economy considers mankind as occupied solely in acquiring and consuming wealth; and aims at showing what is the course of action into which mankind, living in a state of society, would be impelled, if that motive, except in the degree in which it is checked by the two perpetual counter-motives above adverted to, were absolute ruler of all their actions. (Mill 1844)

What concerned those who criticised Mill's *homo economicus* was that it highlighted some of what they considered to be the less seemly aspects of Man's existence. This was an age of high morality, and Mill's construction seemed to many to be against the morality of the day. This was also an age of mass wealth accumulation, and Mill's construction probably showed up a certain truth that some were less than pleased to deal with as it ran contrary to what they considered good behaviour.

By the mid- to late twentieth century, mass consumption had become a way of life and contemporary morality was more accommodative to the *homo economicus.* Indeed, today he seems like a rather natural construction in an age where people constitute their lives through accumulation and consumption. He has also been given more precision. Today, following on from the work of the early marginalists, he is modelled using indifference curves and differential calculus. To a critic of the theory, it is less the morality that stands out as it is the image of Man that is put forward. Man is seen as a sort of automaton with fixed, ordered preferences, a vast capacity for information accumulation and an ability to process this information that would be the envy of even the most powerful of computers. Whereas yesteryear *homo economicus* seemed offensively amoral, today he seems offensively unrealistic.

What is more he seems to crop up in places where he did not crop up before. Almost every contemporary mainstream economic theory seems to have *homo economicus* sitting in the driving seat. These theories, to an altogether obvious extent, stand or fall based on the reasonableness of this single concept, and any serious investigation of this concept shows that it is a very shaky foundation on which to build your house indeed. In a very real sense, if the concept proves to be silly or misleading, then most of mainstream economics crumbles with it. Perhaps never before have the findings and constructions of a whole so-called science depended so much on a concept that few thinking people find remotely credible. That this is taboo to discuss in the profession is due to a profound unease on the part of too many people who have too much invested in this construction to even begin to consider probing its content. What cannot be dealt with on reasonable terms is papered over with a conspiracy of silence.

The fact of this matter cannot be overstated enough. If we turn, for example, to the main macroeconomic model used by the European Central Bank at the time of writing, we find it populated with a plethora of *homo economicuses*. In their key forecasting model which is supposed to represent the Eurozone economy, they write:

> Each household h maximises its lifetime utility in a given period t by choosing purchases of the consumption good, $C_{h,t}$, purchases of the investment good, $I_{h,t}$. (Christoffel et al. 2008, p. 11)

Thus they turn every household into a *homo economicus* and then lump these *homo economicuses* together and spell out their exact behaviour in a series of equations. If the assumption that each household acts like a *homo economicus* can be shown to be nonsense, then the findings of the model will also be nonsense. This cannot be stressed enough: this assumption is at the absolute core of many 'very serious' theories; without it they literally cannot function.[1] Yet if the construction can be shown to be false, and by that I mean if it can be shown to not be a reasonable approximation of the real object of study (economic agents), then the theories themselves must also be false and central banks can be shown to be wasting an awful lot of time and resources employing people to build such theories.

Fixing Preferences

Let us begin with the question of preferences. In order for *homo economicus* to compare various things to one another, he must first be assumed to have fixed preferences. Before we begin to talk about relative prices and so forth, we must first know whether our consumer prefers apples to bananas and we must be able to order these in a numerical way. So, we need to be able to say something like: 'Our consumer likes apples twice as much as bananas and so apples are twice as valuable to him as are bananas.' It is only after positing these fixed preferences that we can then go on to say anything of interest about the effects of prices, changes in budgets and so on. Let us look closer at the reasoning behind the fixity of preferences.

The first step in the process is, as the marginalists say, to 'formulate axioms that are both stable and known'. This statement really does contain what is perhaps the most important part of what follows therefrom. What is an 'axiom' here? Well, in truth it is a tautology. By that we mean it is self-referential and its supposed truth-content is derived only from itself. Read in this light we can see that what this actually means is something like 'we need to first construct a tautology which must be stable and known that hereafter will be beyond reproach'. So far, so good. But what is this clause 'stable and known' all about?

Well, 'known' is known. This is not too complicated. We need to know that the tautology is self-identical—that *X* is indeed *X*—in order to be on firm footing. The criterion 'stable' is more nuanced. The idea here is that the tautology must not only be true right now, but must also be true for the entire period of time which we are concerned with it. So, *X* must not only be *X* at 3.30 pm this afternoon when we first posit it, but it must remain *X* until it ceases to interest us. If we are concerned with *X* from 3.30 pm this afternoon until 8.40 pm this evening, it must not turn into *Y* or *Z* between now and then. When *X* ceases to concern us—say, at 9 pm—it can turn into anything it pleases, but when we are dealing with *X*, it must remain self-identical.

In mathematical terms, we might write this as:

$$X_t \equiv X_{t+n}$$

But let us not allow the form to fool us—indeed, we should never let the form fool us—the key issue here is that *X* must remain constant through time if our theories are to have any meaning. Such a statement, however, does not answer any questions; it merely raises questions regarding the n: how long must these preferences remain stable?

This may strike the reader as gobbledegook, and, in all honesty, it mostly is. But it is also extremely important because we are dealing with a very human element here. This is the exact point on which much of the theory turns; that is, the assumption of fixity of preferences. Samuelson and Nordhaus, in their classic introductory textbook *Economics*, sum this up in more clear language than is typical of the average marginalist:

> What is assumed is that consumers are fairly consistent in their tastes and actions—that they do not flail around in unpredictable ways, making themselves miserable by persistent errors of judgement or arithmetic. If enough

> people act consistently, avoiding erratic changes in buying behaviour, and generally choosing their most preferred commodities, our scientific theory will provide a reasonably good approximation of the facts. (Samuelson 1995, p. 78)

This is an interesting passage and really does deserve to be examined in more detail. Recall that the reason we need to assume the knowability and the stability of the variable—in this case: human behaviour in the face of how to maximise their utility—is so that we can construct a tautological axiom that will thereafter be closed to criticism. So, whatever is tossed into the soon-to-be-sealed black-box at this moment of construction has enormous implications for everything that we try to say in the future when we use this axiom. Now, Samuelson and Nordhaus—and, it should be noted, this is rare for marginalists—are actually trying to give the reason why they are making the assumption of the stability of human preferences. Samuelson and Nordhaus do not appeal to known facts about people, nor do they appeal to common sense. Instead their language is strongly normative or ethical.

Look at the key sentence in the above paragraph that is used to buttress the assumption. If the consumer is assumed to have non-static desires—that is, if their desires for various things change through time—they are said to be 'making themselves miserable by persistent errors of judgment or arithmetic'. The only way they can thus obtain salvation and not be miserable is by fitting into the axioms of the marginalist. Their pronouncements can only remind us of the preacher who tells us that we will be unhappy should we stray from the flock and go against the moral principles being handed down. Personally, I rather like changing my preferences when it comes to choosing new purchases and activities. Indeed, I would think that it would be doing the same thing from day-to-day would be rather tedious and would make me miserable. How the reader feels about this issue is their own prerogative, but my guess is that the majority of people do like to shake things up a bit and try new things. Perhaps then Samuelson and Nordhaus' entire economic theory is based on some very idiosyncratic psychological features of these two men that do not pertain to most of the population—or perhaps they were just making the argument that allowed them an easy means by which to construct their 'scientific' theories.

But let us run with this assumption for a little while longer. Let us allow that people might have fixed preferences and probe a little deeper to see how acceptable this is as a working hypothesis. As we have already seen, we are dealing with the dimension of time here. When we talk about stasis, we are talking about stasis through time; otherwise, we are talking about nothing at all. So, we could be talking here about any number of different things because the marginalist economist is simply not being clear in positing a specific amount of time. Are we saying that a consumer's desire is static in the nanosecond in which they make a decision? Or are we saying that a consumer's desire is static from the moment they emerge from the womb to the moment their heart stops beating? Well, it should be quite clear that the former is an appreciably different statement from the latter.

Again, let us lay this out in formal terms, if for nothing else then to highlight the trickery and silliness that is involved in such an exercise a good part of the time. So, we could be saying that a consumer's desire is static in the nanosecond that they make a decision:

$$X_t \equiv X_{t+\frac{1}{1,000,000,000s}}$$

Or we could be saying that a consumer's desire is static from the maternity hospital to the death bed:

$$X_{baby} \equiv X_{old\ man}$$

If we say that a consumer has static preferences in the moment, he makes a decision we are not saying much at all. Our entire theory will then be fairly arbitrary and will mean something like 'preferences are fixed insofar as they are self-identical in the moment when they are initiated'. Alternatively, it seems unlikely that even the most ardent marginalist would assume that a baby crying for the breast has the same set of preferences as the old man in the hospital bed. So, perhaps we are talking about something in between. But what this something is, we cannot say. More formally, we are saying:

$$X_t \equiv X_{t+?}$$

The theory of the *homo economicus* requires fixed preferences or desires. Without them it cannot function. Yet they can only be appealed to in vague and mysterious ways. If we assume no fixity of preferences, then the whole theory falls apart completely. But when we are told by the likes of Samuelson and Nordhaus that preferences are fixed, they do not really tell us what they mean by this. It seems likely that they remain silent on this matter because if they tried to be more specific, it would soon become obvious that they had nothing to say on the matter at all. This is argument by allusion, a hallmark of mysticism.

But if we investigate further, things get even worse. If we probe a bit more, we will find that the idea of fixed preferences actually renders the theory completely unable to be tested. This is because if the theory is to say anything at all, then it must be saying something about the reaction of individuals to changes in prices or income. So, for example, we might want to see how a consumer reacts to a change in the price of apples. This is the sort of exercise that students are made to undertake in the classrooms at the time of writing. But Joan Robinson noted long ago that this entire experiment rests crucially on the idea that preferences are stable and fixed. She wrote:

> We can observe the reaction of an individual to two different sets of prices only at two different times. How can we tell what part of the difference in his purchases is due to the difference in prices and what part to the change in his preferences that *has* taken place meanwhile? There is certainly no presumption that his character has not changed, for soap and whisky are not the only goods whose use affects tastes. Practically everything develops either an inertia of habit or a desire for change. We have got one equation for two unknowns. Unless we can get some independent evidence about preferences the experiment is no good. But it was the experiment that we were supposed to rely on to observe the preferences. (Robinson 1962, p. 51—emphasis in original)

Again, when we turn to reality—indeed, even if we engage in some simple introspection—we can see quite clearly that preferences are not fixed whatsoever. Our tastes are in a state of constant flux; new goods are constantly entering the marketplace and fads and fashions alight, burn out and fade away. If this is taken into account, it renders the marginalist theory of the utility-maximising *homo economicus* completely hollow and empty. If we observe people actually undertaking various decisions, we can never be sure to what extent these decisions are being undertaken due to a change in preferences and to what extent they are being undertaken due to the normal utility-maximising procedures that pertain when we assume fixed preferences. The empirical testability of the theory—and, some would say, any scientific content of the theory—rests crucially on the unrealistic assumption that consumer preferences are fixed through time.

This criticism was also put forward by the philosopher Hans Albert in a 1963 paper in more refined form. Albert extended the criticism to the so-called law of demand generally. The law of demand, as is well known, states that if the price of a good increases, demand for it will fall, and if it decreases, the demand for it will rise. He noted that the theory contained a *ceteris paribus* ('all else being unchanged') clause that rendered it entirely untestable. He wrote:

> The law appears prima facie to predicate a relatively simple and easily testable relationship and thus to have a fair amount of content. However, upon closer examination, this impression fades. As is well known, the law is usually tagged with a clause that entails numerous interpretation problems: the *ceteris paribus* clause. In the strict sense this must thus at least be formulated as follows to be acceptable to the majority of theoreticians: *ceteris paribus*—that is, all things being equal—the demanded quantity of a consumer good is a monotone decreasing function of its price. The *ceteris paribus* clause is not a relatively insignificant addition, which might be ignored. Rather, it can be viewed as an integral element of the law of demand itself. However, that would entail that theoreticians who interpret the clause differently de facto have different laws of demand in mind, maybe even laws that are incompatible with each other. Here, through an explicit interpretation of the *ceteris paribus* clause, the law of demand is made into a tautology. (Albert 1963, p. 8)

In general, when economists make *ceteris paribus* arguments, they explicitly define all the *ceteris paribus* conditions that are required for their argument to be valid. This allows the theories to at least potentially be testable against empirical content. In the case of the law of demand, however, this cannot be done because preferences, as we have already seen, are never investigated. This produces what Albert calls an 'absolute alibi' against any empirical criticisms of the theory and renders it tautological. He writes:

> Various widespread formulations of the law of demand contain an interpretation of the clause that does not result in a tautology, but that has another weakness. The list of the factors to be held constant includes, among other things, the structure of the needs of the purchasing group in question. This leads to a difficulty connected with the identification of needs. As long as there is no independent test for the constancy of the structures of needs, any law that is formulated in this way has an absolute 'alibi'. Any apparent counter case can be traced back to a change in the needs, and thus be discounted. Thus, in this form, the law is also immunized against empirical facts … If the factors that are to be left constant remain undetermined, as not so rarely happens, then the law of demand under question is fully immunized to facts, because every case which initially appears contrary must, in the final analysis, be shown to be compatible with this law. The clause here

> produces something of an absolute alibi, since, for every apparently deviating behavior, some altered factors can be made responsible. This makes the statement untestable, and its informational content decreases to zero. (Ibid., pp. 9–10)

The microeconomists themselves have gradually realised that their theory is entirely untestable. They now admit as such in the most popular microeconomics textbooks of today. How do they defend themselves against the charge that their theories cannot be proved or disproved? Interestingly enough, they do so by providing a muddled, misleading and simply incorrect characterisation of science itself. Consider this shocking statement from Hal Varian's best-selling textbook:

> Does this prove that the constructed preferences actually generated the observed choices? Of course not. As with any scientific statement, we can only show that observed behavior is not inconsistent with the statement. We can't prove that the economic model is correct; we can just determine the implications of that model and see if observed choices are consistent with those implications. (Varian 2010, p. 129)

Varian here makes extremely large claims. He claims that the theory is perfectly scientific in all sciences all that can be shown is that 'observed behavior is not inconsistent with' the theory. What he does not mention is that in science proper a theory can be *falsified*; that is, it can be proven wrong. In science, it is true that observed behaviour must *not* be inconsistent with a theory; otherwise, that theory will be falsified. But the trick is that properly scientific statements *can* in fact always be falsified. Varian's theory, by contrast, cannot. We can never actually test it in any meaningful sense because if we claim to have falsified Varian's claims about the link between prices and quantities sold, he can always hand wave and say that preferences have changed in the interim to interfere with the price–quantity relationship.[2] And it is for this reason that the theory is not scientific but rather ideological.

In the face of changing and evolving preferences, the marginalist theory can say literally nothing at all.[3] It becomes entirely useless. The only salvageable defence then becomes to insist that it is not applied to markets in which preferences change to any great degree. It must then only be applied to markets in which economic agents are only really interested in prices. There may thus be a case for limited application of the theory in these markets. But it is very likely that these markets are extremely limited, especially in an economic system such as our own where consumer preferences seem ever-changing. What is more, revealing these markets would require a completely different set of tools than the marginalists provide and would require a completely different type of research.

It could be argued that this is what many of the more 'serious' marginalist theories, as opposed to the candyfloss handed to undergraduates, try to do. They do not deal with the ever-changing whims of the consumer and rather seek to find how the *homo economicus* divides his income between consumption and investment. This is called the theory of 'time preference' and it seems, on the face of it, not to suffer from the insurmountable problems of the theory of the marginalist consumer. But when we pry open the lid and look inside, we quickly find that the time preference framework suffers from serious problems of its own.

Breakout Box: Cardinal Utility, Ordinal Utility and Revealed Preference

The history of marginal utility theory is indeed a strange one. The notion of 'utility' can first be found as a rather vague metaphor in the work of the English philosopher Jeremy Bentham. It was developed in more detail in the late nineteenth century by economists like Francis Edgeworth who thought of it as what he called a 'mathematical psychics'. The work of these men, which has become the basis of marginalist economics, was aimed at reducing human behaviour to terms that could be dealt with by techniques borrowed from the physics of the day (Mirowski 1991). In order to do this, they had to conceive of a manner in which they could properly quantify human decision-making.

The early marginalists tended to think of utility as a numerically measurable entity. This is known as the theory of 'cardinal utility'. The idea here is that people assign actual numerical value to the objects they desire. So, for a given person, bananas may have a numerical value of 2 while apples have a numerical value of 1. This implies that the person values bananas twice as much as they do apples. The Italian economist Vilfredo Pareto noted that this was not the right way to view the matter. He insisted that instead of conceiving as people assigning utility to a good by giving it a fixed value, rather we should think of various goods being organised by the buyer in purely relative terms. Thus rather than a plethora of goods assigned specific numbers, we have a list of goods that are ordered relative to one another. This is known as the theory of 'ordinal utility'.

The final innovation in modern utility theory came from Paul Samuelson in 1938. Samuelson was concerned that the theory of utility had too many psychological overtones. He wrote:

> The discrediting of utility as a psychological concept robbed it of its only possible virtue as an explanation of human behaviour in other than a circular sense, revealing its emptiness as even a construction. (Samuelson 1938, p. 61)

Samuelson was concerned that the psychological nature of the theory rendered it a tautological construction. He stated that his overt goal was to actually eliminate the concept of utility altogether. This was a bizarre project and one wonders what on earth Samuelson was talking about. It failed and his later textbook contained numerous references to utility like the ones we have seen in the previous section (Hands 2004). Marginalists later claimed that we could merely observe consumers in the act of purchasing and this would thus reveal their preferences which could then be recorded after the fact. The theory became known as the theory of 'revealed preferences'. This, of course, runs directly into the criticisms raised by Joan Robinson and Hans Albert in the last section: how do we know to what extent behaviour is being affected by price changes and how do we know to what extent they are being affected by changes in the underlying preferences? But it also runs into the problem as to how testable the theory is even if these problems are surmounted.

If preferences are only revealed after the fact—that is, *ex post*—then can the theory of revealed preferences actually make any novel predictions? If it cannot, then what exactly is its epistemological status? If a theory is a statement that can only rationalise already known data from the past and cannot say anything about its objects of study moving into the future, then that theory is surely nothing but a tautology. Viewed in this way revealed preference theory appears to be a sort of narrative structure imposed on already known facts about the past. So, marginalists learn about a given consumer's behaviour and then they retroactively recast and reinterpret this behaviour in light of the revealed preference theory. This sort of game appears entirely arbitrary and an almost purified case of tautological reasoning. One could just as easily apply any arbitrary theoretical framework to interpret the underlying data. Surely this is not science in any meaningful sense of the word.

Time Preference

The time preference theory is the key meeting point between marginalist micro- and macroeconomics. It is the point at which the rubber meets the road and the rational *homo economicus* of microeconomics is assumed to have his macroeconomic effects. The theory is a very simple one. It states that the rate of saving is determined by individuals making decisions about whether they would prefer to consume their income now or they would prefer to consume it in the future. If they decide to consume it in the future, they can lend this income either to people who want to consume in the present or to people who want to invest. The theory then states that the amount of savings in existence at any given moment in time will determine the price of borrowing and the reward for lending—that is, the interest rate.

From its inception, the time preference theory was a conscious projection of the *homo economicus* into the financial realm. Irving Fisher, who came up with the theory, stated quite explicitly that he had taken the idea from the theory of the rational consumer. He wrote:

> Just as in the ordinary theory of prices the ratio of exchange of any two articles is based on a psychological or subjective element—their comparative marginal utility—so in the theory of interest the rate of interest, or the premium in the exchange between present and future goods, is based on a subjective prototype; namely, the preference for present over future goods. (Fisher 1907, p. 88)

Thus we end up once again with a consumer faced with a whole array of goods and, on top of this, an option to save their money and earn interest by lending it out. By lending the money out, they will earn more money and so they will, presumably, be allowed to increase their consumption in the future as interest payments and principle are paid down. Time preference is generally seen as the amount of consumption goods sacrificed now for the amount of consumption goods that will be bought and consumed in the future. But here we already see serious problems emerge. Given that we do not know the future, we cannot really say how much we will value those goods that are available.

Let us say that I decide to save $10,000 for a period of ten years in government bonds at the rate of 5 % interest per annum. It is impossible for me to weigh the utility that I will receive from spending the $10,000 today to the utility I will receive from the principle plus the interest in ten years' time. Why? First of all, because I do not know what goods will be available in ten years' time, nor do I know their relative cost. Thus, for example, there may be all sorts of new inventions that I could never have imagined or the price of oil may have gone up substantially due to supply constrictions. I also do not know how much value the money will have lost through inflation as I will not know in advance the rate of inflation over the next ten years; nor do I know the relative valuations of assets that have changed price in the meantime and this has an impact on the relative price of my bond. Finally, I do not know what other circumstances will be and thus how much utility I will gain from a good or service in any time period. Perhaps the best way to think about this is to consider that in order to know how much utility you will get from a pair of sunglasses over the course of five years, you would have to know where you will be located over that five-year period as well as the weather in each of the locations at the time that you are there. Taken together, these render it absolutely impossible for me to compare the goods that the $10,000 can buy now versus what it will buy, when interest has been accrued and the principle repaid, in ten years' time. The only way we can salvage this is by assuming that the potential saver knows the future trajectory of the economy (and his or her location together with the weather five years out!). But this seems *even more* unrealistic than the assumption that human beings have fixed preferences. Again, we must stress here that this is not a minor point: if the above is correct, then the theory is wrong. It is not 'a bit wrong' and cannot be modified; rather, it is simply incorrect and needs to be abandoned.

Things get worse when we consider how peoples' savings are generally held. In the above example, we considered a person holding their wealth in a government bond which we can assume to be fairly stable and certain. But in the real world, people tend to hold their saved wealth in company stocks and bonds. But when they do this, they have almost no idea as to what amount of money they will hold at the end of the savings period. This is because these shares and bonds are inherently risky. Fisher recognised this in his book, and, like many of his followers today, he said that the risk had to 'priced in' to any measure of time preference (ibid., pp. 99–102). But this assumes that we can give risk a calculable value. In the real world, however, we cannot give such risk a calculable value at all. Investment managers may try to do so, but they will never succeed. This is because of the nature and structure of the financial markets which we will discuss in more detail in later chapters. When this fact is combined with the above-mentioned facts, there seems very little left of the time preference theory of interest. It is clear that trying to determine the macroeconomics of savings based on ideas about individual utility maximisation is ridiculous.

These criticisms cannot be met with the insistence that time preference is merely an approximation.[4] It is quite clear that in marginalist economics, we must take the theory quite literally in order to explain the behaviours of individuals and hence to allow them to play a role in any given economic model. Consider that the European Central Bank model discussed at the beginning of this chapter ceases to function completely if we do not take the time preference theory literally. If we do not, the core rots and the model collapses in upon itself.[5] Those who build these models know this too which is why they explicitly formulate their agents as knowing the future or, at least, being able to calculate the course of future events in the form of probability calculations. If this assumption is removed, nothing remains of the model.

Perhaps old Fisher could have claimed that his theory was only a rather vague metaphor, but his followers today cannot because they have turned the metaphor into a hypothesis that their constructions literally stand or fall based on. Either we take the time preference theory at its word, in which case the models built upon it are valid, or we concede that it is at best a very vague metaphor, in which case the models cease to be relevant to the real world. Why is this? *Because scientific models require extremely precise definitions.* If we replace precise definitions with vague metaphors, we will quickly find ourselves talking absolute nonsense. When an engineer specifies a model, he would never get away with replacing some of the components with concepts that only very vaguely conformed to the object being modelled. If they did so, they would find that their model was distorted to the point of being useless. But the marginalist economists seem to be doing just this. They either assume that ideas like time preference are literally true, in which case they are obviously wrong, or they assume that they are very vague approximate metaphors of reality, in which case any time they try to pin reality down and model it, they will only produce a clumsy piece of rubbish that would result in unemployment for an engineer. Indeed, when economists run the old time preference theory against the data, they get results that are precisely the opposite that they would expect, and yet for some bizarre reason central banks are still using these ridiculous models and economists are still teaching them in classrooms (Canzanori et al. 2007).

The marginalists are in an unfortunate position. Their objects of study—that is, the nature of Man and the movement of history—are some of the most complex things that we as human beings are confronted with. Yet they insist that they can study these things with the precision that the engineer applies to those things that he builds. Nor can they rely on the repeated experiments of the physicist to correct their constructions for any errors that might arise due to external factors. In trying to do gain such precision through the mathematical formalisation of extremely shaky and vague metaphors, they wind themselves into an awful mess indeed. While their unwieldy constructions may appear intimidating to outsiders, most people nevertheless suspects them to be the nonsense that, on closer examination, they obviously are.

The truth of the matter is that if these things could be pinned down in the way that the marginalists claim, then all would be solved. Economists would become perfect fortune tellers. They would be able, like the agents in their models, to rationally dictate to us everything that is going to happen moving into the future. But they obviously cannot do this. And in losing sight of what type of object they study, they are apt to talk the silliest of nonsense. As James Galbraith writes:

> They predict disaster where none occurs. They deny the possibility of events that then happen … They oppose the most basic, decent and sensible reforms, while offering placebos instead. They are always surprised when something untoward (like a recession) actually occurs. And when finally they sense that some position cannot be sustained, they do not re-examine

> their ideas. They do not consider the possibility of a flaw in logic or theory. Rather, they simply change the subject. (Galbraith 2001)

Almost all of these faults can be traced back to their forming very vague and woolly metaphors about how human beings behave that do not stand up to scrutiny and then in the next breath assuming that these vague and woolly metaphors have some sort of validity and, indeed, precision with respect to their real object of study. The marginalists live in a land of make-believe, of fairy tales—a child's dream world. Raising obvious questions about the solidity and reliability of these make-believe constructions is enough to get the student an 'F' on their exam. The marginalists get everything wrong over and over again. They regularly look like fools. Frankly, they render it embarrassing for a person to even admit to being an economist. If the profession was more humble and philosophical, they would not have these problems. There are a lot of smart-alecs in the profession, but there is an absolute dearth of wisdom and insight. The lands of make-believe that the marginalists build in their imaginations allow them to show off to each other with fancy mathematics and flashy simulations, but it is all as hollow as a rotten tree stump.

The true tragedy of much economics today is that it is not even worth criticising because the criticisms are so simple. 'But people do not act like that'; 'But it is not convincing to assume that people know the future'[6]; and so on. You can start playing the game and criticising the models from within, but this is as pointless as playing the game and believing in it. It is simply a waste of energy. Either you believe that the vague metaphors can be used in place of the precise definitions of the engineer and the physicist or you do not. That is the end of the story. If you do not believe in the nonsense, it is best to just move on and try to understand how the real economy works to the best of your ability. Wasting your life trying to convince a man who thinks he is Napoleon that he is not is almost as absurd as insisting that you are Napoleon yourself. The true study of the economy is a fascinating endeavour and an extremely useful activity. That so many receive praise and even positions of power by selling make-believe is a tragedy, but every age has their soothsayers and their priests. There is nothing so useful to a despot as a clown who thinks himself a king. And there is nothing more tragic than someone who could potentially fight against despotism but spends all their time instead chasing the clown around the court trying to remove his silly paper crown.

Appendix: An Example of a 'Consistency Critique'

We have just laid out some fundamental criticisms of the concept of *homo economicus*; in doing so, we have completely undermined the basis of both mainstream micro- and macroeconomics. Both structures rest completely on this idea. If the *homo economicus* falls, so too does most of marginalist economics. While some of the preceding discussions were by no means simplistic, they ultimately rested on two methodological points. The first was an appeal to realism; we examined the idea of *homo economicus* and showed that it was simply not up to the task of explaining human decision-making as it could not integrate change and did not recognise the reality of linear, historical time. The second point was a demonstration that the theory of the utility-maximising agent was tautological and did not contain any properly scientific content; its very structure ensured that it was completely untestable.

These critiques are key. If we are reasonable people who adhere to normal scientific and social scientific methodology, the *homo economicus* must be rejecting as a foundation for any economic theory. That is really the end of the story. Those that adhere to this idea are doing so for completely 'irrational' reasons. Their motivations cannot be scientific and so we must conclude that they are likely ideological. However, it is worth at least mentioning that there has been another tradition of attacks on the *homo economicus* and the intellectual structure that flows from assuming that he exists. These are critiques that take a completely different form to those laid out above. Rather than examining the *homo economicus* on rationalistic, empirical or methodological grounds, they accept his existence and then try to see if the theories that he generates are internally consistent. Some might call these 'hard critiques'. In fact, the critiques laid out above are much 'harder' by anything resembling scientific criteria and so we would be better referring to these as 'consistency critiques'.

As an example of a consistency critique, let us take a brief look at what is generally referred to as the 'Sonnenschein-Mantel-Debreu theorem' (SMD theorem) after its supposed founders, Sonnenschein, Mantel and Debreu. As we shall see, the basic problem was uncovered years earlier by the economist G.L.S. Shackle, so we shall hereafter refer to the theorem as the SMDS theorem so as to recognise Shackle's paternity. The SMDS theorem applies to a branch of economics called 'general equilibrium theory'. General equilibrium theory is to marginalist economics what Einsteinian physics is to physics: a not always useful intellectual construction, but one that generates precision and coherence where the simpler and more practical frameworks break down. In a sense, general equilibrium undergirds the marginalist teachings espoused in textbooks across the world. The critics who attack marginalist economics by scrutinising its consistency claim that any inconsistency that can be uncovered in general equilibrium theory will render all of marginalist economics incoherent and, thus, incorrect.

General equilibrium theory works much like the simplistic fables about supply and demand handed down in the microeconomics textbooks. The difference is that the microeconomics textbooks tend to focus on individual market, while the general equilibrium theorists try to generate coherent results by examining what happens when all individual markets interact together. The general equilibrium theorists effectively seek to show that the fables about individual markets hold for all markets. Note carefully here that the test of the theory is a mathematical and not an empirical test. It is thus *not in any way a scientific test of theory*; rather, it shows that the theory is internally consistent. This is a proof that a mathematician will accept for a theorem; it is not a proof that a scientist will accept for a theory—but we shall leave this point aside for now.

General equilibrium theory is interested in determining what theorists call 'unique results'. Generating a unique result indicates that the general equilibrium has resulted from a determinate outcome. In plain English, it means that the theory is saying something interesting and useful about the model economy which it is describing. A lack of unique results would result in the theory saying nothing that is not arbitrary about the model economy under study; this is why many people refer to the SMDS theorem as the 'anything goes theorem'. A unique result to the general equilibrium model requires that the demand curve for all markets at an aggregate level must be downward-sloping. In effect, the theory requires that the whole economy behave like a macrocosmic reflection of the individual market put forward in the textbook. The SMDS theorem shows that the demand curve for all market is not downward-sloping.

The reason for this inconsistency is what economists call 'wealth effects'. Under marginalist assumptions, the change in the price of a single good has two effects. The first is that the demand for the good increases due to the cheaper price. The second is that the income of the person selling this particular good falls due to the cheaper price. Since the preference of all consumers is obviously not identical, this means that the structure of demand throughout the economy will completely shift. It is this income or wealth effect that throws the model into chaos and ensures that no unique result can occur. In 1972, the economist G.L.S. Shackle had already noted this prior to the SMDS theorem being published in 1973. He wrote:

> [Equilibrium theory] can represent the association of price and quantity offered by [a] plane curve. Then it can assert that price will change until it reaches the point of intersection of the two curves. In such an account one question has not been asked: How can we be sure that price can alter without bodily shifting one, or both, curves and compelling us, at the movement of each price, to redraw them? For a movement along the supposedly stable supply curve, implying a change of both price and quantity, implies thereby a change in the income of the producers of the good. But can a section of society have its income increased without spending more than before on every commodity? And if it does so, what becomes of the supposed stability of the demand curve? Is it not impossible in logic for two curves each to be stable and unshifting, and each at the same time to be meaningful as representing concomitant variation of price and quantity? (Shackle 1972, p. 93)

Those critics who seek to undermine marginalist theory with reference to its internal consistency point to the SMDS theorem as evidence that marginalist theory cannot work on its own terms. The SMDS theorem is not the only consistency critique that exists. There are also the Cambridge Capital Critiques which revolve around inconsistencies in how interest rates impact distribution in marginalist models (Harcourt 1972) and a critique about interest repayments and the distinction between real and nominal variables put forward by Wynne Godley and Anwar Shaikh (Godley and Shaikh 2002). But all of these consistency critiques have similar characteristics; they take the marginalist models seriously and then try to tease out inconsistencies in the structure.

What should we make of these consistency critiques? Well, first of all, we should note that those who make the critiques are correct. A necessary (but not sufficient) criterion for a scientific theory is that it must be logical consistency. Scientists are not politicians and self-contradiction cannot be tolerated. When inconsistencies are uncovered, this is a damning indictment of the theory in which they are found if this theory claims to be self-contained and non-contradictory. But what if, in playing the marginalist game, the critics fall into the marginalist trap? In actual fact, for reasons we will discuss as this book progresses, economics is not a discipline in which singular, unified, self-contained theories work to any great degree. In making consistency critiques, the critics play the game in that they seem to say: 'This grand unified theory is obviously rubbish so we should find a better one to replace it.' But they never find the better theory simply because it does not exist.

The consistency critiques thus tend to generate phantoms. Those who make them are haunted by the need for a unified alternative, while those who are being critiqued simply shrug off the critiques because the critics have nothing better.[7] It is for this reason that the consistency critiques suffer from the same basic problems as marginalist theory itself. The fact of the matter is that, due to the complex and indeterminate nature of the material we deal with, economics can never have access to any grand unified theory. It is simply a phantom; and the phantom is only used to perpetuate ideology and stifle real enquiry. Economic understanding is always and necessarily *partial*. And so the theories themselves will be always and necessarily partial. It is for this reasons that the more methodological critiques laid out in this chapter are far stronger than the consistency critiques. They do not fool us into playing the game. When offered a bat, we simply say 'no' because the game we are being asked to play is never-ending and can produce no clear winner. Rather, it is an interminable ideological distraction that ensures that economics resembles a sort of mathematical metaphysics rather than a meaningful, practical and relevant discipline.

Notes

1. Interestingly, many economists have come to reject the idea of a rational calculating individual due to laboratory experiments undertaken by behaviourist economists who found that people tend to make serious errors in judgements even if we assume that there are no other problems with the underlying theory. Thus the cutting edge of the mainstream seems to be totally in contradiction with much of the 'practical' uses to which the theory is put. There are many such discrepancies in contemporary mainstream economics, and, from the perspective of this outside, it appears that the foundations are rotten and the whole edifice will crumble rather quickly should the wind ever change direction.
2. In one sense we can test it, however. We can simply observe people and see if their preferences change. Or we can see if they possess the calculating capacities and have the access to vast swathes of information that the microeconomists claim they do. If we undertake this test, we quickly see that preferences do change and that people do

not possess the calculating capacities and information that the microeconomists claim they do. If this is the case, one is led to ask: why have the microeconomists not performed this test themselves? Perhaps it is due to the fact that they are defending an ideological rather than scientific theory.

3. Economists might then start looking into preferences, but this would completely overturn the paradigm and replace it with some sort of psychological rather than economic theory. Theorists like Samuelson, as we shall see shortly, were well aware that if this concession was ever made, it would entail that consumer behaviour was basically something that economists could say nothing about and so this field had to be left up to others. The current writer has long insisted (outside of print) that the most promising people to consult about preferences and human behaviour are successful marketing consultants who study and manipulate this behaviour for a living. Anyone who has ever attended a focus group should get a good sense of how consumer preferences are really generated and disseminated in modern capitalist economies. The techniques that one encounters therein are actually derived from clinical psychology and are based on the structure of group psychotherapy sessions. Basically what happens is that consumers are encouraged to discuss their feelings, desires and aspirations and how these relate to a given product. The marketers then structure the marketing of the product in accordance with these feelings, desires and aspirations. If they have done a good job preferences throughout society will be impacted as peoples' psychological associations with the product in question increase and become intensified by the propaganda constructed and disseminated by the marketing departments. For an excellent account of how this occurred in relation to the new aspirations and desires engendered in the cultural revolution of the 1960s, the reader should consult the work done by American cultural historian Thomas Frank (1998). This work is the basis on which the BBC filmmaker Adam Curtis made his popular series of films *The Century of the Self*.
4. Nor can we try to appeal to probabilistic conceptions of the future here. See Chap. 10 for a thorough overview of why probabilistic theories cannot be applied to the material that economics deals with.
5. The modellers will probably insist that time preference is simply a variable that we can estimate based on empirical savings data. But

then they are back using standard Keynesian macro models where aggregated data is used rather than 'micro-founded agents'. And if they start using these, they will come to very different policy conclusions.

6. 'And this cannot be remedied by making allusions to probability theory.'
7. Once upon a time, non-marginalist economists sought in the work of Piero Sraffa an alternative grand unified alternative (Sraffa 1960). But Sraffa's work was wholly negative—its subtitle was 'Prelude to a *Critique* of Economic Theory'. Sraffa's work was rather beautiful in many ways, but it was neither useful nor practical. Eventually, Sraffa's followers were forced to admit that it was really issues of methodology that should be focused on when critiquing marginalist economics and trying to build an alternative (Robinson 1974). We follow them in this book.

References

Albert, H. (1963). Model platonism: Neoclassical economic thought in critical light. *Journal of Institutional Economics* (Trans: Republished, 2012), *8*(3), 295–323.

Canzanori, M. B., Cumby, R. E., & Diba, B. T. (2007). Euler equations and money market interest rates: A challenge for monetary policy models. *Journal of Monetary Economics, 54*(7), 1863–1881.

Christoffel, K., Coenen, G., & Warne, A. (2008). The new area wide model of the euro area: A micro-founded open-economy model for forecasting and policy analysis. *European Central Bank.* Working Paper No. 944. http://www.ecb.europa.eu/pub/pdf/scpwps/ecbwp944.pdf

Fisher, I. (1907). *The rate of interest: Its nature, determination, and relation to economic phenomena.* US & UK: The Macmillan Company.

Frank, T. (1998). *The conquest of cool: Business culture, counterculture, and the rise of hip consumerism.* USA: University of Chicago Press.

Galbraith, J. (2001). How the economists got it wrong. *The American Prospect.* http://prospect.org/article/how-economists-got-it-wrong

Godley, W., & Shaikh, A. (2002). An important inconsistency at the heart of the standard macroeconomic model. *Journal of Post Keynesian Economics, 4*(3), 423–441.

Hands, W. (2004). On operationalisms and economics. *Journal of Economic Issues, 38*(4), 953–968.

Harcourt, G. (1972). *Some Cambridge controversies in the theory of capital.* UK: Cambridge University Press.

Mill, J. S. (1844). *Essays on some unsettled questions in political economy.* http://www.marxists.org/reference/archive/mill-john-stuart/1844/unsettled.htm#ESSAY_V

Mirowski, P. (1991). *More heat than light: Economics as social physics, physics as nature's economics.* US & UK: Cambridge University Press.

Robinson, J. (1962). *Economic philosophy.* UK: Pelican Books.

Robinson, J. (1974). History versus equilibrium. *Thames Papers in Political Economy.*

Samuelson, P. (1938). A note on the pure theory of consumer's behaviour. *Economica, 5*(17), 61–71.

Shackle, G. L. S. (1972). *Epistemics and economics: A critique of economic doctrines.* Cambridge University Press.

Sraffa, P. (1960). *Production of commodities by means of commodities.* Vora and Co. Publishers.

Varian, H. (2010). *Intermediate microeconomics: A modern approach* (8th ed.). USA: Norton.

CHAPTER 5

Methodology, Modelling and Bias

When the poor student enters the economics classroom, they are made to play with models. Yet they are never told what these models represent. Do they represent immediate reality? Or do they amount to a thought experiment that gives us hints as to how reality might be structured? The student is never told. If the student asks their macro or micro professor, they might—I highlight the word '*might*' here—tell them that the model is a thought experiment. But this would seem to be at odds with what they are learning in their econometrics course where they appear to be estimating models—that is, applying them directly to the real-world data. If the student is very lucky, they might have a professor interested in methodology, but they will find that it is altogether likely that their micro, macro and econometrics professors do not want to hear of any of this methodology talk. After all, these people will likely be good Samuelsonians, and good Samuelsonians know that methodology is for wafflers and muddle-heads who cannot do science.

This is a crime, of course. The student is expected to remain blindfolded while they are force-fed various different types of models. The magnitude of this crime should not be diminished in importance; in almost every other social science, these questions are taken very seriously by all involved, but the reader would be wrong to think that the economics classroom is the only place where this brainwashing takes place. Actually, it takes place in pre-school when one is learning numbers and words. These

W.P. Pilkington, *The Reformation in Economics*,
DOI 10.1007/978-3-319-40757-9_5

are taught to be quasi-natural entities but, in actual fact, they bear a far closer resemblance to the models in economics than they do to the objects that we see and hear and taste and smell and feel. Take the number '10'. Now try to imagine this number devoid of particular contents. That is, try to imagine the number without imagining, say, ten dots or ten cats or ten textbooks. You will quickly find that you cannot. The number '10' is an abstraction. It is a signifier that we write down to refer to a general idea that we cannot actually conceptualise.

These questions go right back to the earliest Greek philosophers like Plato, and they were given a new lease of life by more modern philosophers like John Locke, George Berkeley, David Hume and Immanuel Kant. Let us start with Kant as he laid out this problem in an extremely succinct fashion when he wrote in his *Critique of Pure Reason*:

> In all subsumptions of an object under a concept the representations of the former must be homogeneous with the latter, i.e., the concept must contain that which is represented in the object that is to be subsumed under it, for that is just what is meant by the expression "an object is contained under a concept." Thus the empirical concept of a plate has homogeneity with the pure geometrical concept of a circle, for the roundness that is thought in the former can be intuited in the latter. Now pure concepts of the understanding, however, in comparison with empirical (indeed in general sensible) intuitions, are entirely unhomogeneous, and can never be encountered in any intuition. (Kant 1787, p. 271)

Here the 'object' refers to that which we can see, hear, taste, smell or feel while the 'concept' refers to the general idea—like, the number 10. The problem then becomes of applying idea or concepts to empirical objects. We say that the plate is 'homogenous' with the concept or idea of the circle. By that we mean that the two things correspond to some very high degree of precision.[1] But sometimes the object, say, the economy, will be by no means homogenous to a high degree with the idea or concept; in this case, our model of it. Before we pursue this problem and how to deal with it, let us first turn to look a little deeper at the nature of abstraction.

Abstractions and Modelling

The reader might have noted that when we discussed our example of an abstract idea above—that is, the number 10—we did not allow the reader to imagine the signifier *10* (one-zero) as being the general idea that constitutes what we mean when we say 'ten'. This is a very important point and one often lost on people. You see, there are many different signifiers by which we can designate the abstract idea of 10—we can use the English word 'ten', or we can use the decimal sign '10', or we can use the French word '*dix*' or we can use the Roman numeral 'X'. Indeed, we could even go about creating our own personal signifier for the number 10 although doing so would be a rather pointless endeavour unless we could convince others to adopt this new signifier or word.

What the reader might be beginning to see is that this ability to abstract from particulars—say, ten cats or ten trees—and to form general ideas is inherently tied up with language. Indeed, it is only within a given linguistic system—or, more precisely, a system of signifiers—that we can form abstract general ideas. What is more, the capacity for this language of system of signifiers will constrain our ability to generate adequate abstract general ideas for whatever task we have at hand. A wonderful example of this is the fact that the Roman numerical system had no term for 0 (zero). This concept simply did not exist for the Ancient Greeks and Ancient Romans. The lack of existence of 0 caused all sorts of problems. It made any mathematical operations extremely cumbersome and probably restricted the ability of the Ancients Greeks and Ancient Romans to advance their capacity for reasoning and thinking. Eventually, the term 0 had to be imported from India by the Italian mathematician Leonardo of Pisa (Fibonacci) in the thirteenth century.[2]

It was the eighteenth-century Irish philosopher George Berkeley who most clearly noted this ability for language to furnish us with abstractions that could help us to perform operations of thought without which we would be lost. In his *Alciphron*, he wrote:

> But here lies the difference: the one, who understands the notation of numbers, by means thereof is able to express briefly and distinctly all the variety and degrees of number, and to perform with ease and despatch several arithmetical operations, by the help of general rules. Of all which operations as the use in human life is very evident, so it is no less evident, that the performing them depends on the aptness of the notation … Hence the old notation by letters was more useful than words written at length: and the modern notation by figures, expressing the progression or analogy of the names by their simple places, is much preferable to that for ease and expedition, as the invention of algebraical symbols is to this, for extensive and general use. (Berkeley 1732, p. 231)

This quote should speak clearly to any person who has ever dealt with economic reasoning. Much of this reasoning is done by replacing concepts like 'income' or 'exports'—already, in and of themselves, abstractions—with algebraical signs (Y for income, X for exports, etc.). This allows us to then manipulate these algebraic signs to help us think through problems that might be too complex to think through were we not working at such a high level of abstraction. Let us stop here for a moment and examine the level of abstraction taking place in one of the most basic and useful constructions we use in economics, that is, the national income identity which runs as follows:

$$Y \equiv C + I + G + (X - M)$$

Okay, by income (Y) we mean money flows of money to people and business as, well, income of course. If this book sells and the publisher gives me money, that money-flow will count as income. The right-hand side of the identity shows the sources of the flows of income. These are consumption (C), investment (I), government expenditure (G) and exports minus imports ($X - M$). In the example I have already given, the source of the income that I receive from the publisher is due to your consumption of the book. If you receive your income from a factory owner who has paid you wages to build a new machine, the source of your income will be investment spending. If you instead receive your income from the government which hires you to do some public service, say you are a police officer for example, then the source of your income will be from government spending. Income will flow to me if buyers of this book purchase it from abroad as these will be counted as exports, while if I spend some of my income on foreign goods, say coconuts, these will be counted as imports (in other words: money will flow out of the country) and they will subtract income from the domestic economy as the income will accrue to a foreign producer of coconuts.

Note the level of abstraction taking place here. All the measures themselves are high-level abstractions. 'Consumption' encompasses the purchase of this book but also dishwashers, bananas, underpants, blueprints for perpetual motion machines from dubious internet websites and cat-food. These abstractions are not always innocent and digging down into how these abstractions are formed can lead to insights about the macroeconomy that others who take these abstractions at face value will miss. In the USA, for example, Steven Fazzari and Barry Cynamon—two of the best empirical economists working at the time of writing—found that payments for government medical care programmes in the USA such as Medicare and Medicaid are counted as income to households in the national accounts.

This is despite the fact that these households never actually see any cash income from these payments which accrue directly to the healthcare providers (Cynamon and Fazzari 2014, p. 23). There is thus a richness to these abstractions that good economists would do well appreciating. Simple accounting is often more important to understand for empirical work than the most advanced econometric techniques on the market and yet it is often cast off and thought unimportant by those who style themselves as being at the top of the profession—that is, the 'high theorists'.[3]

But we economists are not even content with this high-level accounting abstraction. We go one further: we reduce these accounting terms themselves to algebraic symbols that we can then manipulate and play with. The above accounting identity is income disaggregated into its expenditure flows. But we can also break down income into the elements of income that it generates. We do so thus:

$$Y \equiv C + S + T$$

where we have consumption (C), savings (S) and taxes (T). Here we see that we get the flipside of the previous equation. Savings are the flipside of investment and taxes are the flipside of government expenditure. Investment is the flow of money out of the private sector, whilst saving is the flow of money into the private sector. Likewise, government expenditure is the flow of money out of the government sector and taxation is the flow of money into the government sector. We can then substitute the equations into one another, cancel out the consumption variable that we find on both side and we will be left with:

$$I + G + X \equiv S + T + M$$

The left-hand side of that identity is the source of expenditure and the right-hand side is where it ends up. We can, as we will see in a later chapter, reorganise this identity in a variety of different ways that will tell us interesting things about the macroeconomy that can prove extremely useful in making predictions and policy prescriptions. Let us here take a very simple example. Let us say that we are interested in what makes up private sector saving in an economy. Well, we would just rearrange the identity like this:

$$I + (G - T) + (X - M) \equiv S$$

Now we see that private sector saving is determined by private sector investment, the net expenditure by the government (i.e. the government deficit) and the amount of net exports sent abroad for sale minus the amount of money sent abroad to buy imports (i.e. net exports). If you think this through, it should actually become intuitively obvious that we have thus accounted for all sources of private sector saving.

This provides us with a very clear idea of what is going on when we make algebraic symbols stand in for already abstract concepts. This tendency in economics should never be left unquestioned. A good economist should always be able to justify to him or herself the status of the abstractions that are being used. Are they useful? Do they conform to something we can define in the real world? If we intend to substitute in data can we be sure that the methods used to construct this data are sound? Never take any of this at face value. Such algebraic abstraction is extremely useful, but it can also be used to throw up dust and allow people to engage in sophistical nonsense. An awful lot of microeconomics is precisely this: nice, neat, formal abstractions that have almost a zero-degree of homogeneity with the real world. They are far, far from Kant and his circular plate. Rather, they tend to be made-up stories with no real empirical content. They are, in that sense, fantasy constructions.

Another popular way to use abstractions in economics is through the use of diagrams. Again, Berkeley was keenly aware of such a use of abstract language. He also recognised that it was, when done correctly, rather useful for organising one's thinking. He wrote:

> We substitute things imaginable, for things intelligible, sensible things for imaginable, smaller things for those that are too great to be comprehended easily, and greater things for such as are too small to be discerned distinctly, present things for absent, permanent for perishing, and visible for invisible. Hence the use of models and diagrams. (Berkeley 1732, pp. 232–233)

But Berkeley was always keenly aware that these methods of thought could quickly degenerate. Dull thinkers would begin to believe uncritically in their own abstractions and would take them for having a validity all of their own. In doing so, they would end up talking embarrassing nonsense. Or, as Berkeley put it:

> Be the science or subject what it will, whensoever men quit particulars for generalities, things concrete for abstractions, when they forsake practical

> views, and the useful purposes of knowledge, for barren speculation, considering means and instruments as ultimate ends, and labouring to obtain precise ideas, which they suppose indiscriminately annexed to all terms, they will be sure to embarrass themselves with difficulties and disputes. (Ibid., p. 234)

This is the key problem with economics today. In banishing discussions like the one we have just undertaken, above economists have come to mistake their own abstractions for truth without examining the underlying presuppositions lying behind these abstractions. Economists build models, but they often do not question the form the models take or the ideas underlying the models. The famous applied economist Nicholas Kaldor was extremely concerned about the direction economics took after the war. He wrote:

> In terms of gradually converting an "intellectual experiment" … into a scientific theory—in other words, into a set of theorems directly related to observable phenomena—the development of theoretical economics was one of continual *de*gress, not *pro*gress: the ship appears to be further away from the shore now than it appeared to its originators in the nineteenth century … The process of removing the 'scaffolding,' as the saying goes,—in other words of *relaxing* the unreal basic assumptions—has not yet started. (Kaldor 1972, pp. 1238–1239)

The vast majority of models in mainstream economics are based on highly spurious and often simply made-up foundations; or, as Kaldor goes on to say, they are 'abstract and unreal theoretical assumptions [that] are also increasingly taken on trust' (ibid., p. 1239). What is more, most economists are thoroughly confused about how their models (supposedly) apply to the real world. Are they an approximation of reality that should be treated as a thought experiment; or are they a reflection of reality? Most economists would instinctively say that they are an approximation and a thought experiment, but when they empirically test them using econometric methods, we can only assume that they are thinking of their models as reflections of various degrees of accuracy, with the more accurate reflections 'fitting' the real-world data better than the less accurate reflections. Some gentle probing of the assumptions of most models show that this is a complete lie and farce and thus that a good deal of the profession would be as well off reading tea leaves or engaging in Tarot card reading.

This danger is, as has been pointed out by the fantastic work of Tony Lawson (1997), inherent in the tendency to mathematically model itself. Mathematical modelling leads the modeller to try to 'close' the model. That is, it leads the user to try to build models that are self-consistent and that tell a coherent 'story'. What this entails is that the processes being modelled are, in fact, deterministic. When we assume closure in the case of identities like the national income identity that we worked with above, this is no problem. Identities are identities. They are effectively tautologies that allow us to formalise our thinking about a certain topic but tell us nothing as to how real-world processes are supposed to occur. This is what models seek to do.

But unfortunately, as Lawson argues, economic reasoning is not well suited to such closed-system modelling. Determinism in economics is far different than, for example, determinism in physics or engineering. There are too many all-too-human variables, and humans do not act like the forces we encounter in physics or engineering. Humans are reflexive creatures who make choices that cannot be fully and completely explained. Even if we could explain and thus predict these choices, say by an all-encompassing psychological theory, people would then be given the choice as to whether they would simply stop acting in line with the theory now that they had heard about it and understood it. If I say that my theory says that you will continue reading the words on this page, you, being a creature with some modicum of free will, have the option as to whether you want to confirm my theory by reading on or refute it by choosing to put the book down for a moment and get a drink of water. My theory of you can never take away your freedom to act against my theory. Just the same, my theory of other people can never take away these peoples' freedom to act against my theory.

Thus we need to find a different approach. We need not throw all the models out. Indeed, in the following chapters, we will lay out some basic models that will enhance the reader's understanding of the macroeconomy greatly. But we need to conceive of what we are doing in an entirely different way. Economists have come to think that, just because they have sketched a series of equations on the blackboard and have then managed to solve them, they have said something of value about the real world. We must not do this; instead, we must try to put together an organised and orderly method for dealing with real-world data. Only then will we be able to try to think through how the macroeconomy actually works. This new approach, drawing on terminology from philosophy and psychology, I shall call 'schematism'. Before we move on to describing schematism, however, we will first look in detail at an important, albeit misinformed, debate that has sprung up around abstraction in economics in the 1960s and 1970s and still haunts the profession today.

Microfoundations, Deconstruction and Abstraction

The reader familiar with contemporary economics will likely be more than a little aware of the so-called microfoundations controversy. For the uninitiated, it is this controversy more than any other that has done the most damage to the study of economics over the past four decades. After the Keynesian revolution in the 1930s macroeconomists, even those who claimed Keynes' mantle but did not really follow in his footsteps began to focus on aggregates of individuals. Rather than look at how people maximise their utility and so forth, they would abstract away from these problems and instead look at how aggregate groups of people behaved. They began to talk about aggregates like national income, unemployment, effective demand, the multiplier and so on. This was perhaps the biggest advance that economic theory made since its inception. But because most economists were not willing to follow through this new way of thinking, this was not without contradiction.

As we have seen in Chap. 3, in order to think in this macroeconomics way, the American Keynesians had to basically repress the problems that arose when trying to reconcile the new macroeconomic theory with the microeconomic theory of rational behaviour. As we saw, Paul Samuelson just pretended that the problem did not exist because he wanted his economics to gel with his political preferences in the late 1930s. The true followers of Keynes never had such a problem. They did not believe in rational agents or utility maximisers or anything of the sort. As we saw in the previous chapter, once you take an uncertain future into account, the idea of a utility maximiser or a rational agent completely falls apart. This, as we shall see, meant that the microfoundations controversy was meaningless from the perspective of those who actually upheld the Keynesian revolution.

Basically, the microfoundations controversy arose when some economists, most notably Robert Lucas, lifted the repression that the likes of Samuelson had undertaken in the 1930s and 1940s. Lucas and others began to ask how exactly economists should reconcile the rational, utility-maximising individual with the macroeconomic constructions of the Keynesian era. What they quickly found was that none of the Keynesian (or, rather, pseudo-Keynesian) constructions worked once you threw the rational utility-maximising agent into the mix. If everyone was acting rationally, you would always have what economists call 'market-clearing'.

Thus labour markets, for example, would always clear and thus there could be no unemployment. Similarly, talking about investment falling short of intended savings or financial markets in turmoil made little sense if you assumed that all the actors involved were the crystal ball-wielding economic supermen that microeconomic theory must assume to function coherently. The microfoundations proponents had thus engaged in a rather crude deconstruction of the reigning pseudo-Keynesian models of the day and, in doing so, they had found a vacuum at the core. These models purported to fit together nicely with the old utility-maximising microeconomics but when taken apart and examined they did no such thing. The whole thing was a sham!

The mainstream did not know what to make of this. They had banished expectations and uncertainty all those years ago and had embraced the ridiculous postulates of the old microeconomics. So, they found themselves trapped. They turned instead to trying to work out silly logical reasons for why some people might not, in a given situation, act perfectly rationally. Nobel Prizes were handed out for coming up with ridiculously simple, common-sense reasons why this might not occur. Some said that different economic agents had access to different types of information and this could lead to problems. Others said that changing prices too quickly might be difficult for institutional reasons. This empty and vacuous nonsense, often dressed up in semi-difficult but ugly and unwieldy mathematics, became the basis for debate for decades. Those who may have had interesting thoughts about economics were disincentivised to enter the profession in these years. Seeing the level of what passed for debate, many just avoided the whole dreary game altogether or drifted into obscurity by passing over to the heterodox side of the profession.[4] Those who remained were either extremely mundane, stuffed-shirts who could do a bit of maths but could not think themselves out of a wet paper bag or opportunistic types who played the game without believing in it, all the while trying to slip in a time bomb that they hoped would eventually blow the whole edifice up. The latter never really happened, and, as the mainstream slipped deeper and deeper into incoherence, it was the crisis of 2008 that really led people to question the strange things that were happening within those decades in that crucial era of economic change.

In all this time, the assumption that economics should be microfounded was never questioned by those working in the mainstream of the profession. The very question of what 'microfoundations' actually meant was itself highly obscure, but such questions were rendered taboo (remember what the mainstream think of anything resembling methodological questions!?). For those who built the microfounded models, it typically meant including what came to be known as a 'representative agent'. This representative agent was supposed to be a stand-in for all the other agents in the economy. Since all the agents were assumed to be rational, crystal ball-wielding utility maximisers then, the argument went, you could simply assume that they were also clones of each other. If they were all clones of each other, there was no need to model any of them separately. You just aggregate them into a single individual and lay out this individual's rational, utility-maximising properties. What was being undertaken here, as the careful reader will now appreciate, was an enormous and unjustified act of *abstraction*.

There were a few in the profession who got a rather bad smell from all this. But they seemed unable to articulate themselves in any coherent manner because they remained trapped inside the mainstream cage. Take Alan Kirman, for example. In 1992, he wrote quite rightly that:

> [The]reduction of the behavior of a group of heterogeneous agents *even if they are all themselves utility maximizers*, is not simply an analytical convenience as often explained, but is both unjustified and leads to conclusions which are usually misleading and often wrong. (Kirman 1992, p. 117)

Kirman was completely justified in writing this, of course. But he has not succeeded in breaking out of the intellectual prison that the microfoundations crowd have built for themselves. He genuinely seems to believe in the possibility that the idea of a rational, utility-maximising agent is an abstraction that can meaningfully be applied to the real world. This means, as we saw in a previous chapter, that we must assume that people in the really existing economy effectively know the future and that they can form solid, ordinally comparable preferences when they are making decisions. Faced with what this might mean, Kirman does, at one point, admit that he cannot actually form a meaningful positive programme out of the negative critique that he is laying out. He writes:

> I would ... suggest that the way to develop appropriate microfoundations for macroeconomics is not to be found by starting from the study of individuals in isolation, but rests in an essential way on studying the aggregate activity resulting from the direct interaction between different individuals.

> Even if this is too ambitious a project in the short run, it is clear that the "representative" agent deserves a decent burial, as an approach to economic analysis that is not only primitive, but fundamentally erroneous. (Ibid., p. 119)

This is the typical stance of a theorist who has discovered a massive flaw in a theoretical edifice but, in continuing to believe in the underlying presuppositions of that same edifice, represents the impossibility that his critique has exposed can merely be solved given enough 'time'. A far more promising method of attack that Kirman's criticism opens up in is exploring why we should want to establish microfoundations in the first place. If, as Kirman suggests, the truly interesting phenomenon that we wish to study is the 'the aggregate activity resulting from the direct interaction between different individuals', then we are no longer dealing with microfoundations or microeconomics at all. Rather, we are dealing with macroeconomics proper. Let me be crystal clear on this point: once we move our object to inquiry to the level of 'aggregate activity resulting from the direct interaction between different individuals', we are, by definition, dealing with macroeconomic phenomena. Thus the whole question of microfoundations becomes moot.

Microfoundations, in any true sense, are, if looked at in any detail, impossible. This is because we are dealing with millions, perhaps even billions, of individuals when we study any given economy. Even if we assumed that all these millions and billions of people were rational, crystal ball-wielding economic supermen with fixed preferences, there is absolutely no way we could model them in any conceivable manner. Attempting to do so would be a bit like trying to count all the grains of sand on any given beach; not only would it be pointless, but it would also be hellish and absurd. The only alternative is to begin to aggregate these individuals in some manner or other; that is, the only alternative is to engage in some level of abstraction. But this abstraction will be entirely arbitrary. Why should we lump Jim together with John or Mary together with Martha? What justifies this aggregation? Are we going to deal with an abstraction called 'social class' or are we going to deal with an abstraction that lumps together those that like Marmite and contrasts them with those that do not? Obviously, some of these abstractions are better than others, but they still lead to problems of their own.

Let us take an example that we will deal with in detail in a later chapter: namely, income distribution. In the old Kaleckian literature, it may appear at first glance that individuals were aggregated in line with their social class. Kalecki, like Marx, and those who followed him, regularly talked about 'workers' and 'capitalists'. Workers in the Kaleckian literature received income from wages, while capitalists received income from profits. But, if taken literally, the more you compare this to the real world, the more this distinction becomes blurry. If a worker—that is, someone who receives most of their income from wages—also holds stock options in their pension funds, how do we account for the fact that the dividends that so accrue are clearly profit income? Actually, this is based on a fundamental misunderstanding. 'Workers' and 'capitalists' in the Kaleckian framework do not refer to really existing individuals; rather, they refer to abstractions.[5] Wage income and profit income are merely two types of income. Dividing them up is similar to how, to take an example we have already seen, national income is divided up between consumption, savings and taxes or consumption, investment, government spending and net exports. No one would—or rather, no one *should*—think that these abstractions have any 'real' existence, but they are nevertheless useful, provided that we deploy them carefully and properly. When we refer to social class in economics, we should be doing the same thing; we should not be categorising individuals and forming abstractions; rather, we should be breaking down income flows and forming abstractions about these. What we are discussing here is far closer to accountancy than it is to aggregative sociology or group psychology.

The microfoundations enthusiasts are going down the other path. They recognise, rightly, that when we engage in abstractions in the manner just laid out, we are doing macroeconomics proper. Thus, they seek to try to form abstractions out of actually existing individual human beings as they suppose these human beings to be. But this is completely absurd even on its own terms—that is, it is absurd because, as we have seen, any given level of abstraction will be arbitrary—and it becomes 20 times as absurd if we take seriously the critiques of modelling individuals as rational agents with fixed preferences that we laid out in a previous chapter. The fact of the matter is that this is simply not the way that economics should be done, and any attempt to do economics in this way will only result in absurdities and rubbish.

What is more, the macro approach is far less intrusive and dictatorial. When we start grouping people together based on what you assume to be their behavioural similarities, we are, in a very real sense, engaged in totalitarian thinking. To try to reduce a human being to a fixed set of behaviours or motivations and then to lump them together with other human beings who share these behaviours or motivations is to do enormous violence to the individuality of that human being. Categorising the income flows that individual receives or the type of work they do or their employment status at any given moment in time is far less violent. Put simply, the idea that some hair-brained economist somewhere is assuming that he can say something concrete about my motivations reduce me as a person to these motivations and lump me in with people who he assumes to have the same motivations as me makes me feel violated and reduced to an object. But if another economists somewhere observes that I have been unemployed for a given number of months or that I receive £*x* of my income from wages and £*y* of my income from profits, I really do not feel myself as a human being all that reduced. What has been done to me is no more offensive than what my accountant does to me when he tries to put my accounts into some sort of order. Such abstractions are wholly constructive and simply exist to help us organise our world around us. It is, contrary to what many believe, microeconomics and microfoundations that are the source of totalitarian reasoning in economics, not macroeconomics.

Schematics and Economic Reasoning

What then is the difference between a schema and a model? The term has its origins in the work of Kant. The reader will recall that we discussed above the status of what we mean, for example, by particular numbers, that is, abstractions. The reader might recall that we found that when we tried to understand any given number, say, '10' outside of particular reference points—say, ten dogs or cats or houses or trees—we would find ourselves in great difficulty. Likewise when we examine the signifier we use to describe the number—be it 'ten' or '10' or '*dix*' or the Roman numeral 'X'—we would find that these were rather arbitrary. Indeed, if we so felt, we could invent our own numerical system and give the number 10 a new signifier. What Kant meant by schema was the actual conceptualisation lying behind the number. He wrote:

> The schema is in itself always only a product of the imagination; but since the synthesis of the latter has as its aim no individual intuition but rather only the unity in the determination of sensibility, the schema is to be distinguished from an image. Thus, if I place five points in a row, … , this is an image of the number five. On the contrary, if I only think a number in

> general, which could be five or a hundred, this thinking is more the representation of a method for representing a multitude (e.g., a thousand) in accordance with a certain concept than the image itself, which in this case I could survey and compare with the concept only with difficulty. Now this representation of a general procedure of the imagination for providing a concept with its image is what I call the schema for this concept. (Kant 1787, p. 273)

This is a rather dense passage but necessarily so because what it is describing is an elusive concept. It is not describing a particular instance of the concept—in Kant's example five dots,...—nor is it describing the signifier by which we designate the concept, rather we are trying to describe the concept itself. This process of trying to describe the concept is what Kant calls the 'schema of the concept'. Here we should note that the schema has no empirical existence. What we mean by that is that we shall never encounter the schema of the concept in our lived experience. What we will encounter are only particular instances of the schema of a concept. For instance, in the case of the number 10, we might encounter ten cats today, ten dogs tomorrow and ten houses the next day. We will also encounter the signifier used to designate this concept in multiple forms. For instance, in the above paragraphs we have encountered multiple variations of this signifier: 'ten', '10', '*dix*' and so on. But we will never encounter the schema of the concept '10'.

The reader might then be justly confused. 'This schema sounds very mysterious altogether', they might say, 'If I cannot properly imagine it and I never experience or encounter it what on earth is the it?' Although there is a certain sense of difficulty with schemas, they cannot be avoided. These schemas make up a large component of our thought and are integral to how we understand and interpret the world around us. Consider the advent of the number '0' that we discussed earlier. Before the number '0' was introduced into the West, mathematicians had a very difficult time making calculations. The schema that they were using was ill-suited for making advances in mathematics. But once they had reconstructed their schema by integrating the number '0' into it—that is, when they adopted the decimal system and thus introduced a new schematic structure—they found that they could make serious advances in various sciences much more easily.

So, what use then are schematics in economics? When done properly, all economics is in some sense schematics. When we apply economic reasoning to the world around us, we are effectively engaged in schematics. Again, consider the examples of national income identities that we gave earlier. The abstractions that we dealt with in the form of these identities were schematics proper. We never encounter 'consumption' directly, nor do encounter 'investment' directly. Rather, these are constructions that allow us to organise and understand the world around us. The C and the I in the national income identities have the same status as the number 10 or 0. If the reader thinks about it, they will quickly appreciate that just as when the West integrated 0 into their schema of thought, they made advances, and when we as economists integrated the national income accounts into our schemas of thought, we made serious advances in understanding the economy.

Thinking through schematics in economics allows us to consider better the status of models. Models are not themselves schemas. Rather, they are abstract conceptions built out of various schemas. For example, the ISLM model familiar to students of macroeconomics and that we shall encounter in later chapters is not itself a schema. Rather, it is an abstract conception, a sort of machine, built out of various schemas. These schemas include: savings, investment, liquidity preference, the multiplier, the money supply, the interest rate and output. If we understand that schemas are actually themselves abstract concepts, then it follows that models are abstract constructions built out of abstract concepts. They are abstractions built on abstractions.

This is where we should heed Berkeley's warnings. It is obvious that we must be rather careful when handling abstractions and schemas. Given that they have no empirical or experiential existence, we have to be delicate about how we apply them. But when we are handling models, we are dealing with at least two levels of abstraction. If we are not very careful, we will, as Berkeley wrote, 'be sure to embarrass ourselves with difficulties and disputes' that are not only entirely irrelevant but also entirely silly. We also have to be very careful because if we start taking an abstraction built on abstractions—that is, a model—as an immediate representation of reality, then we will soon find ourselves talking absolute rubbish. Many economists deny that they do this but the fact that many of them try to estimate their models using econometric techniques implies that they are being disingenuous: either they *do* take their models to represent reality in which case econometric estimation is justified, or they do not in which case they are being disingenuous in their use of econometric estimation.

We should not say that models are entirely pointless. They may well be interesting exercises in putting together the various schemas that we hold into a coherent whole. But the schemas that we hold are far, far more important than the models themselves. If these schemas are in conflict with the world of experience, our models will be complete rubbish. This is why we must dismiss any and all schemas that do not hold up to empirical scrutiny. On the other hand, the better the schemas we possess, the better we will be able to analyse the real economy. When new schemas of thought like the multiplier and Keynes' notion of effective demand were introduced in the 1930s, these made economic explanation far easier. The introduction of these schemas was far more important than the models that were later built using them. Indeed, the latter were really only didactic tools built by economists who wanted to see if they had understood the implications of the schema sufficiently. Model building and model comparison, properly understood, is really just economists arguing amongst themselves as to the implications of the schemas they hold at any given moment in time. And, again we stress, the really interesting question is whether or not they hold schemas which display a high degree of homogeneity with the real world.

This is actually recognised by many economists who work in governmental and business institutions. Their voices are rarely heard because of the loathsome elitism that exists at the academic level of the profession, but if you sit down and talk with them, it quickly becomes obvious that it is the basic schemas they are taught that are useful in their day-to-day lives, not the rather silly abstractions that academic economists use to distinguish themselves as 'very clever people' from the simplistic idiot that they often assume the working economist to be. W.R. Allen brought up just this point at a conference in 1974. He actually took the time to talk to economists working at a high level in the government. This is what he said:

> The economic theory [the government economists] are using is the theory most of us learned as sophomores. [They] think the economists' framework is the right one to weigh the advantages and disadvantages as best [they] can see them—but when economists sit down and prepare models to try to trace out these consequences in any sophisticated fashion, [they] think it's just about as apt to be misleading as it is helpful. (Allen cited in Hutchison 1977, p. 169)[6]

Schemas, in a very real sense, dictate how we view the world. They are like lenses in a pair glasses that we look through. Models can dictate how economists view reality too, but only economists who do not appreciate the fact that models are simply thought experiments that should be used in training us as to what implications the schemas we hold have. It is really the schemas that are most fundamental. Another way of thinking about this is that schemas are the building blocks of the narratives we form about the world. We put our schemas together with experience and data from the real world to form coherent narratives about what is going on in the economy. Those economists who do not have a good grasp on their schemas—that is, often, those economists too focused on modelling for its own sake—tend to be unable to form their own narratives about what is going on in the economy and what should be done about it. This leads them to fall prey to 'fads' or 'fashions'; whatever seems popular in economic discourse at any given moment in time will be absorbed into the narrative structure of the second-rate economist. Thus, the same economist throughout his career may have been a monetarist in the 1980s, an adherent of inflation-targeting in the 1990s and early 2000s and a promoter of NGDP-targeting post 2008. Unable to think for themselves, there is a marked tendency in the discipline to follow whatever fashion is in the air at the time. This explains why, as is often noted within the profession, it often matters less *what is being said* in the debate than *who is saying it*. Because economists misunderstand what their theories are and what they mean, economics has marked tendencies to generate cults of personality. Out of these form herd behaviours and fads that are far more extreme and all-encompassing than in other disciplines. Once a fad has set in within the profession to raise questions about this fad critically is often to completely isolate oneself because those involved in the herd movement are completely unable to question whatever pet theory has been handed to them by an authority figure.

In this book, when we turn to reconstruct some aspects of a coherent economic theory, I implore the reader to focus less on any models that are put forward—there are not many—and to more so focus on the schemas that are being expounded, how they work and, above all, what they mean. The goal is not to have a series of equations that 'solve' to tell us something about how the economy operates, but rather to integrate and understand various schemas of thought that becomes tools that we can apply to the really existing economy. The thorough understanding of the ins and outs of a given schema—say, liquidity preference or the multiplier—is far more important for a good economist than combining this schema with other schemas to construct a 'solvable' model. The latter is really only a derivative result of the former—and it can be extremely misleading if good schemas are not chosen, utilised properly and the results are not understood for what they are. In order to understand what we might call the essence of a given schema, it is necessary to look at it from as many directions as possible. This is why, in the chapters that deal with these aspects of economic theory, we have endeavoured to supplement verbal elaboration with algebra, empirical examples, numerical examples and graphics. The reader need not understand all the examples given—although if they do so much the better!—rather they need first and foremost get the thrust of the argument and try to properly integrate a given schema into the way they think about the world.

Economics, properly understood, is not the art of constructing models. Rather, it is the art of furnishing, elaborating, understanding and integrating schemas into one's process of thought. Economics is not about building abstract castles in the sky. Nor is it learned or perfected by engaging in such constructions. It is more like a language that is learned through thorough understanding and practice. You do not learn good sentence construction by studying linguistics; rather, you learn it by becoming as acquainted as possible with language, with words and their multifarious meanings. The vast majority of the problems with economics today are associated with the fact that economists have tried to learn to become masters of prose by consulting the technical manuals on linguistics; and these manuals have themselves been produced by men and women who can barely string a sentence together.

A General Theory of Bias in Science

In 1892, the British statistician Karl Pearson published an epoch-making book entitled *The Grammar of Science*. In the book, Pearson undertook an attempt to survey the key aspects of science in his day—although, given his predilections, the book leans more heavily towards physics and statistics. More importantly, however, Pearson attempted to ground science in a coherent philosophical and epistemological worldview. He attempted what few working scientists attempt today: to integrate their understanding of science into a logical and coherent worldview.

Today scientists and many social sciences with little understanding of philosophy and epistemology have a tendency to fall back on a reactive materialism as their default worldview. This is a materialism that is completely unreflective; the details are never worked out—and if we are to be honest, it more so resembles an ideology than a properly reasoned and considered worldview. Pearson actually gave some consideration of what worldview the discoveries of modern science actually led to and he concluded that it led to what we would today refer to as a rationalistic idealist point-of-view, in the tradition of George Berkeley and David Hume. Pearson's book went on to have a major impact on the development of physics in the twentieth century as it contained the seeds of relativity theory. Einstein adored the book and, after integrating it into his worldview as a young man, went on to recommend it to his friends at the Olympia Academy.

Pearson's book is a masterpiece. No work of scientific philosophy comes close to touching it today. And most scientists arguably do not truly understand the philosophical implications of what their theories tell them because they are so illiterate in the language of philosophy.[7] But Pearson's book was also overly optimistic. Like many of his generation, he truly believed that the language and method of physics could be carried over into all disciplines. This led Pearson to conclude that science could colonise all other spheres. It also led him to integrate certain pseudo-scientific ideologies into his views on morality which in turn led him to becoming a fierce advocate of eugenics.

Pearson's intentions were largely noble. He thought that science represented a wholly disinterested way of looking at the world. His instinctual revulsion at the sight of the poor and the disabled notwithstanding, there was a lot of truth in this view when it was applied to the physics of his day. Here is Pearson himself characterising what he thought of as the scientific mind-set:

> The scientific man has above all things to strive at self-elimination in his judgements, to provide an argument which is as true for each individual mind as for his own. The classification of facts, the recognition of their sequence and relative significance is the function of science, and the habit of forming a judgement upon these facts unbiased by personal feeling is characteristic of what may be characteristic of the scientific frame of mind. (Pearson 1892, p. 6)

This is broadly the view that many have of science today. Yet it is simply not true. Science is, in fact, filled with bias, prejudice and ideology. This is true of some sciences more than others. Lower-level physical theories, for example, are to some extent free from significant bias.[8] But when we move towards the more flimsy sciences, we find that they are dominated by bias. Economics is probably the worst of the bunch.

Since we have already spent so much time on economics in this book, let us turn instead to a study undertaken to examine bias in a different science, one that is on far firmer footing than economic but far less firmer footing than lower-level physics. The study, undertaken by one Brian Martin,[9] focuses on a now long-forgotten debate from the 1970s as to whether high-flying supersonic transports (SSTs) would destroy the ozone layer and in doing so expose the human population of the world to life-threatening solar radiation. Martin chose this particular topic because at the time it was an extremely emotional and politicised topic. As we shall see, this plays a large factor in how much bias a scientific theory will be subject to.

After surveying the arguments, Martin found that the authors were heavily invested in the theories that they were pushing. The side that supported the view that SST pollution was damaging the ozone layer insisted that those who contested the view prove it wrong. While the side that denied that SST pollution was damaging the ozone layer insisted that the onus was on those who held the theory to prove it true. Martin argues that when scientific arguments are shot through with this level of bias, they are no longer scientific arguments; rather, they are political arguments that are using quasi-scientific language as their vehicle. Martin lays down some pertinent general observations on how this bias manifests itself at a psychological or epistemological level:

> People tend to selectively observe and interpret information in a way that supports their preconceived ideas. Because of this, the personal commitments of individual scientists can help to explain the link between the scientists' presuppositions and their pushing argument. In a scientist, this process might operate as follows. The scientist starts with an original idea or hypothesis, perhaps arrived at as a creative solution to a certain problem. In testing or validating the idea, the scientist will tend to notice and use supporting evidence and arguments. Data that seems mainly supportive will be studied, analysed and applied so that every possible advantage can be drawn from it. Seemingly irrelevant or inconclusive items will be filtered from advantageous components, or interpreted in a way that promotes the argument. Evidence that seems mainly to contradict of challenge the argument at hand may be ignored completely or explained away or reinterpreted and twisted in support for the argument. (Martin 1979, Part III)

Our culture tends to instil in us an idea from a very young age that scientists do not do this. Yet every working scientist or academic knows that this is the case. The myth of the purely disinterested scientists is just that: a myth. In reality, very, very few scientists have a temperament that favours pure disinterestedness. Instead, it is the institutional structure of science itself that ensures that biases are filtered out. Yet this filter functions more effectively in some sciences than in others. In some sciences, like lower-level physics, it seems to operate almost seamlessly. Yet in others, like economics, it tends to generate tribal factions, closed-off discussion and generally dogmatic and uninquisitive adherence to the discipline. There have been enough missives written on the institutional problems in the economics profession (see, for example, Lee and Harley 1998). Here we are interested in what is in the nature of economic theory that makes it so prone to bias.

Let us think of bias in terms of a disease and a given science as a body. In order for the disease of bias to not severely damage the body of science, various institutional checks and balances must be in place. Immunisations, if you will. In different sciences, immunisations operate at different magnitudes. Some sciences have healthy immune systems and others have weak immune systems. Those with healthy immune systems tend to not suffer too much from bias while those with weak immune systems are often rendered paralysed by bias.

The first and most important component of a healthy scientific immune system is the repeatable controlled experiment. We must be clear here. By 'repeatable controlled experiment' we do not mean an experiment that can be repeated over and over again like, say, an econometric estimation that can be repeated by various people on the same data. Rather, we are talking about something resembling laboratory conditions. That is, an experiment which can be repeated over and over again so that conditions can be tweaked and possible interfering factors can be isolated. In disciplines like economics, this possibility does not exist. Events in history only happen once. Then they become history. We cannot rewind the clock and run an experiment on economic data over and over again, trying to isolate various polluting influences on the data that we have. Rather, we have to use statistical tricks to try to mimic this procedure. But these statistical tricks never work nearly as well as a true controlled experiment.[10]

The second most important component of a healthy scientific immune system is a small (and preferably shrinking) number of untested or untestable assumptions. Every discipline has some assumptions that are untoasted and untestable. But, as William of Ockham told us long ago: *less is more*. A discipline that rests largely on untested and untestable assumptions—such as economics—will often display a tendency to allow these sorts of assumptions to proliferate endlessly, allowing its practitioners to make basically any claim that they feel like making. This allows for bias to creep into the discipline and, if left unchecked, to metastasise and destroy its body completely.

The third and final component of a healthy scientific immune system is that the discipline remains as unpoliticised as possible. Different disciplines will have different levels of potential for politicisation. For example, Newtonian physics is almost completely bereft of politicisation because, say, the theory of gravity really makes no difference to how we as human beings organise our lives and build our societies. Economics, on the other hand, is all about organising our lives and structuring our societies. For this reason, it is highly prone to politicisation.

Let us try to formalise these observations to some extent.

$$B = \frac{UA + POL}{RCE}$$

where B is bias, RCE is the potential for repeatable controlled experiments, UA is untested assumptions and POL is level of politicisation.

Using this formula, we can construct a graph plotting bias as a function of these variables. Figure 5.1 plots these variables against one another to give us a general theory of bias in science. Note that we are quantifying

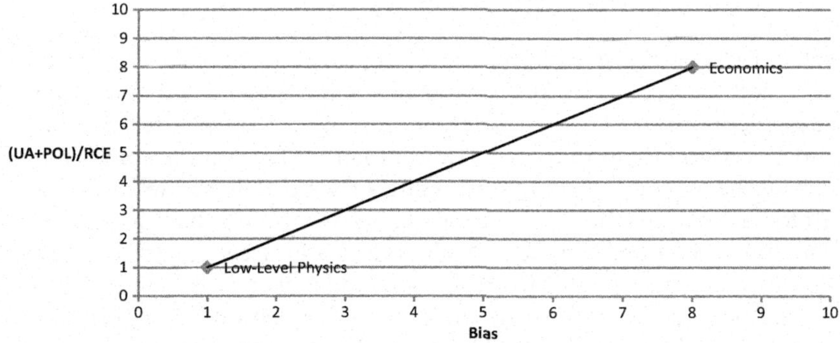

Fig. 5.1 A theory of bias

bias out of ten, with ten being completely biased and zero being completely free from bias.

As we can see, we have placed low-level physics down at the bottom. Since it is a reasonably healthy science with a healthy immune system, it is relatively free from bias. Economics, on the other hand, is far up the scale as it has a very weak immune system and tends to suffer from bias more often than not. We could, of course, attempt to fill in the rest of the graph drawing on other disciplines. But that is far outside of the scope of this present book.

When a discipline has a very weak immune system, it is extremely prone to bias. This means that those in the discipline must be extremely cautious in how they proceed. A man with a healthy immune system does not need to fear catching a common cold, but a man with a very weak immune system must be very cautious during cold season. Economists must be extremely vigilant. Their discipline does not have a very healthy immune system at all. It is extremely prone to bias. If economists are not careful, extremely unhealthy habits of thought will creep into the discipline and destroy it. The discipline will then fall back on authoritarian hierarchies in order to enforce its truth claims. Heterodox economists do not currently suffer as badly from bias as mainstream economists; they tend to be more cautious about their discipline. But they too must remain vigilant. They have just as unhealthy an immune system as the mainstream as they deal with identical material. Because of this, it is just as easy for them to fall ill and for the body of their discipline to fall apart.

Appendix: The Joke

What has been discussed in the foregoing chapter is actually captured, to a very large degree, in a joke that goes around academic and finance circles about economists. The joke goes like this. There is a physicist, a chemist and an economist stranded on a desert island. They are extremely hungry, but suddenly they stumble on a crate of soup that has washed ashore. Unfortunately, all the soup is canned and they do not have a can opener. The physicist suggests that they climb a nearby tree and throw the cans against a large rock until it breaks open. The chemist suggests that they should build a fire and expose the cans to the heat until they burst open. But the economist disagrees. He insists that resources are scarce and that the misled ideas of the physicist and chemist would only lead to wasting some of the soup. The physicist and the chemist ask the economist what his bright idea is to get the soup cans open. He begins: 'Well, let us assume for a moment that we had access to a can opener.'

This joke actually captures a great deal about the underlying methodological problems with economics that we have been dealing with in the preceding chapter. The physicist and the chemist are also assumed to approach the real world with abstractions in their minds. The physicist naturally thinks in terms of relationships of gravitational force while the chemist naturally thinks in terms of the points at which certain chemical compounds will alter their properties. These abstractions, however, are immediately and empirically tied to the real world. The notion that the soup will boil and under the pressure created the can will split open is thought of in highly abstract terms, but it has a corollary in the real world. It is like Kant's perfect circle and the plate. Although the ideas about boiling soup and pressure can nowhere be found directly in the real world, we can nevertheless find a fairly good approximation when we approach reality. Thus, the abstraction proves useful and the chemists training produces a mode of thought that can be utilised for real-world understanding. The economist, on the other hand, completely ignores the real world when he or she makes abstractions. The abstractions are completely self-generated and they need not find a corollary in the real world.

If we thus wanted to carry on the joke, we might say that the economist, after laying down the assumption that the trio had access to a can opener, would then proceed to build a highly abstract model based on a variety of other arbitrary assumptions. Perhaps he would make assumptions about exactly how the trio would act when they had the can open and the soup was flowing. Perhaps he would try to model their relative labour productivities and figure out how the soup should be best distributed when it was opened with the hypothetical can opener. When the whole exercise was over, the fact of the matter would be that the trio have no can opener. The whole endeavour was completely pointless because it started from fallacious first principles. Sigmund Freud once quoted the writer K. Fischer to the effect that 'wit must unearth something hidden and concealed'. In the case of this particular joke about economists, it literally unearths one of the most troubling problems in economics, a problem that accounts much of why the discipline flies high in the clouds away from any contact with the real world.

Notes

1. Note they do not correspond perfectly. You will never be able to find a *perfectly* circular plate in the real world. It will always suffer from some imperfection or another.
2. The history of the number 0 is inherently tied up with the history of Western philosophy. Many of the early pre-Socratic philosophers spent a great deal of time asking essentially 'How can nothing *be* something?' This caused a great deal of confusion for the Greeks. Indeed, even today the status of 'nothing' is a deeply confused concept not just in philosophy, where twentieth-century greats like Heidegger and Sartre have tarried with it in their major works, but also in physics where researchers are constantly finding new particles with ever more confusing properties.
3. This appears to be because prestige within the profession does not accrue so much to careful, humble people who do hard work but rather to flashy theorists who engage in showmanship. These implicit value criteria have done irreparable damage to the discipline in the past few decades.
4. It should be noted that, although the heterodox side of the profession in these years were indeed obscure, they nevertheless managed to do heaps of extremely interesting work. While the mainstream languished in the intellectual cages that they built for themselves, the heterodox pushed ahead forming new theories about the massive institutional changes that were taking place in those years. It is no coincidence that all the interesting debates at the time of writing this book—from financial instability to income inequality—were the focus of heterodox research in those dark days.
5. The same can and will be said of the distinction between 'bulls' and 'bears' in a later chapter on the financial markets.
6. The present author has experienced this first-hand. When I went for interviews in various private sector institutions in the City of London, I usually asked whether the forecasters used models. I was always met with either a smirk or a tirade against modelling. Indeed, I would advise any reader thinking of going into practical work not to do this in interviews as I think that it leads the interviewers to assume that you are an economist overly interested in modelling which seems to me someone who they do not want to

deal with. This also accounts for why, at the time of writing, some prominent private and public sector institutions who hire economists are getting firmly behind the student protest movement calling for curriculum reform. The people I have spoken to in this regard say that they basically have to retrain economists on the job when they hire them out of the present university system. If this were any other discipline, this would be nothing short of scandalous.

7. Today, philosophical illiteracy is actually worn as a badge of honour by some prominent physicists. The astrophysicist Neil deGrasse Tyson is a prime example of a scientist who, perversely, wears his ignorance of a large component of human knowledge as a badge of honour. Reading what he thinks to be philosophy is literally cringe worthy. In one interview, he seems to believe that a serious example of a philosophical questions is: 'what is the sound of one hand clapping?' (Pigliucci 2014). This is the equivalent to thinking that a fair representation of astrophysics can be gleaned from an episode of the *X-Files*. This is truly a sad state of affairs, especially given the increasingly dubious pseudo-theories coming out of disciplines like astrophysics—such as the highly metaphysical and completely unbelievable theory of the 'multiverse'.
8. By 'lower-level physics' we mean aspects of physics like Newtonian mechanics, electromagnetism, thermodynamics, the basic precepts of relativity theory and so on. We seek to distinguish these from, for example, speculations about the origins or nature of the universe which seem more prone to bias. We might also distinguish here between 'practical physics' and 'speculative physics', with the latter often verging on crossing the boundary into metaphysics.
9. Martin has since gotten himself involved in what look to be less noble causes including supporting various anti-vaccination advocates. This does not, to this author's mind, discredit the broad thrust of his 1979 book. Indeed, history appears to have vindicated Martin on this front; people do not seem much concerned with SST pollution destroying the ozone layer at the time of writing—although this could be due to a decline in interest in SSTs. According to Google NGram, interest in questions surrounding the ozone layer peaked around 1991–1992 indicating that there may have been a faddish component to the issues, as Martin's work may have suggested.

In addition to this, it appears to me that some of the controversial stances attributed to Martin—such as his supposed support of conspiracy theories surrounding the origins of the AIDS virus—are not really held by him at all. Rather, he appears to use these theories as case studies to examine how the peer-review process works in science. I quote Martin in the original from a paper he wrote that many have argued shows him supporting conspiracy theories of the origins of AIDs:

> The aim of presenting this story is not to argue that this particular theory is correct. Nor is it to blame any particular individuals. What is at issue is the normal processes of peer review and publication within the scientific community and whether these processes are the most appropriate to benefit society as a whole. (Martin 1993, p. 624)

10. Another way to put this might be to say that a lower aptitude for repeated controlled experiment renders a theory subject to far more uncertainty. Uncertainty and aptitude for repeated controlled experiment are inversely related to one another.

References

Berkeley, G. (1732). *Alciphron or, the minute philosopher*. http://www.cfh.ufsc.br/~conte/berkeley-alciphron.pdf

Cynamon, B., & Fazzari, S. (2014). Household income, demand, and saving: Deriving macro data with micro data concepts. Working Paper. http://papers.ssrn.com/sol3/papers.cfm?abstract_id=2211896

Hutchison, T. W. (1977). *Knowledge and ignorance in economics*. UK: Basil Blackwell.

Kaldor, N. (1972). The irrelevance of equilibrium economics. *The Economic Journal, 82*(328), 1237–1255.

Kant, I. (1787). *Critique of pure reason*. UK: Cambridge University Press.

Kirman, A. (1992). Whom or what does the representative individual represent? *The Journal of Economic Perspectives, 6*(2), 117–136.

Lawson, T. (1997). *Economics and reality: Economics as social theory*. USA & UK: Routledge.

Lee, F., & Harley, S. (1998). Peer review, the research assessment exercise and the demise of non-mainstream economics. *Capital and Class, 22*(3), 23–51.

Martin, B. (1979). *The bias of science*. Society for social responsibility in science (ACT). Republished online at: https://www.uow.edu.au/~bmartin/pubs/79bias/

Martin, B. (1993). Peer review and the origin of AIDS—A case study in rejected ideas. *BioScience, 43*(9), 624–627.

Pearson, K. (1892). *The grammar of science*. London: Adam and Charles Black Publishers.

Pigliucci, M. (2014, May 16). Neil deGrasse Tyson and the Value of Philosophy. *Huffpost Science*.

PART II

Stripped-Down Macroeconomics

CHAPTER 6

Differing Conceptions of Equilibrium

Equilibrium is, as we shall see in the following chapter, a devilish concept when it is applied in economic argument. Yet, it is a concept with such humble roots. The term itself basically means a point in time at which the mutual competing influences of a system are balanced. The roots of the word reflect this too. The word, according to the etymological dictionaries, appeared in Latin in the 1600s in the form of *aequilibrium*, which was made up of the Latin term *aequus* meaning 'equal' and *libra* meaning a 'balance' or a 'scale'. The term had, on occasion, moral overtones. There was much talk about equilibrium being a state of 'balanced mind'. That is, a mind in which various competing influences were well harmonised with one another, ensuring that no unsavoury passions got the upper hand. In this regard, little has changed in the use of the term over the past four centuries.

The economists who first utilised the term in its modern form seemed aware that they were drawing mechanical analogies. In his *Principles*, Alfred Marshall wrote:

> We want first to look at a simple balancing of forces which corresponds to a mechanical equilibrium of a stone hanging by an elastic string, or of a number of balls resting against each other in a basin. (Marshall 1890, p. 269)

The key to this analogy is that equilibrium is seen as a sort of steady state. When the weights on the scales have reached their equilibrium balance,

W.P. Pilkington, *The Reformation in Economics*,
DOI 10.1007/978-3-319-40757-9_6

when the stone no longer pulls on the elastic, when the balls stop at rest against each other in the basin, all movement has ceased. The forces at work have stopped exerting their pull and everything remains at rest. Perhaps, then, the most perfect equilibrium is a ball floating in a spaceship that has broken the orbit of the earth. Here not even gravity exerts any force, and one can imagine, given the right conditions, that such an equilibrium might remain stable for a very long time indeed.

The reader might note that equilibrium is a metaphor that relies on both space and time. The ball hovers, unmoving in space, but it does so only at a given moment in time. The ball can only hover in space for a period of time, say, until an astronaut bats it with his hand or a passing asteroid pulls it into its gravitational field. To extract the notion of time from the equilibrium metaphor is to imagine an area of space that is not inhabited by time, an area of space where nothing moves or changes, rises or falls. Such a conception of space is not to be sought in this world. Perhaps such a space is inhabited by some timeless divine entity and perhaps we might experience such a space when we pass into the Great Beyond. But whatever you believe in this regard, such a metaphor is ill-suited to the world we live in, a world that labours under the weight of time.

Thus we must say that the metaphor of equilibrium in this world of ours rests on our ability to imagine a spatial equilibrium at a *moment of time*. In the case of the ball floating in space, this moment of time might be very long indeed. Under the right conditions, perhaps, the ball will remain unmoved for centuries until it is sucked into the gravitational pull of a passing asteroid. But in the case of the economy, we shall see that this moment in time is often conceived of as an infinitely small instant. This instant should best be thought of, perhaps, as that which is captured in a photograph. The faster the shutter speed, the smaller the instant of time captured on the camera. Economists, when they speak of equilibrium, are referring to a moment captured at a very fast shutter speed indeed. Let us now turn to the different ways in which this metaphor is deployed in economic reasoning.

Pure Static Market Equilibrium

The pure static market equilibrium is the one in which the student of economics is most often first introduced to. In its very basic form, it is the equilibrium of a single market. Samuelson and Nordhaus, for example, describe the concept of market equilibrium to their readers in this manner. Just pages from the introduction to their famous textbook, they write:

> What is a market equilibrium? It represents a *balance among all the different buyers and sellers.* Households and firms all want to buy or sell certain quantities depending upon the price. The market finds the equilibrium price that simultaneously meets the desires of buyers and sellers. Too high a price would mean a glut of goods with too much output; too low a price would produce long lines in stores and a deficiency of goods. Those prices for which buyers desire to buy exactly the quantity that sellers desire to sell yield an equilibrium of supply and demand. (Samuelson 1995, p. 24—emphasis in original)

The reader should note that the authors are referring to a moment frozen in time. Surely, there is always bidding going on in any given market. If you attend a country market, for example, there is constant movement. People are moving from stall to stall making bids on various goods and the bidding only ceases when everyone closes up and goes home. An even clearer example can be seen on the stock exchange or at the horse races. Here screens are set up to display the prices of a given share or a given bet (i.e. the odds) at any moment in time. When the markets open, these prices fluctuate over and over again until the markets close. Equilibrium in such a market can only truly be captured by a person with a camera taking a photograph of the screen at any given moment in time.

The notion of a static market equilibrium, of a moment in time where supply and demand are balanced at a given price, is a very transient one indeed. It undoubtedly exists in those moments when the share price does not move or the odds on the bet stay temporarily the same. But it does not exist for long. Nevertheless, there is a case to be made that the concept is useful here. The problems begin to arise, however, when we try to conceive of the economy as a whole in such a manner.

In order to try to extend this notion of a static market equilibrium outside of one particular market at one particular moment in time, we must recognise that such a notion is of a properly multi-sided act. In order for a market equilibrium to come into existence, there must be some degree of consensus among those participating in the market. In the example we gave of the share prices, this consensus is simply that one person's bid price overlaps with another person's ask price and a transaction thus takes place giving rise to the formation of a market prices. 'I want $100 for this share', I say to you, to which you reply, 'That seems fair, here is $100.' The equilibrium price for that particular type of share is thus, at that moment in time, $100. But this gets a lot more complicated when we assume that such information about the desires of every market participant is transmitted to each and every market participant at each moment in time. When we extend this idea to the economy as a whole, we are back to Samuelson and Nordhaus' definition of market equilibrium as '*a balance among all the different buyers and sellers*' (ibid.—emphasis in original). This sort of equilibrium implicitly rests upon a very specific notion of how information is transmitted through the economy. Shackle summarises this as such:

> Equilibrium is a means by which all persons in choosing their acts can be supposed to have equal and perfect relevant knowledge and equal freedom. Given a list of persons, besides himself, composing the society, and given for each of these persons a list of all the acts possible to that person, each person can be supposed to draw up a list of all the distinct combinations of acts, one or other of which combinations will constitute the circumstances surrounding his own act. For each of these combinations he can be supposed to specify the act that he himself would choose, in case he were assured that the combination in question would prevail. The conditional promises, one for each person, thus derived, can now be supposed to be treated as a system to be simultaneously solved. (Shackle 1965, pp. 12–13)

What Shackle is outlining here is something similar to the idea of a 'Walrasian auctioneer'. This was a trope introduced by Leon Walras, the founder of modern general equilibrium economics. The idea underlying this is that a list of markets bids and asks are drawn up and called out by an auctioneer to all market participants who then formulate their plans in accordance with the best possible outcome (Keen 2011, pp. 178–180). It has been noted many times before that Walras' auctioneer is actually more similar to the existence of a central planner in a command economy than to anything that we find in a market or capitalist economy. But this is embedded in the nature of the approach. In order to assume that perfect information is present to all participants in an economy at any given moment in time, there must be assumed to be some channel of communication through which every agent communicates their 'plans' simultaneously to one another. Unless we assume that the agents are engaged in telepathic communication, we must assume that this channel of communication is external to the agents themselves. Hence, the Walrasian auctioneer or something similar is needed for the market equilibrium argument to remain coherent.

It is difficult to stress this enough: either we accept the argument for some sort of omniscient auctioneer—a sort of benevolent Godlike figure—and hence we can accept at least this component of the market equilibrium argument or we reject it and thus reject the market equilibrium argument. In practice, it seems very difficult indeed to accept the auctioneer argument. It appears to be not merely an abstraction divorced from reality but something like a *deus ex machina*, an external element introduced into the narrative to try to hold it together that cannot be justified in any way beyond simply appealing to the fact that the narrative holds together once it is introduced. The goal here then appears to be less about explaining how the economy might actually work and more about producing a coherent narrative that reflects the theorist's predisposition to thinking in terms of general market equilibrium.

What we have shown is that when we generalise from a static equilibrium period in a single market to a manifestation of static equilibrium in the whole economy, we run straight into the glass wall of how information is distributed. A static equilibrium in a single market really needs no discussion of this. The price is simply set in line with at what price buyers are willing to bid and what price sellers are willing to ask. Early marginalist theorists who had actually thought through the implications of their arguments recognised this. Friedrich von Hayek, for example, wrote:

> I have long felt that the concept of equilibrium itself and the methods which we employ in pure analysis have a clear meaning only when confined to the analysis of the action of a single person and that we are really passing into a different sphere and silently introducing a new element of altogether different character when we apply it to the explanation of the interactions of a number of different individuals. (Hayek 1936)

Clearly applying what works in one market to the whole economy is enormously problematic. The metaphor does not carry over at all easily. In order to try to transfer the metaphor from a single market to the whole economy, we need to, as Shackle says, understand how people will coordinate their activities with one another in such a way that it produces a coherent result. We can only assume that this can be spontaneously done if people are engaged in telepathic communication with one another. Otherwise, we have to introduce an external institution of agent that takes the 'promises' of each individual and draws up an enormous list that all the individuals will then study until they all come to undertake their acts. That such a premise is completely at odds with any theory that can even begin to approach the study of the real economy should be immediately obvious to the reader. The question then becomes why actual academic economists should take such an argument remotely seriously.

This, it would seem, has the same emotional roots as religious instruction. Human beings seem to find emotional solace in telling themselves that there is an omnipresent entity 'out there' that ensures that the world coheres in an organised and functional manner. This, it would seem, is the need that static market equilibrium theories meet. They allow the adherent to form a narrative about the world around them as being spontaneously coordinated by an external, benevolent paternalistic figure: the Divine Auctioneer. Tear away the mask of the general equilibrium theorist and you will typically find lying beneath the face of the priest. And 'believing' that this sort of equilibrium directed by the benevolent, paternalistic figure of the Divine Auctioneer occurs in the real world is, as we shall see, where piety has come to reside in our supposedly Godless world. Walras, properly understood, was the founder of a modern-day secular religion: the Church of the Market.

Dynamic Teleological Market Equilibrium

But today only the most extremist of the marginalists would buy into anything like the pure static market equilibrium conception of how the economy works. Such an approach is often associated with the so-called New Classical or the Rational Expectations school. Just because this group is an extremist faction of purists should not lead us to discount the force that their arguments had on the development of modern marginalist economics. Indeed, it is from the baseline space that they occupy that the mainstream marginalist argument really begins. Most marginalists today only subscribe to a modified version of this theory, but we should be clear that it is this theory that undergirds their conception of how real-world economies work.

The non-purists—often misleadingly called New Keynesians—will introduce various 'rigidities' into the pure static market equilibrium constructions. Thus they might try to show that wages are rigid or that information is imperfect or asymmetric. Most of these arguments are mundane, but some of them tip over into the absurd. The typical manner in which one rigidity is described, namely what has come to be called 'menu costs', is to introduce the idea that if a restaurant wanted to change their prices, there will be costs involved in the printing up of new menus. While this argument is not to be taken wholly literally—the economists who make it are also referring to retagging, updating of computer systems and so on—it is nevertheless rather ridiculous. In effect, many economists in this camp have made their careers effectively pointing out the obvious. They have undertaken pseudo-observations and pushed these as entailing all sorts of revolutionary paths forward for the marginalist research programme. Anyone not heavily indoctrinated in the dogma, however, can see on the face of it that these are not interesting theories, and any reasonably intelligent person could probably come up with tens if not hundreds of similar examples.

What these arguments allow the non-purists to do is to reintroduce some of the ideas from partial equilibrium theorists like Alfred Marshall. Thus they distinguish between the 'short-run' and the 'long-run'. These do not generally refer to any actual period of historical time but are rather to be understood as first and foremost logical and ultimately tautological constructions. The 'long-run' is the period in which the economy reaches its pure static market equilibrium, while the 'short-run' is the period when it is ever in the process of adjusting. This distinction, given that it does not refer to any agreed-upon period of historical time, gives New Keynesian economists an awful lot of leeway. Generally speaking, it will be found that economists in this camp define these periods in line with their political preferences. Strongly interventionist economists will generally think that the short-run is a very long period of time indeed, while more *laissez-faire* economists will tend to think that the short-run is a very brief period of time. This is how many mainstream economists hide their political opinions behind the cloak of the vaguely defined technical language of the short-run and the long-run.

No matter what a given economist's politics those that adhere to this framework, all share one thing in common: namely, that they do not view the economy as being in a perpetual pure static market equilibrium but rather see the economy as always tending towards this state. This is why we might refer to this as a 'dynamic teleological market equilibrium'. It is 'dynamic' insofar as the economy is seen to be moving and evolving through time. But it is 'teleological' insofar as the economy is always seen to be tending towards some always already fixed 'end point' or 'final cause'. In the 'short-run' all sorts of things will interfere with the economy crunching out a pure market equilibrium result, but some unnamed tendency, some spectral entity will always be pulling individuals towards the 'long-run' equilibrium end point. If we examine it carefully, we find, of course, that this unnamed spectral agency is once more the Walrasian auctioneer or the central planner in a new guise.

In the case of a pure static market equilibrium, the Divine Auctioneer draws up a list of all possible actions for all the individuals in the economy and then hands this list out for all these individuals to study before they make their move. The end result is a perfectly harmonious equilibrium in which time and movement have no relevance as everything happens at once. But in the case of a dynamic teleological equilibrium, something slightly different is conceived to be going on. We must still assume that all individuals are provided with information as to what their fellow agents are going to do, but we must also assume that due to some imperfections in the process, some individuals do not act in the way that they told the Divine Auctioneer they would act. For example, all the restaurant owners in our imaginary economy may have told the Divine Auctioneer that they would reduce their prices by $\$x$ if a given amount of demand was forthcoming, but then when the time comes, they simply do not change their price downwards sufficiently due to their incurring of menu costs. The people who wanted to go to the restaurant to eat find that the prices are higher than they were promised by the Divine Auctioneer and so the economy is thrown out of equilibrium.

Nevertheless, because the Divine Auctioneer continues to distribute lists of the subsequent actions of all agents, these firms eventually get competed away. New, more innovative firms eventually enter the market that tell the Divine Auctioneer the true prices of their goods when a given amount of demand is forthcoming. These eventually drive out the 'bad' disequilibrating firms and so the market will tend to smooth itself out in the 'long-run'. Similar cases can be made with regard to labour markets, financial markets and so on. Here we see clearly the leeway given for the economists personal political inclinations. He or she can just as easily argue that the period of adjustment will be weeks or months as they can argue that every time one disequilibrating wrinkle is smoothed out, another one will appear and thus the economy will be in perpetual disequilibrium outside of strict intervention. Thus the theory effectively says everything and nothing. It is so malleable that the person espousing it can basically come to any conclusions about the real economy that they like. This vacuum is typically filled either with that person's particular political proclivities or, if the 'research work' is being done in a key institution, by the Party Line of that institution at any given moment in time which is almost completely determined by politics.

The real problem here is obvious: why on earth should we believe this argument if we did not believe the pure static equilibrium argument? If we think that the Divine Auctioneer is a ridiculous trope, then why should this argument be any more valid than the last one? The answer is that it is not. Rather, it is generally picked up on by marginalist economists because they can generate 'real world' results using it. In the pure static market equilibrium model, unemployment, for example, simply cannot be explained. But the dynamic market teleologists can explain it as a short-run wrinkle that has not yet been ironed out. In effect, the argument is designed to hold the comforting notion of pure static market equilibrium intact and thus reap the emotional rewards that come with it while at the same time not completely and utterly ignoring what might be going on in the real world. Being almost completely a blank slate, due to the undefined but central ideas of 'short period' versus 'long period', the theory makes for perfect ideology. It provides a smokescreen behind which economists and institutions can hide their political preferences, thus lending them an air of legitimacy. But, perhaps, most importantly, it allows the debate to be cast in such a way that people who do not speak economese cannot get a say in the matter. First you must learn Latin, only then can you speak like a priest. But by the time you have learned the Latin, you have likely already come to believe in its Sacred Power.

Dynamic Non-Teleological Equilibrium

Those who followed Keynes largely rejected the pure static market equilibrium story altogether. They circumvented the Walrasian story altogether. They assumed that there was no reason to assume any sort of coordination of individual plans in a given economy unless this coordination was explicitly directed. They simply did not believe in the story of the Divine Auctioneer and thus they came to think that it is not so much instability that needs to be explained as it is relative stability. When stability is generated in a capitalist economy without any central authority—like, say, a government—undertaking explicit plans, it is this phenomenon that we must explain. Indeed, it is highly likely that any time such unplanned stability seems to come about, we should be best on our guard against some particularly poisonous instability that might immediately follow.

Those who worked in this tradition tended to try to posit models with mainly exogenous variables. There are many of these, from the Harrod–Domar growth model of the 1930s and 1940s (Domar 1946) to the stock–flow consistent models of today (Godley and Lavoie 2006). But they all share the same suspicion of the Walrasian story. They do not concern themselves with various micro-level phenomena. They effectively say: 'The economy is enormously complex; we cannot theorise how individuals coordinate based on some fantasy of a benevolent, paternalistic Divine Auctioneer; rather let us just assume that the process of coordination will be a messy one and start our analysis from there.' These economists then go on to produce formal models that can be tested for relative stability.

The notion of equilibrium is not thrown out in this approach. Rather, it is modified. Economists working in this tradition are more so interested in studying various equilibria insofar as these tend towards stability. Here the equilibria are, in a sense, arbitrary. They do not in any way produce some sort of efficient result. Rather, they are recognised as positions that the economy might take in which all forces are balanced and nothing changes. 'If investment is $\$x$ and savings is $\$y$ and the government balance is $\$z$ what level of employment will be produced?' The equilibrium is achieved when the forces that have been 'plugged into' the model from outside produce a result that does not change when left to itself.

This is why we opt to call this is 'non-teleological dynamic equilibrium'. It is a dynamic equilibrium in the sense that we can constantly update the model with new exogenous variables to produce movement in the equilibrium. And it is non-teleological in the sense that we imagine no Divine Force standing behind the economy pulling it in any given direction. Here we say nothing about, for example, the flexibility of wages or prices. A theorist working in this tradition would simply respond that the only way to understand how flexible wages or prices might be at any given moment in time is to examine the available data. Questions such as these are purely empirical and economists working in this tradition see it as a very silly exercise indeed to form logical arguments about Divine Auctioneers first and then approach the data only with these arguments in hand. Rather, they start from the empirical reality of the situation at hand and then try to figure out what changes will appear if certain variable (wages, income, etc.) shift.

Such an equilibrium could also be conceived of as a 'stock–flow equilibrium' (Pilkington 2013c). Thus the equilibrium—that is, the point at which no change takes place—is generated by the level of stocks and flows at any given moment in time. This is similar to how we might view a bathtub that is partially full with the plug open but the tap turned on. If the outflow of water through the plughole is exactly matched by the inflow of water from the tap, the overall stock of water in the bathtub will remain constant until the stock–flow equilibrium is altered by, say, turning off the tap or plugging the plughole. Again, we see very clearly that this is a very different conception of equilibrium than that put forward by those who want to argue that individuals in a market economy will always, through some mystical processes, diverge on the best possible solution when left to themselves.

The two conceptions of equilibrium could not be further from one another. The mystical market equilibrium is odd and bordering on the theological, while the stock–flow equilibrium conception is just a thought experiment that one undertakes in one's own mind to try to get a handle on the varying stocks and flows that we see in any real economy at any given moment in time.

Expectations Equilibrium, Kaleidoscopism and Historical Time

Non-teleological dynamic equilibrium is becoming ever more popular today among non-mainstream economists. Many are attracted to it because it allows them to continue to use their modelling skills but to do so in a far more nuanced and realistic manner. Using these types of techniques, many non-mainstream economists try to build models that integrate real-world processes. These models are so far beyond the market equilibrium models featuring the Divine Auctioneer that we need not even stress this point. For this reason, they are an enormous step forward and should probably be promoted in as many classrooms as possible. But there is another way of doing economics that is gaining less currency today but that still has some supporters and certainly was the manner in which Keynes' own *General Theory* was written, not to mention other great works of twentieth-century economics. This is an approach which we might refer to as the 'expectations equilibrium' approach or the 'kaleidoscopics' approach, and it is one that seeks as best it can to integrate historical rather than simply logical time. It is this type of approach that we will be dealing with in the present book.

All the approaches that we have seen above deal primarily with logical time. What we mean by 'logical time' is time as it plays out in a logical thought experiment that we undertake in our own imaginations. When dealing with logical time, we specify all the variables and follow through our calculations to a given end point. We introduce certain assumptions and evacuate any truly new phenomena from emerging. This latter is key: *in logical time, nothing new or novel can emerge*. Everything that emerges from our thought experiment or systems of equations must be put there prior to the fact. In this sense, we can summarise by saying simply that *logical time is the mode of time that a system inhabits if it is fully deterministic*.

The time we experience in lived reality is not like this at all. While it would be nice to think that we could know the future with certainty from the present conditions prevailing at any moment in time, this is simply not the case. If any reader is not convinced of this, I would simply ask them, if they think that the future is truly determinate, why they are not playing the financial markets and making an awful lot of money rather than reading this book. No, we live in a world where we do not know the future and are thus faced with actually making decisions in the face of an uncertain future. We are not alone in this respect; all other economics actors are in exactly the same position. This is why economics, if it is to properly applied, must come to terms with this uncertain dimension of existence.

It is perhaps worth dwelling on this point a little longer before we consider the equilibrium expectations or kaleidoscopics approach any further. While we will deal in more detail with the implications of decision-making in the face of uncertainty in a later chapter, here we should just point out some implications of the deterministic worldview versus the uncertainty worldview. In the deterministic worldview, there is no choice proper. Indeed, there is no free will. Since every event is already determined by the present situation, we are completely powerless in the face of the future. We are mere puppets having our strings pulled by the hands of Time. Not only is this view rather offensive—indeed, given that our entire legal and moral system is based on the notion of responsibility, it is actually threatening to our way of life—but it is also intuitively implausible. We as humans feel that we are making decisions in the here and now and that these decisions have real effects moving into the future. To feel oneself as having one's decisions completely pre-determined by an outside force is, in our society, a symptom of a serious mental disturbance that could, under present law, be enough to have one forcibly confined.

We must assume that we are not the only ones making such decisions that affect the future. It seems intuitively reasonable to suppose that our fellow human beings also have this capacity. If our fellow human beings have the same capacity for creative decision as we do, then we face uncertainty on two fronts. The first is in the recognition that we do not know exactly what results our decisions taken in the here and now will have in the future. We can try to form some reasonable degree of approximation in this regard, but we can never know for certain. More radically still, we must recognise that since we cannot tell what effects the decisions of other people will be and what effects these will have moving into the future, we are subject to a sort of second layer of uncertainty. Taken together, we can see just how radically we are limited in our foresight of the future. But we are compensated for this by being effectively free beings to a very large extent. We are beings who not only must make creative decisions but also must take responsibility for these decisions.

The question then becomes: how do we integrate this into economic theorising? This is the approach that we will try to develop in this book. We have already laid some of the groundwork in previous chapters, and we can now recognise a bit more what we mean by 'open systems' versus 'closed systems'. As we have previously noted, a closed system is a deterministic system. Since we live in a world of uncertainty and relative freedom of choice, we must instead approach this world through the conceptual framework of an open system. This does not mean that we cannot construct tools that will help us to think about this world. But it does mean that in using these tools, we must, first and foremost, recognise their inherent limitations. In order to do this, we have to be very explicit about which variables are subject to changes in human decision-making. In order to see this clearly, let us take one of the now popular non-teleological dynamic equilibrium models that is currently on the market—namely, the model of Steve Keen. We choose this model for two reasons. First of all, because they are quite popular in the non-mainstream at the time of writings and, secondly, because, due to the nature of the material they deal with, they come very close to being true open systems models.

Keen's goals have long been twofold. First, he wants to build models in which debt matters. He contends, quite rightly, that the mainstream of the profession have not been taking seriously the importance of debt for the functioning of the macroeconomy and this had led them to be blind to the possibility of serious financial crises. The second component of Keen's project is that he wants to explicitly extricate himself from the tradition of equilibrium modelling. For some time, Keen seems to have equated non-equilibrium modelling with using differential equations rather than linear algebra. If this were true, then much of modern mainstream marginalist microeconomics would be non-equilibrium theory due to the fact that they use differential calculus. Obviously, this judgement is untenable. At the time of writing, however, Keen has come to see the utility of introducing, what seems to be, on the face of it, a decision-based distinction (Keen 2014). This distinction is that between *ex post* and *ex ante* that was first introduced into economics by Gunnar Myrdal in the early twentieth century. Myrdal summarised the distinction as such:

> An important distinction exists between prospective and retrospective methods of calculating economic quantities such as incomes, savings, and investments; and ... a corresponding distinction of great theoretical importance must be drawn between two alternative methods of defining these quantities. Quantities defined in terms of measurements made at the end of the period in question are referred to as *ex post*; quantities defined in terms of action planned at the beginning of the period in question are referred to as *ex ante*. (Myrdal 1939, pp. 46–47)

Now, it should be clear from the quote above that Myrdal is here trying to introduce the element of *decision* into his theories. What Myrdal is saying is that people can plan to do one thing and then find that, due to circumstances partly caused by their decision, the end results do not meet with the ones that they planned. A good example of this may be the familiar paradox of thrift in which everyone tries to save together, but because in doing so they consume less, this reduces the income of everybody and hence the total level of savings. Here we see a disconnect between the *ex post* plans laid out by savers (i.e. to save more) and the *ex ante* results that these plans lead to (i.e. to reduce total savings). The reason for this disconnect is because, as we have stated above, people do not know what other people will do at any given moment in time. They must make a decision, in this case the decision to save, in the face of uncertainty about what other people will do and the effects that this will have. The end result is that non-coordinated activity can take place that results in outcomes that no one really aimed at.

Keen, however, appears to have tried to purge these concepts of the elements of decision inherent in them. His reference here is Hyman Minsky, and he notes again and again that the key to Minsky's whole construct is that 'for income to grow, investment therefore had to exceed savings' (ibid., p. 274).[1] Clearly what is going on here that is of key interest to us is that certain decisions must be taking place that may or may not cohere with one another. In the above-quoted sentence, it is clear that these decisions are being undertaken by investors and savers. But rather than focus on these decisions, which is what Minsky did, Keen instead focuses on the passive residual that they produce: namely, the fluctuations in money and debt. These fluctuations are, however, entirely passive. What we are really interested in is the decisions themselves and how closely they become coordinated with one another. The fluctuations in debt or money that result are merely effects of this underlying cause.

The phrase 'I'm pointing at the moon and you're looking at my finger' comes to mind here. Money and debt are mere passive entities in the understanding of economic activity. They are simply the recordings of various human interactions. They are not interesting in and of themselves and to accord them a central place in the analysis is to engage in some sort of anthropomorphic reification, that is, to lend to something that is an abstract or passive medium some sort of concrete human-like agency. This leads Keen to then confuse the functioning of financial markets with the levels of debt or money in existence in these markets at any given moment in time. But again, the level of money or debt in these markets is not the key aspect that we should be interested in here. Rather what are of prime importance are the decisions that are being taken by investors in these markets. Understanding these decisions and what drives them is the key to understanding the financial markets.

We highlight the case of Keen because he has come so close to engaging in theorising that takes into account expectations and historical time, but he nevertheless stops short. He has become entirely focused on what he thinks to be a concrete—and, presumably, measurable—variable in the form of debt or money. But this variable is being driven by something else entirely. In tracking this variable and modelling it, all you are really getting is second-hand information about the past trajectory of expectations. But this past trajectory can already be divined without recourse to the passive entities of money and debt. If we look, for example, at margin debt in the stock market, we see that it expands in lockstep with share price increases (Keen 2013, p. 6). But this is entirely obvious because the same force is driving both: namely, expectations. When investors are confident about the stock market, they both bid up its price and take on higher margins of debt. Keen thinks that he has found a 'causal link' between the share prices and the level of margin debt, but this is really a spurious correlation that tells us all of nothing. Rather, the two are being driven by the expectations of investors in the stock market. This is why Keen's framework can actually tell us nothing about the likely future course of these markets. So long as expectations remain buoyant, the share prices and the margin debt levels can continue to rise. We might say that expectations are currently overheated and that this will likely result in a future collapse, but this is an entirely different argument.

If we want to understand how the real economy operates, we must have respect for the independence of human decisions and expectations. To try to reduce these to a formula or to try to claim that they are 'overdetermined' by some abstract measure of money or debt is only to throw ourselves into an enormous muddle. Rather, we need an open-ended approach where all our theories show is what might happen *if* certain decisions are made by people. This was Keynes' approach at its essence. He allowed for people to make non-coordinated decisions and he then tried to work out what would happen should these decisions be made. He did not try to find concrete explanations for these decisions and nor did he try to find variables within the economy that were imbibed with mystical powers that supposedly held sway over the decision-making of individuals. In the chapters that follow, we will try to lay out a skeleton of such a framework, one which places emphasis on the fact that everything we study as economists is ultimately the result of people making decisions in the face of an uncertain future.

Note

1. There seems to be some major confusion here in Keen's paper. He further writes that 'for effective demand and income to grow over time—the creation of new money had to exceed the fraction of household income saved and not made available for investment'. As we shall see in a moment, this is by no means true. Keen also suggests that this is novel to Minsky's (and his) work. He writes:

   > Minsky's principle thus transcends Keynes on both 'income equals expenditure' and 'savings equal investment', with Keynes's identities applying in the abstraction of equilibrium, but Minsky 's applying in the (normally) growing economy in which we actually live. (Ibid., p. 275)

But this is not at all clear. In Keynes' theory, money that is saved by households and not made available to finance investment is money held for the purpose of liquidity preference which is the centrepiece, as we shall see later in this book, of Keynes' theory of financial markets. Keynes is well aware that if liquidity preference increases—that is, if household saving increases and some of this is not made available for new investment—then either the quantity of money must increase to accommodate this or the rate of interest will rise (Keynes 1936a, b, Chapter 13).

We should be clear, however, in saying that a rise in the rate of interest does not automatically lead to a fall in investment. This is because investment is 'overdetermined' by any number of different factors (animal spirits, future expected profits, etc.). So even if households increase their liquidity preference and no new money creation occurs, firms may still increase their investment at the now higher rate of interest (in doing so, they will speed up the velocity of existing money in the economy).

In this regard, Keen appears to hold a sort of monetarist view of investment. He seems to think that if the available money supply falls, then the rate of investment must also fall. But as we have known since the *General Theory* when the available money supply falls, all that occurs is that the rate of interest—that is, the price on money—increases. What effect this will have on investment depends entirely on other factors. In his paper, Keen states time and again that unlike the monetarists, he does not assume a constant velocity of money. But it is clear from analysing the above statements that they do indeed assume a fixed velocity of money. In the paper, when he finally introduces a non-fixed velocity variable, it becomes unclear why he did not simply, like Keynes and the Post-Keynesians, ignore the question of money in the financial markets and instead turn his attention to the rate of interest.

References

Domar, E. (1946). Capital expansion, rate of growth, and employment. *Econometrica, 14*(2), 137–147.

Godley, W., & Lavoie, M. (2006). *Monetary economics: An integrated approach to credit, money, income, production and wealth.* UK: Palgrave Macmillan.

Hayek, F. (1936). Economics and knowledge. *Ludwig von Mises Institute*. http://mises.org/page/1411

Keen, S. (2011). *Debunking economics* (2nd ed.). USA: Zed Books.

Keen, S. (2013). A bubble so big we can't even see it. *Real World Economics Review*. No. 64. www.paecon.net/PAEReview/issue64/Keen64.pdf

Keen, S. (2014). Endogenous money and effective demand. *Review of Keynesian Economics, 2*(3), 271–291.

Keynes, J. M. (1936a). *The general theory of employment, money and interest*. http://www.marxists.org/reference/subject/economics/keynes/general-theory/

Keynes, J. M. (1936b). *Preface to the German edition of the general theory of employment, money and interest*. http://gutenberg.net.au/ebooks03/0300071h/printall.html

Marshall, A. (1890). *Principles of economics* (8th ed.). New York, NY: Cosimo Classics.

Myrdal, G. (1939). *Monetary equilibrium*. UK: W. Hodge.

Pilkington, P. (2013c). A stock-flow consistent approach to a general theory of pricing. *Levy Institute*. Working Paper No. 781. http://www.levyinstitute.org/pubs/wp_781.pdf

Samuelson, P. (1995). *Economics* (15th ed.). New York, NY: McGraw-Hill.

Shackle, G. L. S. (1965). *A scheme of economic theory*. UK: Cambridge University Press.

CHAPTER 7

Theories of Money and Prices

What is money? That question is one that will never be agreed upon by humankind. The problem here is that a good proportion of people you meet have an idea in their head about what is and what is not money. This is because, like many aspects of economics, people concern themselves with money on a daily basis, thus many of these people will come to some conclusion about the object in question. Lorie Tarshis once remarked that 'most people do not pretend to be physicists. Few of us doctor our own illnesses. When we have to cope with the problems of physics or chemistry, we call in the experts. But we all feel that we are economists' (Tarshis 1947, p. 6). The situation with money is even more extreme than it is with most aspects of economics. Money has a strangely personal character to it, and most people who think about it tend to project their own experiences with it onto the rest of the world. Thus, a man will often take the manner in which he manages his own money as the manner in which money in general should be managed by society at large.

Most economists are not much more sophisticated than this. A good deal of marginalist theory stems from thought experiments that seem more so built, as we have seen, out of a sort of moral reflection on how Man behaves in a perfectly harmonious society than on any attempt to dive into the depths of the economic world as it actually exists. When it comes to the question of money, many economists discuss it, not in a factual manner, but rather in a manner that is conducive to their particular

W.P. Pilkington, *The Reformation in Economics*,
DOI 10.1007/978-3-319-40757-9_7

habit of thought. The meaning of money, for many economists, is the meaning that it *must* assume for their thought experiments and models to work. That is why, in mainstream economics, money is often thought of as a neutral element that has no actual effects on economic activity. The thought experiments are not set up by first studying the factual aspects of the real world; rather, they are set up in a manner that allows the economist to manipulate them in the most simple and convenient way possible. The factual reality of money (and of many other things) are then broken and bent in such a manner that they fit this *a priori* theoretical framework. This is why most textbook discussions of money start from what might be called the 'barter myth'. Take Samuelson on the matter, for example:

> What is money? Money is the means of payment. But more than that, money is the lubricant that facilitates exchange… Just imagine how complicated economic life would be if you had to barter goods for goods every time you wanted to buy a pizza or go to a concert. What goods or services would you offer Sal's Pizza? What goods and services could you offer Madonna? And what about your education—what could you barter with your college for tuition that it needs? Because everyone accepts money as a medium of exchange, the need to match supplies and demands is enormously simplified. (Nordhaus and Samuelson 1995, p. 28)

The idea here is an appealing one. After all, if we had no access to money, we would all be engaged in barter, would we not? And this would be desperately inconvenient, would it not? Behind this explication of the function of money lies a myth, a made-up story taught to every economist when they lie innocent in their cradle. This myth was brought into being a very long time ago by Adam Smith who wrote in his *The Wealth of Nations*:

> When the division of labour first began to take place, this power of exchanging must frequently have been very much clogged and embarrassed in its operations. One man, we shall suppose, has more of a certain commodity than he himself has occasion for, while another has less. The former consequently would be glad to dispose of, and the latter to purchase, a part of this superfluity. But if this latter should chance to have nothing that the former stands in need of, no exchange can be made between them. The butcher has more meat in his shop than he himself can consume, and the brewer and the baker would each of them be willing to purchase a part of it. But they have nothing to offer in exchange, except the different productions of their

> respective trades, and the butcher is already provided with all the bread and beer which he has immediate occasion for. No exchange can, in this case, be made between them. He cannot be their merchant, nor they his customers; and they are all of them thus mutually less serviceable to one another. In order to avoid the inconveniency of such situations, every prudent man in every period of society, after the first establishment of the division of labour, must naturally have endeavoured to manage his affairs in such a manner, as to have at all times by him, besides the peculiar produce of his own industry, a certain quantity of some one commodity or other, such as he imagined few people would be likely to refuse in exchange for the produce of their industry. (Smith 1776, pp. 127–128)

Smith then goes on to tell us how various commodities were likely used as a unit of account for many years until clever people found that precious metals were the most convenient. This, as we shall see, is a hoary old myth. But why did the likes of Samuelson pick up on it? Again, this was because it fit with their *a priori* theoretical conception of the world. The marginalist analysis, at least since the work of Leon Walras, has started from the assumption that people engage in barter. It does this purely for convenience as it provides the economist with a very simple thought experiment. If money is introduced at the outset, this might mess up the little model and that would upset the economist to no end. So, they assume that money enters the picture afterwards—and they find that the Smithian myth fits in with this quite nicely.

This view of money is also implicitly tied up with the tendency for marginalist economists to deal primarily with scarcity and the distribution of resources, in contrast to their heterodox colleagues who lay their emphasis on growth and production. By assuming that money is something that economic agents choose as a convenient store of value, mainstream economists tend to emphasise that money is a sort of scarce factor, like a natural resource for example. This tends to lead to a naturalistic conception of money; rather than being a creature of convention and a human construction, money is rather a natural given, a gift reigned down upon Man from a force external to himself. This will be very important later on when we explore the underlying assumptions of one of the most famous theoretical models in monetary economics, namely, the ISLM. The Post-Keynesian monetary economist Marc Lavoie captures this aspect of mainstream monetary theory when he writes (note that Lavoie calls mainstream economics 'neoclassical' rather than the more accurate term 'marginalist'):

> The neoclassical treatment of money is based on the general neoclassical concern for exchange and the individual. Furthermore money is seen as a given endowment, and therefore as an exogenous variable, as is any input in orthodox general equilibrium theory. Money behaves as if it were identical to any other commodity. Money is thus compatible with the neoclassical view of the world based on scarcity: everything worthy is scarce, including money. The price of money, the rate of interest, is thus market determined, by a supply and demand mechanism, as are all goods in the neoclassical system. (Lavoie 1992, p. 150)

But what is the truth of the matter? In recent years, this has become something of a hot topic. This is likely due to the fact that the man on the street together with the economist in the ivory tower have come to see that in the face of a massive financial crisis their ideas about money might be all wrong. Without beating around the bush too much we can quite clearly and succinctly answer the question as to what is money. *Money is debt.* To the untrained eye, this appears paradoxical. After all, is it not money that we try to acquire to pay off debt? This is true, but that money that we acquire to pay down debt is merely the debt of someone else. Franklin Roosevelt's highly innovative Federal Reserve chairman Marriner Eccles recognised this well. In 1941, as the war raged, Eccles gave testimony to the House Committee on Banking and Currency. He was asked by one Congressman Patman where the Federal Reserve got the money to purchase $2 bn of US government debt in 1933. Eccles' answer was stunningly honest. Here is the relevant part of the exchange:

Eccles:	We created it [i.e. the money].
Patman:	Out of what?
Eccles:	Out of the right to issue credit money.
Patman:	And there is nothing behind it, is there, except our government's credit?
Eccles:	That is what our money system is. If there were no debts in our money system, there wouldn't be any money.

Debt is money. And money is debt. In more formal accounting language: money is always simultaneously one person's (or institution's) asset and another's liability. What is more, it appears that this was always the case. The anthropologist David Graeber makes the case that we never really encounter barter systems in human history—outside of minor examples where people who are already accustomed to money systems are deprived of money, as in the case of prisoner of war camps or prisons. If the famous 'double coincidence of wants' ever does occur, a credit and a debit are created. If I want something that you have and I have nothing that I can trade with you, then I will simply owe you. If I issue a formal IOU, you can then use this IOU to pay off other people if they trust in my creditworthiness (Graeber 2011).

Fiat Money

Today, however, it is clear that in most countries, a single unit of account exists that everyone uses. Whereas in the eighteenth and nineteenth centuries, a wide variety of notes from various trusted (and not so trusted) banks existed side by side in the economy; today in most countries, this has been replaced by a single type of note, typically issued by a central bank. What is more, since the end of the Bretton Woods system in 1973 when US president Richard Nixon suspended the convertibility of the dollar into gold, this money has not been backed by anything. It has rather been 'fiat money'—'fiat' being Latin for 'by decree'. What then is the nature of fiat money?

Keynes saw money wholly as a creature of the state. He was well known for advocating that the governments of the day move away from the gold standard which he viewed as a 'barbarous relic'. For Keynes, money was basically determined by social convention, and with the rise of the modern state-form, the authority to define what money is fell to the state. In his *Treatise on Money*, he wrote:

> [The state] claims the right to determine what thing corresponds to the name, and to vary its declaration from time to time—when, that is to say, it claims the right to re-edit the dictionary. This right is claimed by all modern States and has been so claimed for some four thousand years at least. It is when this stage in the evolution of money has been reached that Knapp's chartalism—the doctrine that money is peculiarly a creation of the State—is fully realized. (Keynes 1930, p. 4)

Keynes, however, never really explained how the state maintained its control on what is and what is not to be defined as money. On this particular point, there is some confusion when people, and even economists, discuss fiat money. There is a myth that circulates among American libertarians, for example, that private money creation is illegal in the USA and only the

Federal Reserve can create money. This is wholly untrue. If we are correct in saying that money is simply a debt relationship, then any time I create an IOU and give it to another person I am creating money. 'Anyone can create money', said the economist Hyman Minsky, 'the problem is in getting it accepted'.

So, what creates the acceptability of state-sanctioned money like the US dollar or the British pound sterling? After all, we know that in these countries there are no 'money police' who travel from door to door making sure that everyone is using the state money as a means of transaction. A group of economists called the Modern Monetary Theorists (MMT) have done perhaps the best work in answering this question. They argue that a sufficient—but not a necessary—condition for giving fiat money its value is for the government to impose a tax on the citizenry that can only be paid in the state currency (Wray 1998, pp. 18–38). While the MMTers do concede that there are other ways of establishing the value of fiat currency—for example, if a state court system says that all contracts brought before it must be in the state's own unit of account—they argue that taxation is usually the most important condition. They sum this up neatly by saying that 'taxes drive money'.

Perhaps the best way to approach this is by laying out an ongoing experiment that MMT economists put in place a number of years back at the University of Missouri Kansas City (UMKC). The university wanted to have the students undertake work in the local community and the MMT economists, under the supervision of Warren Mosler, saw a chance to put their theories into action. They had the university mandate that students were required to accumulate 20 'buckaroo' notes in order to get a certain component of their grade.[1] Each note can be acquired by doing one hour of work for an institution that the university approves. These institutions acquire their buckaroos from the 'treasury' or 'central bank' of the UMKC economics department after they are approved by the university.

The notes themselves are openly traded. So, if one student is bogged down with study while another has all their study done, the latter might choose to work an extra few hours in the registered charity institutions and then sell the notes acquired to their colleague. Thus the dollar value of the buckaroo is determined by the market. It is not 'tied' or 'pegged' to any other currency or commodity. The only thing that drives demand for it is the tax liability imposed on the student at the beginning of the semester; that is, they must earn 20 buckaroos somehow in order to get a portion of their final grade. Mosler, a retired hedge fund manager, reports that the value of the buckaroo has held strong relative to other assets since it was founded in 2001. He writes:

> In the late 1990s, when the program began, it was reported that students had exchanged buckaroo with each other at a price of $5 each. More recently, buckaroos have been reportedly exchanged for $15 each. Therefore, by that measure, the buckaroo has probably been the strongest 'paper currency' in the world, outperforming the S&P and most other investments. (Mosler 2011)

The buckaroo experiment tells us an awful lot about the dynamics underlying fiat money. The fact that the experiment was so enormously successful is not all that surprising. MMT economist Pavlina Tcherneva reports that such experiments were undertaken in the past when colonisers wanted to set those that they conquered to work. Tcherneva writes:

> The British and other colonial powers, interested in African produced cash crops and wage labor, refused to accept inkind payments, instead imposing taxes payable only in their own currency. This turned out to be a highly effective means of compelling Africans to enter cash crop production and to offer their labor services for sale. In addition, as the only local source of British pounds, the colonial authority was also in a position to determine the price it would pay for those goods and services. (Tcherneva 1996)

Obviously this indicates that fiat money can be used for either good or evil, since it is effectively based on an act of force in that the institution issuing it must have power over those whom they impose it upon. But the best way of looking at the 'taxes drive money' approach is to see it as a relatively neutral mechanism through which the demand for fiat money can be generated. Fiat money can be used to build a hospital or to build weapons designed to put people in a hospital, just as taxes can be imposed to construct a civilised society or coerce colonial populations. In terms of economics we really must look at the mechanism first, recognise that this is relatively neutral and then move on to judge each application of this mechanism on its own merits or demerits.

We said above that money is debt. But if fiat money is imposed on people through the force of taxation, then who can be said to be in debt here? Well, in fact, if we look closely, we will see that fiat money sets up a mutual debt relationship. In the example of the buckaroo, we saw that the student had to acquire and hand over 20 buckaroo notes in taxes to the university at the end of the semester. Thus we can say that when the student enters the university for that semester, they are placed in debt to the university for the amount of 20 buckaroos. If they do not repay this debt by the end of the semester, they are penalised. In addition to this, the rules of accounting—which we will deal with in more detail below—state that every time the UMKC 'treasury' issues buckaroos, these count as liabilities on their part. That is, every time the UMKC treasury issues a note, its balance sheet records a debt. Thus we see a two-sided debt relationship set up here: the student is forced into a debt relationship with the university and the treasury must issue a liability of debt in order to allow the student to pay this debt off.[2]

These relationships are very similar to those we encounter in the real world, and the buckaroo experiment actually opens a person up to a very good understanding of the operations of the modern monetary system. If you understand the basic underlying issues of the buckaroo system, you are more than halfway to understanding the accounting operations that central banks undertake on a day-to-day basis, how the broader monetary system operates and why governments that issue their own currency typically run budget deficits.

Basic Monetary Accounting I: Simple Monetary Circuit

The best way to show how the monetary system works in a modern capitalist economy is to set up some simple 'monetary circuits'.[3] These circuits are simplified models that integrate double-entry bookkeeping accounting norms to demonstrate how the monetary system exists in a modern capitalist economy. We will start with the most simple, namely one that only integrates firms, households and banks and then we add in a central bank.

First, some accounting basics. In accounting, we use balance sheets to determine the outstanding assets and liabilities held by various agents in the economy. Every time a loan is created, an asset and a liability are created. An asset falls on the side of the lender and the liability on the side of the borrower. Imagine that I borrow $10 from you and I give you an IOU for $10 with my signature on it. The IOU that you hold is an asset in the sense that, provided my credit is good, you can use it to reclaim $10 at some point in time. Meanwhile, I have a liability insofar as I must eventually pay back $10 to you.

Table 7.1 Simple monetary circuit I

Assets	*Commercial banks*	*Liabilities*
New loans to firms: $R_c + R_i$		New deposits of firms: $R_c + R_i$

Now, back to our monetary circuit. Imagine that we have two types of firms: those that produce consumption goods, R_c, and those that produce investment goods, R_i. Now imagine that these firms must borrow to fund their expenditure. All of this expenditure eventually accumulates as wages to households who are paid to produce the goods. We will also assume that firms only borrow to spend and any time they accumulate revenue from sales, they will use this to pay down debt. When the firm borrows from the bank, the balance sheets of the commercial banks will appear as they do in Table 7.1.

As we can see, the loans have created an asset for the banks—that is, an IOU from the firms to the banks—and a liability for the banks—that is, the deposit to the firms. Why do the banks have a liability on their balance sheet? This is because any deposit held at a bank is an IOU from the bank to the depositor. When you look at your account balance at an ATM, the number on the screen is how much the bank owes you. It is, in a sense, an IOU from the bank to you. This may seem counterintuitive at first, but consider a situation when your account balance was, say, \$100 mn. Do you think that you would be able to extract this amount of money from any ATM? It seems highly unlikely. Even if you went inside the bank and up to the till, they would not be able to give you your \$100 mn straight away. This illustrates clearly that bank deposits are simply IOUs from the banks to the holders of these deposits. In the above example, when the firms take out loans, they hand the banks IOUs and the bank deposits their account; this deposit is then an IOU from the banks to the firms. What we get here is basically a trading of IOUs or debts.

We have already assumed that the firms would not borrow unless they had something to spend the money on. So, the above balance sheets will only exist in that form for a very brief period of time. The firms will soon take their deposits and use them to pay workers to engage in production. Let us say that all the payments are made in the form of wages to households. The identity that will hold here is that investment will equal wages, or:

Table 7.2 Simple monetary circuit II

Assets	*Commercial banks*	*Liabilities*
New loans to firms: $R_c + R_i$		New deposits of households: $W_c + W_i$

$$I \equiv W$$

Thus the deposits that previously sat on the asset side of the balance sheet for firms will be transferred to the households. This will be done in the manner of any bank transfer. When you get paid by your employer, the funds disappear from their deposit account and appear in your deposit account. When this process has taken place, the commercial banks' balance sheets will appear as they do in Table 7.2.

As we can see, the deposits that previously sat with the firms have been transferred to the households which we have designated, W_c, for the households paid wages by consumption good firms and, W_i, for households that are paid wages by investment good firms. Note also that the firms no longer have any deposits, and these do not show up on the balance sheet of the commercial banks. Now let us assume that the households use some of their income for consumption and some of their income for saving. Thus, the income of households will be divided between consumption and saving, or:

$$Y_h \equiv W_c + W_i \equiv C_h + S_h$$

The money that the households spend on consumption will accrue to the firms that make consumption goods in the form of revenue. This will appear to these firms as deposits on their balance sheets. The remaining money that is held as savings by households will appear on the balance sheets of households in the form of deposits with the commercial banks which we have labelled, S_h, to distinguish this action from the action of receiving wages from firms. Once the households engage in consumption, the balance sheets of the commercial banks will appear as they do in Table 7.3.[4]

Recall that we assumed that the firms would use any revenue that they received in order to pay down outstanding debt. In this case, all of the money that was received by firms when households engaged in consumption will be used by the firms to repay their loans to the banks. The only money that will stay outstanding in the system will be the money that is saved by households. So, the balance sheets of the commercial banks will appear as they do in Table 7.4.

Table 7.3 Simple monetary circuit III

Assets	*Commercial banks*	*Liabilities*
New loans to firms: $R_c + R_i$		New deposits of firms: $R_c + R_i - S_h$ New deposits of households: S_h

Table 7.4 Simple monetary circuit w/central bank I

Assets	*Commercial banks*	*Liabilities*
New loans to firms: S_h		New deposits of households: S_h

We can learn an important lesson from this simple exercise so far: in a closed private economy with no government sector, private sector firm revenue after wages or profits will be equal to its investment expenditure minus household savings. Or:

$$\pi \equiv I - S_h$$

where π denotes profits. As we can see from the foregoing circuit, the firm cannot repay all of its loans if the private sector holds money in the form of savings. The insights gleaned from this very simple and striking example will be examined in more detail in a later chapter when we examine the source of profits in a capitalist economy. For now, however, let us build a more complicated monetary circuit that includes a central bank. This will allow us to form a more realistic approximation of how money is created in a contemporary capitalist economy.

Basic Monetary Accounting II: Simple Monetary Circuit With Central Bank

In the above monetary circuit, we have simply assumed that banks create money out of thin air. The idea lying behind this can be summarised in the phrase 'loans create deposits'. As a first approximation, this is entirely accurate and, as we shall see, banks do basically create money out of thin air. In order to understand the full workings of the modern monetary system, however, we must build a slightly more complex monetary circuit that includes a central bank.

Central banks put constraints on commercial banks' ability to lend by imposing reserve requirements. Reserve requirements state that for every deposit of a given size that a bank holds, they must hold some percentage of that deposit as reserve cash. Reserve cash can only be obtained by the commercial banks from either other commercial banks or the central bank, but the central bank is the only entity that can create new reserve cash. Thus the lending activities as a whole should, in theory, be constrained by the amount of reserve cash that the central bank creates.

In practice, the only manner in which the commercial banks as a whole can get access to new cash reserves is by either selling government securities, that is, government IOUs, to the central bank or borrowing from the central bank using commercial securities, that is, IOUs from private firms, as collateral. To make the example simpler, we are going to assume that there is no government sector and thus no government securities. So, in order to get access to new reserves, private banks have to borrow from the central bank using commercial securities as collateral.

Let us call the reserve requirement, t_d, indicating that it is an effective tax on deposits. Let us call the money holdings of household or deposits, M_h. Thus the total amount of reserves that the banks will have to hold will be, $t_d . M_h$.[5] Further let us skip the steps we went through in the last example and imagine that firms have borrowed money from the commercial banks and paid this money out to household who are currently sitting on it. The resulting commercial and central bank balance sheets would then be as they appear in Table 7.5.

Note here that the commercial banks have had to borrow reserves from the central bank in order to extend the loans to firms who then pay them to private households. They back these loans, in our example, with commercial securities. The central bank creates the reserves out of thin air.

Table 7.5 Simple monetary circuit w/central bank II

Assets	*Commercial banks*	*Liabilities*
Consolidated loans to firms: M_h Reserve holdings: $t_d . M_h$		Deposits of households: M_h Borrowing from central bank: $t_d . M_h$
Assets	*Central bank*	*Liabilities*
Loans to banks: $t_d . M_h$		Deposits from banks: $t_d . M_h$

They are literally created on a computer screen. Whether these reserves are created to buy government securities or, as in our example, to extend loans collateralised against commercial securities, it is this act of money creation that is at the heart of the money creation process in modern economies. In our example, what is ultimately happening is that the central bank is creating money to extend loans to banks that are then extending loans to firms which eventually accrue as household deposits. If we carried on our example and allowed households to consume and firms to extinguish their loans, the monetary circuit would be complete. Any money that the households held as savings, however, would require that the central bank creates new money reserves to accommodate these new deposits.

The Misleading Money Multiplier

The money multiplier is a very simple concept that is often one of the first ideas encountered by a student studying monetary economics. It is terribly misleading and leads to very bad habits of thought that are very difficult to remedy. The process itself seems logical and simple. If a bank has to hold, say, 10 % of its deposits as reserves, then it will loan out the other 90 %. This will accrue as deposits ate either another bank or the same bank and a further 90 % of these deposits will be loaned out. Round and round this will go until all possible loans have been made.

In order to illustrate this, let us assume that a new deposit of \$100 is placed in a given bank and the reserve requirements are 10 %. In Figs. 7.1, 7.2 and 7.3, we have laid out various numerical and graphical illustrations of the money creation process that the money multiplier story assumes will occur when this new deposit is lodged.

We can also illustrate this in the form of an algebraic formula as follows:

$$D\left(\frac{1}{rr}\right)$$

where D is the new deposit and rr are the reserve requirements. So the solution to the above example would be as follows:

$$\$100\left(\frac{1}{0.1}\right) = \$1000$$

Period	Deposit	Loan	Reserve	Money Supply
1	100	90	10	100
2	90	81	9	190
3	81	72.9	8.1	271
4	72.9	65.61	7.29	343.9
5	65.61	59.049	6.561	409.51
6	59.049	53.1441	5.9049	468.559
7	53.1441	47.82969	5.31441	521.7031
8	47.82969	43.046721	4.782969	569.53279
9	43.046721	38.7420489	4.3046721	612.579511
10	38.7420489	34.86784401	3.87420489	651.3215599
11	34.86784401	31.38105961	3.486784401	686.1894039
12	31.38105961	28.24295365	3.138105961	717.5704635
13	28.24295365	25.41865828	2.824295365	745.8134172
14	25.41865828	22.87679245	2.541865828	771.2320755
15	22.87679245	20.58911321	2.287679245	794.1088679
16	20.58911321	18.53020189	2.058911321	814.6979811
17	18.53020189	16.6771817	1.853020189	833.228183
18	16.6771817	15.00946353	1.66771817	849.9053647
19	15.00946353	13.50851718	1.500946353	864.9148282
20	13.50851718	12.15766546	1.350851718	878.4233454

Fig. 7.1 Money multiplier I

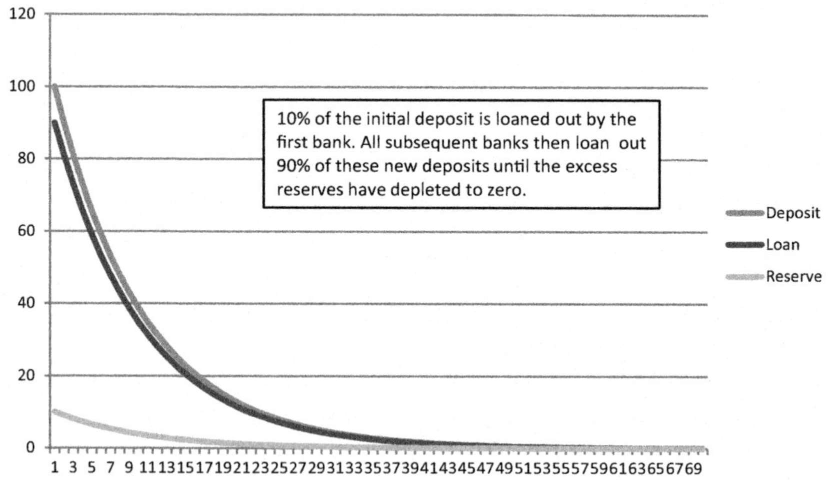

Fig. 7.2 Money multiplier II

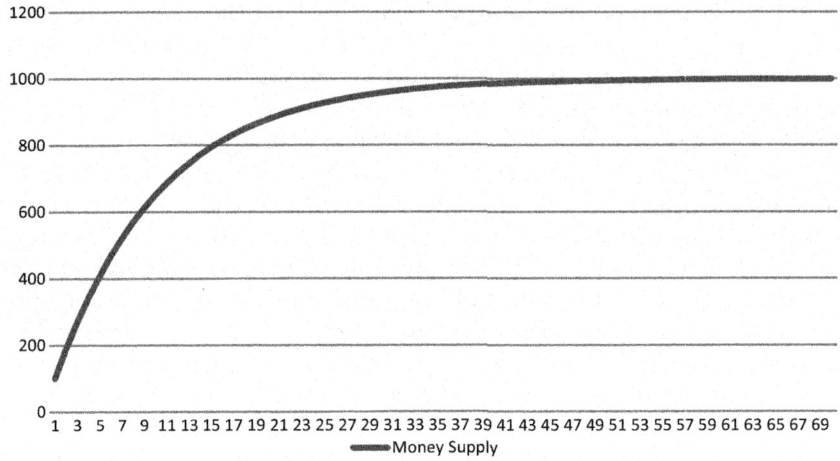

Fig. 7.3 Money multiplier III

Well, this story all looks very nice and neat, but what is the fundamental problem? Actually, it is a misleadingly simple one: *we never said where the original new deposit came from*. Why do economists make such a silly slip? This seems to go back to the old nineteenth-century gold standard system. Under that system a person could literally dig more gold out of the ground and place this as a deposit in the bank. Under those circumstances, it made some sense to assume that a new deposit might come out of nowhere and then be 'multiplied'.[6] But under the current system of credit or fiat money, this makes little sense at all.

The fall-back position for economists is thus to assume that the central bank creates new reserves and these are then 'multiplied up' by expanding new loans into the economy. Take a typical introduction to the concept by Paul Samuelson and William Nordhaus. Before they introduce the money multiplier, they write:

> The central bank determines the quantity of reserves of the banking system… Using those reserves as an input, the banking system transforms them into a much larger amount of bank money. (Nordhaus and Samuelson 1995, p. 490)

The reality, however, is that the central bank has no ability to determine the quantity of reserves in the system. Rather, it sets the rate of interest and then commercial banks make loans based on this rate of interest in a very similar manner to that which we laid out above in the second of our monetary circuits. If there are reserve requirements in place, and we should note that in many countries like Canada and the UK there are no such reserve requirements, the central banks will buy government securities or extend loans to the banking system as they need them. If they did not, banks would continue making loans regardless and would start to bid up the interest rate as they all scrambled for the limited number of reserves available. The central bank would thus lose control over the rate of interest that they target. Instead of allowing such a disastrous and chaotic process to take place, they release the new reserves on demand. This turns the 'money multiplier' into a 'credit divisor'. It is not that new reserves are 'multiplied up' but rather that extensions of credit call the new reserves into existence on demand.

This alternative theory is known as 'endogenous money' theory, and thanks to a number of devoted bloggers, it has become more and more popular since the financial crisis of 2008. This led central banks to start paying attention. Economists at the Bank of England (BoE), for example, have formally conceded that the mainstream textbook account of money creation is deeply misleading. In a quarterly report entitled 'Money creation in the modern economy', BoE economists wrote[7]:

> Whenever a bank makes a loan, it simultaneously creates a matching deposit in the borrower's bank account, thereby creating new money… The reality of how money is created today differs from the description found in some economics textbooks:
>
> • Rather than banks receiving deposits when households save and then lending them out, bank lending creates deposits.
>
> • In normal times, the central bank does not fix the amount of money in circulation, nor is central bank money 'multiplied up' into more loans and deposits. (McLeay et al. 2014, p. 1.)

Unfortunately, most economists have the old money multiplier theory firmly stuck in their heads. This leads them to make any number of practical errors. Take the most obvious example of 'crowding out'. The idea behind 'crowding out' is that there is a fixed supply of money, presumably set by the central bank, and thus when the government engages in borrowing to fund deficit spending, this leads to the rate of interest rising. This rise in the rate of interest then discourages private firms to borrow and invest.

Thus, public investment is said to 'crowd out' private investment, and the debate typically moves to whether we want the moribund government or the more efficient private sector engaging in investment and spending. From an endogenous money point-of-view, this is entirely incorrect. In fact, there is no fixed supply of money because *loans create deposits.* When a loan is made, new money comes into existence. If the government engages in borrowing and this leads the interest rate to begin to creep up, the central bank will step in automatically in order to defend their interest rate target. They will create the new reserves and interest rates will stay at the point where they were previously.

The money multiplier story highlights some very typical aspects of mainstream economic theory: while it is logical in its own right, many aspects of it are entirely disconnected from the real world. This leads those who study it to be grossly misled when it comes to real-world policy questions. Many economists who argued in favour of austerity, for example, invoked the crowding out argument. Even those who defended fiscal stimulus during economic crises, like Paul Krugman, accepted that crowding out would occur when the economy had exited what they referred to as a 'liquidity trap', that is, when people stopped hoarding money and not investing it. But none of this is true. In a modern capitalist economy with a modern banking system, there is never a shortage of money. Modern central banks do not even try to control the money supply. Rather, they set the price of money—the interest rate—and let the quantity of money demanded 'float' at this price. The quantity demanded depends on any number of factors: the state of expectations, the price of money (i.e. the interest rate), innovations in the financial markets. We will look at some of these in a subsequent chapter.

Breakout Box: The Quantity Theory of Money

Richard Nixon once famously said that 'we are all Keynesians now!' In that spirit, one might be tempted to argue that we are, in a sense, all Quantity Theorists now; except for one key difference: in the case of the Quantity Theory, the intuition is one that comes not with experience but rather as a matter of instinct. The Quantity Theory of Money is classic 'man-in-the-street economics' in that it is something that makes so much intuitive sense to people that they find it very difficult to question even when they think in depth about economic theories. After all, if more money is produced, then it will be worth less, right? Supply and demand and all that, no? In order to examine the old Quantity Theory, let us turn to its modern-day source.

Although the Quantity Theory was set out many times in a rather vague and undefined manner—Copernicus was apparently one of the first, while David Hume was the most famous early exponent—no one gave the theory more clarity than the American economist Irving Fisher. In his 1911 book *The Purchasing Power of Money* (Fisher 1911), he put forward the now famous equation:

$$MV \equiv pQ$$

where M is the quantity of money, V is the velocity of money or the amount of times it circulates in a given period, Q is the quantity of goods and services sold and, most crucially, p is the price level. In actual fact, Fisher, being a fantastic expositor of ideas, makes the case even more clearly. Given that the right-hand side of the equation is dealing with the prices and quantities of heterogeneous goods and services, he writes[8]:

$$MV \equiv \sum pQ$$

Fisher is far more cautious in interpreting the equation than later economists who endorsed the theory. Indeed, he sees it more so as an identity rather than as a behavioural equation—which is why we have used the triple-bar sign in the above equations. In his book, Fisher considers a whole host of possible influences on the price level. He considers what might happen if M changes, what might happen if V changes and even what might happen if Q changes. This is a far cry from the later monetarist economists who would interpret Fisher's identity in a wholly different manner. Milton Friedman and his followers made a strong claim that the velocity of money and the quantity of goods and services were somewhat constant and so any increase or decrease in the supply of money would lead to an increase or decrease in prices (Kaldor 1982, pp. 17–39). This turned Fisher's identity into a behavioural equation proper which we might write as such:

$$M\dot{V} = \sum p\dot{Q}$$

Here we are holding both *M* and *Q* constant (as noted by the lines or 'hats' drawn above the variables) and considering *M* to be the causal variable in the equation. That is, we are holding both *M* and *Q* constant and reading the equation from left to right. The assumption here is that the economy is at maximum capacity (i.e. more goods cannot be produced) and thus any increase in the money supply will simply translate into higher prices. As Fig. . 7.4 shows this is simply not true empirically and should be disregarded as such.[9] In actual fact, both the velocity of money and the degree of capacity utilisation are extremely volatile.

Fisher's treatment of the equation, as we have stressed, was in line with interpreting it as a simple identity. This, he thought, meant that

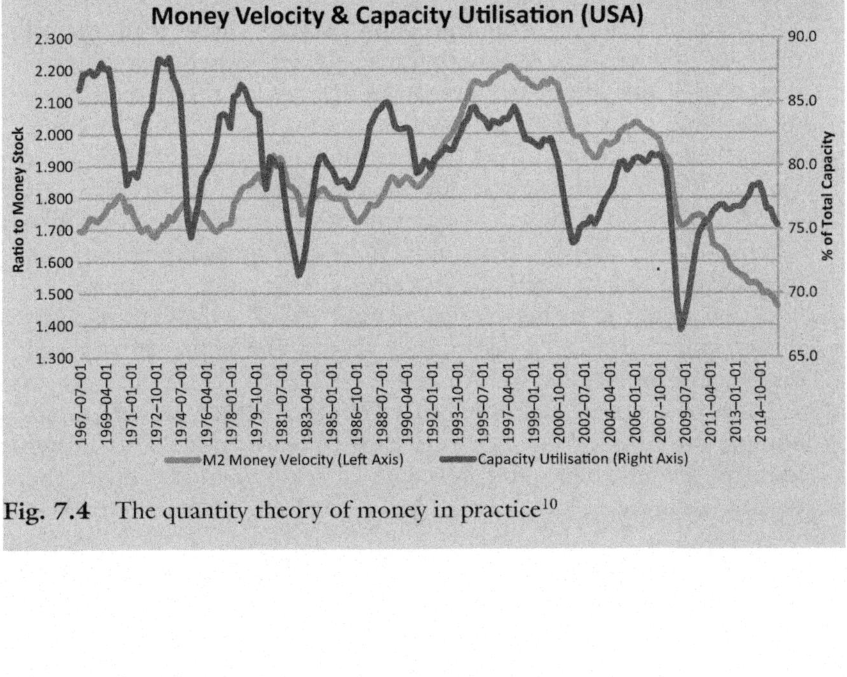

Fig. 7.4 The quantity theory of money in practice[10]

it was an entirely neutral presentation completely above reproach. This is not true, however. At no point in the discussion of his identity does Fisher ever state that the price level may have an effect on the quantity of money and the velocity of circulation. But this seems to be a rather obvious point and casts serious doubt on the usefulness of the framework.

Imagine that a price increase began in a given economy due to an external shock; say, the price of oil increased precipitously because the supply of oil in the economy fell.[11] In the Fisher identity, this would be synonymous with a fall in Q which would in turn increase p just as the identity states. But in reality, the process would not stop there. Prices would increase across the board. Capitalists would see their input costs (energy etc.) rise and they would pass these on to consumers in the form of higher prices. Workers, especially those in heavily unionised industries, would likely view this as an attack on their living standards and would demand higher money wages. This, in turn, would further increase the costs of the capitalists (labour is probably the most important input in any economy, after all) and they would again try to offload these costs onto workers through price increases.

As this wage-price spiral set in, both the velocity of circulation and the money supply would probably increase (or, at least, one of these would increase). Although firms would be experiencing higher nominal revenue due to the increase in their prices, they would experience rising costs before they actually received this higher revenue. Thus they would be forced to open up lines of credit with their banks which would increase the money supply (Moore 1983). It is for this reason that, as early nineteenth-century economists like Thomas Tooke and his Banking School colleagues recognised, an increase in prices may lead to an increase in the money supply. The equation might then be read from right to left which is not what Fisher intended and certainly goes against the entire theory laid down by his monetarist followers.

Those who adhere to the Quantity Theory of Money are, of course, completely blinded to this very real phenomenon. The Fisher identity, even when interpreted as a strict identity, gives the reader the impression that the price-level component is passive with regard to the rest of the equation. But this is simply not true. Prices, as we have seen, may have an active effect in leading to the quantity of money (and its velocity of circulation) to rise. Fisher himself came close to recognising this mechanism in a later chapter of his book but ultimately fell back on a rather silly theory of the rate of interest to place an airtight seal on his erroneous theories and keep his framework intact (Fisher 1911, pp. 57–58).

Today those who uphold the Quantity Theory of Money—and they are legion—completely veneer over the fact that this theory, which purports to explain to them everything they need to know about the change in prices (inflation) in a given economy, actually explains nothing about this phenomenon. And given that this silliness is propagated in both classrooms and the popular press across the globe, it is only a rare and inquiring mind that ever tears back the curtain to examine why a particular inflation is actually taking place.

Inflation and All That

In the next chapter of this book, we will try to look at prices in a very abstract manner. We will provide a highly intuitive schema that describes a particular type of inflationary process, namely, 'demand-pull' inflation. It is probably best to treat inflation in this chapter because, thanks to an economist named Milton Friedman, most people have got a very silly idea into their heads: they think that inflation is always and ever a monetary phenomenon. The reader will already have gotten a sense why this is not the case from what has previously been said about the quantity theory of money. The theory is actually not a theory at all, but rather an identity. This identity can be read in any number of different ways and has no set causal interpretation. When we do try to give it causal significance by holding fixed the velocity and the quantity produced—this is basically what Friedman and the monetarists did—we quickly find that this interpretation runs completely contrary to the data. Let us now turn to the types of inflation that can actually take place in an economy. To summarise before digging into them these are:

1. Demand-pull inflation
2. Cost-push inflation
3. Speculative inflation
4. Exchange-rate inflation.

As we shall see, there will always be some overlap between the four types, but such a taxonomy is useful insofar as it allows us to draw out their core features. Let us explore these one by one. Demand-pull inflation is the type of inflation that most people are familiar with. We assume that there are a certain amount of resources available in the economy and that if the demand for these resources outstrips the supply, we assume that prices will rise. Despite being a rather simple tale in the real world, it is actually not altogether clear that these ideas bear out. First of all, it should be pointed out that when we make this case, we are implicitly assuming that the market mechanism works perfectly. That is, we are assuming that when more demand manifests itself in the system, all prices will adjust upward in response to this new demand. We might think of this as people with more income going to an auction and bidding higher prices that reflect their higher incomes. If the market mechanism does not work perfectly, however, we would merely see shortages and we would see no price changes; that is, in the language of economics: quantities, not prices, would adjust. This is a point that is not often raised, but it is an important one because shortages actually do occur on quite a regular basis in capitalist economies. In areas of high population density, large chain stores often find their shelves without stock in periods of very high demand (usually at the end of the working day when people shop for necessities). This is by no means a temporary phenomenon and can often occur day after day, even in a capitalist economy. Personally, I encounter this all the time living in London—although I almost never encountered it living in Dublin. It has less to do with a shortage of resources and more to do with shops being unable to keep the physical space of their shelves stocked during periods of very high demand. This is a form of shortage that occurs literally due to the lack of physical geographical space in large cities. The most typical instance of shortages for those living outside of big cities can be seen around Christmastime when people rush to buy gifts and shops run out of many types of goods.

This is worth looking at in slightly more detail because it can tell us a lot about the assumptions needed to make a case that a given inflation might be demand-led. If I go into my local shop at a time of very high demand and I spot the last loaf of bread, what happens? Do all the shoppers who want bread form a circle around the loaf and start making bids for it, the highest bidder ultimately receiving the loaf? No, of course not. The person who gets the loaf first gets the privilege of buying it at the marked price. During the Second World War many countries, including the UK and the USA, recognised that high inflation was undesirable for the stability of the macroeconomy, so they fixed prices and distributed ration cards. They knew that if they did not do this, those people with more purchasing power would price poorer people out of the market for basic goods, especially those people, like pensioners, on fixed incomes. Black markets did develop in response to the shortage economy this created, but the rationing was a rational response to the problem of shortages during the war. Some of these black markets were on a limited scale and helped to iron out the inefficiencies of rationing (Dunstable Town Centre 2005) while some of them were exploitative and treated very harshly by the authorities (Office of War Information 1944). All in all, the rationing worked rather well and prices did not rise to dangerous levels.[12] Of course, outside of serious social emergencies, rationing is unlikely to be desirable. Although in certain contexts, it does make a great deal of sense and import-control policies designed to ensure exchange-rate stability can be seen as effective rationing policies designed to maintain the international purchasing power of a given country's currency.

Considering all of this, it begins to become clear how demand-pull inflation might actually work. It might occur in periods when the supply of goods is being soaked up by other, more pressing requirements. In modern capitalist economies, demand-pull inflation rarely exists outside of wartime. As we have already said, in the Second World War, demand-pull inflation was contained through rationing. The same was the case in the Korean War. During the Vietnam War, however, the US government tried to run a 'guns and butter' economy because of the unpopularity of that war. This gave rise to the first pangs of the inflation of the 1970s which we will discuss in more detail below. But the key point that should be understood here is that *demand-pull inflations are the exception and not the rule in modern, developed capitalist economies and will usually only occur during a social emergency.*

It should also be noted that demand-pull inflation should not be thought of as some crude 'expansion of the money supply'. While it is typically money that is being used to bid up prices during such inflations (although local sources of credit can also be used), it is the demand that really matters and that we should focus our attention on. Demand has three sources: the private sector, the public sector and the external sector. The private sector demands goods and services for both consumption and investment, as does the government sector. The external sector demands goods through exports and increases the supply of goods through imports (which is functionally equivalent to a negative demand pressure). We can highlight these sources of demand in a slightly modified version of the familiar GDP identity which is far more sophisticated than the crude quantity of money identity.

$$(C+I)_P + (C+I)_G + (X-M) \equiv p.Y$$

Here we denote the price level p and the level of output supplied Y,[13] private sector consumption and investment $(C+I)_P$, government sector consumption and investment $(C+I)_G$, and the external sector's exports and imports $(X-M)$. This is effectively a nominal GDP identity and is a far more powerful way of thinking about the potential effects of demand on the price level than the old quantity of money identity. Money does not spend itself; it requires some conscious acting agent to spend it. The above identity makes clear the peoples and institutions in society that actually spend the money or credit and in doing so produce demand. The quantity of money equation has certain animistic tendencies in that it seems to ascribe agency to the passive medium of money. Anyone who reflects on this will see the immediate absurdity of pretending that money is anything but a passive force that is brought to life only in the hands of real people. The modified GDP identity has no such problems and encourages us to think in real-life, institutional terms about the sources of demand. This will help us to avoid the bad habits of thought that arise when people think about inflation in terms of the quantity of money.

It is worth further reflecting on the mechanism through which real-life demand-pull inflation actually feeds into prices because, as we have said, shoppers in modern economies do not typically bid up prices in supermarkets. The way in which demand-pull inflation actually works is that, rather than raise their prices, shops typically increase their orders to factories as they run out of certain types of goods. If these factories are operating at full capacity and all of the labour force is employed, the workers are asked to work overtime and the equipment is pushed to the limits of its ability to produce. This leads to increased costs for the factory as the machines will need more maintenance and the wage-bill will be substantially higher due to the overtime payments. These costs are then passed through to the shops in the form of higher prices which are, in turn, passed on to the end consumer. Thus, demand-pull inflation when encountered in the real world generally has a substantial component of the second type of inflation: cost-push inflation. Let us now turn to this second type of inflation.

In a modern capitalist economy, cost-push inflation is by far the most prevalent type of inflation. The manner in which it works is quite simple: the cost of one good needed to produce another good rises and so the producer raises the price of their own good. In order for a cost-push inflation to take place, some factor of production that is used throughout the economy should see its price rise. This may be a raw material, like oil, but the most typical and important factor of production that might raise its prices is labour. The majority of inflationary pressures that we see in modern capitalist economies are due to wages rising and producers passing on the cost to consumers.

This aspect of cost-push inflation has come to be known to non-mainstream economists as 'conflict inflation' (Rowthorn 1977). Conflict inflation can be found in the work of many writers from Marx (1867) to Keynes (1940) to the original article lying behind the famous Phillips Curve by Phillips himself that was later distorted to a large extent (Phillips 1958). The basic idea here is that a good deal of inflation in modern capitalist economies is due to the conflict between capitalists and workers trying to divide up the pie between wages and profits. Workers bid up their nominal wages in order to gain more of the social product, but capitalists then respond by raising prices in line with their new wage-costs that would otherwise eat into their profits. This can then develop into a 'wage-price spiral' as workers realise that their real wages—that is, the amount of goods and services their wages can buy—did not rise at all due to the price increases that their wage increases called forth. This leads to another round of rising wages and another round of price-hikes and so on. Wage-price spirals are, as we shall see, the most dangerous source of inflation in modern capitalist economies (Galbraith 1973, pp. 187–197). They are also typically accompanied by strikes, social upheaval, discontent and political upheavals—usually political upheavals that aim at dismantling the workers' movements that are insisting on higher wages. From the point-of-view of trade unions, they are one of the most self-defeating and silly strategies ever conceived.

The third type of inflation is speculative inflation. This is actually a variant of straightforward demand-pull inflation but is probably more prevalent in modern capitalist economies and usually confines itself to particular markets where the supply is fixed over the course of a few months. As we saw in Fig. 7.4, modern capitalist economies typically operate with excess productive capacity because businesses build in this additional capacity in case demand changes unexpectedly. This means that if the demand for a certain good suddenly increases, manufacturers can usually increase production to meet this response. This provides for a great deal of flexibility and accounts for why we do not see violent price swings as the economy grows. Such flexibility is not available, however, in markets where the producer cannot increase supply at short notice. The economist Michał Kalecki made this distinction most firmly when he wrote:

> It is clear that two types of price formation arise out of different conditions of supply. The production of finished goods is elastic as a result of existing reserves of productive capacity. When demand increases it is met mainly by an increase in the volume of production while prices tend to remain stable. The price changes that do occur result mainly from changes in costs of production. The situation with respect to raw materials is different. The increase in the supply of agricultural products requires a considerable time. This is true, though not to the same extent, with respect to mining. With supply inelastic in short periods, an increase in demand causes a diminution of stocks and a consequent increase in price. (Kalecki 1965, p. 11)

Speculative inflation can arise when speculators realise that this dilemma presents them with an opportunity to make money. They notice that these markets are supply constrained and that if they buy up a portion of the goods in these markets, they can hoard them and sell them at a higher price in the future (possibly even to other speculators!). Sometimes speculators may not even realise what they are doing because they may just be following the trend set by other speculators. But this can have an enormous impact on prices. What is more, it is extremely difficult—if not impossible—to detect the level of speculation in such markets at any given moment in time. This is because we must allow for some speculation in these markets because a certain amount of speculation serves the public good as it evens out inconsistencies. If, for example, too much grain is produced one season, a speculator can support the price and then release it on the market (for a tidy profit) when there is a shortfall of grain

(Kaldor 1939). Economists have no concrete way of separating these two types of activity and thus trying to detect speculative price inflations is very difficult. Nevertheless, many within regulatory institutions seem to think that at the time of writing, a good deal of financial activity taking place in such markets might be speculative. Ben Bernanke, the former head of the US Federal Reserve, argued that such a component was extremely important in driving up oil prices (Bernanke 2004), while researchers at the Federal Reserve have argued that speculation is the second most important driver of oil prices after real fundamental demand (Juvenal and Petralla 2012). While we should not take such studies at face value, it is curious that this phenomenon is not more discussed in the popular press and in policy circles and one would be forgiven for thinking that it might have to do with what passes for economic discourse today. We would find out rather quickly whether speculation was taking place in such markets if well-funded investigations that were not hampered in their powers were unleashed on the markets. In order to understand the dynamics of speculative inflation, we must view certain commodities not as typical goods but rather as assets. Thus, these goods should be treated similarly to how we treat financial markets in Chap. 11.

The fourth and final type of inflation is exchange-rate inflation. Exchange-rate inflation typically occurs after a currency crisis, that is, when a currency loses much of its value on the foreign exchange market. Often economists conflate currency crises with balance of payments crises, but this is fallacious. A balance of payments crisis occurs when a country has been running deficits on its trade (current) account and suddenly finds itself unable to meet payments. This may lead to that country selling their currency on the foreign exchange market which will drive down its value and possibly cause a currency crisis, but these are logically distinct phenomena. In fact, today most currency crises are due to capital or 'hot money' inflows that then reverse when asset markets collapse within a country. So, for example, lots of money rushes in to buy up stocks during a boom. Because these stocks are denominated in the domestic currency, investors have to buy up this currency to purchase the stocks. This drives the currency's value skyward. Then when the stock market collapses, the money rushes back out of the country and the exchange value of the currency collapses overnight (Harvey 2009).

These currency crises cause inflation through a very simple channel: when the value of a currency falls, the cost of imports go up, and when the value of the currency falls very sharply, the cost of imports can go up quite significantly. Typically the country's industry and consumers will still require these imports and cannot switch to domestic goods immediately—perhaps because these imports are natural resources or perhaps simply because it takes time for industries that produce these goods to open for business. This leads to inflation which will then feed through the system in the form of cost-push inflation. If worker bargaining power is strong, this can then initiate a wage-prices spiral as the workers and capitalists try to push the price increases onto one another. This can generate a particularly vicious type of inflation that proves very difficult to tackle.

There are a multitude of different ways in which a currency crisis can occur, and we will not list them here. But it is worth noting that the famous Weimar hyperinflation, which is typically thought to be a case of money printing, was actually an exchange-rate inflation followed by a wage-price spiral (Robinson 1938). Under the terms of the Treaty of Versailles, the German government had to make outrageous and unrealistic reparation payments to the Allies. Since the Allies did not accept German marks (the German currency at the time) in payment, there was only two ways to make these repayments. Either the Germans could export sufficient goods to the Allies and then effectively turn over the money that they received for these exports. Or they could create marks and use them to buy foreign currency and gold in the international markets which they could then turn over to meet their repayment obligations. Because the Allies' demands were so unrealistic, the Germans found that they could not export sufficient goods to meet the reparations. They then had the choice of either creating marks and selling them in the foreign exchange markets or allowing the Allies to occupy the country for not meeting the reparations payments that they had agreed to. Naturally, they took the more reasonable path and used newly issued currency to buy foreign currency in the exchange markets: the value of the mark collapsed, a violent wage-price spiral set in and hyperinflation ensued. When they were unable to meet their repayments, the French invaded the Ruhr valley; this cut off much of Germany's industry, and the hyperinflation got even worse as the supply capacity of the domestic economy contracted. The lesson here is that this was a wholly *political* hyperinflation. If the reader looks properly into various hyperinflations in history, they will find this to very often be the case. Hyperinflations are typically exchange-rate inflations followed by wage-price spirals, and they are usually brought about when the fever breaks of an underlying sickness that is a manifestation of unrealistic, absurd and unsustainable political arrangements (Montier 2013a, b).

Actually Existing Inflation: The Case of the 1970s

The most dramatic inflationary episode seen after the Second World War was that which took place in the 1970s across most of the world. This inflation led directly to what we might call the 'neoliberal revolution' in political and economic thinking. Here we will briefly examine the causes in the USA, although similar causes can be found elsewhere. This inflation, being multifaceted and rather chaotic, is a perfect test case for our theories set out above because there were aspects of each type present, although, as we shall see, the most important was cost-push inflation.

The inflation had its roots, as we alluded to earlier, in the pressure put on the US economy by the Vietnam War. In the late 1960s, the USA was experiencing some of the highest growth it had ever achieved. The unemployment rate, which is a good approximation for how slack the economy is at any given moment in times, was hovering around 3.5 %.[14] The economy was running at full steam. But President Lyndon Johnson wanted to ramp up spending in order to fund the war in Vietnam and he did not want to increase taxes because that war was already extremely unpopular among US citizens. In the first quarter of 1968, the government budget registered a deficit of $24.6 bn which amounted to 2.7 % of GDP. This was not a particularly large deficit, but when the economy is running at full steam, it might be easily enough to cause demand-pull inflation. And indeed, inflation began to climb. It was running at about 4.1 % year-on-year in mid-1968, but, as wages began to rise when workers did more overtime to meet the orders coming in, it accelerated to 5.5 % in mid-1969. By the time the recession of 1970 hit the US economy, inflation was running at 6.5 % year-on-year.

As unemployment rose in response to the recession of 1970, pressures on the US economy eased and inflation subsided to a low of 3 % in mid-1972. As the economy recovered, the government budget registered a deficit of 1.8 % of GDP in the third quarter of 1972 and 1 % of GDP in the first quarter of 1973. The civilian unemployment rate, while not as low as it had been in the late 1960s was still relatively low at 4.8 % to allow workers to raise their wages. In the third quarter of 1973, wage-hikes had driven the year-on-year inflation rate to the high level of 8.4 %.

This might have subsided, but then another unexpected shock hit the US economy. In the first month of 1974, Arabian oil producers in the OPEC cartel doubled the price of oil from around $4.30 a barrel to around $10.10 a barrel. The Arab oil producers did this because US president

Richard Nixon had ordered airlifts of weapons to support the Israelis in the Yom-Kippur war against Syria and Egypt. This rise in the price of oil caused further price rises, and since unions had indexed their wage agreements to the inflation index, this automatically called forth wage increases. As workers and capitalists effectively fought over how to distribute the new higher prices brought about by the oil embargo inflation hit a high of 12 % in the fourth quarter of 1974. After a brief readjustment and a fall in inflation, this process repeated itself when a crisis in Iran led to the second oil shock in 1979. Throughout this period, the US dollar was also falling in value, thus causing import prices to rise. The key events can be seen having their economic effects on the US economy in Fig. 7.5.

This crisis gave rise to a vulgar sort of monetarism that became a sort of ideology in the USA and around the Western world in this era. The ideology of monetarism was used by the head of the Federal Reserve Paul Volcker in the late 1970s to raise interest rates substantially and create a recession.[15] The recession that ensued, the worst seen since the Great Depression, together with Ronald Reagan's tough union reforms broke the back of organised labour in the USA and reigned in an era of stagnant real wage growth. As workers produced more and more due to technology allowing productivity to rise, their purchasing power never really grew. This, together with the rise in the strength of the dollar due to the high

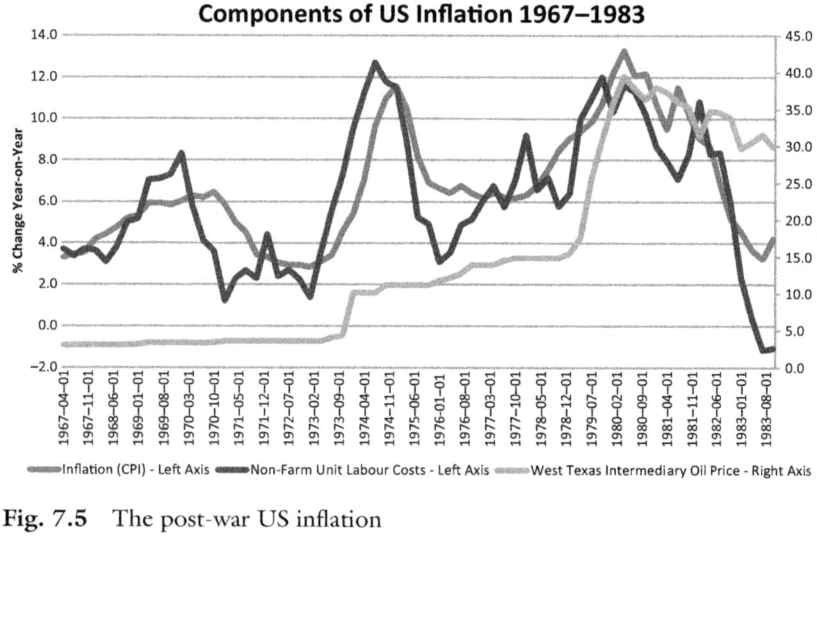

Fig. 7.5 The post-war US inflation

interest rates, kept a lid on inflation for the period known as the Great Moderation, but created a highly unstable economy in which households took on enormous amounts of debt in order to bolster consumption. This house of cards collapsed in 2008, and, at the time of writing, the economy remains in stagnation.

The inflation of the 1970s should be understood as a cost-push inflation. The conditions needed for it—that is, the strain put on the real economy prior to it taking off—were demand-led and were, as are most demand-led inflations, due to a government trying to fund an unpopular war that could not be funded by either taxation, rationing or price controls as other wars had been. In this inflation, we see two types of cost-push inflation: a supply shock and a wage-price spiral. The former exacerbated the latter which then tended to feed upon itself. This inflation also highlights some of the major inflationary risks to the advanced capitalist economies today, namely, real supply shocks, wage-price spirals, and, although it was never a deciding factor in this particular instance, a fall in the exchange value of the currency.

Rather than saying that inflation is always and everywhere a monetary phenomenon, it is far better to say that inflation is always and everywhere a complex phenomenon. During inflations, it is natural that the money supply should grow (and, often, the velocity of circulation speed up). But correlation is obviously not causation. And money does not walk around the streets bidding up prices. Every instance of inflation is unique and must be studied carefully for its unique properties. Any other approach is just ideology plain and simple, and is ultimately no better than 'man-in-the-street-economics'. That the majority of the economics profession at the time of writing have some variant of this ahistorical nonsense baked into their brains is a testament to the fact that it is unclear as to whether the discipline is actually doing economics any more.[16]

Demolishing the ISLM Framework I: The LM-Curve

At this point, we can begin our demolition of the famous ISLM model. The ISLM framework, as most interested people know, was the major macroeconomic model used by those teaching economics before they moved to microfounded models in the 1970s and 1980s. Because these models have proved to be functionally useless, the ISLM continues today to be the 'workhorse' of mainstream macroeconomics. Every time you

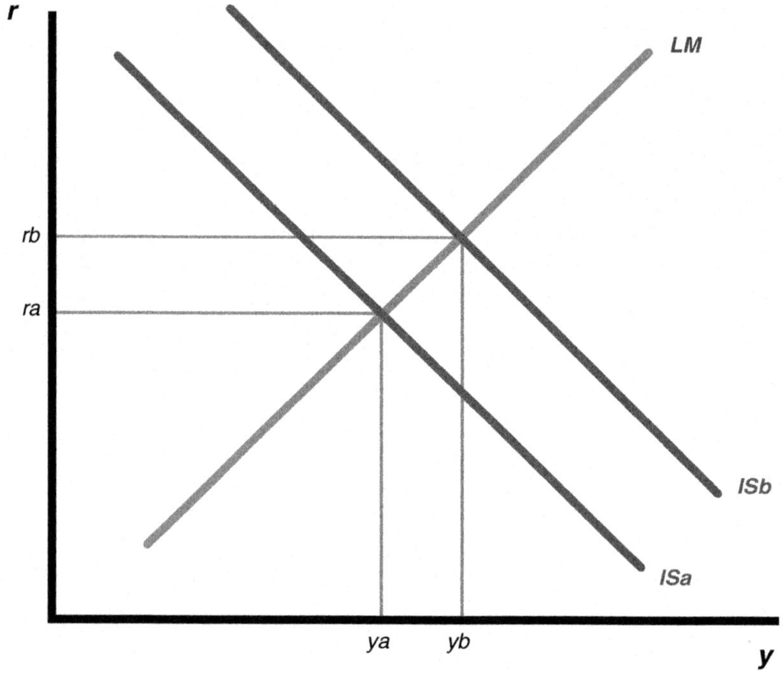

Fig. 7.6 Basic ISLM model

have a policy discussion with a mainstream economist, you can be sure that behind his or her eyes a little ISLM model is being manipulated in his or her brain. If you understand correctly the flaws and limitations of the ISLM model, you will basically understand the flaws and limitations of mainstream economic policy advice.

We will not here spend the rest of the chapter deriving the ISLM. Rather, we will assume familiarity with it. If the reader is not familiar with it, they can consult a textbook, Google or even YouTube for an easy 'how to manual'. We can see the basic ISLM diagram laid out in Fig. 7.6.

This ISLM diagram shows what happens in the basic model when investment and savings are increased. When someone, say the government, increases investment by running a deficit, they push the IS-curve from point IS_a to point IS_b. The increase in investment is assumed to be funded by borrowing. In the case where, for example, a government ran a deficit, they would fund this by selling bonds in the open market.

The increase in investment leads to increased income, y, and this can be seen by the fact that we move from point y_a to point y_b. According to the ISLM, however, there is no free lunch. If the government, or anyone else, increases their borrowing, this will lead to an increase in the interest rate as borrowers scramble for money. We see this in Fig. 7.6 where the interest rate, r, increases from point r_a to point r_b.[17]

But we have seen from the foregoing discussion that this is entirely false. When borrowing increases, the central bank will automatically increase funds into the banking system so as to counteract any pressure put on interest rates by borrowing. The ISLM model is misleading because it is implicitly based on a money multiplier view of the economy. It is based on the view that Samuelson and Nordhaus express in their textbook: namely, the idea that central banks control the money supply. In truth, as the BoE has stated quite clearly, the central bank does no such thing. Rather, they set the interest rate and allow anyone, the government included, to borrow at that rate. Reconstructing the model assuming that the central bank sets the overnight rate and allows the quantity of money demanded to adjust, we get a very different picture indeed. We have laid such a picture out in Fig. 7.7.

As we can see, we have flattened the LM-curve to indicate that when lending increases, the interest rate does not move. Now income can increase from point y_a to point y_b without an accompanying rise in the interest rate. The central bank will simply keep the interest rate wherever it sets its target and adjust the amount of reserves needed in line with this.

This shows up a number of absurdities in mainstream policy analysis. The first is the idea that lending crowds out other lending by raising interest rates as borrowers scramble for funds. This is manifestly untrue, as we have already discussed. Another implication is that reserve requirements are, as many central banks have found in recent decades, completely irrelevant. This shatters proposals by many prominent economists, including some at the IMF, that we might stabilise the banking system and stop it engaging in excess lending by imposing 100 % reserve requirements (see Benes and Kumhof 2012).[18] If this were done, it would have almost no effect. The central bank would merely beef up its open market operations and extend more reserves to hit its target interest rate. If it did not, the banks would scramble for reserves and find them completely lacking and interest rates would go haywire. Imagine if a central bank raised reserve requirements from 10 % to 100 % and refused to extend the needed reserves. What would happen? The banking system would find itself with

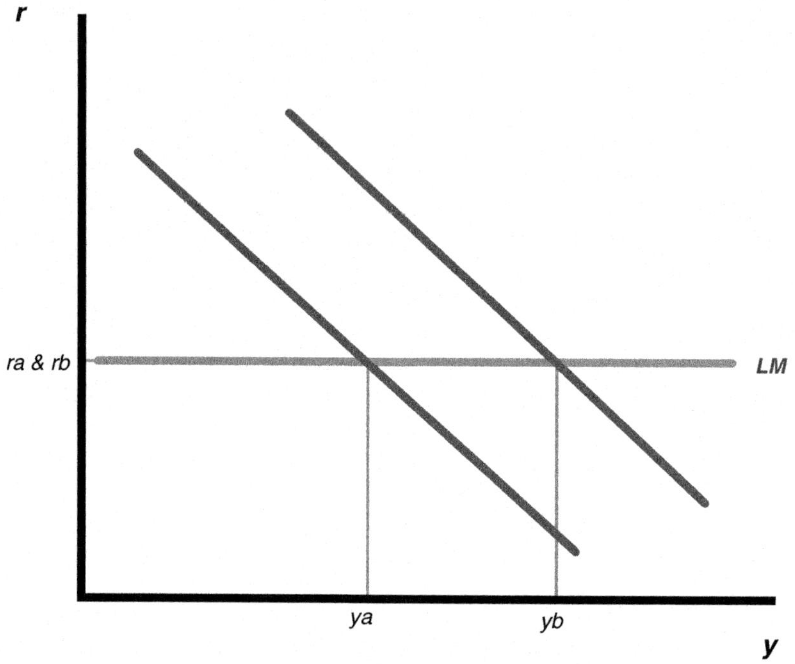

Fig. 7.7 ISLM model modified for endogenous money

only 10 % of the reserves it needed to meet the new reserve requirements. The upward pressure on interest rates would cause chaos.

Yet another implication is that we should not be surprised that the Quantitative Easing (QE) programmes put in place first in Japan in 2001 and then in the USA and the UK in 2009 proved to have basically no effect on bank lending. Although since then central bankers and others have claimed that this was not their goal, if you look back on their statements at the time, it quite clearly was one of the main goals. But if we understand that banks do not control the money supply and only control interest rates, it should be simple to see that once interest rates are at zero, any excess reserve cash pumped into the system will just sit on the balance sheets of banks. Yet many economists thought that the QE programmes would lead to an increase in the money supply, presumably through some 'money multiplier' effect, and that this would lead to an uptick in income and inflation. Indeed, some even warned that the QE programme would lead to hyperinflation![19]

During the crisis, an interesting and forceful narrative emerged directly from the ISLM framework. This was the 'liquidity trap' narrative that was popularised by Paul Krugman. Krugman had formulated his liquidity trap argument in the late 1990s when he was studying the downturn and subsequent stagnation that had occurred in Japan after the housing and stock market bubbles burst in the early 1990s. Before we examine this argument and how it is affected by the preceding discussion in detail, we should first note that Krugman's definition of the liquidity trap, which he derived from the work of John Hicks, the British economist and inventor of the ISLM (1937).[20] We will not deal with this issue here but rather broach it in the next chapter. The reader should here merely keep in mind that, if the arguments in this and the next chapter of this book are accepted, the 'liquidity trap' explanation of economic stagnation is flawed in two absolutely fundamental ways which renders it largely useless as an explanation of macroeconomic phenomena.

It should also be noted that Krugman's interpretation of the liquidity trap is an idiosyncratic one. In his key academic paper on the matter, he uses a microfoundations approach and assumes deterministic expectations on the part of agents. This leads Krugman to some rather strange policy conclusions; notably, that if a central bank can convince people that it will act 'recklessly', the economy will recover.[21] After examining his regular columns and his recent turn against microfoundations, Krugman should probably be given the benefit of the doubt in this regard; it is likely that he never believed in this approach and was merely trying to make Hicks' point using tools that allow economists to get published in mainstream journals.

These differences should be noted only in passing as the functional mechanism of the liquidity trap in both Krugman's and Hicks' paper is identical. And so whatever flaws we can find in the basic ISLM model can also be found, possibly even in amplified form, in modified versions thereof. In his paper, Krugman defines a liquidity trap exactly as it was defined in Hicks' original formulation. He writes:

> A liquidity trap may be defined as a situation in which conventional monetary policies have become impotent, because nominal interest rates are at or near zero: injecting monetary base into the economy has no effect, because base and bonds are viewed by the private sector as perfect substitutes. (Krugman 1998, p. 141)

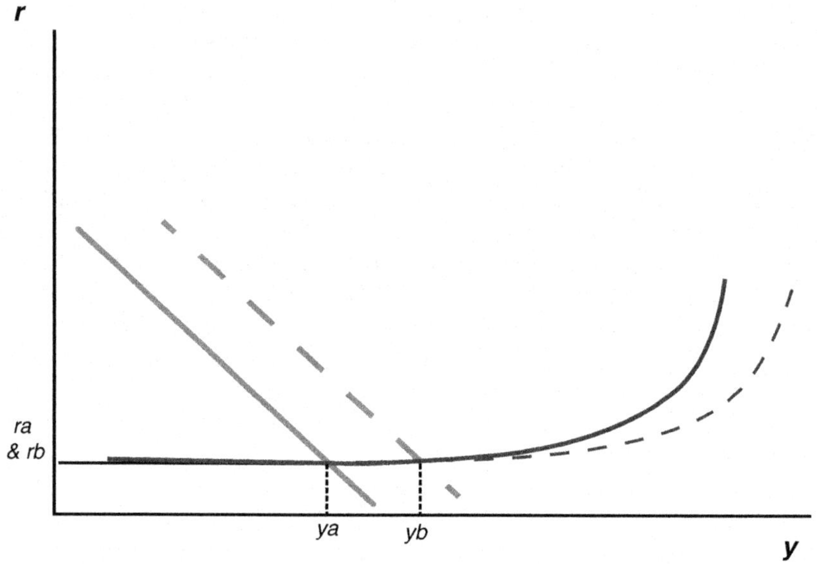

Fig. 7.8 ISLM model w/liquidity trap

We can demonstrate this graphically by flattening out the left-hand side of the LM-curve, as is done in many macroeconomics textbooks. We can see this in Fig. 7.8.

What the graph in Fig. 7.8 shows is that moving the LM-curve to the right-hand side will have no effect on the level of activity. It also shows that if we shift the IS-curve to the right-hand side, not only will we see an increase in income and economic activity but we will not see a rise in interest rates. Mainstream economists who support fiscal intervention in times of severe downturns like Krugman consider this to be a sort of free lunch situation. You can see this clearly if you look at the far right-hand side of the graph. When the IS-curve moves to this point, the normal ISLM emerges intact. Thus, outside of a liquidity trap, interest rates will rise if the IS-curve is pushed to the right and some borrowers (like, say, the government) will crowd out other borrowers (like, say, private firms).

It should be manifestly obvious why this is incorrect. As we have seen in Fig. 7.5, *the LM-curve is always flat and so a rise in investment never leads directly to a rise in the money interest rate*. If we turn back to Fig. 7.5, we must imagine that if the central bank raises or drops interest rates, they will merely move the LM-curve up or down rather than right or left.[22] So, provided we accept the shape of the IS-curve (for the purposes of this chapter, at least), we can still discuss the effect that shifting the LM-curve has if we take it to be a strictly independent policy function that moves up or down at the whim of the central bank rather than left and right. But clearly, talking about a liquidity trap leading to a situation in which increased borrowing and investment by, say, the government does not provoke a rise in interest rates is nonsensical because, given the manner in which modern banking systems are set up, an increase in borrowing and investment ***never leads directly to a rise in interest rates.***[23] Even though some proponents of the liquidity trap argument, like Krugman in his 1998 paper, do use a slightly different model to the ISLM, they nevertheless come to make the same incorrect predictions as to what should happen when investment increases outside of a liquidity trap. In reality, once we accept endogenous money theory, then the LM-curve is always flat and the liquidity trap theory loses one of the legs on which it stands.

If you make the above arguments to many mainstream economists, they will look at you patronisingly and say that they know all this already. But listen carefully to that very same persons next time they talk about concrete policy issues and you will hear them quickly revert to all the old fallacies within just a few seconds. While it is true that the ISLM can be interpreted in a number of different ways, the basic model in the form it was presented above sears itself into the minds of mainstream economists and can rarely be truly removed. Like all economic models, the ISLM structures the manner in which those who are trained to use it think. It is not an innocent model. Even if it can be pulled apart and put back together in any number of different ways, in its basic form, it shapes the minds and arguments of those who learn it and it leads to incorrect conclusions about any number of very important issues.

The inherently conservative aspect of the ISLM device is that it places a limitation, a sort of taboo, in the mind of the person who uses and adopts it. Everyone has surely heard some politician or some economist claim that a country has run out of money or that the government cannot spend because it will simply be taking money from the private sector. These hoary of myths are the result of the taboo imposed by devices like the ISLM. In that sense, the ISLM is like a sort of updated version of the Quantity Theory of Money, but one that is far harder to attack or deconstruct because it hides its assumptions so well. The underlying myth of the LM-curve is basically that money is scarce. And when the untruth of this is peeled back, the reaction is generally to fall back on the taboo that if money is not created in line with some very rigid, mystical and usually arbitrary rule or set of rules, something awful will happen. Typically, as is the case with taboos in most primitive tribes, a doomsday scenario of hyperinflation is posited to steer the enquiring mind away from such dangerous ideas.

As throughout the rest of this book when I use the term 'conservative', I am only somewhat referring to what might be called the 'right-wing ideology'. While it is true that the right loathes social change more than the left and is thus far more suspicious of intellectual constructions that imply that social change is a rather simple process, the left also tends to ingrain conservative taboos into its collective mind-set. These are then converted into policy proposals that are more amenable to the spirit of equality on the left. A good example of this is the idea, deeply ingrained on the left, that taxation is an end in itself and should be required for any government expenditure. I have come to call this stance 'balanced budget socialism' and it is a deeply destructive conservative aspect of left-wing ideology in the twentieth century which puts a serious limit on the extent to which those on the left can engage in debate regarding economic issues.

This chapter should have shown conclusively that the LM-curve is completely misleading and should be jettisoned immediately. In the next chapter, we will explore the issues of finance and investment, and when we discussed them in sufficient depth, we will show why the IS-curve is also highly misleading and should also be thrown onto the rubbish-heap of bad ideas. With that the tired old 'workhorse' of mainstream macroeconomics will be confined, as he should have been long ago, to the knacker's yard where he will sit quietly waiting to be turned into glue.

Notes

1. This is a fusing together of the American slang for the US dollar—the 'buck'—and the school's mascot, the kangaroo; hence the name 'buckaroo'.
2. Some people might think this coercive. They might not like the idea that charity work is being monetised. But consider this carefully. Imagine that the university did not use the buckaroo system. Imagine they simply stated that in order to get a certain percentage

of their grade, the student must turn up for 20 hours of community service work. The university would then check in to see if this had taken place.

In actual fact, the exact same relationship has been set up: the student *owes* the university 20 hours of community service work to *earn* their grade just as they *owe* the university an exam of a certain quality to earn another part of their grade. Now, the reader might be against the very idea of coercing university students into doing community work to *earn* their grade. But that is an entirely different matter. What this example shows is that many of the relationships we enter into with social institutions have a debt-like quality. Typically when we say we have an 'obligation' to do something, it basically means we 'owe' doing this to someone or some institution. The only reason we do not often notice this explicitly is because we do not always monetise these debt relationships.

To be clear: this does not mean that we should monetise all these relationships. Much of the time having these relationships as informal debts is a far better way to run a society. But monetisation is a powerful force and can be used to promote the social good provided we are careful about how we deploy it.

3. The following two subheadings will be derived in some part from Lavoie (1992); see especially, Chap. 4 of that book. For a more comprehensive account of some of the issues dealt with in this chapter, the readers would be well advised to consult that book.
4. It might be noted by the reader that if households engage in consumption, all of this revenue will accrue only to the consumption good firms, R_c. Here we are implicitly assuming that the investment goods are being used by the consumption goods sector and so the latter passes on a share of its revenue to the former.
5. The symbol t_d is understood here as a fraction. So, if reserve requirements were 10 %, then $t_d = 0.1$. If we assume that deposits are \$1000, then according to our formula, $t_d . M_b$, we would get 0.1(\$1000), and the reserves required would be \$100.
6. Whether the process ever actually worked like this is an entirely different question. Studying the banking system of the nineteenth century, this appears to be very doubtful.
7. The reader can also find video presentations of this on the BoE's website at: http://www.bankofengland.co.uk/publications/Pages/quarterlybulletin/2014/qb14q1prereleasearticlemoney.aspx.

8. The upper-case sigma, Σ, means 'summation of'. That is, the sum of all individual prices and quantities in the economy.
9. Note that at some points in his career, Friedman admitted that these two variables might indeed not be constant. If we accept this, then we are back to interpreting the Fisher equation, as Fisher himself did, as a simple identity and so what follows in the rest of the discussion with regard to Fisher equally applies to Friedman and the monetarists.
10. All data from the Federal Reserve of St Louis.
11. We will explore this in more detail below.
12. The period of rationing during the Second World War is fascinating from an economic and an anthropological point-of-view. The rise of YouTube has allowed for many of the old propaganda films to be shown once more. Some of the best include (Office of War Information 1942) and (Office of War Information 194x). The former is a surprisingly informative dramatisation based on a Hollywood film script with all the typically Freudian overtones that scripts from that era manifested, while the latter is a film based on the 'new emerging science of nutrition' and warns against poor eating habits among Americans.
13. The variable Y here is functionally equivalent to the Q in the quantity theory of money; it is just a different notation. The reason that we have used the denotation is to make clear the connection between the above identity and the familiar GDP identity $[Y = C + I + G + (X - M)]$ wherein GDP or income or Y (these are all equivalent) can be interpreted as total demand for goods and services.
14. All data used in this section is sourced from the Federal Reserve of St Louis.
15. Note that Volcker himself denies that he adopted monetarism as an ideology to cover over the fact that he was raising interest rates, although he admits that many around him saw it that way. If you read how he conceived of what he was doing, however, it was clear that he had a far more objective view of the situation than the monetarist True Believers (Volcker in Mehrling 2000, pp. 445–446).
16. Consider a phrase that one often hears from economists: 'Inflation is when too much money chases too few goods.' A moment's reflection will confirm that inflation could potentially be

accommodated through a large increase in the velocity of money without any need for an increase in the money supply should the spending decisions of agents in the economy so demand it—or, more formally, $\bar{M}V = p\bar{Q}$. The only conclusion one can draw from the fact that trained economists continue to make such crude statements is that the contemporary economics of inflation is dominated by ideology and not critical, rational thinking.

17. Note that the ISLM was originally taken to represent all interest rates in the economy. In practice, however, economists generally assume that the interest rate represented by the model is the overnight interest rate that the central bank targets. On occasion, economists will make the case that the ISLM is actually representing long-term interest rates—that is, ten-year government bond yields. We assume here that the ISLM is representing the overnight interest rate, but our discussion will not be much altered if we assume that it is representing long-term interest rates, as these tend to simply 'follow' short-term interest rates. The fact that the ISLM only discusses a single interest rate and considers this to be some sort of aggregate will be examined in more detail in the following chapter. This is seriously problematic because interest rates in other markets are subject entirely to their own dynamics and are only partially responsive to the central bank interest rate.
18. Note that the Benes and Kumhof paper is particularly fascinating for those who want to understand properly the limitations of mainstream economic methodology. Benes and Kumhof, having been made vaguely aware of the ideas of endogenous money, have attempted to integrate the so-called Chicago Plan for 100 % reserve requirements into a 'modern' DSGE framework. Unfortunately for the authors, they have clearly shown that they are completely and utterly unable to grasp the essence of the endogenous money argument, and they instead spend over 70 pages, including references, building a highly complex mathematical model on completely incorrect assumptions.

    Once again, the mainstream methodology shows its major limitations: namely, that its practitioners become obsessed with the idea of modelling as a game in itself and do not bother to examine the actual economic issues in any detail. Their actual argument can be addressed and refuted in literally a paragraph but instead of engaging with the actual argument they sat down in a room and built a model. When dealing with such issues, I always have the feeling that we are dealing with the same methodological problem as Keynes alluded to in his critique of Tinbergen's econometric method: 'I have a feeling that Prof. Tinbergen may agree with much of my comment, but that his reaction will be to engage another ten computors and drown his sorrows in arithmetic' (Keynes 1939, p. 568).

In the world of giant microfounded super-models, communication on actual issues of interest becomes an entirely secondary issue and arcane mazes full of unnecessary puzzles and riddles becomes the order of the day. This calls to mind another wonderful quote on the perversities of certain types of academic discourse, this time from Montaigne: 'Let him remove his academic hood, his gown and his Latin; let him stop battering our ears with raw chunks of pure Aristotle; why, you would take him from one of us—or worse. The involved linguistic convolutions with which they confound us remind me of conjuring tricks: their sleight-of-hand has compelling force over our senses but it in no wise shakes our convictions. Apart from such jugglery they achieve nothing but what is base and ordinary' (de Montaigne 1993).

19. It should be noted that some mainstream economists have realised this to some extent. They have proposed that we replace the LM-curve with a simple Taylor Rule to show how the central bank sets its interest rate (Romer 2000). While there are a number of problems with this approach, perhaps the most pressing is that central banks do not set their interest rate in line with a Taylor Rule! What's more, the author's insights, as he notes himself in the paper, do not seem to have penetrated the ever impenetrable mind of the profession at large, a mind that is tied, as ever, to antiquated dogma.
20. It should be noted in passing that towards the end of his life, John Hicks actually repudiated the ISLM model and said that it was an impoverished representation of Keynesian macroeconomics (Hicks 1980). While Hicks was indeed a marginalist economist, he remains one of the most interesting monetary economists of the twentieth century to emerge from that school. It is tempting to say that while Hicks was marginalist in his economics, and suffered from all the wounds that such a view inflicts on the mind, he was a truly eclectic and interesting Keynesian in his monetary economics.

21. The QE programme initiated by the Japanese government three years after his paper would probably meet his criteria of a central bank 'credibly' acting 'recklessly', and it did not foster the promised economic recovery, so if Krugman did hold these beliefs in 1998, we can only assume that they have since become untenable.
22. This is assuming, of course, that we allow the IS-curve to have a downward-sloping shape. We will argue that this is absolutely not the case in the next chapter, but for now we are merely taking the IS-curve as a given.
23. Note that one potential response to this is that outside of a so-called liquidity trap there is assumed to be full employment. Thus, a rise in investment in these circumstances will lead to inflation and nominal interest rates will thus rise of their own accord. This is simply not true. The central bank has full ability to control nominal interest rates no matter what the level of inflation; see (Pilkington 2012a, b, 2014a).

    Another line of argument might be to make the same argument about full capacity and say that central banks will raise the rate of interest automatically in the face of inflation. This is identical to the Taylor Rule argument put forward by Romer (2000). First of all, it should be stated that this is never explicitly explained by liquidity trap theorists like Krugman. And secondly, the reader is reminded that, as previously stated, central banks do not actually operate in line with the Taylor Rule.

References

Benes, J., & Kumhof, M. (2012). The Chicago plan revisited. IMF Working Paper. https://www.imf.org/external/pubs/ft/wp/2012/wp12202.pdf

Bernanke, B. (2004). Oil and the economy. *Distinguished lecture series.* Darton College, Albany, GA. http://www.federalreserve.gov/boarddocs/speeches/2004/20041021/

Dunstable Town Centre. (2005). Rationing and the black market. *BBC: WW2 Peoples' War.* http://www.bbc.co.uk/history/ww2peopleswar/stories/59/a3914859.shtml

Fisher, I. (1911). *The purchasing power of money: Its determination and relation to credit, interest and crisis.* USA, UK & Canada: The Macmillan Company.

Galbraith, J. K. (1973). *Economics and the public purpose.* UK: Andre Deutsch.
Graeber, D. (2011). *Debt: The first 5,000 years.* USA: Melville House Publishing.
Harvey, J. (2009). *Currencies, capital flows and crises.* USA: Routledge.
Hicks, J. (1980). ISLM: An explanation. *Journal of Post-Keynesian Economics, 3*(2), 139–154.
Juvenal, L., & Petralla, I. (2012). Speculation in the oil market. *Research division: Federal reserve bank of St. Louis.* Working Papers Series. http://research.stlouisfed.org/wp/2011/2011-027.pdf
Kaldor, N. (1939). Speculation and economic stability. *The Review of Economic Studies, 7*(1), 1–27.
Kaldor, N. (1982). *The scourge of monetarism.* UK: Oxford University Press.
Kalecki, M. (1965). *Theory of economic dynamics: An essay on cyclical and long-run changes in capitalist economy.* USA: Monthly Review Press.
Keynes, J. M. (1930). *A treatise on money, volumes I and II.* USA: Harcourt, Brace & Co.
Keynes, J. M. (1939). Professor Tinbergen's method. *The Economic Journal, 49*(195), 558–577.
Keynes, J. M. (1940). *How to pay for the war. The collected writings of John Maynard Keynes Vol. IX.* UK: Royal Economic Society.
Krugman, P. (1998). It's Baaack: Japan's slump and the return of the liquidity trap. *Brookings Paper on Economic Activity,* 137–205.
Lavoie, M. (1992). *Foundations of post-Keynesian economic analysis.* USA: Edward Elgar.
Marx, K. (1867). *Capital: Volume I.* New edition by Penguin Books, 1976.
McLeay, M. Radia, A., & Thomas, R. (2014). Money creation in the modern economy. *Bank of England.* Quarterly Bulletin 2014 Q1. http://www.bankofengland.co.uk/publications/Pages/quarterlybulletin/2014/qb14q1prereleasearticlemoney.aspx
Mehrling, P. (2000). An interview with Paul A. Volcker. *Macroeconomic Dynamics, 5,* 434–460.
Montier, J. (2013a). Hyperinflation, hysteria and false memories. *GMO White Paper.* http://s3.amazonaws.com/presspublisher-do/upload/567/JM_Hyperinflations_213-1.pdf
Montier, J. (2013b). Hyperinflations, hysteria, and false memories. *GMO White Paper.*
de Montaigne, M. (1993). *The complete essays.* USA: Penguin Classics. Reprint Edition.
Moore, B. (1983). Unpacking the post Keynesian black box: Bank lending and the money supply. *Journal of Post Keynesian Economics, 5*(4), 537–556.
Mosler, W. (2011, September 20). The UMKC buckaroo: A currency model for world prosperity. *Huffington Post.* http://www.huffingtonpost.com/warren-mosler/the-umkc-buckaroo-a-curre_b_970447.html

Nordhaus, W., & Samuelson, P. (1995). *Economics* (15th ed.). USA: McGraw-Hill.

Office of War Information. (194x). Wartime Nutrition. *US Government Wartime Propaganda Film*. https://www.youtube.com/watch?v=RRQH59_xdgs

Office of War Information. (1942). Prices Unlimited. *US Government Wartime Propaganda Film*. https://www.youtube.com/watch?v=UXRZgVm11pA

Office of War Information. (1944). Black Marketing. *US Government Wartime Propaganda Film*. https://www.youtube.com/watch?v=VaCEGhAjHjw

Phillips, A. W. (1958). The relationship between unemployment and the rate of change of money wages in the United Kingdom 1861–1957. *Economica, 25*(100), 283–299.

Pilkington, P. (2012a, March 8). Policing the economists from within their own minds—ISLM as a model of intellectual control. *Naked Capitalism*. http://www.nakedcapitalism.com/2012/03/philip-pilkington-policing-the-economists-from-within-their-own-minds-%E2%80%93-islm-as-a-model-of-intellectual-control.html

Pilkington, P. (2012b, February 28). Sexual politics and child's play—The absurdity of game theory. *Naked Capitalism*. http://www.nakedcapitalism.com/2012/02/philip-pilkington-sexual-politics-and-child%E2%80%99s-play-%E2%80%93-the-absurdity-of-game-theory.html

Pilkington, P. (2014a, May 16). Why Thomas Piketty is wrong about inflation and interest rates. *Fixing the Economists*. http://fixingtheeconomists.wordpress.com/2014/05/16/why-thomas-piketty-is-wrong-about-inflation-and-interest-rates/

Robinson, J. (1938). Review of *The Economics of Inflation* by C. Bresciani-Turroni. *The Economic Journal, 48*(191), 507–513.

Romer, D. (2000). Keynesian macroeconomics without the LM-curve. *Journal of Economic Perspectives, 14*(2), 149–169.

Rowthorn, R. E. (1977). Conflict, inflation and money. *Cambridge Journal of Economics, 1*(3), 215–239.

Smith, A. (1776). *The wealth of nations books I–III*. UK: Penguin Books.

Tarshis, L. (1947). *The elements of economics: An introduction to the theory of price and employment*. USA: Houghton Mifflin Company.

Tcherneva, P. (1996). Critical review of soft currency economics. Working Paper No. 7, Soft Currency Economics. http://www.mosler.org/docs/docs/pavlina.htm

Wray, R. (1998). *Understanding modern money: The key to full employment and price stability*. USA: Edward Elgar.

CHAPTER 8

Profits, Prices, Distribution and Demand

For the engine which drives Enterprise is not Thrift, but Profit.

—John Maynard Keynes

To the person not trained in economics, or to the interested student entering an economics course for the first time, the above quotation from Keynes would seem to be a self-evident truth. After all, is not capitalism based on the profit motive? Is this not what politicians, especially those on the right-wing of the political spectrum, tell us is the very essence of the entire system? Yet the student who enters an economics course for the first time is likely to have dust thrown in their eyes with regard to the source and importance of profits in capitalist economies. A survey of the introductory textbooks in the 1990s published in the *Cambridge Journal of Economics* concluded that the 'reader leaves the textbooks more confused about what determines the profit rate in neoclassical theory than when s/he began' (Aslanbeigui and Naples 1996, p. 54). The textbooks appeared to provide explanations of profits that were not only contradictory amongst themselves but also internally contradictory. Rather than emphasising that marginalist theory has no agreed upon, consistent explanation of profits the authors appeared to barrage students with various partial and conflicting explanations that were, taken together, incoherent.

W.P. Pilkington, *The Reformation in Economics*,
DOI 10.1007/978-3-319-40757-9_8

Why all this confusion? It seems that at this point many critical-minded students become suspicious of the ideological motivations of mainstream economic theory. They tend to get a strong sense that something is amiss. What is more, they may have heard somewhere, perhaps in a sociology lecture, that Karl Marx had found the true source of profits in his 1867 classic *Das Kapital*. They might saunter down to the university library and crack open a well-worn copy of that tome and find it stated that 'the rate of profit is … the ratio of the surplus-value to the capital advanced' (Marx 1867, p. 660). Well, this all seems rather abstract. So, the inquisitive student begins to read and read to try to discover what this 'surplus-value' is all about. After some digging, they eventually begin to understand that Marx divides the working day into two parts, and this explains the source of surplus-value and hence of profits.

The first part of the working day is for Marx the part that produces all the goods and services necessary for the worker to maintain their standard of living, or what Marx calls the workers' 'means of subsistence'. The idea here is that if the worker were able to work for himself or herself and not for someone else—that is, in the Marxist narrative, the capitalist—then they would only be required to do this amount of work, and then they could put their feet up or enjoy the fruits of their labour. The second part of the working day is, for Marx, of an altogether different character. Here it is worth quoting the original in full to give the reader a flavour of the theory:

> During the second period of the labour-process, that in which his labour is no longer necessary labour, the workman, it is true, labours, expends labour-power; but his labour, being no longer necessary labour, he creates no value for himself. He creates surplus-value which, for the capitalist, has all the charms of a creation out of nothing. This portion of the working-day, I name surplus labour-time, and to the labour expended during that time, I give the name of surplus-labour. (Ibid., p. 325)

But Marx did not stop there. He believed that he had found a sort of Universal Truth about all human societies. Indeed, he thought that he had found the truth of all forms of economic domination and exploitation throughout human history. He wrote:

> The essential difference between the various economic forms of society, between, for instance, a society based on slave-labour, and one based on

> wage-labour, lies only in the mode in which this surplus-labour is in each case extracted from the actual producer, the labourer. (Ibid.)

This is heavy stuff indeed. And, it would seem, on the face of it, a call for revolution. After all, the worker is having his/her labour-time 'extracted', and that does not sound nice at all. If this labour-time was not being extracted, then would not the worker have either more wealth or more free time? And would not everyone but a person with an interest in said extraction be in favour of this? But perhaps our student is not so hot-headed as to join the university's Communist Party quite yet. Perhaps he or she is more interested in economic theory than politics—for now, at least. In such a case, he or she might ambush their professor after class and ask what all this 'profit' stuff and all this 'surplus-value' stuff are about. Here the student will likely only have their suspicions strengthened. The professor will likely have a very shaky view of what determines profits in a capitalist economy. And if the student presses the point the professor may well become agitated and say that these are questions that only Marxists and other disreputable people ask.

The student will then become very suspicious indeed. They might quite reasonably ask themselves: 'Is the mainstream of the profession throwing up all this dust because Marx put his finger firmly on the pulse of capitalism nearly 150 years ago and since then economists have been acting as agents of the bourgeoisie by trying to cover up this fundamental truth?' Well, before the reader mounts the barricades and learns the chorus of *The Internationale*, let us go back to those mainstream theories of profits and try to see if they stand up to scrutiny. Who knows? Maybe there was something of worth in that seeming fog of confusion.

Marginalist Theories of Profit

While it may be surprising to many, in standard marginalist theory, profits should not really exist at all. If they do, they are likely the result of some anomaly or other and probably indicate a so-called inefficiency of some kind. Profits may, as it is held, be the result of a nefarious monopolist bullying others out of the market to ensure that resources are not distributed efficiently. A recent popular microeconomics textbook is remarkably candid about this when the author writes that 'the only reasonable long-run level of profits for a competitive firm that has constant returns to scale at all levels of output is a zero level of profits' (Varian 2010, p. 355).[1] And yet profits continue to exist regardless.

The previously mentioned survey of eight leading textbooks in the 1990s was able to tease out all the major explanations of why profits remain. The first was, rather unsurprisingly, the role of entrepreneurship. While this does not seem on its face a particularly bad argument—indeed, it appears to chime with common sense—the authors noted that they were hard-pressed to find any coherent explanation of what this entrepreneurship actually entailed. Even the fragmentary answers that did appear seemed rather unsatisfactory. For example, some authors seemed to equate entrepreneurship with 'human capital'. On the face of it that seems intuitively plausible but the authors of the survey point out that there are problems with this. They write:

> Why then is entrepreneurship treated separately from other kinds of human capital? Why does the entrepreneur receive extraordinary returns rather than wages that reflect a normal return on their human capital? None of the textbooks answers this question. (Aslanbeigui and Naples 1996, p. 56)

As the authors note, this cannot simply be glossed over when using a theoretical framework the entire *modus operandi* of which is based on the market automatically finding some sort of optimal allocation of resources. This leads to all sorts of strange statements some of which verge on mysticism; indeed, the authors of one popular book refer to entrepreneurship as 'a "rather mysterious" factor of production' (ibid.). Others refer to the particular action of entrepreneurs as that of 'confronting strife'. Still other authors attribute profits to innovation. But since, as the authors point out, these authors appear to be talking about innovations undertaken by researchers in the Research and Development labs of large corporations, it is not altogether clear who these 'innovators' are. It seems far more reasonable to assume that in a modern economy it is the scientists in the lab or the designers in the design room that actually innovate. It seems altogether doubtful that the stockholders add to this innovation, yet it is to them that the profits accrue (ibid., p. 57).

One particularly interesting approach that some textbooks take is to assert that profits might accrue due to the risk that investors take by placing their investment in the first place. This, however, raises the familiar issue of risk versus uncertainty. In order to assume that profits are a compensation for something measurable, some authors insist that investors are able to determine the risk of a given investment in line with a probabilistically well-behaved future. That is, we might be able to say that this or that investment has, say, a 50/50 chance of succeeding and then invest money in it in line with these risks versus the potential profit rate. If this was the case, however, it seems that profits accruing to one group of investors in the aggregate would be perfectly balanced out with losses accruing to other investors and profits in the aggregate would melt into thin air.[2] Thus, we are effectively back once again to the problem we started with, namely, the problem of a rate of profit that disappears in theory but does not seem to disappear in practice. Another aspect of this theory that seems problematic is that there are many ways to derive profits in the real economy that do not seem to entail much risk at all; investing one's money in high-grade or blue-chip stocks would be one obvious instance of this.

Others, however, argue that profit arises as a result of the fact that investors must throw their money into an enterprise in the face of a completely unknowable future. The authors of the survey note that Frank Knight appeared to be making an argument along these lines (ibid., p. 58). Knight's conception of uncertainty is very close to Keynes', and so we may here be dealing with a properly Keynesian theory of profits that could be of great interest. However, once this particular can of worms is opened up, most of the marginalist edifice—based as it is on precise calculations about the future in the here and now—goes completely rotten and begins to fall apart. We may well accept the explanation provided by the Knightians that profit is a result of the fundamental uncertainty of investment decisions, but only on the condition that they allow us to burn the rest of their books due to their theoretical frameworks being completely unable to deal with uncertainty. While very damaging to the underlying epistemological foundations of marginalist economics, lines of inquiry involving questions of uncertainty are actually rather promising but, being effectively financial theories of profit and investment, they will have to wait until our later chapter on the financial markets.

How Firms Actually Derive Their Profits

The marginalist theory of profits (or lack thereof) assumes as its underlying framework a theory of perfectly competitive markets. Building on this, it can then go on to explore monopolies and firms engaged in monopolistic competition. These distinctions all seem trivial. The assumptions underlying the perfect competition models are completely unrealistic. As is the underlying sin with almost all marginalist economics, too much is required from the real world in order for it to live up to the models. In the real world, all firms, no matter how big or small, operate in a manner that might be taken by marginalists to resemble something like oligopoly. In their seminal 1939 paper, Hall and Hitch of the Oxford Economic Research Group surveyed businessmen and found that they did not set their prices in line with marginal revenues at all. Rather they set their prices by adding together direct material costs, labour costs and overhead costs determined at a 'standard' volume of output.[3] After these were calculated, the firms would add a percentage-based 'mark-up' that included both a profit element and also took into account any costs related to selling goods together with any interest payments the firm had to make (Lee 1984, p. 152).

The mark-up is generally conceptualised as follows:

$$(1+\theta)AVG = p$$

where p are prices, θ is the percentage mark-up and AVG is the average costs discussed above. We might then further break down the mark-up, now expressed not as a percentage but rather as a money value, as follows:

$$i + SAL + \pi \equiv \Theta$$

where Θ is the mark-up in money terms, i is payments on interest incurred, SAL is costs incurred during selling (transaction costs) and π is the actual profit component for the firm in question. What interests us here, of course, is the profit component. This, as it was reported, was generally set in line with a sort of customary norm. Businesspeople, no matter what size their business was, tended to look to other businesspeople in the same industry as them and effectively copy their profit margin. The reasons they did this were varied but the majority of them tied into the need by the businesspeople to maintain a sense of stability. All of the businesspeople feared that, on the one hand, trying to extract a higher profit margin might lead to others undercutting them and putting them out of business while, on the other hand, lowering their price too much would trigger a price war and at the same time would not increase their market share all that much (ibid.).

Here we see in full force the problem with the marginalist tendency to base their models not on a psychological view of the human being existing in a world full of uncertainty and other human beings whose motivations are not known, but rather on robotic calculators that act exactly as the economist's models and equations tell them they should. Such a view of human beings, while it may seem an innocuous simplification when it is introduced, quickly leads to a proliferation of errors that completely undermine any insights that economic theory might provide. In situations of business, as in situations of life in general, people often simply conform to the environment around them to avoid having to tarry with uncertainty proper. When we enter a new work environment, for example, the first thing that we do is try to determine how everyone else behaves and then reflexively tailor our own behaviour accordingly.

The mark-up theory of profit, simple though it is, provides us with a very firm reason explaining why profits do not simply disappear over time. Profits margins are conventions, and they exist in the form that they do so long as people believe that they should exist in this form. Yes, it is conceivable in theory that human beings might one day wake up from what the marginalists must see as their slumber, become the rational calculators that they are in the classroom theories and forcibly undermine these convention-based profits. But then why on earth can we not equally argue that after this Great Awakening has taken place just about every human convention in existence is seen for the arbitrary frauds that the marginalists must see them to be? We need not even refer to the shocking implications that such a Great Awakening might lead to mass outpourings of nude people onto the streets in hot weather or to the mass, indiscriminate copulations in parks and fields across cities throughout the world. No, we need only refer to the fact that the most obvious of the arbitrary conventional frauds that people will do away with will surely be paper currency.

Profits, and we will explore the implications of this in the conclusion of this chapter, are a creature not so much of competition as they are of convention. The fact of the matter is that businessmen and businesswomen will try to derive as much profit from their activities as they feel is the customary norm at any given moment in time. What determines this customary norm at any given moment in time? On the one hand, it seems determined by how low businesspeople are willing to tolerate their profit margins and on the other hand how high consumers are willing to tolerate the prices they pay for goods and services. In a situation where businesspeople, in the aggregate, moved to raise their profit margins by increasing their prices by too much consumers, who are also workers, would feel that their real wages were being eroded and would demand wage increases. This, in turn, would increase the average costs that businesspeople incurred and thus lower their profit margin. The opposite would likely happen if workers decided, in the aggregate, to lower the profit margin by trying to increase wages. It is this tension—this properly class tension—that ultimately determines the profit margin in a capitalist economy, and it is also this tension that often gives rise to either a stable path of low-inflation equilibrium growth (as in the USA in the 1990s) or an unstable path of high-inflation disequilibrium growth (as in the USA in the 1970s[4]).

Before we move on, a final word should be said about mark-up theories of profit in the marginalist literature. In this literature, readers will find something that is remarkably similar to the mark-up pricing theory put forward above when they encounter discussions of pricing and profits in the case of pure monopoly (Varian 2010, p. 443). The marginalist theory states that it is only in the case of monopoly that such pricing occurs. Monopolies in this literature arise mainly due to the size of the 'minimum efficient scale' (MES) (ibid., pp. 454–455). This is tied up with the idea of economies of scale and basically predicts that it is only in markets for goods that require large firms to minimise costs that monopolies and hence mark-up pricing will appear. The problem with this is that it is simply not confirmed by the evidence. In reality, all firms, including those that marginalists would assume to exist in perfectly competitive markets, employ mark-up pricing.

The reason for this is rather simple: the real world does not conform to the thought experiments taught in marginalist economics. In the real world, even firms in small markets employ mark-up pricing for any number of reasons—for example, because they all want to maintain their profitability so that they can grow and expand. Those who operate the firms also, as we have said, tend to emulate those already in the markets or in similar markets. Pricing is thus, as Roy Harrod said, based largely on 'ritual' (Harrod cited in Lavoie 1992, p. 134). Once again we are back to the simple fact that the marginalist theories completely misunderstand the nature of human beings; they are neither rational calculating machines nor implicit marginalist economists, rather they are creatures of habit trying to maintain islands of custom and stability in a vast ocean of uncertainty and change. Another aspect of the findings of studies like Hall and Hitch's is that prices are set by businesspeople long before the goods are even produced let alone brought to market (Lee 1984, pp. 159–160). Yet, in the marginalist framework, prices are set in line with a sort of bargaining procedure that ensures goods are produced and then tossed on to the market. This is simply not how the real world works. In the real world, prices are set by businesspeople who plan prior to their engaging in production. This completely overturns any idea about 'market-clearing prices' and introduces a far more realistic view of how economic actors are actually confronted with the movement of time and how they undertake decisions in the face of this.

Marginalists seek to do enormous violence to the real world with their ideal view of mankind as a large group of homogenous, rational calculators. It is a mode of thought that is inherently totalitarian in that an *a priori* view of how humans *should* act is conceived of first, and then the real world, which does not conform to such ideational constructions, is simply assumed to function in this manner. The violence that such a mode of thinking can do varies by degrees. As far as empirical work goes, violence is done to the data by squeezing it into the *a priori* framework out of which nonsense and untruth emerge; when considering the effects that such modes of thought have on students, it does violence to their rational faculties in that it encourages them to view the world not as it is, but rather in a twisted and distorted way that is at odds with observed reality; while in the realm of policy when these ideas are attempted to be put into practice, enormous violence is done to the societies and people upon which they are imposed.

Aggregate Profits, Prices, Demand and Distribution

The search for the theory of a normal rate of profit is a bit like looking in a dark room for a black cat that probably is not there.

—*Joan Robinson*

If we are to be honest, we must admit that how firms determine their profit margins is, from a purely economic point-of-view, in many ways uninteresting. It is, as we shall argue at the end of this chapter, largely a political, cultural or social question. The question as to where profits in the aggregate come from is a far more interesting and relevant one from the point-of-view of pure economics. This is because we can say something quite tangible and useful about it which we can then apply quite directly to the real world. As we laid out in the first chapter of this book, it is on these questions about which we can actually say something that we as economists should focus. On issues that we as economists cannot say anything of particular interest, we should perhaps not say anything at all; or at the very least, we should not say anything that we insist to be objective and therefore beyond the scope of our particular opinion. We should not be greedy on what our discipline might have to offer; rather we should follow Wittgenstein's famous dictum:

> Whereof one cannot speak, thereof one must be silent. (Wittgenstein 1922, p. 90)

So, let us turn now to an issue on which we have no need at all to be silent: aggregate profits. Perhaps the best manner in which to approach this is through a parable.

Imagine for a moment that there exists an island. Not a particularly paradisiacal island, mind you, but an island all the same. On this island, there exists a capitalist, a bank and a banker, a government with two competing politicians and ten workers. Five of our worker friends are bakers, and five of them are builders. We make some rather silly assumptions here which we explain with recourse to the fact that this is, after all, a magical island (oh, did we not mention that!?).[5] These silly assumptions are that the capitalist does not require food or sustenance, neither do the politicians nor do the bankers; also the capital goods that are produced do not suffer from wear and tear and are thus not subject to depreciation. Finally, there are no input costs to production apart from those of labour. Two additional not-so-silly assumptions will also be put in place: the government has mandated that there is a minimum wage law which dictates that workers must be paid at least $1 a week in nominal wages and the workers have a stock of food sufficient to sustain them for a week of work.

In the first period, say a week, the capitalist hires the five builders to build him a factory and hires the five bakers to enter the factory and make bread. The $10 he spends on weekly wages is raised from the bank—this is, as we have explained in a previous chapter, created out of thin air—which thereafter charges him $1 interest a week. At the end of the week, the workers have eaten all their food and have produced for the capitalist a giant loaf of bread which he turns around and sells to the workers, who get 10 % of the loaf each for the $1 that they have earned that week. This 10 % share sustains them for a week of healthy work. Before moving on, we should note here that the price of the bread is completely determined by the aggregate expenditure of the workers in the economy—that is, the bread is priced at $10 as the ten workers with their $1 wage packets offer their earnings to buy the bread.

Anyway, at the end of the period, the capitalist has laid his hands on $10 in profits out of which he pays the bank $1 in interest payments. In the next period, he again decides to produce a large loaf of bread. But this week, since he already has his factory, he only needs to pay the five bakers and does not need to hire the five builders. If the week had progressed in this manner, two things would have happened. On the one hand, the capitalist would have found himself with diminished profits at the end of the week. Since he invested only $5 this week, he would only see $5 in profits. This is due to the fact, and this is an extremely important point, *in a closed economy with no net government spending profits are equal to investment.* Another result of this lower level of investment spending by the capitalist would be that the price of bread would fall. Because there would only be five workers each with $1 willing to buy the bread, they would now get 20 % of the bread for the same price at which they had gotten 10 % of the bread the previous week. Thus, a general price deflation would occur.

But let us assume that such a tragedy does not occur. A new president is elected, call him Roosevelt II, and this president has heard from the capitalist's own mouth that the latter has decided only to employ five men this week. Roosevelt II knows well that the other men will simply be left to starve and when the deflation and low profits appear to the capitalist he may get scared and not hire anyone at all the next week. So, Roosevelt II sets up the Works Progress Administration (WPA) which hires the five builders to do various odd jobs which include cleaning up the island and staging artistic productions. Roosevelt II adheres to his own minimum wage laws and pays each of the five builders $1 a day which he has the government's central bank create out of thin air. At the end of the working week, the builders join the bakers at the factory door, and each gets his 10 % of the giant loaf of bread for his $1 weekly wage. The capitalist is ecstatic. He has spent on $5 this week, and he has received a total profit of $10 minus $1 in weekly interest payments to the bank.

Here we should stop and note two things. First of all, since the government has engaged in net money creation, profits are no longer solely dependent upon private sector investment. Rather *they are determined by private sector investment plus government sector investment.* Secondly, the capitalist is quickly building up a *stock* of profits or saving out of the *flows* of profits he receives every week. In the first week, he borrowed and invested \$10 out of which he received the same \$10 and paid \$1 as interest to the bank. In the second week, he used \$5 of the remaining \$9 to invest and at the end of the week received a full \$10 in profits. At the end of the second week, after making his \$1 interest repayment, he had a total stock of wealth of \$13. The banker is also accruing a flow of \$1 profits a week which compound to a stock of profits of \$2 at the end of the second week. Table 8.1 shows the evolution of profits if the current situation were imagined to go on for a number of periods.

Now this may seem rather simple and even rather trite, but even with this highly simplified little model we can explore some key aspects of the distribution of profits. Let us imagine, for example, that the capitalist decides to repay his debt to the bank in full at the end of the third week. That way he will only have to make the interest payment for the third week, and he will never have to make any more. The outcome is shown in Table 8.2.

Here we see some interesting dynamics emerge. Obviously, the banker's profits stop accumulating after the last interest payment is made at the end of the third week. But note what happens to the stock of the capitalist's profits. It is only in the 13th week that his stock of profits catches up

Table 8.1 Simple profits model I

Week	*Private investment*	*Government investment*	*Capitalist profits (flow)*	*Interest payments*	*Capitalist profits (stock)*	*Banker profits (flow)*	*Banker profits (stock)*
1	10	0	10	1	9	1	1
2	5	5	10	1	13	1	2
3	5	5	10	1	22	1	3
4	5	5	10	1	31	1	4
5	5	5	10	1	40	1	5
6	5	5	10	1	49	1	6
7	5	5	10	1	58	1	7
8	5	5	10	1	67	1	8
9	5	5	10	1	76	1	9
10	5	5	10	1	85	1	10
11	5	5	10	1	94	1	11
12	5	5	10	1	103	1	12
13	5	5	10	1	112	1	13
14	5	5	10	1	121	1	14
15	5	5	10	1	130	1	15
16	5	5	10	1	139	1	16

Table 8.2 Simple profits model II

Week	*Private investment*	*Government investment*	*Capitalist profits (flow)*	*Interest payments*	*Capitalist profits (stock)*	*Banker profits (flow)*	*Banker profits (stock)*
1	10	0	10	1	9	1	1
2	5	5	10	1	13	1	2
3	5	5	10	0	12	1	3
4	5	5	10	0	22	0	3
5	5	5	10	0	32	0	3
6	5	5	10	0	42	0	3
7	5	5	10	0	52	0	3
8	5	5	10	0	62	0	3
9	5	5	10	0	72	0	3
10	5	5	10	0	82	0	3
11	5	5	10	0	92	0	3
12	5	5	10	0	102	0	3
13	5	5	10	0	112	0	3
14	5	5	10	0	122	0	3
15	5	5	10	0	132	0	3
16	5	5	10	0	142	0	3

to what it would have been had he kept making the interest payments and it is only in the 14th week that it surpasses what it would have been in that alternate reality.[6]

Okay. But let us leave that all behind and rewind a bit. Let us imagine that we are back at the end of the second week (i.e. before we even looked at the above tables). Further let us imagine that another president has seized power in a coup. Let us call this president Nixon II. Now, let us imagine that in order to solidify his reign he has to turn all the builders who were previously working for the WPA into soldiers. Furthermore, in order to secure their loyalty, he must pay them more than they were previously paid. So, at the beginning of week three, he has the central bank create double the money that Roosevelt II would have and pays his soldiers $2 each for their weekly salary. At the end of the third week, the soldiers turn up at the factory door and buy their share of the loaf of bread but in doing so they bid up the price. They receive a 13.333 % share each for their $2 while the bakers only receive a 6.666 % share each for their $1. The capitalist, however, sees his profits increase to $15 this week and is altogether very happy.

But his happiness is short-lived because the bakers feel like they have been short-changed. They say that if the capitalist does not now pay them $2 a week they will go and join Nixon II's well-paid army. And so at the end of the fourth week, the capitalist is forced to pay his workers at the new higher wage. All that has now happened is that we have seen a rise in the price level due to Nixon II's irresponsible government spending. The dynamics have been laid out in Table 8.3.

We should note here one or two interesting points before we move on. First of all, as we can see, the capitalist's total nominal profits have increased at a far faster rate than they would have if Nixon II had not ramped up spending; also, the price level has risen significantly in the two periods where the rate of investment increased.[7] In the third and fourth week, the capitalist would see his stock of profits erode in real terms as it was hit by inflation. But after this initial two-period hit the inflation rate stabilises and the stock of profits eventually surpasses its would-be level had the inflation not occurred due to diminished real interest payments. The inflation-adjusted measurements of the evolution of the capitalist's and banker's profit stock can be seen in Fig. 8.1.

In Fig. 8.1, we are measuring profits in real terms. In the case of our model, this means in terms of how much bread—which makes up the 'basket' of goods—these profits can purchase. As we can see, capitalist profits initially take a hit relative to what they would have been due to the price increases which erodes the previous stock of profits held by the capitalist. Once the effects of the price increases have been felt in the system, however, the growth of the stock of profits stabilises and finally catches up with what it would have been without inflation in the 20th week. In week 22, it actually surpasses what it would have been had there been no inflation. The reason for this can be seen in the lines representing the stock of the banker's profits. Because the banker has fixed his debt contract with the capitalist in nominal terms, the inflation eats away at his interest payments in real terms. This means that the capitalist has to pay less interest on his loan in real terms and thus we see the inflation actually increases his stock of profits in the long-term (i.e. over the course of more than 20 weeks). This actually teaches us an important lesson about real-world inflation dynamics: *in an inflation real wealth will be redistributed from creditors to debtors.* (A deflation, of course, will have the opposite effect.) Since bankers are typically net creditors, this goes a long way towards explaining why they hate inflation above just about everything else.[8]

Table 8.3 Simple profits model III

Week	*Private investment*	*Government investment*	*Capitalist profits (flow)*	*Interest payments*	*Capitalist profits (stock)*	*Banker profits (flow)*	*Banker profits (stock)*	*Price level (Index = 100: Week 2)*	*Inflation rate (%)*
1	10	0	10	1	9	1	1	0	0
2	5	5	10	1	13	1	2	100	0
3	5	10	15	1	27	1	3	150	0.5
4	10	10	20	1	46	1	4	200	0.333333333
5	10	10	20	1	65	1	5	200	0
6	10	10	20	1	84	1	6	200	0
7	10	10	20	1	103	1	7	200	0
8	10	10	20	1	122	1	8	200	0
9	10	10	20	1	141	1	9	200	0
10	10	10	20	1	160	1	10	200	0
11	10	10	20	1	179	1	11	200	0
12	10	10	20	1	198	1	12	200	0
13	10	10	20	1	217	1	13	200	0
14	10	10	20	1	236	1	14	200	0
15	10	10	20	1	255	1	15	200	0
16	10	10	20	1	274	1	16	200	0

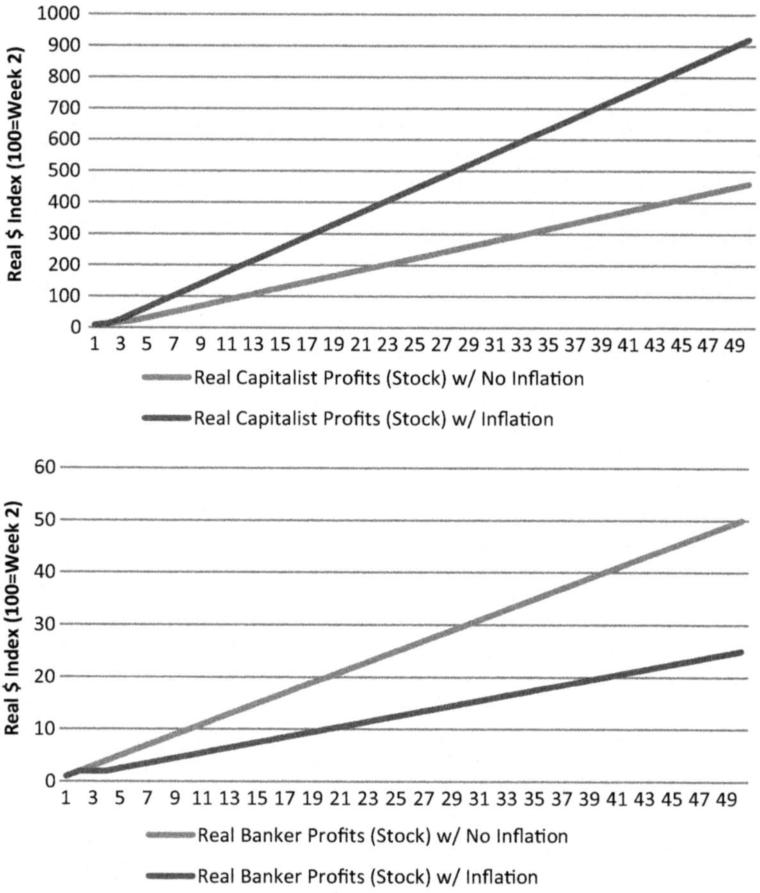

Fig. 8.1 Simple profits model IV

Breakout Box: The Multiplier

Up until now, we have been merely interested in the money that accrues to various sectors of the economy. While this can tell us a great deal about income distribution, it does not tell us very much about the level of economic activity that results from spending and investment. In order to get a better grasp on this, we have to introduce what is usually called then Keynesian multiplier but which is more accurately called the Kahn multiplier after the person that discovered it, R.F. Kahn.

The multiplier is perhaps one of the most useful mathematical tools in the whole of the economist's toolbox. It was first published by in 1931 but since then historians have found many predecessors (Kahn 1931). Kahn's multiplier is based on the idea that an increase in spending in one part of the economy gives rise to increases in spending in other parts of the economy. Kahn was not concerned with the fact that investment spending can give rise to additional output. This is why he used the case of road building in his famous example. He wanted to investigate what would happen when workers were compensated in wages when they were paid to build the road. Kahn noted that they would save some of the money and spend the rest on goods and services. The recipients of the workers' spending would then also save some of the balance and spend the rest. This gave rise to a sort of chain-effect where one person's spending becomes another person's income, part of which would then be spent which would then accrue as another person's income, part of which would then be spent and so on.

Kahn simplified this by taking the tendency to spend by those who receive the new income as a whole. Thus, we can imagine that we group all the end recipients of income together and then aggregate their tendency to consume out of the new income. Doing this, we can write the familiar multiplier relationship:

$$\frac{1}{(1-MPC)}$$

where *MPC* is the marginal propensity to consume out of additional income. So, for example, if the average person receiving new income spends 80 % of it and saves 20 % of it, the *MPC* will be 0.8, and the multiplier will be:

$$\frac{1}{(1-0.8)}=5$$

This means that for every \$1 in extra spending that is undertaken initially—say, by a government engaging in road building—the additional spending this will generate down the line will result in a total of \$5 of extra income.

Many people confuse the Kahn multiplier with the idea that extra money is being generated within the economy. This goes back to the highly misleading quantity theory of money that we presented in the previous chapter. Actually some reflection will show that this is not at all the case. While the initial injection of, say, \$1 in the form of wages paid by the government to the road builder may come from newly issued money, it will generate \$5 of additional income as it is passed around the economy like a hot potato in line with the multiplier.

When we are discussing the multiplier, we are not interested in money as such. Rather we are interested in how much extra output is being produced. We are interested in how much a given amount of extra spending calls forth extra expenditure on consumption goods, for example. The amount by which the money supply increases is, from this perspective, far less interesting than the amount by which peoples' spending is increased on consumption goods. While it is clearly true that when \$1 of new money is created only \$1 of new savings can be generated, we are focused on how much economic activity this new spending creates rather than the balance sheets of the firms and households at the end of the period.

The Levy–Kalecki Equation

In the previous sections, we have explored some key issues relating to aggregate profits, prices, demand and distribution using a very simple economy model. Let us now ignore the question of prices and focus on the relationship between profits, demand and distribution. Although we will not be saying much here that has not already been demonstrated in the previous section, we will be able to formalise much of this in a manner that makes it far easier to keep 'on hand' when thinking about the real world. We should also note that from now on we will also cease to discuss the financial sector and train all our focus on the real, productive sector.

This is because the framework we will be using was not built to accommodate a financial sector.

First, a historical note. The following theory of profits is, in a very real sense, the first modern macroeconomic theory to have ever been conceived. It bears many similarities to Keynes' schema but it was conceived of long before. The first person to have claim to inventing it was the American businessman Jerome Levy in 1914 who derived it from his intense study of the balance sheets of businesses.[9] Michal Kalecki, drawing on the work of Karl Marx in Volume II of *Das Kapital* (Kalecki 1965, p. 47), derived a similar equation in 1935. Levy's version of the equation is actually more interesting as it has a far superior breakdown of the components of profits but we will here be dealing with Kalecki's version as it is generally the version more often discussed and it is much simpler to get one's head around (Levy 2000).

Let us begin with a closed economy with no government sector and no financial sector. In such an economy, the gross income of the economy as a whole (GDP) is equal to gross profits plus wages and salaries. This gives us the income side of our identity:

$$Y \equiv \pi + W$$

where Y is income, π is profits and W is wages. We can determine what generates profits in a similar fashion:

$$I + Cp - Sw = \pi$$

where I is gross investment, Cp is consumption out of profits (i.e. capitalists consumption) and Sw is workers' savings (i.e. wages minus consumption of workers, or $W - Cw$).[10] Note that in the above equation we have dropped the identity symbol ($\equiv$) and replaced it with the symbol that denotes causality ($=$). This is because we are trying to make clear that it is the left-hand side of the equation that determines the right-hand side.[11] Kalecki makes the argument as such:

> What is the significance of this equation? Does it mean that profits in a given period determine capitalists' consumption and investment [and worker saving], or the reverse of this? The answer to this question depends on which of the items is directly subject to the decisions of the capitalists [and workers]. Now, it is clear that capitalists may decide to consume and

invest more in a given period than in the preceding one [and the workers may decide to consume or save more out of their income], but they cannot earn more. It is, therefore, their investment and consumption [and saving] decisions which determine profits, and not vice versa. (Kalecki 1965, pp. 45–46)

In such an economy, the determinants of profits are the level of gross investment, capitalist consumption decisions and worker's saving/consumption out of their previous income. But we should note carefully that, as we showed in our example in the previous section, the key variable here is really investment. It is only through prior investment, which allows for production and income generation in the first place, that capitalists and workers are allowed to consume and save. This leads to Kalecki's famous conclusion that, in a closed economy with no government, it is the investment decisions of capitalists themselves that determine the levels of profits that those capitalists receive. This is precisely what we have already seen in our verbal exposition.

Let us now open the economy to outside flows and include a government sector that can spend money on consumption and investment by borrowing rather than collecting this money in taxes (i.e. a government that can engage in deficit spending). National income is now determined as such:

$$Y \equiv (\pi - T_\pi) + (W - T_w) + (T_\pi + T_w + T_i)$$

where $T\pi$ are taxes on profits, T_w are taxes on wages and T_i are indirect taxes. The final profit equation for such an economy will be as follows:

$$I + (X - M) + (G - T) + Cp - Sw = (\pi - T_\pi)$$

where $X - M$ is net exports (i.e. exports minus imports) and $G - T$ is the budget deficit (i.e. government expenditure minus taxes). Again, we have turned our identity sign ($\equiv$) into a sign denoting causality ($=$) to show that the variables on the left-hand side are active decisions taken by various economic agents that then determine the outcome of the variables on the right-hand side. In order to get a clearer view of what determines gross profits in this economy, we might write:

$$\textit{Gross Profits net of Taxes} \equiv \begin{cases} +\textit{Gross Investment} \\ +\textit{Net Exports} \\ +\textit{Budget Deficit} \\ +\textit{Capitalist Consumption} \\ -\textit{Worker Saving} \end{cases}$$

Here the plus and minus signs denote whether the variable adds to or subtracts from gross profits.

The above series of identities and equations are by no means exhaustive. We can write these relationships in any number of different ways. But if the reader is able to become quite familiar with them in their mind and integrate them, as it were, as they might integrate a new series of words into their vocabulary they will find them very helpful in thinking through how incomes flow through an economy. Again, the mainstream economists will claim that all that has been said above is glaringly obvious but again I ask the reader to then listen to these same people discourse on actual policy issues and note their ignorance of obvious truths that would become apparent if they had properly digested the above material.[12]

Profits: A Moral Dilemma

Now that we have properly examined some of the very objective things that we can say about profits in the macroeconomy, let us now turn back to where we began: to Marx and the marginalists. Has the above discussion told us anything about the source of profits in a capitalist economy? Yes, indeed it has but only in very abstract terms. It has not told us anything about what might be called the moral dimension of profits. The moral dimension is, of course, what preoccupied Marx and marginalists. They wanted to determine what led to the distribution of income. In our discussion of macroeconomic profits above, we said nothing about this although there is an obvious link between the two in that the relationship between wages and the mark-up will determine to what extent income is distributed between wages and profits. The profit identities that we discussed assumed a given distribution of income, and this distribution is, of course, given by the relationship between wages and the mark-up. When we discussed the mark-up, we concluded that the distribution between profits and wages was ultimately one of convention.

Conventions are not immutable. They are subject to moral or ethical evaluation and the political change that may result from such an evaluation. When discussing profits—both profits in the real, productive economy and profits in the financial sector—and how these determine the share of national income and wealth, we can never lose sight of the moral dimension. Marx and the marginalists sought to hide this moral dimension behind a veil of what can only be described as metaphysics, in the most pejorative form in which that word can be used. The marginalists sought to justify the existence of profits as a sort of transitory phenomenon stimulating entrepreneurship that had nothing to do with power or underlying social relations. Marx, on the contrary, completely ignored that profits might stimulate entrepreneurial activity and instead insisted wholly on power relations. His implicit working premise was that only labour adds value to goods produced and those who come up with the idea and take the risk in putting it into action by investing and hiring workers are vile leeches. Both parties then constructed rather meaningless abstract narratives or fictitious 'stories' to justify their underlying point-of-view.

From a moral perspective, both of these stories, so far as my particular opinion is concerned, have an element of truth to them. Entrepreneurship is, as it seems to this writer, stimulated by profits but profits also result from power relations that are ingrained in social conventions. To me, profits play a role in both of these phenomena and cannot be completely disentangled from either. My preference would be to extract this element of truth from both sides of the debate. But we would be suckers if we simply bought into either story at face value. This is because each story seeks to justify an *a priori* political position that the authors and champions of both have hidden from view. The marginalists hold the position that a free market system, preferably with very limited monopoly, will result in a fair and efficient distribution of resources, while Marx holds the position that only a society in which profits have been completely abolished can be free to produce optimally. It is not my job here to convince the reader of the truth, untruth or partial truth of either statement—we have enough Gospels in economics and I have no desire to write another—but I do feel that it is my job to highlight that both are effectively moral judgements. Moral judgements are, unfortunately, rather subjective which is evident in the fact that different people hold to different moral judgements. If they did not, we would have no need for politics or for democracy; but in entering such a stationary state we would also be giving up our ability to be individuals with individual opinions, preferences and ultimately our freedom as individuals.

We have a name for those who seek to impose on people single moral truths that are in some sense perfectly objective: they are called zealots. Zealots are different from moral philosophers in the sense that moral philosophers help us to think through and explore certain moral dilemmas while zealots try to impose their particular moral proclivities on others as objective truths. Economics needs no more zealots. Indeed, it needs far fewer of them as they are toxic and they have taken over the discipline. They cloak their zealotry in the robe of objective science and wrap it in the language of mathematics but it is still zealotry. The dilemma that profits and income distribution raise is a properly political or moral dilemma but it is one over which the zealots currently have control.[13]

What the above section has sought to show is that as economists we can say an awful lot about profits that non-economists cannot insofar as we can have a discussion of where these profits come from and how they work their way through the system. But there is really nothing that we can say with regard to the justness or unjustness of profits that a non-economist can have just as valid an opinion on. Economists may be able to point out the practical flaws in a certain policy. For example, if a given policy expressly aims at reducing profits, we may be able to point out that the direct effect will be nothing of the sort. In that very specific sense, we can be objective about profits and income distribution. But anything that we say about the moral or political implications of the policy in question has no more objective validity than a similar statement made by, for example, a trade unionist or an anarcho-capitalist. Let us not fool ourselves into thinking otherwise.

Those readers that are politically inclined may find this disappointing. After all, had we not said before that this book sought to show the non-conservative nature of macroeconomic thinking? But again we must stress what we mean by 'non-conservative'. What the above implies is that the system as it is stands can be changed. It is based on conventions, opinions and evaluations of what is good and bad in a given society at a given moment in time. It is not immutable or 'natural' and, above all, catastrophe will not occur if it is tampered with—provided we do so in a carefully thought-through way. This should be what we expect from economics. It gives us the tools we need to make changes to the system to produce desired outcomes. It does not tell us that we should definitively make particular changes as we should follow the Ten Commandments or that we cannot make particular changes lest the Four Horsemen mount their steeds and ride into the night causing death and chaos in their wake. If this makes the politically inclined reader anxious, I would encourage them to embrace that anxiety. Despite the fact that they will not find definitive answers to those particular questions here, nevertheless, as the song says, 'Power comes to them that enjoy the thrill of fear.' Moving into the twenty-first century, mankind should have no more need for those silly pseudo-objective stories told by the marginalists and the Marxists. Those stories sought to buttress certain political tendencies while shutting down the debates surrounding them. Anyone who requires such stories to justify their political proclivities is likely not someone who has much to contribute to real, practical and moral political debate.

Notes

1. Note that making explicit what this author means by 'long-run' does not help us here solve the mystery. Elsewhere in the book, he writes that the long-run is characterised by the fact that 'all factors of production can be changed'. This is in contradistinction to the short-run in which 'there will be some factors of production that are fixed at predetermined levels' (ibid., p. 340). Thus, we should assume that when a given firm has sufficient time to change its factors of production then it has entered the author's 'long-run' and should no longer been profitable.

   Given that the average Standard & Poor's 500 company has ranged from 60 to 15 years old between 1958 and 2011 (Innosight 2012)—surely both of which qualify as 'long-run' periods—and the average real earnings of this period were $44 a share**, then it follows that either the author's theory of zero profits in the long-run does not live up to the real world or the real world does not live up to the theory.

   **Calculation made using Robert Shiller's data, available at: http://www.econ.yale.edu/~shiller/data.htm.
2. In a world of rational investors, for example, equal amounts of money would pour into all investment projects with a 50/50 chance of succeeding. Half of these investors would derive profit and the other half would, presumably, experience losses of an equal amount. Thus, on balance there would be no net income creation for the profit-making class in society.

3. Note that this 'standard' level of output was derived from taking previous levels of output and projecting them into the future. An empirical example from General Motors (GM) might prove pertinent here:

   > Since [GM] does not know how many autos will be sold in a forthcoming year, and hence what the average cost per unit (including prorated overhead) will be, it calculates costs on the assumption of a *standard* volume—that is, operation at 80 per cent of conservatively rated capacity. (Scherer 1970 cited in Lavoie 1992, p. 132)

   The careful reader will note that it is assumed, in keeping with the empirical evidence (see: Fig 6.4 in Chap. 6), that firms operate consistently below full capacity. We can imagine that in very uncertain times, as when the economy is in a very serious recession, these standard volume measures are supplemented concrete short-term market demand analyses.
4. On this point, the reader may want to consult the previous chapter or Pilkington 2013a.
5. The critical reader will here probably experience a 'gotcha' moment. They will say that I am engaged in rank hypocrisy in that I here insist on unrealistic assumptions but have spent a good deal of this book attacking unrealistic assumptions. The difference, however, is that the theories that I criticised for their unrealistic assumptions literally collapse when these assumptions are removed. The building blocks for the marginalist approach to profits or marginal utility are, after all, the assumed behaviours of the actors involved. Remove these unrealistic behaviours and the entire edifice crumbles.
   In the above example, the unrealistic assumptions can be removed rather easily and the narrative structure remains intact. These assumptions are not vital to the theory expounded. Rather I make them for the sake of brevity and ease of exposition. At the end of our rather silly little parable, we will, unlike in the marginalist theories, have a tangible working tool that can be applied to the study of the real economy.
6. Note that we have not engaged in very consistent accounting here. We have not noted, for example, that the government is accruing a dollar liability for every dollar of money that it issues. Nor are we recording the liabilities (or assets) of the capitalist of the banker.

These are important issues if we wanted to make our model stock–flow consistent but we have left them out because our main intention here is to discuss profits in the most basic form that we possibly can.

7. That is, the rate of government investment increased in the third week and the rate of private sector investment increased in the fourth week; this led to an increase in aggregate demand and thus, because the supply of buyable goods was fixed, to price increases.
8. Some readers, especially those who have taken a course in economics, will claim that the above exercise is highly misleading because there is no wage and price flexibility. Their economics lecturer will have told them that when the capitalist lays off five workers, wages will fall together with prices and the capitalist will hire the workers at the new lower wage. First of all, this is not at all clear even in theory. If the wages and the prices fall together, then the real profits will remain the same—this is because the wages are the capitalist's key source of demand. Secondly, investment relies mainly, as we shall see in the next chapter, on confidence. Assuming some mechanical relationship between the wage rate and the rate at which capitalists employ labour is apt to be very misleading. This ties back into the first point: if wages and prices fall together capitalists will see lower nominal profits. Even though they see a cheaper pool of labour, it is by no means clear how this new situation will affect their confidence which is key to their making final investment decisions. Thirdly, even with a lower wage rate, it is by no means clear why capitalists will hire more workers. Marginalists typically make some dodgy assumptions here about capital-labour substitution. But these are very rarely explained in anything approaching realistic terms. While it may have been easy to substitute labour for capital on a nineteenth-century farm where 'capital' consisted of a plough, it is far less clear that a modern factory or supermarket could stop investing in new machinery or cash registers and instead double their labour force. At the very least, it would surely require years of unemployment and falling wage rates for capitalists to restructure the process of production. Meanwhile, the negative effects this would have on the economy in the meantime would be enormous. Finally, this is probably the most important point: in modern economies, we see almost no downward wage or price flexibility. Even in the worst recessions, we rarely see price deflation of more than a

percentage point, and wages will typically not fall at all. What is more, when unemployment is not dealt with through government action, it can persist for years and even decades. In this regard, our highly oversimplified model above captures many of the real world dynamics far better than the marginalist models that incorporate wage and price flexibility. Why the profession continues to make the assumption of wage and price flexibility the starting point of any acceptable economic theory rests completely on a dogmatic belief in the forces of supply and demand. As an empirical starting point, it has been completely out of date probably since the end of the nineteenth century.

9. The subsequent history of Jerome Levy might also be of interest to the reader. Using the profit equation, Levy gained access to information which nobody at the time could have hoped for (given that the national accounts were not invented in this period). Using this information, Levy became a very successful investor and, ultimately, a very wealthy man. Much of his wealth was left to promote the pursuit of what would today be called 'heterodox' economics. This is done today through the institution that bears his name: the Levy Institute at Bard College.

   The Levy Institute is a seminal institution that has unfortunately not received the attention it deserves. In recent decades, it has supported and, in some measure, helped produce the seminal heterodox work of Hyman Minsky, Wynne Godley and what has come to be known as Modern Monetary Theory. The reader interested in alternative approaches would be well advised to look into the institution which has an extensive and accessible website. The present author has also (proudly) published both empirical and theoretical papers through the institutions. The Levy Institute is quite literally the most open-minded and progressive economics institution in the world today, and the fact that it is not better known, despite its producing much seminal and important work, is a testament to the grim state of the profession.

   The reader might also note that Jerome Levy's sons and grandsons became successful investors in the vein of their progenitor. His grandson, an ex-hedge fund manager, currently runs the Jerome Levy Forecasting Center which utilises the profit equation to make sophisticated forecasts about the macroeconomy for various financial institutions.

10. The reader will note that we have dropped some of the simplifying assumptions we made in our verbal exposition. We need no longer make these as our formalisation allows us to be far more thorough without damaging the readability of our exposition.
11. We can derive the above formula quite simply if we consider income in terms of expenditure (recall that $Y \equiv E$). So:

$$E \equiv I + C_p + C_w$$

And:

$$W \equiv C_w + S_w$$

It follows that:

$$I + C_w + C_p \equiv \pi + C_w + S_w$$

Cancelling out workers' consumption, rearranging and changing the sign to denote causality rather than identity we get:

$$I + Cp - Sw = \pi$$

12. Even otherwise competent policy economists suffer from blind spots caused by failing to properly digest the above equations and identities. See, for example, Pilkington 2013a.
13. Some readers may find it unusual that a self-proclaimed heterodox economist has written an entire chapter on income distribution without once mentioning the Cambridge Capital Controversies. Well, it should be said that all that I have just written is, I think, perfectly in keeping with the spirit of the heterodox side of the debate. What they were trying to show—and what Sraffa was trying to do with his neo-Ricardian framework—was to overturn the zealotry implicit in the idea that income is distributed in line with the marginal productivities of capital and labour.

    The Cambridge UK side of the debate, on this reading, was rightly seen as engaging in an act of demolition by the Cambridge US side of the debate. This is exactly what the Cambridge UK side was trying to do. They were trying to demolish any deterministic distribution theory and put forward the idea that the distribution of wealth in any given society is a moral, political and historical issue. This opens up the space for us to have a real discussion as to whether any given income distribution is fair or not, and it prevents the zealots from telling us that left to itself the system will largely determine this distribution in some sort of efficient manner which, if we tamper with it, will result in chaos and disorder. For a decidedly politically partisan view of the question, although one that does succeed in getting to the heart of the issue in a way that economists are generally unable to do see (Ackerman 2014). As the author summarises nicely (again using the less-than-accurate term 'neoclassical' rather than the more concise 'marginalist'):

> Once this neoclassical story—where the relative demands for labor and capital are dependent on their relative prices—is "debunked," to use Paul Samuelson's contrite term, the competitive market economy no longer contains any necessary mechanism pushing the various wage rates or the profit rate to any determinate level. Rather, history and custom, as well as politics, laws and struggle, will determine who gets what. It's a system of grab what you can. (Ibid.)

References

Ackerman, S. (2014). Piketty's Fair-Weather Friends. *Jacobin*. Blog 5.29.14. https://www.jacobinmag.com/2014/05/pikettys-fair-weather-friends/

Aslanbeigui, N., & Naples, M. I. (1996). What *Does* determine the profit rate? The neoclassical theories presented in introductory textbooks. *Cambridge Journal of Economics, 20*(1), 53–71.

Innosight. (2012). Creative destruction whips through corporate America. *Executive Briefing Winter*. http://www.innosight.com/innovation-resources/strategy-innovation/upload/creative-destruction-whips-through-corporate-america_final2012.pdf

Kahn, R. F. (1931). The relation of home investment to unemployment. *The Economic Journal, 41*(162), 173–198.

Kalecki, M. (1965). *Theory of economic dynamics: An essay on cyclical and long-run changes in capitalist economy*. USA: Monthly Review Press.

Lavoie, M. (1992). *Foundations of post-Keynesian economic analysis*. USA: Edward Elgar.

Lee, F. (1984). Full cost pricing: A new wine in a new bottle. *Australian Economic Papers, 23*(42), 151–166.

Levy, S. J. (2000). Profits: The views of Jerome Levy and Michal Kalecki. *Levy Institute Working Paper Series*. Working Paper No. 309. http://www.levyinstitute.org/pubs/wp309.pdf

Marx, K. (1867). *Capital: Volume I*. New edition by Penguin Books, 1976.

Pilkington, P. (2013a, August 6). Animism and monetarist thinking: The inflation in the US in the 1970s. *Fixing the Economists*.

Varian, H. (2010). *Intermediate microeconomics: A modern approach* (8th ed.). USA: Norton.

Wittgenstein, L. (1922). *Tractatus logico-philosophicus*. UK: Kegan Paul, Trench, Trubner & Co., Ltd.

CHAPTER 9

Finance and Investment

True prudence recognizes human limitations and does not strive to leap beyond them; it is willing to run with the herd, to overlook faults tolerantly or to share them in a friendly spirit. But, they say, that is exactly what we mean by folly. I will hardly deny it—as long as they will reciprocate by admitting that this is exactly what it means to perform the play of life.

—*Desiderius Erasmus*

Finance and investment are at the very heart of macroeconomic theory. Investment is what drives any economy that does not exist in a stationary state and which exhibits a tendency to grow. Finance is that which enables investment to take place, and one peculiar aspect of capitalist economies is that they have very extensive and sophisticated financial apparatuses. Unfortunately, however, even though finance and investment are the heart of macroeconomic theory, they are also the most slippery and indeterminate elements. They are determined by a mixture of custom and emotion and the outcomes these rather labile 'variables' produce is often something of a *comédie humaine*. Some economists may be disheartened by this but if they are I would encourage them to pursue another field of study. There are many such fields that have nice, relatively 'well-behaved' variables that can be fit into a comprehensive and fully deterministic framework. The material we deal with in economics is nothing like that, and any attempt to turn it into this is an act of intellectual violence. What is more, it is completely wrong-headed. The Americans have a saying that states that if you put lipstick on a pig, it is still a pig. Likewise, if we treat markets

W.P. Pilkington, *The Reformation in Economics*,
DOI 10.1007/978-3-319-40757-9_9

for finance and investment as well-behaved physics-like systems, they will nevertheless remain the labile and contingent markets that, in reality, they always and everywhere are.

To study finance and investment is to be, as Erasmus had it, 'willing to run with the herd, to overlook faults tolerantly or to share them in a friendly spirit'. For it is in the field of finance and investment that little exists that is not subject to an unwitting burst of emotion among large groups of people or, conversely, a sinking feeling of depression felt at a societal level.[1] This is because it is in the field of finance and investment that human decision-making is most immediately subject to uncertainty proper. Reading the financial press or watching the financial news channels on television gives the reader/viewer the most immediate sense of people talking about things about which they are well aware that they have no objective standard of belief. They speak in terms of their own emotions, their 'gut feelings', and weigh these against what they perceive to be the opinion of the herd. The same is true if you speak with someone about to undertake an extensive investment or perhaps someone who has just quit his/her job and taken on a substantial burden of debt in order to open a business. One component of this may be somewhat rationally calculated—indeed, they would be fools if they had not thought through to some extent whether the good or service they sought to offer will be sought by consumers—but the main determinant of the decision will be a 'gut feeling', one that will be affected and weighed up against what each person perceives to be the opinion of the herd.

Mainstream Theories of Finance and Investment

The careful reader might have noted what appears to be something of a discrepancy in the title of this chapter; yes, I have noted finance and investment but why on earth have I not mentioned savings? In most presentations of this topic, finance is the vehicle through which savings are converted into investment. For example, in his best-selling macroeconomic textbook, Greg Mankiw defines the financial system as such:

> Financial system: the group of institutions in the economy that help to match one person's saving with another person's investment. (Mankiw 2011, p. 256)

This, of course, ties back to the idea that savings equals investment. Or, in equation form:

$$S \equiv I$$

Note that we have used the identity symbol ($\equiv$) here rather than the causality symbol ($=$). This is, of course, a truism. In any given period, in a closed economy with no government sector, investment and savings must be equal. If I borrow \$1000 and then invest in, say, a machine and I buy this machine from you for \$1000, then you will have a saving of \$1000. My investment is equal, to the penny, to your savings. But note that Mankiw's statement quoted above, and this is typical of how marginalist economists view this issue, implies something entirely different. It implies that savings drive investment, or:

$$S = I$$

The intuition here is that we must save before we invest. So, for example, if we want to plant more corn as an investment, we will have to stop consuming as much corn as we are currently consuming and plant this corn in the ground. We 'save' corn in order to make an investment in future corn. The same applies to money in the marginalist framework. Either I must save up money before I invest or you must save up money that I will then borrow from you before I invest.

As we will argue later in this chapter, and as the reader might already have guessed from the presentation in Chap. 7, this is simply not true. Rather, the causality is reversed. I hope the reader appreciates what a difference the removal or addition of one little bar from or to the equals sign makes in this case. It literally determines how we as economists view the money markets. If we view them in the same way as Mankiw, then these are just passive intermediaries channelling a given society's desire for saving into productive investment. But if we fundamentally disagree with Mankiw's causal argument, then the money markets become something different altogether.

So, what is the mainstream theory of financial markets? How is it that these act simply as intermediaries between savers and investors? This is actually not often discussed in any detail. In most macroeconomic models—and, as we shall see later in this chapter, the ISLM model is representative of this confusion—it is simply assumed that the money markets are populated by rational agents who channel savings into investment projects that they have something resembling perfect information about. This is probably the biggest weakness of contemporary mainstream macroeconomic theory, and it is this weakness that gives rise to much myopia and general silliness.

If we reconstruct the argument lying behind marginalist models, we will quickly find that what they actually assume is something like an Efficient Markets Hypothesis (EMH) in its strongest form (Pilkington 2013c, pp. 19–22). The EMH basically states that financial markets are 'efficient' in the sense that investors possess perfectly transparent information about potential investments in the form of probabilities as to whether they will succeed and fail and that they will act perfectly in line with this information in a rational manner (Fama 1970). They will then assign high-risk projects a higher rate of interest (or yield) than lower-risk projects. Meanwhile, firms and entrepreneurs will be trying to get the lowest possible interest rate they can for the given riskiness of their particular investment project. In this way, the financial markets set a price on the money they loan out—that is, the interest rate or yield—in line with objective riskiness of the investment projects being undertaken in the economy at any given moment in time. We have given this relationship visual form in Fig. 9.1.

The lines here represent the supply of and demand for a given asset or series of assets. On the horizontal axis is quantity while on the vertical

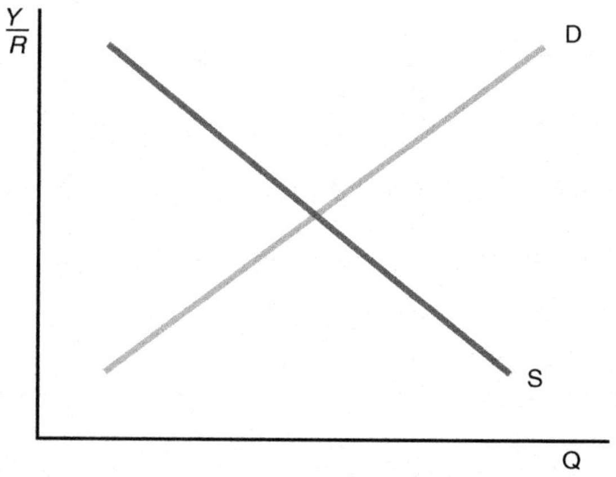

Fig. 9.1 The EMH in supply-demand space

axis is the yield or interest rate, Y, divided by risk, R. As we can see, as the interest rate rises relative to risk, less of the asset is supplied (because issuers do not want to pay high interest payments for low-risk assets) while more of the asset is demanded (because buyers want high-yielding assets with low risk). The equilibrium point at which the two lines meet is the series of interest rates at which the financial markets allocate funds to the series of investment projects weighted by their relative riskiness. This interest rate—or, more properly, these series of interest rates for there are as many as there are investment projects—might be familiar to the reader by a different name. It is (or they are), in fact, the so-called natural rate(s) of interest that balances an economy at the optimum level of full employment output (Pilkington 2014b).

Note that, so far as I am aware, this connection has never been stated explicitly before.[2] But it is clear that if the marginalist theory of financial markets which states that these markets are simply a passive medium allocating the savings of a given society to various investment projects means anything, then it must mean this. If we assume that it means anything else, for example, if we assume that financial markets are dominated by non-efficient decision-making, then we must also assume that financial markets are not simply passive intermediaries. Rather, they must be seen as entities with actual agency in determining the amount of investment made by society at any given moment in time. Think about this carefully. If savings 'cause' investment, then the actual process through which the investment takes place must in some sense be 'neutral'. That is, the decisions taken with regard to investment expenditure must not be very important. What is important is rather society's desire to save rather than consume.

Again, the corn example is instructive. If we as a society increase our corn savings by 50 % in a given period, then investment in corn will rise by 50 % (provided we are not simply hoarding corn). The manner in which this is done probably does not matter all that much. We simply assume that the corn is planted, and we also know roughly how much extra corn it will yield when it grows. If, however, we are dealing with investment in new capital projects—say, research and development on a new method of production—we are dealing with something entirely different altogether. In this case, we cannot really say what the correct 'price' of this investment should be because we do not know what its outcome will be. We are taking a chance on the investment, and thus it is difficult to do a profit–loss calculation.

If this is indeed the case then, as we hinted at above, the causality that Mankiw puts forward must be reversed, and rather than writing $S = I$, we must instead write:

$$I = S$$

This implies that the financial markets and the investment function are completely independent of a given society's savings decisions. In such a framework, it is the level of investment that determines the level of savings. This is what we might call the properly Keynesian theory of investment and savings, and it is this that we saw in the previous chapter when we examined profits in a capitalist economy. In this theory, interest rates (or yields) in the money markets are set entirely independently of savings, and at the same time, the rate of investment is determined not by the 'rational' or 'efficient' decisions of various firms and entrepreneurs but rather based on something else entirely. But before we get more deeply into this, let us first turn to the current state of opinion in the mainstream literature to really get a feel for how seriously the argument laid out above as the mainstream argument is taken.

Mainstream Opinions on Finance and Investment

The rather odd thing about the above explication of the mainstream theories of finance and investment is that it does not seem to square with what appears to be the majority opinion among mainstream economists. We can see this clearly in the evolution of the literature on the EMH. Back in the 1970s and the 1980s, most mainstream economists basically believed in the EMH as accurately representing how money markets in capitalist economies functioned. But already in the early to mid-1980s, doubts had begun to creep in. The first instançes of this were in papers by the likes of later Nobel Prize winner Joseph Stiglitz (Grossman and Stiglitz 1980) and the famed financial economist Fischer Black (1986). Although the argument was dressed up in fancy mathematics and statistical language, it was actually a very simple one indeed (as is so often the case when it comes to fundamental theoretical issues among mainstream economists). Basically, the authors were saying that if markets were perfectly efficient and were always in a state of equilibrium, then no trading would ever take place, and these markets, in a very real sense, would cease to exist.[3]

But in this era, the time was not yet ripe to try to overturn the EMH. Stiglitz and Grossman wrote quite explicitly that they 'were seeking to redefine the EMH, not destroy it' (ibid., p. 404). Of course, what the authors wrote and what they believed were likely at odds with one another. But this is what characterises debate among mainstream economists. Because the discipline is largely based on fashion and authority, new developments are only accepted gradually and with the sanction of members with certain credentials. This is reflective of the fact that deep down the profession knows that what it is doing is not science in any real sense—or at least it not the social science version of the hard sciences that it pretends to be—and this in turn makes the entire profession very wary about raising criticisms that cannot be dealt with from within the research programme. Finding logical flaws within the accepted framework—one built on a mixture of assertions about how the economy actually functions and a bit of maths—is perfectly acceptable and is how one makes one's career.[4] But calling any of these foundational assumptions into question on either logical or empirical grounds is completely taboo. At some deep, perhaps unconscious level the profession knows that if they do not keep a tight lid on this, the whole edifice would crumble in perhaps a few years.

After economists like Stiglitz and Black had laid the groundwork in the early and mid-1980s, others could then come in and challenge the EMH as a theory. This work was done by Robert Shiller who showed that there was no real agreement between the EMH and the real world financial markets (Shiller 2003).[5] In doing so, Shiller opened up the field of what would become behavioural finance. The mainstream press and policymakers, on the contrary, continued to appear to believe in the EMH right up until the financial crisis of 2008. But after this, majority opinion seemed to turn against the idea (note again the fact that it is fashion not argument or fact that drives opinion in mainstream economics). This was perhaps best seen in former Federal Reserve Chairman Alan Greenspan's famous speech in front of the US Congress wherein he stated that he had found a 'fundamental flaw' in his worldview—which, of course, was basically that financial markets were fully efficient (PBS 2008). In 2013, Robert Shiller won the Nobel Prize thus lending institutional recognition to the death of the EMH.

Beyond his empirical work on the EMH, which was almost entirely negative, Shiller basically rewound the clock back to something resembling the theories of Keynes and G.L.S. Shackle. Although Shiller does not mention uncertainty as such (and often misuses the term 'animal spirits'), it is quite clear from his books that he considers the financial markets to be driven by a mixture of convention and emotion (Shiller 2005). It also appears that much of the profession have come to accept something similar to this conclusion, especially in the face of the events of 2008. But then how do they square these beliefs with those that are implicit in their discussions of finance and investment? The answer to that is rather simple: they have not and they cannot. This may strike the reader as a strange statement, and in order to try to explain it, I will again have to go on something of a tangent about the psychological and sociological make-up of the profession as a whole.

Especially since the 1970s, the mainstream of the economics profession has been in a state of gradual fragmentation. Economists have sought to become more and more specialised, and prestige is no longer won by having a coherent, overarching view of how the economy functions but is rather won by specialising in a niche area closed off from the rest of the discipline. This leads to a certain amount of what we might call, borrowing from psychopathology, compartmentalisation. Compartmentalisation is a psychological defence mechanism in which certain feelings and thoughts that should be related to one another are kept apart. One of the key reasons why some people compartmentalise is because they do not want to encounter what might be called cognitive dissonance. They do not want certain thoughts or feelings to encroach on their general view of either themselves or the world around them. Something similar happens in marginalist economics with regard to any number of different issues. But the link between the existing, widely accepted theories of investment and finance and the ones that are integrated into their basic macroeconomic models is perhaps the most glaring and damaging compartmentalisation that the profession is currently engaged in. Frankly, if the compartmentalisation were ever undone, the mainstream edifice as it stands would likely collapse, and all the current textbooks would have to be burned.

Liquidity Preference and Interest Rates

During the whole course of the twentieth century, there were perhaps only two economists who truly understood the nature of the financial markets and made substantial theoretical contributions. They were John Maynard Keynes and Hyman Minsky. A good portion of the rest of the profession—I would argue: anyone who did not follow the work of either of these men directly—were completely blind to how the financial markets function.[6] Why is this? I think that the explanation is quite simple. When other economists approached the study of the financial markets, they approached it with their *a priori* tools in their hands. They believed that they had already learned the truths of markets in their microeconomics classes and that all they needed to do was to take these intellectual constructions and apply these to financial market data. Keynes and Minsky, on the contrary, allowed the financial markets themselves to inform their theories. They formed their theoretical frameworks and concepts through careful inductive observation.

Beyond understanding these concepts, the reader would be advised that if they want to understand financial markets properly to follow them for an extended period of time. Read high-quality financial press for perhaps 12 months. But do so from a rather detached point-of-view. Never assume that some writer in the *Financial Times* actually knows what is going on in the markets—if they did they would be making money on that knowledge and not writing about it in the press—rather treat these opinions themselves as the ebb and flow that needs to be studied. Above all, try to get a feel for how the markets move from day-to-day. Be advised that there are few, if any, truly linear relationships that hold through time. Even in a relatively short period of time—say, a few months—the markets will change and evolve. What led to a fall in interest rates in the first quarter of a given year might lead to a rise in interest rates in the next quarter. The markets are somewhat but not completely chaotic. Observing them is not like observing the working of a well-ordered machine but there is a sort of shifting, changing, ever-evolving logic to the whole thing. Thinking of this strange logic, one is reminded of Shackle's metaphor of a kaleidoscope to characterise the dynamic thought process that you can find in Keynes' writing.

> There is a toy called a kaleidoscope, in which three mirrors face inwards in a tall pyramid and repeat in symmetrical reflections the random mosaic of colour formed by loose pieces of stained glass on the floor of the instrument. This toy seems strangely apt as an analogue of Keynes's method. Even the randomness of the disposition of the coloured pieces at any moment of repose suggests the *conventional* character of the economy 'at rest'. The economy is in the particular posture which prevails, because particular expectations, or rather, particular agreed formulas about the future, are for the

> moment widely accepted. These can change swiftly, as completely and on as slight a provocation as the loose, ephemeral mosaic of the kaleidoscope. A twist of the hand, a piece of 'news', can shatter one picture and replace it with different ones. (Shackle 1965, p. 48)

This, indeed, is also a nice picture of the financial markets. A change in sentiment—what Shackle calls 'the news'—can shatter all the relationships that were until that moment in time seeming to hold together. Yet there are some tools that we can equip ourselves with to try to think such processes through in a properly coherent and orderly way. Of course, with the caveat that these tools must be applied not under the supposition that the financial markets are a closed, deterministic system but rather under the supposition that they are open, evolving and non-deterministic.

The key tool in this regard is Keynes' theory of liquidity preference. As is well known, Keynes thought that financial investors often hold money rather than other financial vehicles for three distinct reasons. These reasons are as follows:

> The three divisions of liquidity-preference which we have distinguished above may be defined as depending on (1) the transactions-motive, i.e. the need of cash for the current transaction of personal and business exchanges; (2) the precautionary-motive, i.e. the desire for security as to the future cash equivalent of a certain proportion of total resources; and (3) the speculative-motive, i.e. the object of securing profit from knowing better than the market what the future will bring forth. (Keynes 1936a, b, Chapter 13)

We might add that the financial system has evolved somewhat since Keynes' own time. Today there are instruments in existence that are looked upon as perfect substitutes for cash. These instruments are, of course, Treasury securities in countries with floating exchange rates that issue their own currency and that are denominated in this currency. As the Modern Monetary Theorists rightly insist, in a country that issues its own currency and issues its national debt in this currency, Treasury securities should simply be viewed as interest-bearing money. This is so because these securities are not convertible into anything except the money of the country in question, and since the government, through its central bank, issues this money, there is no real non-political risk of this country ever defaulting on these obligations (Wray 1998).[7] The amount that investors hold in the form of money substitutes rather than money is probably best described in terms of the transactions motive that Keynes puts forward above. Although money substitutes typically yield a rate of interest, they cannot generally be used for transactions. For this reason, investors may hold cash on hand rather than money substitutes.

Financial markets have long since recognised that money substitutes should be treated as cash. The investment firm, Charles Schwab, highlights this clearly in a short article on their website entitled 'What About Cash?' that economists really should read before they go around talking about interest rates, cash and bonds. The author of the article writes:

> Many people think of cash as physical currency—actual bills and coins in circulation. For practical purposes, however, the term "cash" also includes traditional bank deposits, such as checking and savings accounts, where you generally have access to your funds on demand and without risk of losing any principal (up to FDIC limits). *In an investment context, however, the definition of cash expands to other types of cash investments, including short-term, relatively safe investment vehicles such as money market funds, US Treasury bills (T-bills), corporate commercial paper and other short-term securities.* (Williams 2012)

This creates all sorts of problems for the textbook theory that tends to treat 'cash' as separate from highly liquid Treasury Bills. But in order to understand the markets properly, we must accept this definition as it is the correct one. In an investment context, 'cash' basically means any very safe asset that might be held rather than riskier assets, that is, 'cash' is any asset with a very high degree of liquidity.

The textbooks teach the liquidity preference theory as some sort of stable formula but this is only to blunt it and render is useless for analysis of the financial markets. The two key components of the liquidity preference are the precautionary motive and the speculative motive. It is these two components that allow the ever-shifting winds of financial change into Keynes' theory of interest rates. When people become nervous about riskier assets—either risky bonds or stocks or both—they dump these assets on the marketplace and engage in a 'flight to safety',[8] that is, to both cash and perfectly liquid financial assets (like Treasury bills from a country with a sovereign currency that denominates its debt in that currency). This is seen most dramatically when markets as a whole flee from almost all financial instruments apart from those that are completely safe. In such a situation, which Keynes calls a 'liquidity trap', even if the central bank creates more and more money, the panic within the markets will be so acute; this will have little or no effect on the interest rates across markets.[9] But on a more minor scale investors in various markets are fleeing towards liquidity every day. It is really just a matter of degree.

In the USA and other countries in 2007–2009, we saw a liquidity trap proper where the central bank temporarily lost much of its influence over market interest rates. The best way to see this is by looking at the TED Spread which financial analysts use as a measure of perceptions of systemic market risk. The TED Spread, which is shown in Fig. 9.2, is the spread between the three-month US Treasury Bill and the interbank lending rate (specifically the LIBOR rate). It shows clearly the dynamic where banks become nervous of the risk of lending to other banks—generally the second safest place to lend after a sovereign government—and flee into cash and Treasury securities. Also shown in Fig. 9.2, is the VIX Volatility Index of the S&P 500—also known as the 'fear index'.[10]

In Fig. 9.2, we see clearly a period between 2007 and 2009 where the central bank lost much of its influence over the interest rates across the economy. This coincided with a sharp uptick in volatility in the stock market. If we overlaid the actual S&P 500 index in Fig. 9.2, we would see that the peak in the stock market volatility coincided with the trough of actual share prices. This is why we know that the period between 2007

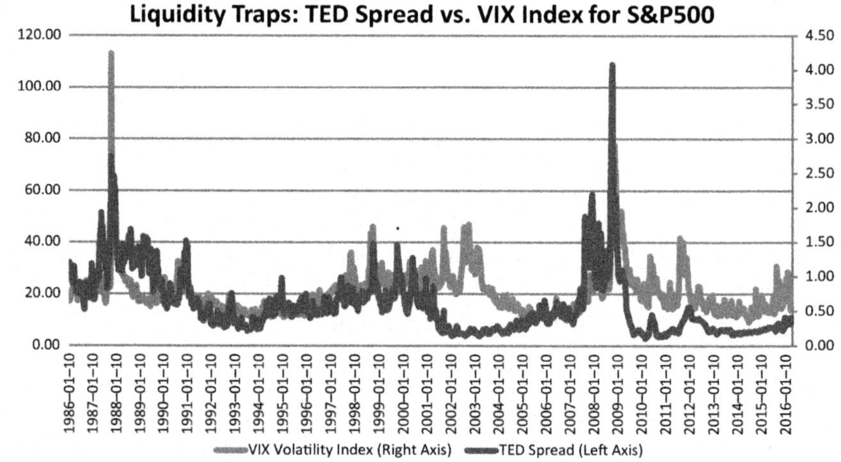

Fig. 9.2 Liquidity trap measurements

and 2009 was a liquidity trap proper; investors were not simply fleeing the private bond market into the bosom of the market for risk-free Treasury securities (and when they could not get their hands on these immediately, cash), they were also fleeing the stock market *en masse*. We see a similar phenomenon occur during the stock market crash of 1987 when asset markets seized up and money pulled back into safe assets.

Figure 9.2 also shows clearly the kaleidoscopic nature of the markets. As we can see, there is no hard and fast correlation between the TED Spread—that is, perceived private market bond risk—and the VIX index—that is, the 'fear index' for the stock market. In the period 2000–2003, for example, the VIX was quite high (this was, after all, just after the dot-com stock bubble burst) but the TED Spread remained at quite low, yet when a major event like the credit crunch of 2008 occurred, both responded in kind. What we therefore know is that in the period 2000–2003 stock investors' liquidity preference remained high while in the interbank lending markets' liquidity preference remained low. This illustrates nicely how we can use the liquidity preference theory in analysing the financial markets.[11]

So then, how should we conceive of liquidity preference in relation to interest rates? That is simple: *when liquidity preference is high, either in any given market or across markets, then interest rates will also be high and vice versa*. Liquidity preference is a like a vacuum sucking the air out of a given market and thus deflating it. Liquidity preference is basically a reflection of the fear in any given market or markets, and this fear manifests itself as a rush for safe assets—a flight to safety. Before we move on to providing an analytical framework in which to cast the liquidity preference theory let us first discuss the two key components of the liquidity preference theory, that is, the precautionary motive and the speculative motive.

Keynes himself seems to have given more attention to the speculative motive. This probably reflected his own experiences of the market as a speculator. The speculative motive is basically manifested in the feeling that one knows better than the market where the market is going to go next. Now, after looking at Fig. 9.2, the reader will probably get the impression that the speculative motive plays little role since the market moves appear herd-like. After all, given that the markets tend to move in a herd-like fashion, should it not be said that the speculative motive plays a minor part? This would be to misunderstand the psychology of the market completely. Every speculator within the market thinks that he or she knows better than the market. If they did not, they would, by definition, not be engaged in speculation. This is because the very act of speculation is engaged in by thinking that you know something that the market as a whole does not. This is, of course, massively ironic because the markets can only really move when a consensus has been formed among the majority of investors as to which way it is going to move. And given that every speculative investor thinks that they know better than the market, then any large-scale shift driven by speculative investors will be driven by a large herd of objectively conformist investors who subjectively hold the view that they are contrarians.[12]

If all the markets were indeed driven by speculation pure and simple, this simple logical evaluation would show rather quickly what a farce this particular *comédie humaine* actually is. Fortunately for both the market participants themselves and, perhaps, the sanity of the reader this is not the case. Only a few markets at any given moment in time are driven by speculation pure and simple. Thus, it is only in speculative bubbles that the whole thing turns into farce pure and simple, with conformist-cum-contrarians thinking that they are beating the 'fools' who surround them, 'fools' who are, in actual fact, also thinking that they are the smart ones beating the 'fools' all around them. The majority of the time markets are actually being driven by the precautionary motive and because of this there also exist speculators who are not engaged in purely farcical behaviour. Instances when the clowns truly take over the circus, while by no means a rarity, are generally the exception rather than the rule.

As previously noted, Keynes himself did not actually recognise this. He tended to emphasise the speculative motive.[13] It was Roy Harrod, an economist far better known for the growth theory that bears his name than for the astounding work he did on the money markets, who truly brought out the importance of the precautionary motive in the liquidity preference theory and how it relates to the real world of modern finance. First of all, Harrod argued that precautionary demand for money was just as labile to changes in the 'news' or sentiment of the market as the speculative demand, something that Keynes appears to have denied. He then went on to distinguish between two subcomponents of the precautionary motive, both of which were rather similar in form but distinctly different in motive these were: *covering* and *hedging*.

Covering is the action taken by businesses, typically large businesses, so that they should be able to 'cover' all their known future commitments as soon as they are entered into. Basically, they hold money back in order to make sure that they can meet any obligations that they make at any given point in time. These businesses then seek advice from professional financial advisers, often economists and financial economists, who try to spot developing trends. If, for example, the financial advisers think that a given currency which their clients require to pay out for imports is going to rise in value; they may advise companies to buy this currency in the future market so that they will be 'covered' in the future and will not have to pay the higher price. Hedging is very similar to covering but is undertaken for a slightly different motivation. Hedging is tied up with the fact that companies and individuals hold financial assets from various different countries. If, for example, investors from outside of the UK own a lot of sterling assets and their financial advisers believe that the sterling might decline in the future, then they will likely hedge against this decline. They would do this by selling the sterling in the forward market in equal amount to the amount of sterling assets that they hold. By doing this, they ensure that if the sterling does decline in the future; the profit that they make on the forward sale will balance out with the losses that they will incur on their assets (Harrod 1969, pp. 79–86).

Modern financial systems are dominated by these sorts of transactions. Indeed, it is these types of transactions that give large parts of the financial sector an excuse for existing beyond the extraction of rent and the turning over of speculative profits. In the cases of currencies described above, the manner in which liquidity preferences functions is rather clear and transparent but something similar is at work when we consider investment advisers who try to balance their clients' portfolios. A perusal of the websites and advertising literature of investment management firms—together with the handbooks they use to train students in their courses—show just how concerned they are with managing funds, or at least being perceived to manage funds, in a non-speculative, low-risk manner. Yes, there are more flamboyant high-risk firms that try to flog riskier investments, usually in the form of some sort of great monetary adventure, to the higher end of the market. But the majority of the market is made up of risk-averse technocrats. Despite what popular culture may tell the lay person, the vast majority of investment managers are rather dull people, and the vast majority of the process of investment is a rather dull business. The majority of investment managers less so resemble the buccaneering pirate-capitalists we see in the movies and more so resemble a Soviet bureaucrat sitting in an office counting beans on a spreadsheet.[14]

It is this great architecture that shakes and sways when it hears, collectively, of changes in the 'news' and in sentiments. Every time the winds of euphoria and fear change their course, tens of thousands, perhaps even hundreds of thousands, of bean counters shift their balance sheets to accommodate what they think that everyone else is thinking. It is not generally the speculators that move the markets but rather the more humble spreadsheet managers across the major financial capitals of the world. Good speculators, contra Keynes,[15] are generally concerned with anticipating the moves of these people rather than of other speculators.

Bulls and Bears

The question then becomes: how should we get a better handle on this process? Well, first let us say something about the price of, say, a bond which, recall, stands in inverse relationship to its interest rate or yield. The price of a bond, or any given asset, is determined by the last bid offered on that bond or asset. So, if you had a bond worth, say, \$5 and for some silly reason I offered you \$10,000 until the next bid had been made on another of those bonds the price would be \$10,000.[16] Of course, if I tried to disrupt a financial market in this way, I would quickly get burned. The next bond would sell for, maybe, \$6 or \$7; the price would fall to this level, and I would find myself with a loss of over \$9990 while the happy person that I bought the bond from would find himself with a profit of the same amount. Meanwhile, everyone will make a gain to the tune of how much the asset increased by after it had stabilised to some extent (i.e. \$6 or \$7).

These profits or losses will be counted among the community's capital gains or losses. It is important to note a few things about the nature of capital gains before we move on. First of all, we should note clearly that *capital gains/losses are not counted in the national income* (i.e. GDP or GNP). There are very good reasons for this. If they were then national income would increase every time, there was a boom in the stock market in lockstep, that is, for every \$1 in capital gains on the stock market national income would increase by \$1. Under the current accounting norms, national income can increase when the stock market booms but only in an indirect manner. For example, when the stock market booms, this might lead to firms increasing investment or holders of stock increasing their consumption (the latter is called the 'wealth effect'), and these increases will be counted as increases in national income. What we seek to measure in national income is income generated, broadly speaking, from actual economic activity and not due to price increases.[17] This is why capital gains are not included in national income.

Nevertheless, if we are careful to keep in mind that capital gains are not and should not be counted in national income, we can observe that aspects of these capital gains do, in fact, have many similar properties to increases in real income. The most important of these properties is that when the price of a capital good rises, this must be due to a bid being made that then required a transfer of funds from a buyer to a seller. This is precisely the same as what happens when money changes hands, for example, in an act of consumption or investment. If we refer to the actual money that changes hands due to financial transaction as financial expenditure or financial income, then we can say, again being careful to distinguish from *real* expenditure and income, that:

$$E_F \equiv I_F \equiv Y_F \equiv S_F$$

When I hand over \$100 to you for a bond, I am engaged in what we might call 'financial expenditure' (E_F), or alternatively, we might call the same transaction 'financial investment' (I_F). Meanwhile, when you accept the \$100 from me and hand over the bond, I receive what might be alternatively called 'financial income' (Y_F) or 'financial saving' (S_F). The reason that we use the language of the national accounts here is simply to make clear that much of what goes on in the financial markets, while again we stress that it does not add or subtract from national income, nevertheless in many ways resembles what happens in the real economy.

Let us get back now to formalise somewhat how prices are formed in these markets (or, indeed, in any market that has flexible prices). We have already given a practical example of how the market price is determined by the last bid made on the asset. Note here that we are necessarily taking the price of the asset at a given moment in time when the last highest bid has been made. We are taking a sort of snapshot of the price of the asset at one point in time among many in an ever-evolving dynamic process. Thus, we might write:

$$P_1 \equiv B_2$$
$$P_2 \equiv B_2$$
$$\ldots$$
$$P_n \equiv B_n$$

As we noted previously, the last successful bid made increases the market price, not just of the particular asset on which the bid was made but rather all assets of this particular type. That means that the resulting total capital gains from a given bid will be:

$$Capital\ Gains_{t+1} \equiv A_{t+1}.B_{t+1} - A_t.B_t$$

where A is the number of assets of a particular kind in existence at the moment in time when the final bid in a given period is made. So, if there are 100 of this asset in existence and I bid up the price from \$100 to \$110 dollars, then the capital gains accruing due to this bid will be \$1000. But this raises the question as to what determines the bid. This should be a combination of two things: first of all, the state of liquidity preference in any given market which is negatively related to the price of an asset, and secondly, the quantity of money available to participants of that market which is positively related to the price of an asset.[18] Or, we might write:

$$\frac{1}{Lp}.M = A.B$$

Now we must say something about what determines the liquidity preference in any given market at any given point in time (recall that this variable is shifting literally second-by-second in many markets). The liquidity preference is ultimately determined by what we might call the amount of bulls and the amount of bears in that particular market at any given moment in time. For those unfamiliar with these terms, they refer to people in any given market that are optimistic about future price increases (bulls) and those that are pessimistic (bears).[19] Note that these are not distinctly different people; a person may turn from a bull to a bear after some news or other emerges (on the contrary, those familiar with the markets will be quick to spot the rather silly character of the perma-bull or perma-bear, the stubborn investor in a given market known for not changing his opinions on a given asset no matter what the state of the news). So, when we refer to bulls and bears, we are really discussing in what proportion those in the market are net selling and to what extent they are net buying. The manifestation of bulls and bears represents the market as a whole liquidity preference at any given moment in time. As liquidity preference rises bulls turn to bears and as it falls bears turn to bulls. So, the liquidity preference rising leads to a heavier weighting of bears in any given market than of bulls and vice versa, or:

$$Lp \equiv Bear / Bull$$

We can then insert that equation into our previous equation relating the liquidity preference and the money/money substitute supply to the bid price at any given moment in time. So:

$$\frac{1}{Bear / Bull}.M = A.B$$

What this tells us is that the bid will increase when bulls increase relative to bears and decrease when bears increase relative to bears. Note that, when the bear/bull ratio is unity, we assume that liquidity preference is having no effect on the price. In such a situation, the interest rate is purely determined by the quantity of money held by market participants. Alternatively, we could say that when the bear/bull ratio is unity, the market is in a 'risk-neutral equilibrium' and the price of assets in that market is purely determined by the amount of money being held by participants in that market.

Let us take an example of a market for a given type of bond. The interest rate on bonds in such a market will be the inverse of the price of those same bonds. So:

$$i \equiv \frac{1}{B}$$

where i is the interest rate. The formula to calculate the final bid on the bond will be as follows:

$$\frac{\frac{M}{Bear\,/\,Bull}}{A} = B$$

So, alternatively, we can write the formula for the interest rate as such:

$$\frac{1}{\frac{\frac{M}{Bear\,/\,Bull}}{A}} = i$$

Table 9.1 shows the evolution of the price and interest rate as first the bear/bull ratio (i.e. the liquidity preference) changes and then the supply of money changes. In periods 1–10, the bear/bull ratio changes, and the money supply is held constant, while in periods 11–20, the bear/bull

Table 9.1 Simple interest rate model I

Period	*Bear/ bull*	*Quantity of M*	*Bid × no. of bonds*	*No. of bonds*	*Bond price*	*Bond yield*
1	**1**	100	100	10	10	0.1
2	**0.5**	100	200	10	20	0.05
3	**0.25**	100	400	10	40	0.025
4	**0.5**	100	200	10	20	0.05
5	**0.75**	100	133.3333333	10	13.33333333	0.075
6	**1.25**	100	80	10	8	0.125
7	**1.75**	100	57.14285714	10	5.714285714	0.175
8	**0.5**	100	200	10	20	0.05
9	**2.5**	100	40	10	4	0.25
10	**2**	100	50	10	5	0.2
11	1	**200**	200	10	20	0.05
12	1	**300**	300	10	30	0.033333333
13	1	**325**	325	10	32.5	0.030769231
14	1	**250**	250	10	25	0.04
15	1	**125**	125	10	12.5	0.08
16	1	**500**	500	10	50	0.02
17	1	**600**	600	10	60	0.016666667
18	1	**135**	135	10	13.5	0.074074074
19	1	**110**	110	10	11	0.090909091
20	1	**100**	100	10	10	0.1

ratio is held constant at the risk-neutral equilibrium level and the money/money substitute supply is changed. (Note that the boxes highlighted in bold are the variables that are fluctuating.)

We can see two distinct dynamics here that will perhaps better be brought out in graphical form. Figures 9.3 and 9.4 show these dynamics.

Before moving on, we should note that the bear/bull ratio (i.e. liquidity preference) is actually synonymous with the velocity of money in the market in any given period. As the amount of bears increases relative to bulls, the velocity of money in the market slows down as those bears hoard money and the price of securities in that market falls. As the amount of

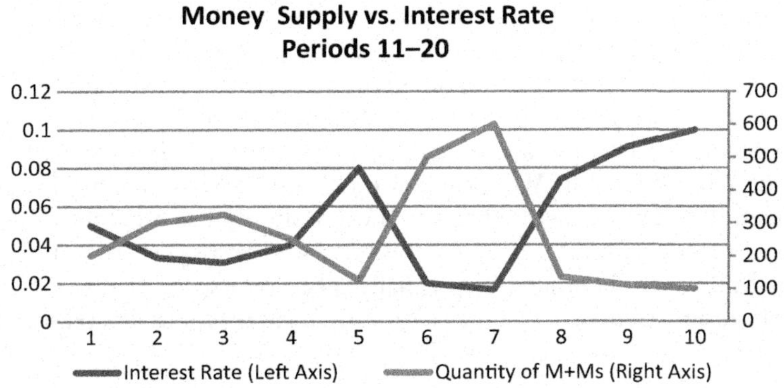

Fig. 9.3 Simple interest rate model II

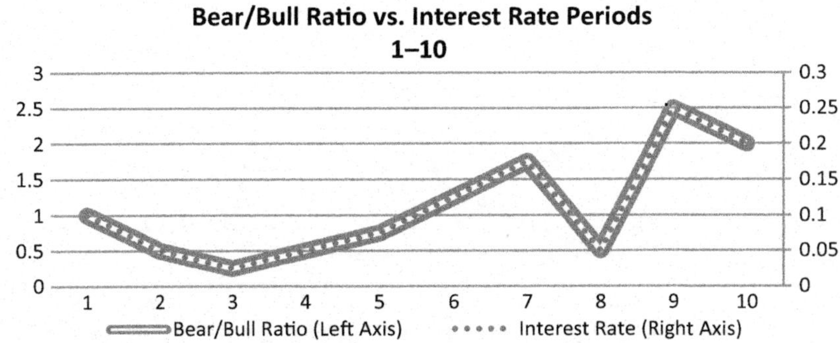

Fig. 9.4 Simple interest rate model III

bulls increases relative to bears, the velocity of money in the market speeds up as bulls increase their expenditure of money and the price of securities increases.

The example in periods 11–20 seems particularly unrealistic. While we may be able to conceive, to some extent, of a market in which the supply of money is constant, it seems highly unlikely that a market for bonds will always have a risk-neutral stance with regard to liquidity preference. In Table 9.2, we supplement periods 11–20 above by allowing the bear/bull ratio to fluctuate so that both the liquidity preference of the market and the supply of money are allowed to fluctuate simultaneously.

In this graph now that both the variables that determine the interest rate are moving in tandem, everything has gotten a bit more chaotic. But we can still get a broad sense of going on if we represent the key variables in the table graphically as we have done in Fig. 9.5.[20]

As we can see, the two major forces are acting in opposite directions against the interest rate. A rising money supply, ceteris paribus, causes the interest rate to fall. While a rising, bear/bull ratio, *ceteris paribus*, causes the interest rate to rise. We should also note from what happens in periods 5 through 8 that it seems that the money supply has a greater influence on the interest rate than the bear/bull ratio. This suggests that, unless the bear/bull ratio becomes exceptionally large or exceptionally small (e.g. in a liquidity trap or a speculative boom), increases or decreases in the

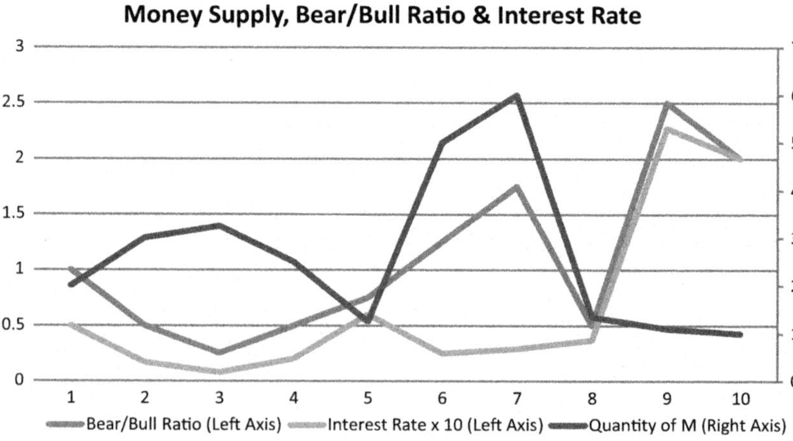

Fig. 9.5 Simple interest rate model V

Table 9.2 Simple interest rate model IV

Period	*Bear/bull ratio*	*Quantity of M*	*Bid × no. of bonds*	*No. of bonds*	*Bond price*	*Bond yield*	
1	**1**	**200**	200	10	20	0.05	0.5
2	**0.5**	**300**	600	10	60	0.016666667	0.166667
3	**0.25**	**325**	1300	10	130	0.007692308	0.076923
4	**0.5**	**250**	500	10	50	0.02	0.2
5	**0.75**	**125**	166.6666667	10	16.66666667	0.06	0.6
6	**1.25**	**500**	400	10	40	0.025	0.25
7	**1.75**	**600**	342.8571429	10	34.28571429	0.029166667	0.291667
8	**0.5**	**135**	270	10	27	0.037037037	0.37037
9	**2.5**	**110**	44	10	4.4	0.227272727	2.272727
10	**2**	**100**	50	10	5	0.2	2

Table 9.3 Simple interest rate model VI

Period	*Bear/ bull ratio*	*Quantity of M*	*Bid × no. of bonds*	*No. of bonds*	*Bond price*	*Bond yield*
1	1	200	200	10	20	0.05
2	0.5	300	600	15	40	0.025
3	0.25	325	1300	20	65	0.015384615
4	0.5	250	500	8	62.5	0.016
5	0.75	125	166.6666667	6	27.77777778	0.036
6	1.25	500	400	25	16	0.0625
7	1.75	600	342.8571429	20	17.14285714	0.058333333
8	0.5	135	270	12	22.5	0.044444444
9	2.5	110	44	15	2.933333333	0.340909091
10	2	100	50	10	5	0.2

quantity of money will likely drive the interest rate downwards or upwards rather easily.

Finally, we will present a table similar to that of Table 9.2 but we will also allow the amount of bonds issued to fluctuate. We can see what happens in this regard in Table 9.3.

We need not dwell on this example too long. Needless to say, as the number of bonds issued increases, the price of these bonds tends to fall, while as the number of bonds issued decreases or bonds are retired from the market, the price of these bonds tends to rise.

Finally, we should say a word on the very general case that operates in most financial markets most of the time. Most financial markets today are characterised by two important dynamics: (1) the overnight rate of interest—that is, the rate at which risk-free money can effectively be borrowed—is set by the central bank and (2) the central bank does not intervene directly in these markets by engaging in asset purchases.[21] We shall call a market that adheres to these dynamics an 'IRT market', short for 'interest rate targeted market'. These markets are extremely simple in that the rate of interest is simply by placing a mark-up on the overnight rate of interest in line with liquidity preference. In these markets, the interest rate is determined thus:

$$i_{rt} + T_c + Lp_{irt} = i$$

where i_{rt} is the overnight target interest rate, T_c is transaction costs for borrowing money and Lp_{irt} is the liquidity preference in an IRT market as defined by (i) and (ii) above. Liquidity preference in an IRT market operates along much more simplistic lines than liquidity preference in a non-IRT market such as the ones that we have been describing in the previous section. In an IRT market, liquidity preference operates as such:

$$Lp_{irt} \equiv D_r^e + \Delta i_{rt}^e$$

where D_r is perceived default risk and Δi_{rt}^e is the expected change in the overnight target interest rate.[22] Therefore:

$$i_{rt} + T_c + D_r^e + \Delta i_{rt}^e = i$$

If we want to use the bear and bull terminology we put forward earlier, we can simply say that in such a market bullishness is characterised by liquidity preference tending towards zero which will cause the interest rate to line up with the overnight target interest rate, while bearishness is characterised by liquidity preference tending towards infinity which will cause the interest rate to move further and further away from the overnight target rate of interest. Again, we must stress that, even though the dynamics in such markets appear rather simple, liquidity preference remains an inherently subjective judgement. That is, perceived default risk $\left(D_r^e\right)$ and the expected change in the overnight target rate $\left(\Delta i_{rt}^e\right)$ are based on the subjective evaluations of financial market participants.

This all seems rather tidy, of course, but the readers should not be fooled by the tidiness of the examples and equations given above because they all contain a rather pesky and unpredictable variable. In the real world markets for bonds of various kinds, the liquidity preference is constantly shifting from here to there. Every time the news changes, for example, the prices too will change as liquidity preference shifts.

What Determines the Interest Rate?

We have just explored how liquidity preference determines interest rates in capital markets. But we should not take this to suggest that interest rates are primarily a market phenomenon. Capital markets do exist—and probably always have existed in some shape or form—but they are derivative of deeper forces. Capital markets allocate wealth to various different types of assets; in doing so, they determine the relative return on these different types of assets. Mainstream economists tend to think of the entire capital market as a sort of emergent order from untenable chaos. The idea is based on probability theory, as we have already discussed in relation to the EMH.

To summarise once more, the mainstream view is that there are an uncountable number of individuals in the economy that are looking to either save or borrow money. The savers then 'loan' the money that they have saved to the borrowers in exchange for a return. This return might be thought of as an interest rate. The interest rate is determined, as we discussed earlier with respect to the EMH, by the relative riskiness of the borrower. The idea here is that the saver has a fixed probability distribution for all borrowers in the markets and then allocates their saving in accordance with their risk appetite together with an objective assessment of these probabilities. When all savers allocate their wealth, the capital market as a whole is formed and with its interest rates.

The problem, as we have seen above, is that there are no objective probabilities, and so liquidity preference determines how savers allocate their money in the capital markets. This leads us to the question: why then are capital markets not more chaotic than they appear to be in reality? Part of this can be attributed to social norms within the investment communities. Optimism and pessimism tend to come in waves of relatively low frequency—maybe seven to ten years—and during these waves, swings are somewhat bounded. But there is a deeper explanation, and it is one that economists like James Steuart and Karl Marx knew well: the interest rate is a question of distribution grounded in legal, social and political norms. The interest rate—or the rate of return on accumulated wealth—is determined by the relative social power of creditors.

If we step back and consider this carefully, it soon becomes obvious. Let us imagine a basic creditor-debtor relationship. This consists of a creditor and a debtor—and these can both be individuals, or small entities like firms, or large entities like whole countries. The creditor has a certain amount of information about the debtor that he will use to determine what interest rate they should charge the debtor. In the mainstream theory, this information may be thought of as the debtor's income (y) and the debtor's default rate (dr). The interest rate will then be determined as such:

$$i = \frac{dr}{y}$$

Recall that the mainstream theory assumes that both future income and probability of default are thought to be known as objective probabilities. These assumptions are entirely untenable. But a more pragmatic economist might take the mainstream parable as containing a grain of truth. 'After all', they might argue, 'although these are not objective probabilities and although there are probably waves of optimism and pessimism in the credit cycle, surely we can say that these are the two key determinants in determining the interest rate'. This is simply not true. There is another variable that is extremely important in this regard: extractive power.

Think about this for a moment. There are a number of small borrowers in an economy at any given moment in time that have no access to official capital markets. When their income and credit history are taken into account, no credible lender will lend to them. Yet they are able to obtain loans from loan sharks. Why? This is because loan sharks operate outside of basic laws. If the borrower does not repay a bank, the worst the bank can do to the borrower is seize their assets or force them into bankruptcy. The loan shark, meanwhile, can break the borrower's legs or perhaps threaten their lives or the lives of their loved ones. What this tells us is that the relative extractive power, *ep*—the threat—that the lender holds over the borrower also plays a role in interest rate determination. The lower the magnitude of the threat, the higher the interest rate will be and vice versa.[23] So:

$$i = \frac{dr}{y.ep}$$

From the example of the loan shark, we also learn something else about interest rates: they are primarily determined by law. Since the loan shark operates outside of the law, his extractive power is higher than that of the bank which operates inside of the law. This means that interest rates are always determined by the prevailing legal structures of the era. This is completely and utterly unavoidable and always and everywhere must precede the existence of capital markets. For example, in ancient times, it is well known that debtors could be taken into slavery if they failed to repay their debts. Yet today slavery is illegal. The banning of debt slavery had an immediate and tangible impact on the interest rate and the relative share of the economic pie enjoyed by borrowers as it lowered their extractive power. Bankruptcy laws are another example of how the interest rate is always embedded in the legal frameworks that structure it. There is no separating the two. Even if we assume a world totally without laws, we are still assuming, in a sense, a certain regulatory regime.[24]

This leads to a rather startling conclusion: interest rates are always and everywhere regulated. By their very nature, they must be. Capital markets may distribute wealth to various assets within this structure of rules, but this structure of rules must exist in order for capital markets to function. When central banks today seek to control the interest rates, this is really no different an operation than when the Babylonian King Hammurabi set the maximum interest rate on grain at 33.5 % and on silver at 20 % in 1800 BC. It also explains why many legal systems actually started through the regulation—or rather, establishment—of capital markets. Homer and Sylla write that 'the Romans began their legal history with a body of laws regulating credit' (Homer and Sylla 2005, p. 3—my emphasis). Finally, it explains why the existence of central banks or the IMF, which intervene in capital markets, is not anomalies; they are simply modern versions of Babylonian or Roman law. Something resembling them must exist in order for capital markets to exist.

The key determinate of interest rates is the relative social power of creditors. We as a society determine this relative social power. If a society is set up in such a way that the creditors control the mechanics of power then the relative return on wealth will likely be high; if a society has decided that the relative return on wealth should be low, then it will be low. What is more, there is no 'market rate of interest' prior to these arrangements. A capital market can only come into existence with these arrangements already in place. Certainly, there are various market rates of interest within a given legal-institutional but there cannot logically be any market at all prior to the legal-institutional arrangements being in place.

This leads us to another strong conclusion: because mainstream economics can say nothing about the relative power of creditors in society, its theories of capital markets are, quite literally, vacuous and tautological. Even abstracting from the their incorrect assumptions about capital markets being subject to known probability distributions, their theories are still completely irrelevant because they say literally nothing about the relative power of creditors in the economy.[25] Now that we have concluded our discussion of financial markets and interest rates, let us turn to the market for real investment that provides employment and produces output.

Animal Spirits and Investment

So we find ourselves back at where we started with Mankiw and the marginalists. If we agreed with them, we would say that savings determine investment. But, as we said clearly above, it is quite the other way around. Investment comes first and pulls new money in the form of debt out of the banking system, and when this new money is spent into the system it creates savings. We can now also say that it is not savings that even determines the interest rates across the markets. Rather, these are set in line with subjective evaluations of riskiness in various markets, and they ultimately converge in some sense—but not, it should be stressed, in any linear manner—around the risk-free rate set by the central bank (in the case of an IRT market as defined above). This is because what we have above referred to as financial investment, I_F, which ultimately determines the interest rate in any given market, is ultimately set by subjective expectations undertaken in the face of an uncertain future. As we shall see, the same is also true of real investment, and this is why we must introduce another term borrowed from Keynes, namely, 'animal spirits'.

Animal spirits are the liquidity preference of the real investment market. They are, however, the inverse of liquidity preference. Whereas an increase in liquidity preference led financial investors to draw back their purchasing power and seal it up in highly liquid assets or 'cash', an increase in animal spirits gives rise to a burst of real investment as investors in plant and equipment draw down money, liquidate financial holdings or borrow money outright from the capital markets in order to create new productive capacity. Animal spirits can be written in the same manner as liquidity preference if we reverse the bear/bull ratio to form a bull/bear ratio and also always keep in mind that when we are referring to the animal spirits, we are referring to the markets for real investment rather than financial investment (we have denoted this below by a large *R* subscript to avoid confusion).

$$As_R \equiv Bull / Bear_R$$

Thus, as the ratio of bulls to bears increases, the animal spirits in the real investment market increase. Money is drawn down; borrowed or financial assets are liquidated and new plant and equipment is built. Does this mean that animal spirits are the only component dictating real investment decisions? No. Important too are the interest rate given by the market to any particular borrower—an interest rate determined, as we now know, by the state of liquidity preference and the quantity of money in that particular market at any given moment in time—and the expected rate of profit that will be yielded by carrying out the real investment (Keynes called this the 'marginal efficiency of capital' which we will discuss later in this chapter). So:

$$\left(As_R\right).\left(\frac{1}{i}\right).Q_R = I_R$$

where As_R is the animal spirits, i is the interest rate in the particular market and Q_R is the expected profits that will flow if the investor makes the investment. Since we know that the interest rate is determined as a negative function of the liquidity preference in a given market together with the amount of money, and that animal spirits are the result of the ratio of bulls to bears in the market for real investment we can thus write:[26,27]

$$\left(Bull\,/\,Bear_R\right).\left(\frac{1}{\frac{1}{\frac{M+Ms}{\frac{Bear\,/\,Bull}{A}}}}\right)_F.Q_R = I_R$$

Before moving on, let us note one interesting feature of this formulation: namely, *that it is almost completely determined by subjective evaluations on the part of the investors.* The animal spirits term is completely dominated by subjective expectations (i.e. the bull/bear ratio in the real investment market); the interest rate term is half determined by subjective expectations and half determined by the amount of money held by the market and the expected profits term is also, being 'expected', subject to subjective evaluations. Indeed, even if we assume that expected profits are determined by the last periods actual profits—an assumption with some degree of truth[28]—once we investigate this a little deeper, we will find that these profits, as we showed in previous chapters, are determined by investment, and this investment function will, in turn, be determined by subjective evaluations and so on and so on *ad infinitum*.[29]

The above presentation is a formalisation of Keynes' marginal efficiency of capital argument. But there is good reason to suspect that this is not an altogether accurate depiction of how investors make investment decisions and needs to be modified. Shackle reports that when he interviewed businessmen, they did not think too much about the levels of interest rates when making investment decisions (Shackle 1966, pp. 150–159). This seems to be a proposition that, rather strangely, is accepted by even some mainstream economists (see Mishkin 1996).[30] Shackle found that businessmen typically make decisions based on whether a given piece of capital equipment can pay itself off (amortise) over a short period of time—usually about three years. This, again, is based on their subjective evaluation or their animal spirits but these are cast over the short term because they believe that they are completely uncertain with regard to the long-run. It seems likely, however, that different people within a modern firm undertake investment decisions to the people who allocate internally generated funds and seek to borrow money. Thus, it is likely that the people who make decisions about how much to invest are typically given a sort of menu of the funds available to them at any given moment in time. They then, as Shackle says, likely weigh up their potential profits against their potential losses and try to come to a decision about how much to invest (Shackle 1966, pp. 166–167).[31] This means that the above framework is probably still a good starting point to understand the complexities of the investment decision-making process. But these complexities cannot be dealt with in any more detail here. Rather, the idea is to simply give readers a general framework to begin to understand the investment process.

Breakout Box: The Natural Rate of Interest

Here is a good place to bring up once again what was noted in passing above: namely the so-called natural rate of interest. The natural rate of interest was first devised by the Swedish economist Knut Wicksell (1898). In the above discussion of mainstream theories of finance and investment, we said that they implicitly relied on the EMH which in turn is the implicit basis of the natural rate of interest. In light of what we have written in relation to liquidity preference and animal spirits, we might now be able to clarify some of this.

In Wicksell's formulation, he distinguished between two rates of interest: the *natural rate of interest* and the *money rate of interest*. The natural rate of interest, Wicksell claimed, is the rate of interest at which net investment and net savings are perfectly balanced. That means that for every \$1 invested in real goods and services, there is \$1 saved. If we assume a full employment equilibrium, this means that there will be no inflationary pressure from the additional demand created by the new investment (Leijonhufvud 1979). Already from our above presentation, there are serious problems with this conception. It assumes that as money is saved the interest rate falls, and this fall leads to an offsetting increase in investment. But even if we assume this to be true, the presentation assumes that the bull/bear ratio on the side of our animal spirits term is always in a risk-neutral equilibrium. Not only is this false with respect to the real world but it also means that there should not be any profits in our model if we allow that profits are generated through people take risks on real investments—that is, that they are a reward for engaging their animal spirits.

Wicksell then discussed the *money rate of interest*. This is the rate of interest that the banks actually lend at, and it is assumed to be determined by the central bank setting its rate of interest which the other rates of interest in the economy then gravitate towards (Leijonhufvud 1979). Wicksell's construction implies that the central bank should set its rate of interest in line with the natural rate of interest. But even if we ignored the problems with the natural rate of interest narrative that we have just highlighted, we still cannot avoid the fact that, due to liquidity preference, the private bank rates of interest will not necessarily converge with the central bank rate.

This is because they are set partially in line with the bear/bull ratio in these markets at any given moment in time.

This is why in the previous section we said that the natural rate, and indeed, the marginalist theory of finance and investment relies on the EMH. Indeed, it rests on two implicit assumptions that are two manifestations of the EMH. First, it assumes that those investing in real goods and services have a list of investments about which they have perfect information and then weigh these against the market rate of interest. Secondly, it assumes that those in the money markets also have perfect information and will lend money to the investors in real goods and services at a market-clearing rate of interest. Once we introduce animal spirits and liquidity preference, this whole construction falls apart completely (Pilkington 2014b). Despite this, Wicksell is no relic. The predominant theory of setting interest rates is today known as the Taylor Rule, and it is based on the assumption that there does indeed exist a natural rate of interest that the central bank should target (Arestis 2011).[32] In addition to this, central banks all over the world actually try to estimate this natural rate of interest (Beenstock and Ilek 2005). Perhaps, they should have read their Keynes.

Demolishing the ISLM Framework II: The IS-Curve

As we saw in a previous chapter, one of the two legs that the famous ISLM model stands on—that is, the LM-curve—is completely at odds with the nature of present-day monetary systems. But the problem does not end here. The IS-curve too is completely at odds with the reality of investment decisions in real-world capitalism. Again, in this section, we will assume that readers are familiar with the ISLM diagram. We repeat that it is a rather simple construction, and you can find both written and video guides on the internet to get a feel for how the contraption works.

The IS-curve in the ISLM diagram basically shows the relationship between the interest rate and the rate of investment. Before we go into this relationship, let us first ask a few questions about the interest rate. Note that the ISLM considers only the interest rate. But if we have gleaned anything from what has been discussed above, it should be that there are a whole multitude of interest rates. So, we can only really conceptualise the ISLM diagram in two ways. The first is to assume that the interest rate that is being depicted is a sort of average of all interest rates in the economy. The second is to assume that the interest rate in question is the short-term policy interest rate that the central bank set and that every other interest rate in the economy gravitates around this single interest rate.

The first approach simply does not square with the rest of the model. Those familiar with the model will know that the LM-curve shifts when the quantity of money increases (this is because, and this is another key problem with the model, it assumes that liquidity preference is constant). This implies that the central bank—that is, the money-issuing authority—is in control of the interest rate. So, we can only assume that the interest rate being discussed is the overnight interest rate as set by the central bank and that all the other interest rates are then gravitating around this rate. But as we now know from the previous discussion, this is simply not true. Interest rates in different markets respond in different ways to changes in the central bank interest rate. This is because liquidity preference is a many-headed beast that changes as the 'news' in the market changes. Whereas liquidity preference may be increasing in one market, it may be falling in the other. This leads to contradictions if, for example, we want to raise the interest rate in a market for an asset class in which liquidity preference is falling while lowering the interest rate in a market for an asset class in which liquidity preference is stable or rising. A good concrete example of this is the case of the USA after 2004. The Federal Reserve began to raise the interest rate to choke off overheating in the economy but the interest rate for the one market that was actually overheating—that is, the housing market—was responding more so to a falling liquidity preference within that market than to the rate hikes.[33] We can see this dynamic play out in Fig. 9.6.

Even at this stage of examining the model, we are struck with what might be called a 'spurious aggregation'. The model insinuates that the interest rate depicted—that is, the overnight interest rate that is set by the central bank—is the important one. But that really depends on the particular economic problem that you are trying to tackle. Often raising the overnight interest rate is a bit like using a chainsaw to try to undertake delicate surgery; even if you succeed in destroying the disease, it will only be because you have killed the patient stone dead. Once again, the economists will say that they know all this already, that the model is a simplification and that we are saying nothing new. But there are simply too

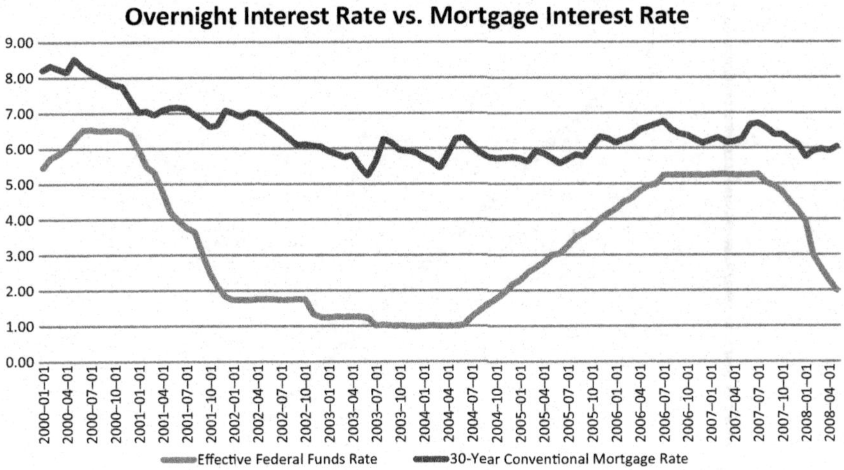

Fig. 9.6 Real world interest rate dynamics

many examples where prominent economists have given stupid advice or commentary because they engage in this spurious aggregation. Also, we quickly see that it is only those non-mainstream economists who take this argument seriously that actually advance interesting policy measures that might help to alleviate these problems (see Palley 2004). The manner in which one sees the world has an enormous limiting effect on one's ability to engage with it, and nothing shows this more clearly than the blind spots that so many economists suffer from due to their love for the ISLM framework.

Things get really awful when we leave behind the question of which interest rate is being depicted and examine how the model depicts the transmission mechanism that supposedly runs from interest rates to investment. In Fig. 9.7, we have laid out the standard ISLM diagram and how a shift in the LM-curve is supposed to affect investment. Note that although we have already definitively shown in a previous chapter that the LM-curve is not, in fact, downwards-sloping, we will pretend for the rest of what follows that it is. We will therefore leave it to the reader to put the two criticisms of the two separate curves together for themselves. If they get a good handle on both, they will quickly see that the ISLM framework is completely misleading on basically every account, and they will quickly do away with it.

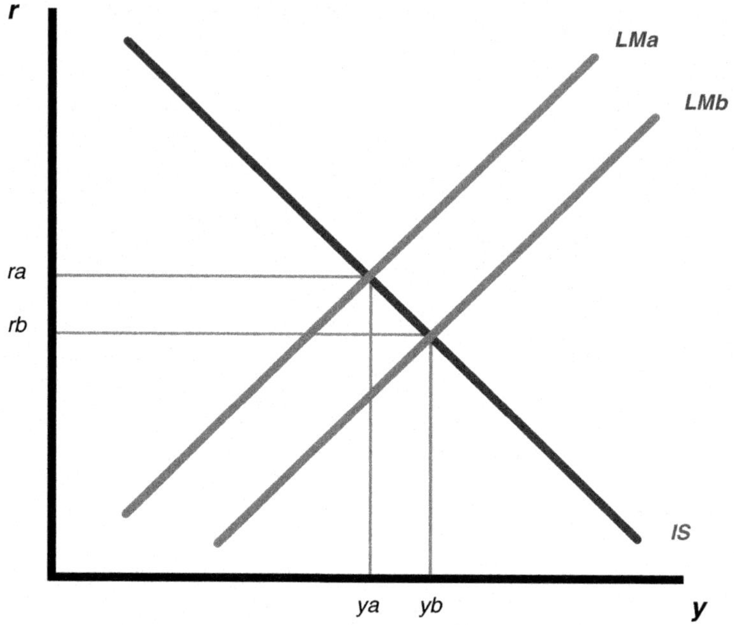

Fig. 9.7 Basic ISLM model

As we see in Fig. 9.2, when the LM-curve is shifted to the right—that is, when the interest rate is lowered—the amount of investment follows suit and expands. Those familiar with how the IS-curve is derived will know that this because there is assumed to be a mechanical relationship between the interest rate and the rate of investment. Famously, the ISLM model is supposed to depict the basic theory that Keynes laid out in the *General Theory*. But it does no such thing. Keynes was very much so arguing in line with our discussion above. He thought that investment was determined by the 'animal spirits' of investors at any given moment in time. This was not to say that he thought that the interest rate played no role. But he was quite clear that this role was not the mechanical one depicted in the ISLM diagram. Rather, Keynes discussed the interest rate and its effect on investment with respect to his theory of the 'marginal efficiency of capital'.[34]

The marginal efficiency of capital is the relationship between the supply price of a capital asset—that is, the price that would induce an investor to actually buy the asset—and its prospective or expected yield in the future. Keynes is very careful to note that the yield on such an asset is not known in advance. Since the future cannot be known, it is inherently tied up with expectations about the future.

> The reader should note that the marginal efficiency of capital is here defined in terms of the *expectation* of yield and of the *current* supply price of the capital-asset. It depends on the rate of return expected to be obtainable on money if it were invested in a *newly* produced asset; not on the historical result of what an investment has yielded on its original cost if we look back on its record after its life is over. (Keynes 1936a, b, Chapter 11—emphasis in original)

Keynes then goes on to argue that the marginal efficiency of capital will tend to equality with the rate of interest available to investors at any given moment in time. Think of it this way: if investors have money they can either invest this money in real capital assets or they can lend it out at the going rate of interest. When they think that it will be more profitable to invest in capital assets than it will be to lend it out, they will engage in such real investment. However, since the future yields of the capital assets cannot be known with mathematical precision, their ability to formulate an estimate of these future yields and to compare these with the going rate of interest will be dependent on their expectations about the future. These expectations about the future are what we refer to as the 'animal spirits'. As we saw in our previous discussion, these animal spirits can best be thought of as the ratio of bulls/bears in the market for real investment at any given moment of time. When there are a lot of bullish investors and companies making investments in real capital assets, then the animal spirits of the market as a whole will be high, and when there are a lot of bears, it will be low.

Now, a further point can be drawn from our previous discussion of profits. The source of the yields on any given real capital asset will be, of course, profits. To some extent, then the marginal efficiency of capital should respond to the level of profits in an economy at any given moment of time. This is making the assumption that investors will project future trends forward (adaptive expectations) and that they will consider high profits in the present to be indicative of high profits in the future. As we have noted previously, there is some truth to this idea—although the reader would only be fooling themselves if they thought it a mechanical description of the investment process. What this means is that the marginal efficiency of capital will tend to rise relative to the interest rate as investment and hence profits increase. This is known as the accelerator effect and can tell us rather a good deal about why economic booms and slumps tend to be self-reinforcing. This effect is, of course, completely elided by the ISLM model because of its static nature. The ISLM model leads economists to think that the effects of investment will take place within a set, static period. But the truth of the matter is that they will have dynamic, knock-on effects and produce cyclical upswings and downswings. The accelerator principle accounts, to some degree, for the rocky nature of Really Existing Capitalism.

It is this irreducible idea of expectations that the IS-curve in the ISLM model lacks. For the sake of tidiness, the model implies that changes in the interest rate[35] will have mechanical effects on the rate of investment. To try to understand investment without understanding expectations, however, is a mug's game. It literally eliminates the single most important determining element in the causal chain. The author of the ISLM model himself, John Hicks, conceded this in later life. He came to recognise that the ISLM model had done an awful lot of damage to the way many economists conceived of the manner in which the economy works. Hicks wrote:

> The ... difference [between the ISLM and Keynes' theory] is more fundamental; it concerns the length of the period. Keynes' (he said) was a "short-period," a term with connotations derived from Marshall; we shall not go far wrong if we think of it as a year. Mine was an "ultra-short-period"; I called it a week. Much more can happen in a year than in a week; Keynes has to allow for quite a lot of things to happen. *I wanted to avoid so much happening, so that my (flexprice) markets could reflect propensities (and expectations) as they are at a moment.* So it was that I made my markets open only on a Monday; what actually happened during the ensuing week was not to affect them. This was a very artificial device, not (I would think now) much to be recommended. (Hicks 1980, p. 141—my emphasis)

As we can see, Hicks explicitly wanted to freeze time to an almost static moment where expectations were given. He says that he realised later that this was 'not much to be recommended'. This is because expectations and their influence on investment are absolutely key to the whole Keynesian edifice. They are also absolutely key if we want to understand how investment actually works in the real world. We might be able to give the ISLM some leeway if we considered it to be a highly formalised or stylised model—say, in the vein of a General Equilibrium model—but it is today generally treated as an *applied* model. But the model, as Hicks makes clear in his retrospective paper, is not actually an applied model at all, and any attempt made to apply it to the study of the real economy will be fraught with difficulties. In this regard, it provides the reader less with a reliable map guiding the way towards a better understanding of how a capitalist economy functions and more with a misleading signpost that has been turned in the opposite of the intended direction to play tricks on unwitting tourists.

An Outlier: The Case of Hyman Minsky

Along with Keynes, the other economist who made a major and substantial contribution to the study of financial markets in the twentieth century was probably Hyman Minsky. Minsky's work is quite varied, and he is certainly an economist worth reading in his own right. But his most fundamental contribution to financial economics was probably his idea of hedge, speculative and Ponzi investments as put forward most succinctly in his classic paper, 'The Financial Instability Hypothesis' (Minsky 1992). Of these, Minsky writes:

> Hedge financing units are those which can fulfil all of their contractual payment obligations by their cash flows: the greater the weight of equity financing in the liability structure, the greater the likelihood that the unit is a hedge financing unit. Speculative finance units are units that can meet their payment commitments on "income account" on their liabilities, even as they cannot repay the principle out of income cash flows. Such units need to "roll over" their liabilities: (e.g. issue new debt to meet commitments on maturing debt). Governments with floating debts, corporations with floating issues of commercial paper, and banks are typically hedge units. For Ponzi units, the cash flows from operations are not sufficient to fulfil either the repayment of principle or the interest due on outstanding debts by their cash flows from operations. Such units can sell assets or borrow. Borrowing to pay interest or selling assets to pay interest (and even dividends) on common stock lowers the equity of a unit, even as it increases liabilities and the prior commitment of future incomes. A unit that Ponzi finances lowers the margin of safety that it offers the holders of its debts. (Ibid., p. 7)

What Minsky did was he applied a sort of accelerator principle to the idea of financial investment. He saw the market for finance as one that was characterised by cyclical upswings and downswings. As we have already noted, a key determinate of investment in real capital assets will be current profitability. Following Minsky, we can say that these profits will also be a key determinate of the propensity to invest in financial assets. In a boom, profitability rises and riskier assets become more attractive to investors. This tips the market towards increasing its levels of risky assets relative to relatively risk-free assets. When the bottom falls out of the market for any given reason, the entire house of cards has a strong proclivity to collapse. This leads to massive money-issuing operations by the central bank to prop up the money markets because, as we have seen, one of the key determinates of asset prices is the stock of money in existence in a given market at any given moment in time.

It is important to note that Minsky was very much so working in a world of shifting expectations and ever-evolving institutions. Minsky's methodology was very much so reflective of what we refer to, with Shackle, as Keynesian kaleido-statics. In the wake of the financial crisis of 2008, there have been many misguided attempts to formalise Minsky and build so-called Minsky models. Some of these are being built in a more heterodox framework, and some of these are being built in a more orthodox framework but they all share a characteristic that Minsky's work lacks: they are closed deterministic models that evade the question of expectations. But Minsky himself famously said that 'Keynes without uncertainty is like Hamlet without the prince'. The same could be said with respect to Minsky and expectations. Minsky, himself originally trained as a mathematician, wrote:

> In [my] view relevant theory is not a compendium of propositions derived from axioms assumed to be universally true: economic theory is not a subdivision of mathematics. Relevant theory is the result of the exercise of imagination and logical powers on observations that are due to experience: it yields propositions about the operation of an actual economy. *The current methodological fashion, where artificial economies are first specified, then simulated and finally deemed satisfactory (unsatisfactory) if it can be said that the general characteristics of simulation are similar (dissimilar) to the general characteristics of a time series of constructs based upon observations (such as GNP) would most certainly have been anathema to both Keynes and the Institutionalists of his day.* (Minsky 1996, p. 1—my emphasis)

This really cannot be stressed enough. Minsky's work is a prime example of an instance where mathematical and logical rigour are not utilised as ends in themselves. Rather, they are used when it is required, and they are deployed, as we have tried to do throughout this book, in an open-ended manner. There is no desire in Minsky to 'close the model'. He simply does not see the point in engaging in such a logical game. For Minsky, economics is, as it should be, an open-ended system of ideas that need to be applied to the world in a deeply intuitive manner. Building closed models and, most especially, estimating these closed models against the data using econometric techniques is perhaps one of the worst plagues that the mathematicians have unleashed on the economics profession. Further discussion of these issues, which are perhaps the most important issues for how economics will evolve moving into the future, will be dealt with in the next chapter of this book.

Appendix: Tautological Nonsense: The Efficient Markets Hypothesis

Trying to get a handle on the EMH is like trying to pick up a wet bar of soap. It is notoriously slippery. Its proponents have a remarkable ability to make it say anything and everything. But when you really probe the idea deeply, you find that it is remarkably hollow. It either makes proclamations that can easily be proved wrong or mistakes simple statistical truisms for insight. Let us first deal with the proclamations that can easily be proven wrong.

The EMH basically states that financial markets always process and price in information in an efficient manner. This view of information appears to have been derived from the computer sciences (Mirowski 2002) in that it seems to imply that there is only one 'correct' way to interpret information. This is an extremely crude view as information in a human world is inherently relational and relative. Is the number ten a large or a small number? That depends, of course, on what you are referring to. It may be a large number of children in a modern-day family, but it may be a small number of pages for a book to have. All information that we human beings process has this characteristic. It is not in some sense fixed or static. For this reason, there is typically no 'correct' way to establish an opinion on information. The EMH, together with much of information-based economics, appears to hold to the idea that human beings process information in the same way as computers do. You simply plug in an input, and an output comes out the other side. If you plug in the same input, you will always get the same output.

But when we turn to the real world even if we accept this highly limiting view of how we as human beings deal with information, we see strong evidence to the contrary. In 2008, the House Oversight Committee of the US Congress held a hearing to examine what had been occurring in the ratings agencies in the past few years. Market participants use ratings given out by these agencies to evaluate products and so they have a direct impact on market price. The ratings agencies are a key place in which information is processed in markets. The results of the hearings are now legendary. The House Oversight Committee uncovered numerous instances in which the people making the ratings were simply ignoring problems with the deals that they were rating. The most famous example was the response of one employee to his colleague who said that the model they were examining did not capture half of the risk and that they should not be rating the deal. The employee replied: 'It could be structured by cows and we would still rate it' (Jones 2008).

No one could seriously argue that this is an instance of the market correctly processing information. It is quite clear that the employees at the ratings agency were wilfully overlooking the fact that the model was extremely misleading with regard to how much risk there was in the product. Instances like this are constantly uncovered whenever there are investigations into financial markets activity, especially when there are investigations into activity during times of financial bubbles. These instances completely disprove the hypothesis that markets correctly price in all relevant information. Studies published in mainstream economics journals seem to confirm this intuition that financial markets are not driven by some sort of 'neutral' capacity to process information objectively but are rather driven by the most basic group dynamics familiar to both the expert in group psychology and the casual observer of herd behaviour.

> Our evidence that some groups of agents [in the mortgage securitisation industry] were particularly aggressive in increasing exposure to housing suggests that job environments that foster groupthink, cognitive dissonance, or other sources of overoptimism are of particular concern. (Cheng et al. 2014)[36]

When facts like these are raised to EMH proponents, they typically fall back on another interpretation of the theory. They say that what the really interesting part of the theory states is that investors cannot beat the market over the long-run. The EMH states that market prices are a random walk and since all information is priced in anyone who beats the market will only do so by luck. The market is seen as a giant roulette wheel. An investor may be able to beat the other investors on the first or second spin but if he keeps playing he will eventually have the same pattern of winning and losing as all the other investors. A leading proponent of the EMH puts it as such:

> Many of us economists who believe in efficiency do so because we view markets as amazingly successful devices for reflecting new information rapidly and, for the most part, accurately. Above all, we believe that financial markets are efficient because they don't allow investors to earn above-average risk adjusted returns. In short, we believe that $100 bills are not lying around for the taking, either by the professional or the amateur investor. (Malkiel 2003, pp. 60–61)

Now, if we take this at face value, it is a testable proposition that can be falsified. If we can find a number of investors that beat the market over and over again, year in, year out, then the EMH will be falsified. Can we find such investors? Indeed, we can. The famed investor Warren Buffet wrote a fantastic article in 1984 where he showed the returns of nine investors—ten if we include Buffett himself—who consistently beat the market by large margins for decades (Buffett 1984). What is more all these investors shared a common characteristic: they were all students of the father of an approach to investing known as 'value investing' called Benjamin Graham. While they did not undertake identical investments, they did use an identical framework when they approached investing. And this framework, Buffett argued, allowed them to consistently beat the market thus proving the EMH wrong. There was another rather well-known investor who managed to beat the market for a long period too. His name was John Maynard Keynes. In the 1920s, Keynes' investments effectively tracked the market. In this period, he was using a macroeconomic approach. But when he switched in the 1930s to something that greatly resembles the value-investing strategies that Buffett discusses, his returns consistently beat the market (Chambers and Dimson 2012).

When confronted with this evidence, the EMH proponents put this down to luck. As we shall see in a moment, this makes absolutely no sense but even if we take this explanation at its face value what should we make of it? Is it a coincidence that one of the greatest financial economists of all time also managed to achieve higher-than-market returns? To put this down to pure chance seems absurd. And what about the nine investors that Buffett discusses? Is it simply a coincidence that they all manage to beat the market consistently? Again, such an explanation seems far-fetched. As Buffett says in his article:

> If you were trying to analyse possible causes of a rare type of cancer—with, say, 1,500 cases a year in the United States—and you found that 400 of them occurred in some little mining town in Montana, you would get very interested in the water there, or the occupation of those afflicted, or other variables. You know that it's not random chance that 400 came from that small area. (Buffett 1984, p. 6)

So even from the perspective of probability and chance, these explanations seem stupid. But if we dig a little deeper, we see that they are also tautological nonsense that are based on confusing statistical averages with theories of financial markets. In order to understand this, we must note carefully that the criteria of proof for the EMH has been subtly shifted. No longer does the EMH say: 'No investor will beat the market over the long-run.' It now says: 'Most investors will not beat the market over the long-run but a small few may beat the market simply by chance.' If we examine this carefully, we will find it to be a tautology.

Let us start from the beginning to see why this is so. The market is made up of investors. Statistically speaking, most of these investors will be average; a small number will be highly above average and a small number will be highly below average. This is a simple statistical truism and is based on how we construct an average. Thus, the fact that only a few investors are able to beat the market over the long-run is just reflective of the fact that only a few investors will be, statistically speaking, really good investors.

Consider the analogy of poker. There are millions and millions of poker players around the world. People typically set up games with their friends and colleagues in their kitchens. But there are only a small number of poker players who play at the tournament level. Why is this? Well, it is rather obvious really. The fact is that the majority of poker players will fall somewhere around the average. There will only be a small number that are really good poker players. This has nothing at all to do with the game of poker being in any sense 'efficient'. It has to do with the fact that only a small number of people in any given field, in this case poker, will be really phenomenal players. Most people will just be average, and their poker game will be average.

In order for the EMH defence to make sense, they would have to show that this small number of investors that beat the market in the long-run are not doing so because they are skilled but rather that they are lucky. How would you show this? Frankly, it is impossible to prove this either way. But it strikes me as a very silly argument. We could just as well apply it to the poker players. We could say 'Oh, they are not really skilled, they are just lucky. They are just a statistical anomaly.' Moving on from this, we could say this about anything and everything. We could say this about professional football players, master chefs and seminal guitar players. None of these people, by the EMH logic, should be seen as skilled. Rather, they just get lucky over and over again. The professional football players are just getting lucky time and again when they play well; the master chef is getting lucky every time he cooks a fabulous meal; and the seminal guitar player is just fortunate that his hands move in the way they do.

At this point, the reader will appreciate the vacuity of the EMH argument. The proponents start by saying that markets are efficient information processers. When evidence comes to light of various biases, herd behaviour and tangled incentives, they wave their hand and say that this is not the important component of the EMH. They then go on to argue that no one will beat the market in the long-run. When they are shown evidence to the contrary, they modify this and say that a few people may beat the market in the long-run by chance or luck but these are just a statistical anomaly. But at this stage, the reasoning becomes absurd and even a bit deranged. How do they know that these investors are getting lucky and are not skilled? They do not. They just assume it so that they can continue to believe in the EMH. But in doing so, they could just as easily assume it about everything and anything. In their bizarre desire to believe in a world full of rational, calculating clones, the EMH proponents have tied themselves up in logical knots and, when their statements are examined carefully, they are quickly revealed to be the clownish nonsense that they are.

Notes

1. Did the reader honestly think it a coincidence that the word 'depression' is used at once to describe a mental state and at the same time a contraction of economic output? And did they also honestly think it a coincidence that these two phenomena are generally positively correlated (Gatapoulos 2013)?
2. Apart from in all the previous writing by the present author already cited.
3. Such an argument is shallow in the extreme. It can be made more general quite easily by pointing out that this applies to any and all economic phenomena. Carried in this direction, it leads rather simply to the plain fact that static equilibrium modelling cannot be applied to a real economic world where everything is always in a state of flux and change. If we carry the argument in this direction, we actually raise issues of genuine interest. Yet, in mainstream economics, this argument seems more so deployed in a tactical manner any time a mainstream economist wants to make a minor change to some arcane and irrelevant theory at whose feet the profession, ever subject to the whims of fashion because they cannot hope to attain the truths of science, at any given moment in time worships.
4. Although, it should be said that when logical flaws are found that undermine the entire edifice, these are indeed buried under the rug. This is precisely what happened after the famous Cambridge Capital Controversies (see Cohen and Harcourt 2003).
5. There was also some more work done in the vein of Grossman and Stiglitz. This work was generally referred to as 'noise-trader models' and rested on the idea of 'redefining the EMH, not destroying it'. This work was entirely derivative and unremarkable even by marginalist standards. Indeed, the champion of deregulation himself, Larry Summers, was a key author in this field, and so we can only conclude that the general consensus was that such considerations did nothing to damage the empirical conclusions of the EMH. See, for example, Delong et al. 1990.
6. We cannot really include in this people who did purely historical work on financial markets like J.K. Galbraith.
7. In cases where the Treasury securities are issued in a foreign currency denomination or the country does not have a national

central bank and thus cannot issue its own money, then these securities can no longer be seen as perfect money substitutes. This, of course, has been the case in the Eurozone and is precisely what accounts for the sovereign debt crisis that took place there after 2008 (Mosler and Pilkington 2012).

All of this should be seen as part and parcel of the kaleidoscopic nature of financial markets which are constantly evolving and changing. One would readily imagine that, in 50 to 100 years, there will be altogether different instruments in existence that will be treated as cash equivalents by the financial markets.

8. It might be worth stressing here a point well known to readers of textbooks: the price of a bond is inversely related to the interest rate or yield on that bond. Thus when the price rises/falls, the yield will fall/rise. This is, however, not the case with stocks. Stocks do not have interest rates per se. Rather, they pay out dividends and the relationship between the price of a stock, and its dividend is by no means simple. The reason that economists historically discuss bonds rather than stocks is because of the simple price/interest rate trade-off that characterises the market. The stock market is a far more complicated beast but the basics can still be understood by utilising the liquidity preference theory. Just remember that *while when the price on a given bond rises, its interest rate declines while when the price on a stock increases its dividend should not be directly affected*.
9. This is, of course, a very different meaning of the 'liquidity trap' that economists like Paul Krugman push (Krugman 1998). But this is Keynes' own meaning, and it is a meaning with far more usefulness and theoretical cogency. For more information, see Pilkington 2013d.
10. Both TED Spread and VIX data are from the Federal Reserve Bank of St. Louis.
11. In line with the kaleidoscopic nature of the financial markets, we would, of course, have to examine each market in turn relative to perfectly safe assets to see to what extent liquidity preferences were dominating in these markets. Indeed, many financial statistics services carry statistics comparing the spread between Treasury securities and various other securities that are not risk free. In practice, many financial analysts are probably measuring liquidity preference on a day-to-day basis without even being aware of the theory.

12. Those readers who are relatively detached observers of social behaviour and have spent any time among market participants—especially those engaged in speculation—will be all too familiar with the figure of the 'subjectively-perceiving contrarian, objectively perceived conformist' investor, that is, the investor who sees themselves as a contrarian but who is clearly tied to some tribe or other.
13. As much respect as I have for Keynes, this lionisation of the power of the speculator may have gone a long way to explaining the overconfidence and hubris that allowed him to get himself caught up in the stock market bubble in the 1920s.
14. Perhaps, the imagery of the buccaneering pirate-capitalist helps people to cope with the inherent instability of the modern financial system. If people knew the truth of the matter—namely, that the system is made up of bean counters—then it would be very hard to anthropomorphise (and place blame on) the system itself. The pirate-capitalist is, it seems, a sort of soporific fed to the layperson by the contemporary media to help them conceive of the instability of the system in a manner which they can immediately comprehend. To equate heavily financialised capitalism with a personality type that revels in excess and transgression, in a sense, soothes the soul. Even Keynes fell for the bait.
15. I am referring, of course, to Keynes' famous 'beauty contest' theory of financial markets (Keynes 1936a, b, Chapter 12).
16. The dynamics are actually slightly more complicated than this. When I make a bid in a given market, in order for this to actually become the market price my bid price must line up with your ask price, that is, the price you require to sell the asset to me. Market prices are determined when a given bid price meets a given ask price. In what follows, we will simplify by imagining that we are in a perpetual buyers' market where the highest bid determines the price.
17. This is also why we tend to take real GDP—that is, GDP adjusted for inflation—as a measure of economic growth rather than nominal GDP—that is, GDP with price increases counted in. Although it should be noted that, in recent years, a school of thought known as the 'market monetarists' have sprung up in response to the recent financial crisis and subsequent depression/stagnation who hold that the economic institutions of any given society should

actually target nominal GDP growth rather than real GDP growth. I do not want to get into the reasons for this here but, from the perspective of the present author, such ideas strike me as being somewhere between pointless novelty and crank ideas proper. Most of the arguments that these economists make—some of which are completely misguided—can be made in normal language and basically amount to saying 'in times when deflation threatens, some inflation is probably a good thing'.

18. Note that these discussions often raise conceptual problems for those familiar with the theory of endogenous money that we laid out in a previous chapter. The confused person typically says 'but I thought we stopped talking about the money supply because it is endogenous so why are you reintroducing this here?' We reintroduce this here because it is a very useful way to understand the dynamics of financial markets. At the end of this section, we will examine markets that can be studied from a pure endogenous money perspective. To anticipate, these are markets where the central bank targets an overnight interest rate and where the central bank does not intervene directly in the asset market being discussed.
19. Note that Keynes used this terminology in his *Treatise on Money* but we are here using it in an entirely different way, one which incorporates Keynes' more mature ideas about liquidity preference (Keynes 1930). The present usage is more similar to the manner in which Joan Robinson used the terminology in her monetary theory but she abstracted away from the existence of bulls proper which, in the present author's opinion, was an enormous step backwards (Robinson 1951). Perhaps, the closest to the present usage is G.L.S. Shackle whose theory of financial markets is very much so in line with the author's own (Shackle 1965, pp. 76–95).
20. Note that because we only have two axes to represent our data, we have multiplied the interest rate by 10 to make the numbers similar to the numbers of the bear/bull ratio. This makes no real difference to the results and merely allows to see the relationships better in Fig. 9.5. Just imagine that a 0.5 reading for the interest rate is 5 % rather than 50 % and so on.
21. Today most central banks target the overnight interest rate. But in the past, especially in the late 1970s and early 1980s, many central banks tried (and failed) to control the money supply. Thus, the

majority of financial markets today meet the criteria: (1) Recently (at the time of writing), more and more central banks are interested in targeting certain asset markets directly thus disqualifying them from meeting criteria. (2) Quantitative Easing was one instance of this but it is very likely that this will become more prevalent moving into the future. Thus, our discussion of the quantity of money in markets earlier in this chapter may have practical as well as didactic usefulness moving into the future.

22. Note that we are no longer discussing the amount of bonds in existence—that is, *A*—this is because we assume that default risk will increase, *ceteris paribus*, as the number of bonds increases. So:

$$D_r^e = f\left(A^+\right)$$

23. Of course, the real world situation is obviously more complicated than this. Loan sharks, for example, often charge very high rates of interest because their customers have no other choice. This leads to the broader conclusion that we must face below: the interest rate is ultimately determined by the relative power of creditors in a society.
24. In such a world, creditors would, of course, have no legal recourse to property rights, and so they would have to enforce these themselves. Such a world would be total anarchy, and the 'economy', for what it is, would consist of perpetual warfare.
25. Anwar Shaikh's neo-Marxian formulations are extremely odd in this regard. Shaikh seems convinced that he can determine interest rates in some sort of a vacuum through recourse to his theory of 'real competition'. In his recent book, he seems to try to capture what determines interest rates prior to a central bank coming into existence. He writes:

> We know, of course, that the rise of central banking has gone hand in hand with the manipulation of interest rates … in order to move them away from their market levels… [We] need to understand where the market would have taken them in the first place. (Shaikh 2016, pp. 443–444)

Shaikh is engaged in the same mythic search for an 'unregulated interest rate' as the mainstream. As we should now understand, this is simply a Holy Grail quest that will turn up nothing; it is based on a complete misunderstanding of the object of inquiry. Shaikh is driven by the same desire as the mainstream to formalise his theory of economics completely, and it is this that leads to a rather bizarre situation where a self-avowed Marxist seems to completely ignore the key dimension of social power.

26. Note that we have clearly distinguished between the real and financial markets here by their respective subscripts.
27. If we assume an IRT market, this formula can be modified to read:

$$\left(Bull\,/\,Bear_R\right).\left(i_{rt}+T_c+D_r^e+\Delta i_{rt}^e\right).Q_R=I_R$$

28. Readers will note here that we are assuming something like an 'accelerator principle' where investment is determined by past rates of investment. In reality, the accelerator principle performs rather well empirically but it fails to explain why investment every now and again simply falls. This can be explained much better using a framework that integrates liquidity preference and animal spirits.

    We should also note that while the above is a good way of thinking about the economy, it is not entirely accurate. After the 2008 financial crisis and the subsequent recession, corporate profits in the USA soared due to the large government deficits that were being run at the time. Nevertheless, investment was extremely slow to pick back up. This was because the firms were able to meet their present orders without needing to expand their productive capacity, and so they turned to wash their profits back into the financial markets. In Keynesian terms, we might say that the marginal efficiency of capital was very low relative to the going interest rates in the financial markets at the time. This example shows quite clearly that it is to oversimplify to say that profits determine investment in some mechanical manner. The reader would be well advised to never take mechanical theories of investment at face value. We have only laid out the above provisional account as a sort of guide which is by no means definitive. In order to understand the real nature of investment, one must be appreciative of the kaleidoscopic nature of investment decisions in capitalist economies and be prepared to fully engage with the 'state of the news'. This is why economics can never aspire to being a 'hard' science like physics or chemistry. The subjective and evolutionary element therein is simply far too great.

29. We know that in a closed economy with no government sector profits are determined thus (see Chap. 7):

$$I_R + Cp - Sw_R = \pi_R$$

We now also know that investment is determined as we have laid out above. So:

$$\left(Bull / Bear_R\right).\left(\frac{1}{\frac{1}{\frac{M+Ms}{\frac{Bear / Bull}{A}}}}\right)_F .Q_R + Cp - Sw_R = \pi_R$$

If we assume that expected profits is determined by the previous period's profits, then it follows that:

$$\left(Bull / Bear_R\right)_t.\left(\frac{1}{\frac{1}{\frac{M+Ms}{\frac{Bear / Bull}{A}}}}\right)_{F\,t}.\left(\left(Bull / Bear_R\right).\left(\frac{1}{\frac{1}{\frac{M+Ms}{\frac{Bear / Bull}{A}}}}\right)_F .Q_R + Cp - Sw_R\right)_{t-1} = I_{Rt}$$

We could, of course, keep substituting in lagged series of variables like that in the large bracket above into the expected profits term until the equation grew to an infinite size.

30. Note that in this paper Mishkin confuses Keynes' argument as outlined above with the ISLM argument which we shall criticise below.

31. Note that this does not mean that they weigh up numerical probabilities. This is because they do not know all the potential events

that might happen in the future. Thus, they must use their imaginations to come up with such events and invest in line with these. Since the number of these events is as limitless as the imagination of the investors in question, probabilities cannot be assigned as probabilities require a limited list of possible events to even be calculated in an arbitrary, subjective manner. We will deal with these aspects of decision-making under uncertainty proper in the following chapter.

32. The Austrian School go one further: they claim that the central bank will always allow the money rate to diverge from the natural rate, and they therefore insist that the markets should be left to themselves to set the rate of interest. There is an assumption here—one, so far as I can see, based wholly on Faith—that the markets will somehow get line the money rate and the natural rate up with one another automatically. This is a completely bizarre belief given that this school of thought claims to explicitly recognise the existence of Knightian uncertainty proper.

    It should be said, however, that this school of thought has degenerated massively since its founders lay out their rather confused precepts in the early to mid-twentieth century. The school seems to be so fragmented and confused as to what it is they do and do not believe that it is no wonder that they continue to articulate self-contradictory theories. It should also be said that this particular school of thought seems to have become more so a vehicle for political ideology than an actual school of economics. Thus, the Faith that the market should naturally find the correct rate of interest might be more properly read as an assertion of a wholly political nature the goal of which is not to do analysis but rather to push the so-called libertarian political philosophy down the throat of those that disagree. It is not surprising that this school of thought has degenerated into a propaganda machine given that one of its major founders stopped doing economics soon after the school was founded and turned to doing political propaganda; see Pilkington 2013e.

33. This was the era when there was a major bull market in the likes of supposedly triple-A rated Mortgage-Backed Securities (MBS).
34. Hyman Minsky was also scathing on this point about the ISLM, going so far as to call it a 'caricature' of Keynes' theory. He wrote:

> [The] core of *The General Theory* is the theory of investment and why it is so prone to fluctuate. The glib assumption made by Professor Hicks in his exposition of Keynes's contribution [i.e. the ISLM] that there is a simple, negatively sloped function, reflecting the productivity of increments to the stock of capital, that relates investment to the interest rate is a caricature of Keynes's theory of investment. (Minsky 1975, p. 92)

35. Outside of what the ISLMists incorrectly refer to as a 'liquidity trap', which we have shown in a previous chapter, makes no sense anyway.
36. In fact, the authors are far too generous to those working in the mortgage securitisation industry, and this is because they continue to adhere to 'rational agents' assumptions even when they move to disprove them. They assume, for example, that, if the portfolios of those working in the industry did worse after the housing crash due to exposure to housing relative to their colleagues outside the mortgage securitisation industry, this constituted clear evidence of simple ignorance. Undoubtedly, ignorance and groupthink did play a role. But from examining the qualitative evidence, it seems that there were high degrees of cynicism in this industry.

    For example, at the height of the crisis in August 2007, the *New York Times* reported the following:

> Oddly, the credit analysts at brokerage firms now being pummeled were among the Cassandras whose warnings were not heeded. "I'm one guy in a research department, but many people in our mortgage team have been suggesting that there was froth within the market," said Jack Malvey, the chief global fixed income strategist for Lehman Brothers. "This has really been progressing for quite some time."… "All of the old-timers knew that subprime mortgages were what we called neutron loans—they killed the people and left the houses," said Louis S. Barnes, 58, a partner at Boulder West, a mortgage banking firm in Lafayette, Colo. (Babel and Scwartz 2007)

    Such examples—and they are legion—do not fit with the quantitative framework of the authors who seem to assume that portfolio managers would act on all available relevant information. By assuming that those with foreknowledge of the meltdown would position their portfolios accordingly, the authors' framework relies too strongly on the assumption of human beings as 'rational', 'neutral' information processors.

References

Arestis, P. (2011). The new consensus in macroeconomics. In E. Hein & E. Stockhammer (Eds.), *A modern guide to Keynesian macroeconomics and economic policies*. USA: Edward Elgar.

Babel, V., & Scwartz, N. (2007, August 19). How missed signs contributed to a mortgage meltdown. *The New York Times*.

Beenstock, M., & Ilek, A. (2005). Wicksell's classical dichotomy: Is the natural rate of interest independent of the money rate of interest?. In *Discussion paper on monetary studies*. Bank of Israel Monetary Department.

Black, F. (1986). Noise. *Journal of Finance, 41*(3), 529–543.

Buffett, W. (1984). The superinvestors of Graham-and-Dodsville. *Hermes*. http://www.bestinver.es/pdf/articulos_value/The%20Superinvestors%20of%20Graham%20and%20Doddsville%20by%20Warren%20Buffett.pdf

Cheng, I. H., Raina, S., & Xiong, W. (2014). Wall street and the housing bubble. *American Economic Review, 104*(9), 2797–2829.

Cohen, A., & Harcourt, G. (2003). Whatever happened to the Cambridge capital controversies? *Journals of Economic Perspectives, 17*(1), 199–214.

Delong, B., Scleifer, A., Summers, L., & Waldmann, R. (1990). Noise trader risk in financial markets. *Journal of Political Economy*, 703–738.

Fama, E. (1970). Efficient capital markets: A review of theory and empirical work. *The Journal of Finance, 25*(2), 383–417.

Gatapoulos, D. (2013, September 10). Suicides in greece spike during financial crisis. *Huffington Post*. http://www.huffingtonpost.com/2013/09/10/greece-suicides_n_3900906.html

Grossman, S., & Stiglitz, J. (1980). On the impossibility of informationally efficient markets. *The American Economic Review, 70*(3), 393–408.

Harrod, R. (1969). *Money*. UK: Macmillan and Co.

Hicks, J. (1980). ISLM: An explanation. *Journal of Post-Keynesian Economics, 3*(2), 139–154.

Homer, S., & Sylla, R. (2005). *A history of interest rates* (4th ed.). USA: Wiley Finance.

Jones, S. (2008). Rating cows. *Financial times alphaville blog*. http://ftalphaville.ft.com/2008/10/23/17359/rating-cows/

Keynes, J. M. (1930). *A treatise on money, volumes I and II*. USA: Harcourt, Brace & Co.

Keynes, J. M. (1936a). *The general theory of employment, money and interest*. http://www.marxists.org/reference/subject/economics/keynes/general-theory/

Keynes, J. M. (1936b). *Preface to the German edition of the general theory of employment, money and interest*. http://gutenberg.net.au/ebooks03/0300071h/printall.html

Krugman, P. (1998). It's Baaack: Japan's slump and the return of the liquidity trap. *Brookings Paper on Economic Activity*, 137–205.

Leijonhufvud, A. (1979). The Wicksell connection: Variations on a theme. *UCLA Working Paper No. 165.*

Malkiel, B. (2003). The efficient markets hypothesis and its critics. *Journal of Economic Perspectives, 17*(1), 59–82.

Mankiw, G. (2011). *Principles of macroeconomics* (6th ed.). USA: South-Western Cengage Learning.

Minsky, H. (1992). The financial instability hypothesis. *Levy Institute of Bard College*. Working Paper No. 74.

Minsky, H. (1996). Uncertainty and the institutional structure of capitalist economies. *Levy Institute of Bard College*. Working Paper No. 155.

Mirowski, P. (2002). *Machine dreams: Economics becomes a cyborg science*. US & UK: Cambridge University Press.

Mishkin, F. (1996). The channels of monetary transmission: Lessons for monetary policy. *NBER Working Paper Series*. http://myweb.fcu.edu.tw/~T82106/MTP/Ch26-supplement.pdf

Mosler, W., & Pilkington, P. (2012). Tax-backed bonds—A national solution to the European debt crisis. *Levy Institute Policy Note*. http://www.levyinstitute.org/pubs/pn_12_04.pdf

Palley, T. (2004). Asset-based reserve requirements: Reasserting domestic monetary control in an era of financial innovation and instability. *Review of Political Economy, 16*(1), 43–58.

PBS. (2008). Greenspan admits 'flaw' to congress, predicts more economic problems. http://www.pbs.org/newshour/bb/business-july-dec08-crisishearing_10-23/

Pilkington, P. (2013c). A stock-flow consistent approach to a general theory of pricing. *Levy Institute*. Working Paper No. 781. http://www.levyinstitute.org/pubs/wp_781.pdf

Pilkington, P. (2013d, July 4). What is a liquidity trap? Fixing the economists. http://fixingtheeconomists.wordpress.com/2013/07/04/what-is-a-liquidity-trap/

Pilkington, P. (2013e, January 8). The origins of neoliberalism, part I—Hayek's delusion. *Naked Capitalism*. http://www.nakedcapitalism.com/2013/01/philip-pilkington-the-origins-of-neoliberalism-part-i-hayeks-delusion.html

Pilkington, P. (2014b). Endogenous money and the natural rate of interest: The re-emergence of liquidity preference and animal spirits in the post-Keynesian theory of capital markets. (Forthcoming).

Robinson, J. (1951). The rate of interest. *Econometrica, 19*(2), 92–111.

Shackle, G. L. S. (1965). *A scheme of economic theory*. UK: Cambridge University Press.

Shackle, G. L. S. (1966). *The nature of economic thought*. UK: Cambridge University Press.

Shaikh, A. (2016). *Capitalism: Competition, conflict, crises.* Oxford: Oxford University Press.

Shiller, R. (2003). From efficient markets theory to behavioral finance. *Journal of Economic Perspectives, 17*(1), 83–104.

Shiller, R. (2005). *Irrational exuberance* (2nd ed.). USA: Broadway Business Books.

Wicksell, K. (1898). *Interest and prices: A study of the causes regulating the value of money.* UK: Royal Economic Society.

William, R. (2012). What about cash?. *Charles Schwab.* http://www.schwab.com/public/schwab/nn/articles/What-About-Cash

Wray, R. (1998). *Understanding modern money: The key to full employment and price stability.* USA: Edward Elgar.

PART III

Approaching the Real World

CHAPTER 10

Uncertainty and Probability

If you do not expect the unexpected you will not find it, for it is not to be reached by search or trail.

—Heraclitus

The two things that I found most confusing when I started studying alternative approaches to economics were interest rates and uncertainty. Interest rates brought up all those terribly entangled issues that we broached in Chap. 8. It would not surprise me in the least that of all the chapters in this book it will be this one that will most perplex the casual reader. The only advice that I can give them is to persevere as the question of finance and interest rates is one of the most pressing in economics and it is the question to which mainstream theory, which generally conceives of interest rates as some sort of 'reward for waiting', has the most unsatisfactory and oversimplified answer. The confusion that uncertainty brought up for me was of a different nature. It did not seem to me to be a particularly difficult concept to grasp. Rather, I was confused about why it was so important and why it seemed to crop up everywhere in the alternative literature.

We should start with the question of what we mean by uncertainty. In this sense, our usage of the term in economics will not stray too far from common usage. The uncertainty we deal with in economics is the same uncertainty experienced by the teenager experiencing the onset of puberty or the student of economics uncertain if they have grasped the essence of a particular argument. Uncertainty is the gnawing sense of doubt that we all

W.P. Pilkington, *The Reformation in Economics*,
DOI 10.1007/978-3-319-40757-9_10

face when we intuitively sense that we cannot be sure of a given outcome. 'Oh dear', thinks the economics student, 'I think that I have grasped the essence of the argument but because I cannot be sure I do not want to risk embarrassing myself by talking what might prove to be a load of nonsense in front of my peers.'

Human beings, quite understandably, spend an awful lot of time trying as best they can to bury this uncertainty. They seek habits of behaviour and systems of explanation that give them relative certainty. When it comes to habits of behaviour, we can safely say that these often work. If I brush my teeth every morning and every night before bed, avoid very sugary food and do not break these habits too often, I can be at least somewhat certain of the outcome upon my dental health. Most of the process of socialisation is to provide children with habits by which they can at once behave themselves in a manner deemed socially and morally acceptable and at the same time give them a framework through which they can live their lives not perpetually subject to uncertainty.[1] Similarly, many of the public and private institutions that human beings build have the primary aim of eliminating uncertainty as best they can. A large corporation, for example, will engage in large-scale market research to try to eliminate the uncertainty around launching a new product; or a government will provide unemployment insurance to ensure that citizens never fall below a certain income threshold. So far as habits and institutions go, the elimination of uncertainty that they may provide is very real indeed. But when it comes to systems of explanation that seek to eliminate uncertainty, we should be far more wary. These are far more likely to be fantasies. If we undertake certain actions in line with particular habits, we may well ward off uncertainty to some extent, but, when we think that have mastered it in thought, we are probably fooling ourselves.

Much of contemporary science is an attempt to eliminate uncertainty as best scientists practically can. This is why one of the key tools of the scientific method is the replicable experiment. If we undertake an experiment once, we can be by no means sure that the results are certain. So, what scientists do is design experiments that can be repeated over and over again. Each time we repeat the experiment and get the same result, we gain a higher degree of certainty as to this result. But as the British philosopher David Hume pointed out long ago, we can never be completely certain as to the result for that would require an infinite number of experiments which would in turn require an infinite amount of time to undertake them (Hume 1739, Part III Section II).[2] So, while contemporary science does try as best it can to reduce uncertainty to as small a point as is practically possible, it can never eliminate it altogether.

The key problem with economics and that which renders it fundamentally different from the hard sciences is that, in economics, we cannot repeat experiments. Yes, we can examine data and look for trends. We can even use sophisticated econometric estimation techniques to try to detect these trends as best we can. But we can never attain a very large degree of certainty when doing this because we simply cannot repeat an experiment. Economics is not alone in this regard. This is a problem for all the social sciences. In these disciplines, we are dealing with material that is fundamentally different to that which is dealt with in the hard sciences. Thus, we may be able to get a very high correlation coefficient between two variables in economics—and we may get a high t-statistic to boot—but this does nothing to assure us that the correlation is not in some way spurious. After all, it may be a third of forth variable that we have excluded that is causing the correlation. Or, more radically still, the correlation may disappear in the period after the one we have just studied. Indeed, this happens in financial markets all the time because, by the time people have discovered a correlation, they engage in activities which seek to eliminate said correlation. The fact is that things change; what has been true for a year, ten years, one hundred years may not be true for the next year, ten years, one hundred years.

Nor is this simply a problem with econometrics. This is a problem that goes right to the heart of how we must think about the economy. This is because the problem with uncertainty is not a problem with the techniques some economists use to try to eliminate it. Rather, it is a problem that is buried deep within the structure of the material we deal with. Again, this mainly has to do with the fact that we cannot engage in replicable experiment in economics. And this renders anything we say about the data somewhat speculative. But it also arises because, in the social and economics world, relationships are constantly changing and evolving. Man evolved from the ape. Through studying various remains, we can reconstruct what he looked like at each stage of the evolutionary process. But this tells us little about his future evolutionary trajectory. The material we deal with in economics is identical in this regard.

Uncertainty versus Probabilistic Risk

Before we move on, we must first distinguish between uncertainty proper and probabilistic risk. In more formal terms, the former is often known in economics as 'Keynesian uncertainty' or 'Knightian uncertainty'.[3] Uncertainty proper is the recognition that the people we study in economics do not have knowledge about the future and that, in part because of this, we as economists do not possess this knowledge either. Because the world is changing in any number of different and contingent ways, there is no way that people can be sure as to what will happen next. The flow of historical time is, by its nature, a flow of largely contingent events. No one could tell years before the fact, for example, that terrorists would attack New York City on 11 September 2001, and yet this event changed the course of world history in that it led to the Iraq war and a completely new perception of the USA in the eyes of the wider world.[4] Nor can we tell, for example, who will be president of a given democratic country 20 years from now. About these potential future happenings, we are completely uncertain.

Probabilistic risk, on the other hand, is an entirely different beast. If I have a balanced coin and I flip it, I can, in fact, make a mathematical estimation as to what the future course of this particular event will be. Likewise, if I have a balanced six-sided dice and I roll it, I can estimate mathematically the probability that the event will turn out in a given way. All I have to do in these instances is to take the number of potential 'indifferent' events—that is, events that have equal likelihood of occurring—and divide this number into the number one. Thus, given that there are two potential events that can occur with the coin toss (heads or tails), I get a mathematical estimation that the chances of either occurring are $\frac{1}{2}$ or 50 %. In the case of the balanced dice, the mathematical estimation of each potential event occurring is $\frac{1}{6}$ or 16.666667 %.

In the old days of economic theory, economists used to simply model the economy assuming that the people within their model economies had perfect knowledge of the future but, in the second half of the twentieth century, economists began to assume that, rather than perfect knowledge of the future, the people in their economic models had objective, numerical probabilistic estimates of future events (Davidson 1996). This has become known as the 'ergodic hypothesis' in economics. While the older economists used to assume a very crude determinism in that they assumed that the economy simply did not change through history, the more recent mainstream theorists instead assume that the economy is indeed changing through time but that it is changing in line with objective probabilities. This means that people within the economy can nevertheless make numerical and rational predictions despite the fact that the future would not be a simple mirror of the past. Davidson summarises this as such:

> Reality is, therefore, immutable; the future path of the economy and the future conditional consequences of all possible choices are predetermined (i.e. programmed by natural laws). This does not preclude an economy that is moving or changing over time. It does mean that all future movements and changes are already predetermined by the fundamental real parameters of the system and cannot be changed by human action. (Davidson 1996, pp. 479–480)

As Davidson implies, this means that humans do not have free will and any attempts to consciously change their environment is fruitless—indeed, such attempts are already, in some way, pre-determined. This view of the world carries with it older religious views on, for example, Predestination and is in some sense similar to the Intelligent Design (ID) version of evolutionary theory. It assumes what in philosophy is called a 'teleological process' in that there is assumed to be an end point far in the future, but already set in stone, on which all events in the present will inevitably converge.[5]

Beyond being a very arcane and old-fashioned view of the world, it is also inherently conservative. It carries the message: 'There is no point in trying to fight against certain economic tendencies because these are inevitable and, anyway, in some sense your desire to fight against them has already been taken into account by the Great Computer that is the economic universe.' This is in striking contrast to the view generally adopted by other social scientists who, to a greater or lesser extent, tend to follow Marx's dictum:

> Men make their own history, but they do not make it as they please; they do not make it under self-selected circumstances, but under circumstances existing already, given and transmitted from the past. The tradition of all dead generations weighs like a nightmare on the brains of the living. (Marx 1852, Chapter 1)

Modern economics relies instead on deterministic and teleological notions to an extent beyond any other social science discipline. Of course, these ideas do not conform to reality. If I am asked who will be elected president of the USA in 20 years' time and what economic consequences this will have, it is quite clear that I cannot give this event a numerical estimate or series of numerical estimates. Yet, mainstream economists claim that they must make this assumption in order to render their discipline a science. To the present writer, such assertions appear less as scientific explanations or assumptions and more as derivatives from religious systems of belief in the discernable benevolent authority of some entity totally and completely directing human life. If this latter characterisation is more accurate than that of science, it would appear that those making proclamations based on the idea that they have access to either numerical estimates about the future or theories that assume people make evaluations based on these numerical estimates are very close to cultic religious figures of the past like the haruspices who cut open the stomachs of goats to gain access to divine foreknowledge of events to come. This explains, to a very large extent, why the general public often find economists to be figures of fun and make jokes about them. It is the economists' own fault that they have assumed sometimes the position of the court jester or clown in this regard. Many are quite literally people who live in a different intellectual age.

Probability and Possibility

The key reason that the idea of numerical probability does not work when trying to conceive of future states of the economy is because people form their expectations using their *imaginations*. In the examples above of the coin and the dice, we saw clearly that there were a given number of possible events—in the case of the coin, two, while in the case of the dice, six—and that the probability of each event occurring was assumed to be 'equiprobable' (i.e. they are all just likely to happen). But when we are dealing with the future in terms of historical time, this cannot be said to be the case. The future possible outcomes or events are literally as numerous as you or I can imagine them. If you or I can imagine it, then it becomes a possibility. The number of future outcomes or events then becomes potentially infinite, limited only by the amount of time that one spends concocting possible future universes and the extent of our imaginations. Clearly, here we are in a completely different space to that inhabited by the coin, the dice and the objective probability measures.

When human imagination and storytelling comes to the fore, we are no longer in a world of the probable, rather we are in a world of the possible (Shackle 1966, pp. 94–95). In such a world, the number of possible futures is literally as limitless as our imaginations, and our evaluations of their likelihood are entirely subjective. This does not mean that we cannot say anything about possible future events. It seems far more likely, for example, that the current British government will be re-elected in the next election cycle than that I will grow a tail next week. Thus, in the face of an uncertain future, we can separate sense from nonsense, at least to some extent. We can put aside conjectures that we find improbable to the point of ridiculous and try to construct a number of possible imagined scenarios. Shackle calls this ability 'bounded uncertainty' (ibid., p. 86).

If uncertainty were not bounded, our imaginations would literally run away with us. We would be unable to sort sense from nonsense, and imaginary scenarios would proliferate to the point that, potentially, we went mad. But human beings seem able to form relatively coherent narratives about what they expect the future to possibly hold, and these narratives allow them to take action in the world. This process is largely a negative one. The first thing that the human mind must do to separate sense from nonsense is to label the nonsense. It appears to do this largely automatically in most cases. Thus, it actually took for me some psychic effort to come up with the nonsensical idea that I might grow a tail next week. This shows that it actually takes psychic effort to retrieve instances of nonsense, thus suggesting that the mind automatically throws the nonsense stories that are largely useless or renders them unconscious. Indeed, society compensates writers of fantastical fiction to come up with such nonsense for our amusement thus reflecting that doing so requires some labour.

When the human mind whittles away most of the nonsense, we are generally left with some limited number of imaginary narratives that describe possible futures. We then try to organise these relative to one another by dint of what we perceive to be their relative likelihood, that is, we organise these narratives ordinally. Next, we try to discern which of the outcomes we favour and which we do not favour and weigh this against the likelihood we have assigned the possible event of taking place. When we have formed this structure in our mind, we can then either use it to undertake a decision or communicate it to others to try to influence their decisions.

It is important to note that just because (some) people have this ability, it does not mean that all people undertake such reasoning before they make decisions. In fact, I do not believe that most people do undertake decisions in this way. Rather, many people appear to 'outsource' their decisions to outside people or institutions that they trust or they just do whatever they feel like at a given moment in time. When the majority of people are doing the former, the world displays a fair degree of consistency; when the majority of people are doing the latter, the world displays a large degree of chaotic inconsistency and becomes almost impossible to rationally analyse.

To try to reduce possibility to probability is farcical if one understands the inherently different natures of the two things. To form a probability judgement, one must know all the potential future events and what probability weighting they each have relative to one another. This is reflected in the fact that all the potential future events must sum to 1. So, tossing the coin can yield heads or tails with equal probability. We thus assign a 50 % probability to each. The sum of the two probabilities—0.5 + 0.5—adds up to one. The case of the dice is the same but rather with six potential future events. With possibility, on the other hand, we do not possess a complete list of possible future events. Even by the time, we have arrived at something resembling a list—that is, when we have separated sense from nonsense—we would still be misled if we thought that we had a proper complete list in the same sense we do in the case of the coin or the dice. And even though we must, to some extent, organise these possibilities relative to one another, it would appear very silly indeed to assign them a numerical probability. Anyone who does so and takes such numerical probabilities seriously should probably not themselves be taken in any way seriously.

Oh, Nihilism

At this point, many economists annoyed that you have pointed to an obvious and damning flaw in their methods and theories will accuse you of nihilism. But it is not altogether clear that they understand the meaning of the word. Presumably, when they say this, they have the following dictionary definition in mind: 'Nihilism, an extreme form of skepticism: the denial of all real existence or the possibility of an objective basis for truth.' But is this actually what we are saying when we talk about uncertainty? It appears to this writer that we are not talking about this at all. What we are really saying is that there are no very objective ways in economics to proclaim the truth or falsity of a statement. But this is also the case in many other disciplines and professions. In law, for example, there is no ready-made method using which we can establish Truth with absolute certainty. Rather, we have institutions in place that try to render judgement based on the best and most convincing argument (or, at least, we should hope that this is how these institutions work). Does this render law to be a fundamentally nihilistic profession and our legal system a fundamentally nihilistic institution? I would imagine that many hard-working lawyers and judges would be very offended indeed if we made such a statement. I would also put forward that it should be on the person making this claim to provide the outline of a better system of legal justice.

It seems that many economic policies are decided in a similar way to the way we set up our justice systems. Monetary policy is set, for example, by taking a cross-section of opinions from people assumed to be experts. Sometimes, we may disagree with these people, and we may even think that their expertise are somewhat lacking but we cannot deny that this is how things are generally done. I do not know of any central bank in the world that has a single manner in which to objectively define what the optimum rate of monetary policy is. I know of plenty of theories that purport to do this—note that I wrote 'theories' plural thus indicating little consensus—but I do not know of any economic institutions that completely subordinate themselves to a supposedly objective number crunched out by a particular theory. Does this then make the practice of central banking nihilistic? Again, that strikes me as being absurd.

Perhaps, then the only way we can understand the charge of nihilism is to look closely at what those who make it actually do on a day-to-day basis. They seem to want to build models, methods or systems of explanation that will tell them with absolute certainty how human society should be governed. This strikes me as being very dangerous indeed. There is an element of hubris here that comes across as bordering on totalitarian. There is a desire for a sort of Godlike control that strikes me, in its more pronounced moments, as being somewhat megalomaniacal. Indeed, examined closely the desire underlying the need for certainty in economics may well manifest highly authoritarian tendencies that should be pointed out to anyone who aspires to democratic impulses. But in its more resigned moments, this desire does not manifest as Evil but rather as Folly. It is the desperate need for someone to obtain a certainty that renders him/her useless in the real world. Just as I can lead a very certain existence if I stay indoors all day and eat the same thing at the same time every day, I can also obtain a very certain conclusion if I stick closely to logical games and puzzles and econometric estimation techniques. But in both instances, my value when it comes to partaking in real world activities diminishes immeasurably. Indeed, one might say that to confine oneself to such an existence is, in some ways, rather nihilistic. Nihilism is, in the last instance, in the eye of the beholder.

Coping with Uncertainty: In Theory

In economics, there are three broad types of possible models each with its own subheadings. The first of these are the static models. An example of a static model in macroeconomic theory is the ISLM that we have looked at in previous chapters. This is what we might call a Marshallian static model, after Alfred Marshall.[6] This particular static model is characterised by the fact that it is subject to manipulation by the user to produce some sort of supposed intuition. That is, the user is given the flexibility to alter the parameters and see what effects policy is supposed to have on the economy. Other types of static models, like those found in microeconomics textbooks, are not subject to such manipulation at all. They are characterised by a fixed, teleological end point. In these models, the outcome is already built into the prior assumptions, and rather than trying to change up some of the variables to see what different results we get, the whole idea is instead to 'solve' for some equilibrium end point. The idea here is not to fiddle with the model to see what changes take place but rather to 'prove' an equilibrium result.

The static models are the most useless in economics. In their extreme general equilibrium form, they seem like nothing but an exercise in intellectual construction, a game played for its own sake. Sometimes, their practitioners and the results derived from them lead one to question whether building and studying these models are actually doing economics at all. In their less extreme form, they are slightly less offensive in that they seek to actually tell us something about the real world. Thus, the ISLM actually tries to tell us something about what will happen when, for example, investment increases or when the supply of money is reduced. But because of the static limitations of models like the ISLM, they often give us information that is completely at odds with reality. This is why their own creator, as we have seen in previous chapters, came to reject them.[7]

The second type of broad economic model is the self-contained, dynamic model. The most famous of these is the Harrod–Domar growth model.[8] The very simple profit model laid out in Chap. 7 of this book is perhaps the closest laid out here to a dynamic model. Popular models that purport to be dynamic, like the Dynamic Stochastic General Equilibrium

(DSGE) models, are not actually dynamic at all. Rather, they are an amalgamation of general equilibrium models that allow for comparative static comparisons. The truly dynamic models are very interesting in their own right. What they do is to provide the user with a highly simplified, bare-bones analytical device to help them think through certain relationships. Harrod's approach was to lay out some basic conditions for balanced economic growth to take place. Although these models are self-contained, they are generally used intuitively against the real world as a sort of very general guide. G.L.S. Shackle wrote of them:

> Such models in their most precise and uncompromising form are not intended for exact prediction: for only such exactness can be got out of them, as is put into them in selecting the form, and numerical values of the co-efficients, of their equations. And statistical resource does not yet, and possibly never will, make it possible to be precise … Such models are tools of insight, not foresight. (Shackle 1965, p. 98)

These models are necessarily false in that they oversimplify to an extent that is, frankly, unforgivable. But they are false in a way that can nevertheless provide some insight if used delicately. This puts them in contrast with the static models which provide very little if any insight and, in their more extreme modern conceptions, actually make the user think in perverse and unusual ways that are completely at odds with reality. We only presented our very simplified dynamic model very briefly because we were more interested in this book in the third type of model.

The third type of broad economic model is the open-ended, kaleidoscopic Keynesian model. The chapter in this book on finance and investment was written in the vein of such a model.[9] They are also the type of model that we find laid out in Keynes' *General Theory*. What characterises these models is that they are properly open-ended. Shackle again provides an extremely useful gloss on this type of model:

> At the other extreme of the range of dynamic models we have those whose design deliberately leaves out some of the linkages which would be needed in order to calculate the future from the past. A very notable example of such 'open' or non-self-contained models is Keynes's *General Theory of Employment*, where net investment, the flow whose size is treated as the actively dominant feature of the situation, is deliberately left free of any simple determining formula involving only other 'internal' variables of the

> system. The whole spirit of Keynes's book insists on the unfathomable subtlety, complexity and mutability of the influences which bear upon decisions to invest. To build a self-contained dynamic model would have been, for him, to contradict the very essence of what he was trying to say, namely, that it is uncertainty, the feeling of helpless inability to know with assurance how a given course of action will turn out, that inhibits enterprise and the giving of full employment. (Shackle 1965, p. 8)

It is these models and these models alone that deal with uncertainty proper. In these models, we have variables with two distinct characteristics: (1) they can never, by their very nature, be measured or estimated in any way before the fact and (2) they actually refer to what we have called 'the news' and thus rely on the analyst's own ability to actually follow historical events which affect the economy as they unfold in real time. These variables were, of course, liquidity preference, the animal spirits and the marginal efficiency of capital, and they all rely on highly contingent judgements on the part of various actors within the economy; the key defining feature of whom is that they must make decisions in the face of proper uncertainty.

What then is the point of all this? Before giving a positive answer to that question, it is first necessary to turn it upon those who will likely ask it. If uncertainty holds in the real world and your models evacuate uncertainty in order to obtain closure, then what is the point of your models? In the end, the only point seems to be to obtain the closure itself for some sort of psychological reward. The key point here is that we cannot simply wish away uncertainty if we want to engage with the real world. Yes, we can pretend that uncertainty does not exist so that we can build little self-contained models that give us precise, but also precisely meaningless, answers. But this does not assist us in any way of understanding the world around us. Rather, it is the simple playing of intellectual games, a sort of mental onanism, which does not, like the useless Onan, provide us with any legitimate heir.

The point then of real economic thought is not so much to provide a model but to provide a 'schema', as we have laid out in a previous chapter. A schema is an organised pattern of ideas that help us to organise and interpret real world data. It provides us with a coherent and organised basis with which we can approach the world around us. This is what Keynes spoke in favour of in contrast to closed-system modelling when he wrote in the *General Theory*:

> The object of our analysis is, not to provide a machine, or method of blind manipulation, which will furnish an infallible answer, but to provide ourselves with an organised and orderly method of thinking out particular problems; and, after we have reached a provisional conclusion by isolating the complicating factors one by one, we then have to go back on ourselves and allow, as well as we can, for the probable interactions of the factors amongst themselves. This is the nature of economic thinking. (Keynes1936a, b, Chapter 21)[10]

The ability to do this will, in a very real sense, separate the men from the boys—if the reader will excuse my rather sexist metaphor—leaving those who feel the need for 'infallible answers' to play with their toys while leaving the rest of those who seek out this 'orderly method of thinking about particular problems' to make real advances in economic theory and, most importantly, apply this thinking to questions of real world policy. This will be massively complicated, however, by the fact that those of the next generation who do try to break away from the 'methods of blind manipulation' will quickly find themselves being pushed back into it by the previous generation who have formed a sort of cult that punishes those who challenge certain drab formalistic principles that have become ingrained in the profession over the past several decades.

Coping with Uncertainty: In Practice

The key to applying the principles of economic analysis in practice must always be some mix of intuition and induction. That much seems obvious. Rather, less obvious is what specifically the focus should be on. If you examine a good deal of the work done by empirical economists, you will find a strange tendency among them: there is a marked proclivity to try to figure out how the economy, or some section of the economy, will remain stable at any given moment in time. There are a number of reasons why this tendency seems prevalent but the most simple is that analysts tend to try to project the present conditions into the future, and since the present is more often stable than it is unstable, the future is generally thought to be stable too. The only time that most analysts become interested in instability is when instability is actually occurring—and then it is usually too late.

The key to good analysis is to go against the grain in this regard. In periods of stability, one should always be searching out, to use the late forecaster Wynne Godley's term, 'unsustainable processes' (Godley 1999), that is, aspects of the economy that do not appear to be logically sustainable moving into the future. The idea is to try to figure out what effects these are going to have when their sustainability runs out. Conversely, when the economy is in a period of turmoil—that is, when the unsustainability of an unsustainable processes becomes manifest—the good analyst should always be looking for the point at which the economy is going to restabilise. There is always a bottom or a floor that an economy will hit no matter how deep a downturn and when a downturn occurs, and everyone is scrambling to explain what is going on (you should have been keeping an eye on those unsustainable processes guys!); a good economist should be looking for that floor. In modern economies, with strong countercyclical government institutions, there are any number of ways of doing this, from looking at the size of the government deficit to trying to pick up on when the banking system will have sufficient liquidity to stymie a liquidity trap within the system.

The reason that most analysts try to project the present into the future is that they fail completely to recognise the element of uncertainty. Many economists even insulate themselves in bad times by assuring themselves that these bad times will go on forever. At a time when the economy is in meltdown, economists often obtain comfort from Doomsday warnings. They engage in projections of the current crisis into the future. These, strangely enough, provide a certainty all of their own, the certainty that everything is going to Hell in a handbasket. But this certainty is just as illusory as the tendency to project periods of calm into the future.

This raises the further question of what these analysts are actually doing. Are they in fact even doing economic analysis? There is a strong case to be made that they are not. Rather, they are engaged in a sort of 'economics storytelling' in which they tell themselves, the media and policymakers the stories that they want to hear. In a very real sense, these people provide the narrative that acts as the engine driving unsustainable processes—and when these unsustainable processes run out, they provide the narratives that buttress and sustain the downturn. In the case of the unsustainable boom, they cover over the inevitable changes that are going to take place with their narratives that reinforce the present. Indeed, in a certain sense, these people generate the narratives that actually move the economy in the direction of stability or instability. When these narratives are believed, the processes that they foretell actually come about, and it is only when they hit the rock of reality—that is, when the process becomes unsustainable—

that they are forced to change. Likewise, it is only when the economy stabilises after a downturn that they begin to talk about stabilisation.

When engaged in good economic analysis analysts, should not concern themselves too much with precision. Precision is usually the harbinger of serious error. Precision will also make you look like a clown when the results of your crystal-ball gazing do not come true. General trends and spotting unsustainable processes in either a downswing or an upswing are far more important. As Keynes said, 'it is better to be roughly right than precisely wrong'. Plugging a self-contained system of equations into an econometric model in order to get a number is a sure-fire way of coming out the other side looking like a fool. Indeed, there is very little difference between doing this and shaking a magic eight-ball in order to give oneself a concrete answer.

Another key aspect of good analysis is to try to understand the possible paths that an economy might take in the future. This ties into the idea of unsustainable processes laid out above. The analyst must ask themselves 'if this process is unsustainable what potential paths are there that the economy can take when the unsustainability becomes manifest?' Economies are very robust entities, and there are always a multitude of different directions in which they can evolve. An unsustainable process might be adjusted for by, for example, a substantial currency devaluation or rapid contraction in domestic income. Again, this is tied to not trying to give a definitive answer. Rather, the analyst should present possible scenarios that might occur moving into the future. 'Well, if policymakers let this go on for any longer the result is either going to be *x*, *y* or *z*…'

The key to good analysis is to turn uncertainty into your friend rather than your enemy. The economic storytellers—and these people will always exist because they are integral to the system—will be fighting as hard as they can to eliminate uncertainty by projecting the present into the future. But this provides ample space for the good analyst to get ahead of the crowd. Key here is to become very familiar with the narrative that the storytellers are telling at any given point in time and then examine the data in detail to find holes in this narrative. The holes in this narrative are the key to identifying unsustainable processes. These sorts of analyses are what we might call 'anti-conservative analyses'. As we have pointed out again and again the key to the conservative mind-set is to try to hold things stable and keep them as they are. This is precisely what the economic storytellers are doing with their narratives. But the non-conservative economist will always be looking for that point of change, that traverse, where the economy moves from one point of activity to another. Once this traverse is identified, it should then be studied to reveal what paths the economy can take when it bumps up against it.

None of this precludes, of course, having a cogent and realistic theory or schema of ideas about how the economy works. This present book is not an exercise in criticism pure and simple, and its message is in no way that those interested in economics should engage in some free-for-all of economic theorising. It is very important that a coherent, realistic, flexible and accurate theory is adopted by the economist. It is imperative that they understand and appreciate changing institutional dynamics and political tensions. Basically, the economist must be a practical theorist who never allows rigid theoretical construction built for the sake of tidiness and simplicity to dominate his or her thinking about the real world. Keynes put it nicely when he wrote:

> The study of economics does not seem to require any specialized gifts of an unusually high order. Is it not, intellectually regarded, a very easy subject compared with the higher branches of philosophy or pure science? An easy subject at which few excel! The paradox finds its explanation, perhaps, in that the master-economist must possess a rare combination of gifts. He must be mathematician, historian, statesman, philosopher—in some degree. He must understand symbols and speak in words. He must contemplate the particular in terms of the general and touch abstract and concrete in the same flight of thought. He must study the present in the light of the past for the purposes of the future. No part of man's nature or his institutions must lie entirely outside his regard. He must be purposeful and disinterested in a simultaneous mood; as aloof and incorruptible as an artist, yet sometimes as near to earth as a politician. (Keynes 1924)

Breakout Box: Unsustainable Processes: Wynne Godley and the Financial Crisis of 2008

Wynne Godley was a Post-Keynesian macroeconomist and forecaster who became known through his career as the 'Cassandra of the Fens' for his famously prescient and unheeded warnings. For much of the latter half of his career, he was on the outside of economic debate. This appears to have been mainly a reflection of the Dark Ages that began in economic policy circles starting in the late

1970s. In the early to mid-1970s, Godley was actively partaking in a very interesting series of debates within Her Majesty's Treasury in the UK about the future trajectory of the British economy. Godley and his colleagues—which included other Post-Keynesian economists (then known as 'New Cambridge') Francis Cripps and Nicholas Kaldor—intervened in this debate with new approaches to empirical policy research that had been developed by Keynes' students and their students at Cambridge, UK, in the post-war years (Maloney 2012).

The Post-Keynesians were soon run out of the government institutions, however, by the monetarists. The monetarists were already getting traction within the Bank of England in the mid- to late 1970s, but, with the election of Margaret Thatcher in 1979, they became entrenched.[11] After this, they wrote largely from the standpoint of opposition against the government policies of the day (Kaldor 1982; Kaldor 1983). Godley was not able to fall back on his independent forecasting at Cambridge because the Economic and Social Research Council (ESRC) under Thatcher cut off funding, presumably as part of the anti-Keynesian push of that government (RES 2010). Eventually, Godley continued his forecasting work with the Levy Institute at Bard College where he published seminal and prescient analyses. Here we will examine the most important of these to get a sense of his overall method.

The paper in question was entitled 'Seven Unsustainable Processes'. It was written in 1999 and predicted that the Clinton boom—otherwise called the 'goldilocks boom'—was completely unsustainable.[12] At the time, the economy was being driven largely by confidence buoyed on the back of a massive stock market bubble. But beneath this, Godley found an even more important unsustainable process at work. Before we examine his method in detail, however, let us understand first the perspective he was taking. In the paper in question, he wrote:

> This paper makes no short-term forecast. Bubbles and booms often continue much longer than anyone can believe possible and there could well be a further year or more of robust expansion. The perspective taken here is strategic in the sense that it is only concerned with

developments over the next 5 to 15 years as a whole. Any recommendations regarding policy do not have the character of 'fine-tuning' in response to short-term disturbances. They ask, rather, whether the present stance of either fiscal or trade policy is structurally appropriate looking to the medium- and long-term future. (Godley 1999, p. 1)

This is key. If you read the paper today, you can see that Godley was very much so roughly right rather than precisely wrong. His approach is a very general one, and in the first half of the paper, he does not engage in crystal-ball gazing.[13] Rather, he tries to tease out processes that he does not think will be sustainable in the next five to ten years. Godley utilises a very simple framework that has become known as the 'sectoral balances approach'. The sectoral balances approach is an accounting truism that we derive from the identities of the national accounts. First, we break income down in accordance with expenditure:[14]

$$Y \equiv C + I + G + (X - M)$$

Then we break it down in accordance with income:

$$Y \equiv C + S + T$$

Then we combine the two identities by substitution, cancel out the consumption element and rearrange and we get the sectoral balances identity:

$$(S - I) \equiv (G - T) + (X - M)$$

We can then plug real data into this equation from the national accounts. Since Godley was using the US data, we have displayed it (updated for the periods after 1999 when he was writing) in Fig. 10.1.

What Godley noted was that the private sector had gone into substantial deficit in the early to mid-1990s. This completely defied the trends of private sector surpluses in the post-war era. When he dug into these numbers, it quickly became clear that it was the private household sector that was accumulating much of this debt. This increase in debt was due to the fact that the US government was sucking money out of the economy in the form of budget surpluses while the foreign balance was sucking money out of the economy and sending it overseas in the form of a trade deficit. As the sectoral

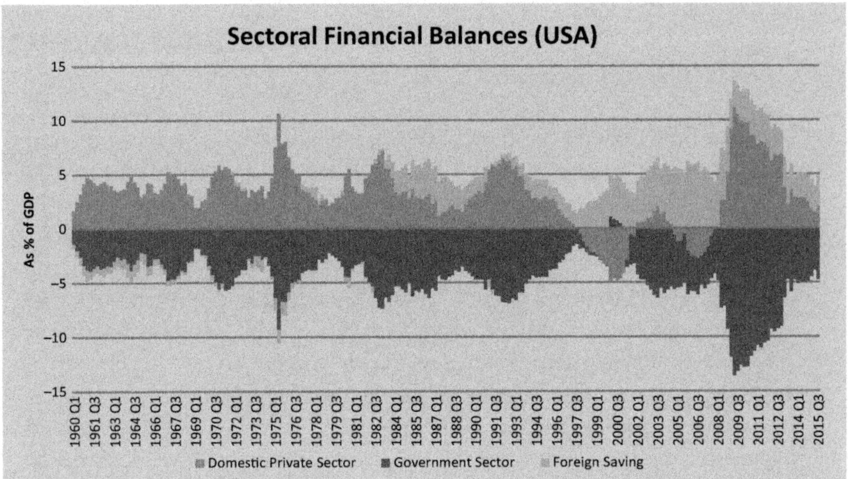

Fig. 10.1 Sectoral balances

balances identity shows, by accounting identity, this must mean that the household sector is going deeper and deeper into debt in order to fund the expenditure that is keeping the economy ticking over. Godley's conclusion was extremely prescient. Nearly ten years before the financial crisis of 2008, he wrote:

> The central contention of this paper is that, given unchanged fiscal policy and accepting the consensus forecast for growth in the rest of the world, continued expansion of the U.S. economy requires that private expenditure continues to rise *relative to income*. Yet while anything can happen over the next year or so, it seems impossible that this source of growth can be forthcoming on a strategic time horizon. The growth in net lending to the private sector and the growth *in the growth rate* of the real money supply cannot continue for an extended period. Moreover, if, *per impossibile*, the growth in net lending and the growth in money supply growth were to continue for another eight years, the implied indebtedness of the private sector would then be so extremely large that a sensational day of reckoning could then be at hand. (Ibid., p. 5)He was right, of course. His 'impossible' scenario more or less unfolded over the next few years. As we can see from the more recent data after the collapse of the stock market bubble, private sector debt accumulation came to a halt briefly before picking back up again during the housing bubble. When this finally came to a halt

in 2007–2008, a 'sensational day of reckoning' was indeed at hand, just as Godley predicted.

In the first half of his paper, Godley followed the approach that we have been laying out above. He tried to detect trends that he did not think could continue. While the Central Budget Office (CBO) was projecting the present trends into the future, Godley was looking for the breaking point that would change the trajectory of the US economy. He was cautious in his words. He knew that unsustainable processes could continue for a long time. But his logic was solid. He saw that these private sector debt trends were an historical anomaly, and he also reasoned that it was very likely that households could not go into debt indefinitely. The CBO was engaged in economics storytelling of the most noxious kind while Godley was undertaking a properly dynamic analysis. He was not making any silly proclamations on human behaviour—on whether people behave 'rationally' or whatever other silly moral narrative the other economists of the day were peddling to public—he was just looking at historical trends and engaging in some very basic logical reasoning about how much debt households could be burdened with before they became insolvent. Using some very simple but powerful tools, he tracked down the engine of the Clinton boom and found it to be running on fumes. Meanwhile, all the other forecasters, barring maybe a handful, were inhaling the poisonous emissions coming out of the exhaust pipe.

Must We Scrap Econometrics?

In the second half of the Godley paper, the whole thing goes completely off the rails. Godley tries to use a computer model, an early version of the models he would later write about in his book with Marc Lavoie (Godley and Lavoie 2006), to run predictive econometric regressions on the data he has collected. Prior to this, he was happy with simply picking holes in the CBO projections by showing what dynamics they implicitly entailed for private sector debt build-ups. But then he goes on to make some projections of his own. He gives us six of these and, in retrospect, they look fairly ridiculous. Without getting too much into the details, the most accurate projection for 2003 was 2.9 % for the government deficit and 2.8 % for the trade deficit, and this was thought to coincide with an unemployment rate of 9.6 % (Godley 1999, p. 8). In actual fact, due to the onset of the Iraq war—an event so unforeseeable in 1999 that it in itself underscores the silliness of such quantitative predictions[15]—the budget deficit in 2003 stood somewhere just below the 5 % mark; the trade balance too was just below 5 % and unemployment peaked at around 6 %.[16]

This is not the fault of Godley's models. They are surely some of the best and most comprehensive large-scale economic models built today. Rather, it is the fault of the misguided attempt to apply them directly to the data using econometric techniques. This simply does not work. While the CBO and other forecasters were prancing around saying how great everything would be now that the Clinton boom had set in, Godley's macroeconometric projections do not actually look all that much less silly. They strike the reader as being just as wrong as those that he is attacking. Yet, in contrast to the Panglossian optimists, the first half of his paper where he makes a more rough and ready prediction about the rising levels of household debt looks so much more salient. The only reason that his projections take a pessimistic tone in contrast to the optimism of the other forecasters is because he has taken account of the unsustainable build-up of private sector debt. But formalising this intuition and running regressions using it tells us nothing new. In fact, it gives Godley's otherwise classic paper a dated quality that it by no means deserves. Reading the first half of the paper is like reading a pioneer in an emerging field of philosophy or science; reading the second half of the paper is like reading a dusty old tome filled with meaningless numbers and graphs on eugenics or phrenology or some other pseudoscience.

Keynes, of course, was scathing in his criticism of econometric modelling; a field which first emerged in the late 1930s as his theories were gaining traction. He likened it to 'those puzzles for children where you write down your age, multiply, add this and that, subtract something else, and eventually end up with the number of the Beast in Revelation' (Keynes 1939, p. 562). Godley's projections, which spoil his otherwise timeless and brilliant paper, cannot but strike one as being something like the number of the Beast in Revelation. He has indeed added this and that, subtracted something else and come up with a number that is by no means from this world of ours. Estimating models, whether to test the models themselves or make predictions about the future, is an awful and embarrassing game, and it is high time that economists gave it up. It is also a desperate waste of time. There is so much real policy work to be done; so many real issues to be examined and studied; but with the current impetus to do macroeconometric modelling, many economists are literally contractually obliged to engage in make-work. The most unfortunate and cynical thing is that many of those who are seasoned from working in this particular field know just how bogus it is.

Does this mean that all econometrics should be scrapped? Not really. Keynes' pointed criticisms of the field have been roughly felt by the discipline but those that read the paper often miss a comment at the end. Keynes writes:

> This does not mean that economic material may not supply more elementary cases where the method will be fruitful. Take, for instance, Prof. Tinbergen's third example—namely, the influence on net investment in railway rolling-stock of the rate of increase in traffic, the rate of profit earned by the railways, the price of pig iron and the rate of interest. Here there seems a reasonable *prima facie* case for expecting that some of the necessary conditions are satisfied. (Ibid., pp. 567–568)

Keynes had spent an awful lot of his life putting together statistics. He had done a lot of what would today be considered the 'dirty work' of economics.[17] He had also written a great deal on the philosophy and methodology of statistics (Keynes 1921). He knew that there were some relationships within economic statistics that met the criteria required to use them in an econometric study. But these were extremely limited. In order to fit the bill, there had to be an immediate relationship known basically before the fact. Keynes laid this out explicitly in response to a letter from a statistician called Szeliski who worked on the problem of demand for automobiles.

> You have chosen just the sort of problem where multiple correlation methods may be useful. You are dealing with details of a specific problem where the main causes are pretty well known *a priori*, and where the statistics are definite and precise. The method is always full of danger, but, in my opinion, it is the kind of problem to which you have applied it rather than in those to which Tinbergen has applied it that the method is properly in place. (Cited in Garrone and Marchionatti 2004)

'What then', the reader will ask, 'is the point of running regressions? If we already know that a very immediate relationship exists, then why use econometrics?' The answer is: because econometrics should be used less to establish causality and more so to present statistics supporting a causal argument in a clear and concise manner. Thus, econometrics is less a manner of doing empirical work and more so a means of clearly presenting statistical relationships that are basically known in advance.

Take a very simple example. We know for a fact that, at the time of writing, Scotland is heavily reliant on oil exports. We know this because, among other reasons, the oil revenues are included in the Scottish national accounts and make up part of the overall trade statistics (Pilkington 2014c). We can then use regression techniques to estimate how reliant Scottish oil and gas exports are in the price of oil. The results can be seen in Fig. 10.2.[18]

Note that the regression here is not being used to verify or falsify a truth-claim that I am making. Rather, it is used as a means to *present statistical data*. 'We know', I say, 'that Scotland is heavily reliant on oil revenues for its trade surpluses. Now here is a number showing in a neat way just how dependent it is on the price changes in oil.' Nor are we making a prediction using the regression techniques. Rather than making concrete numerical predictions, we might say: 'Now that we are aware of how dependent the country's trade is on changes in the price of oil we can discuss the dangers that there might be if the price of oil were to decline in the future.' Again note that we are not making forecasts as to what such

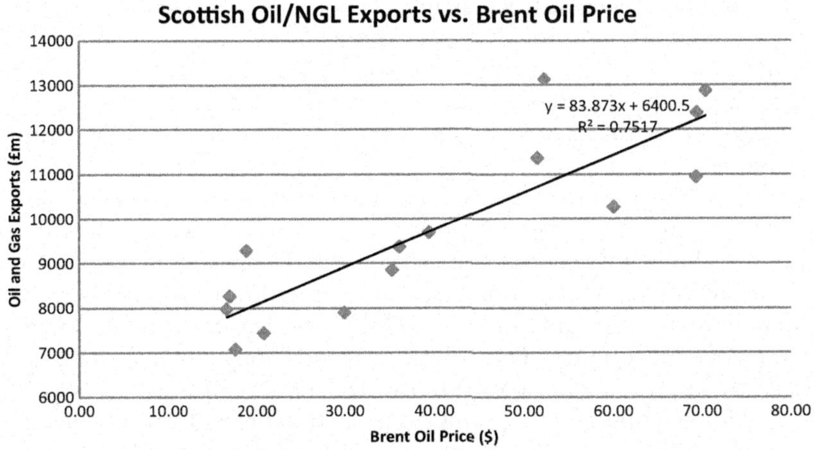

Fig. 10.2 Utilising regressions robustly

a future price decline may be. Nor are we making forecasts about what a given price decline will have on the trade balance (while not completely outlandish, we are already moving into murky territory here). Rather, we are just presenting the statistics and warning the Scottish that they had better keep a close eye on how they are structuring their economy because a shock to the price of oil might lead to a serious deterioration of their trade balance. This is the direction in which the usage of econometric techniques should be moving. Right now, driven by a silly need to give off an air of false precision, the profession is engaged in nothing but what Keynes referred to as 'black magic' and 'statistical alchemy'. And it is far better to be roughly right than precisely talking nonsense.

Building Robust Institutions

Up until now, we have really only been referring to how to deal with uncertainty in doing economic work. But surely if economic work is to do anything, it is to build institutions that help the economy to function better. This is an absolutely key point that many economists do not seem to grasp: as we have laid out earlier in this chapter, *uncertainty may exist, and we may have to live with it, but we can nevertheless take precautions to control it.* Robust economic institutions do precisely this; they help to steer the economy away from disaster in the face of uncertainty. Central banks, for example, perform many functions, including deposit insurance. Not only does this insurance assure people who hold deposits in a bank that their wealth will not disappear due to some unfortunate economic event but it also ensures that these same depositors do not engage in bank runs, should they think that their deposits may be threatened. Such is one of many protections against uncertainty that good economic institutions provide.

This is where much mainstream economics goes completely off the deep end and often becomes a defence of absolute insanity. Because the currently dominant economic theory tends to favour explanatory methods that assume away uncertainty, economists often try to push governments and policymakers to undertake actions the objective consequence of which is to *increase* uncertainty. The irony here is enormous. The economists construct themselves a fantasy world in which they abolish uncertainty. They do this for any number of reasons: to make themselves feel empowered, to make their thought experiments work and so on. But then, this misleading fantasy construction allows them to assume that uncertainty does not exist *in the real world*. Thus, they go into the real world and start peddling policy advice that they think will make the economy work better but will actually just create chaos as the amount of uncertainty in the world increases.

We can give all sorts of examples of this. From the call of the economists for flexible wages and prices to the insistence that financial markets are best left self-regulated (whatever that means).[19] But let us stick with our very simple and clear example above, namely, deposit insurance. After the economic meltdown of 2008, a lot of economists claimed that one of the key problems was 'moral hazard'. What they meant by this was that, because the central banks were standing behind certain financial institutions backing them if they failed, this incentivised these same institutions to engage in reckless activity. Many of the more muddle-headed economists came to see deposit insurance itself as the problem. To be fair, most of the profession did not buy into this awful argument. But if you understand the essence of economic theory and how it banishes uncertainty, it is not hard to see that people who spend too much time in classrooms and in front of blackboards might arrive at this conclusion. In reality, the problem is not with deposit insurance at all. Rather, the problem is with the fact that financial markets have been substantially deregulated. Deposit insurance mitigates uncertainty and helps prevent banking crises. But deregulation increases uncertainty and promotes banking and financial crises.

Even some more level-headed commentators fell into the trap of seeing deposit insurance as some sort of 'double-edged sword'. An IMF report shortly before the financial crisis stated:

> Deposit insurance is a tightrope act. On the one hand, explicit deposit insurance can significantly reduce the incidence of bank runs or even stop runs altogether in countries with strong institutions and proper safeguards. On the other hand, when not done carefully, explicit deposit insurance can fuel bank crises by giving banks perverse incentives to take unnecessary risks. (McCoy 2007, p. 1)

This is absolutely the wrong way to look at deposit insurance. It is not a 'tightrope act'. It is an institution that decreases uncertainty and helps mitigate financial and economic catastrophe. If banks are undertaking unnecessary risks, this probably has little to do with deposit insurance—indeed, unnecessary risk-taking and financial crises existed long before deposit insurance was ever dreamed up—rather the undertaking of unnecessary risk-taking is due to the fact that the markets themselves are structured and regulated in such a way that promotes uncertainty. In an environment of uncertainty, people become completely blinded to anything that they cannot immediately see. Confronted with the bottomless pit that is the far-off future, they engage in highly destructive activities for short-term gain that can ultimately bring an economy to its knees.

Again, we give the example of deposit insurance because it is such an extreme one in which economists will actually make arguments the logical result of which would increase uncertainty in the economy. But many arguments that economists deploy in favour of so-called flexible markets would only result in heightened uncertainty and economic catastrophe, were they ever taken seriously. The vast majority of economists, for example, believe that flexible wages and prices would be good for the economy. In fact, as Keynes noted so long ago, they would likely produce chaos in developed, mature economies where large firms need to make projections of future prices if they are to engage in the planning necessary for large-scale corporate investment. Flexible prices may work well in a village market where everything is immediately visible to both the buyer and the seller. But in a world in which economic processes remain in the dark to most actors, flexible prices and wages would be an absolute nightmare to live with. This is precisely why large corporations generally fix their prices and workers' organisers tend to fix their wages.

Good economists should work to build institutions that protect against uncertainty as best is practically possible. This was something that Hyman Minsky came to write about more and more towards the end of his life, and he took this in quite brilliant and revolutionary directions, such as suggesting the idea that people should be insulated from the uncertainty of being unemployed by being guaranteed a job. Of course, government guarantees can indeed foster abuses, and this point is not to be avoided. But the best economic policies are those that get the balance right between preventing abuse while at the same time minimising the level of uncertainty in the economy. Because it is uncertainty that is the major culprit that destabilises economies, and if uncertainty can be held in check, economic stabilisation can and probably will follow. Can we say this with absolute, 100 % confidence? Of course not! That is, after all, the nature of uncertainty. But we can be fairly certain that this is true, just as we are fairly certain of many of the best things in life.

Appendix: Questions for a Bayesian

If you move in economics circles, you are likely to come across or have come across someone calling themselves a 'Bayesian'. They will likely have told you that they recognise the existence of uncertainty and that they do not believe in objective probability measures of future events. But they will also tell you that you can nevertheless use probability theory to forecast the future. They will, in essence, recognise the existence of the devil but nevertheless promise you a simple path to salvation. But in truth, what they are saying is empty with regard to the content of economics, and what they are really trying to sell is old wine in new bottles. Let us here first examine Bayes' theorem; then we will put forward some questions that you, dear reader, can put to your Bayesian friends. The present writer has done so many times and has never gotten a solid answer.

Bayesians deny that probability is objective. What does that mean? In the frequentist interpretation of probability—which is (supposedly) the arch nemesis of the Bayesian interpretation—probabilities are supposed to be objective. Often statistical theorists point to Aristotle's definition in order to think about what this means; Aristotle wrote that 'the probable is that which for the most part happens' and that is a fairly good approximation of the frequentist approach. Thus 'objective' means to these people 'things that happen'.[20]

What about the Bayesian interpretation? Well, the Bayesian interpretation of probability is what its practitioners call the 'subjective interpretation'. It basically means that probabilities are degrees of belief that we, the statistical theorists, hold about the world. While this does not appear to me to be 'subjective' in any philosophically important way, we can quite clearly see the difference between the two approaches. In all honesty, the Bayesian interpretation is probably better grounded in any meaningful philosophical or epistemological framework. Imagine you get a DNA test to find out if your father is indeed your father. When the probability is handed back to you showing whether you were lied to all those years, the Bayesians would inject some doubt into the situation by saying that this probability only represented a degree of belief on your part and was not in any true sense 'objective' in their terms.

The Bayesians start with Bayes' theorem—which is also used by non-Bayesians but which acquires a new degree of meaning with the Bayesians. Bayes' theorem is a method of calculating probabilities for any given event or situation. In its own terms, it is both useful and inoffensive. Perhaps an example will suffice.

Imagine that there is a curtain behind which you are told is a person. You have to guess whether this is a man or a woman. You are told that there is a 50 % chance that it is a man and that this represents the fact that 50 % of people in the country are men. Now, assume that you are told that the person is over 5' and 9" and that 75 % of men are over 5' and 9" (175 cm) while only 15 % of women are. So, we are trying to calculate what the probability is that this is a man given that we know the person is over 5' and 9" (175 cm) tall. Or:

$$P(Man|\, 175\ cm)$$

Bayes' theorem tells us that this should be done as such:

$$P(Man|175cm) = \frac{P(175cm|Man).P(Man)}{P(175cm)}$$

We can further expand the theorem so that we can calculate it with our current known information. So:

$$P(Man|Tall) = \frac{P(175cm|Man).P(Man)}{P(175cm|Man).P(Man) + P(175cm|Woman).P(Woman)}$$

Now we can plug all our available information in, and we get our answer. So:

$$P(Man|175cm) = \frac{(0.75).(0.50)}{(0.75).(0.50) + (0.15).(0.50)} = 0.83$$

And now, we know that, given the information we currently possess, there is an 83 % chance that the person behind the curtain, standing at over 5' 9" (175 cm) tall, is a man.

It seems to me that what characterises people that refer to themselves as 'Bayesians' is that they basically believe that the above theorem—or some modified version thereof—basically has the answers to all life's questions. In more advanced models, they typically make some further modifications in that they add in some random variables for unknown quantities. Then they put in what they call their 'priors', that is, already held knowledge about the probabilities of certain events. Then the Bayesians begin to calculate and recalculate the probabilities. They then add in more data when it becomes available and use the previous calculations as priors. In this way, they can continually update the model. This, they think, tells them the most rational probability to believe at any moment in time for whatever is being modelled.

The first question when looking at this technique is: what is actually being modelled? Are we dealing with something that is amenable to probabilistic calculation or are we not? Most of things we deal with in our day-to-day lives are not amenable to such calculations. There are simply too many variables. This is why, for example, financial markets still hire analysts and do not simply set up a load of computers crunching out Bayes theorems. Yes, these analysts may use Bayes' theorem—they may even think themselves to have drank from that Well of Truth known as Bayesianism—but there is nevertheless a human element that cannot really be avoided in these matters. Again, this is because human beings have a remarkable capacity to sort out the data of what we have called 'historical time' in a manner that computers and formulae simply cannot.

The reader should try an experiment on themselves in this regard. They should try to actually form numerical probabilities about all the things they encounter on a day-to-day basis and then try to conceive of how they could possibly plug these into a formula. What they will quickly find is that the number of possible events that might occur in the future will become only limited by the imagination of the person thinking of these possible events. So, if we ask ourselves if we would like to go for a walk in the park today, we must then calculate the probabilities of all the possible events that might occur, should we decide to go for the walk. But these possible events are only limited by our imagination, and any probabilities that we do apply to them will be entirely arbitrary. While it is conceivable that we could go to the same park every day and observe what goes on there and then, after a huge amount of effort, calculate relatively accurate probabilities one day, this is still potentially as limitless as the aspects that we choose to focus on, which are ultimately limited by our imaginations and the time we allot to conceive of them.

Consider this carefully. Imagine that you went to the park every day and spent hours making observations of the frequency of various events. What events would you focus on? Perhaps, the first would be the probability that you will encounter men or women. The next might be the various cultural backgrounds that the people you encounter come from. But where does this end? At the colour socks that people wear? At the average pitch of peoples' voices? At the average speed at which they walk? The multitude becomes potentially limitless—or, at least, limited by our imaginations and our time on this earth—and undertaking such activity every day would probably not be an indicator of sound mental health. What our minds do is focus out most of this irrelevant detail automatically; so that, when we are not in a state of distress, we only notice a few stylised facts—usually very broad ones about the type of people around us, whether we identify with them or feel alienated from them and so forth.

Bayesianism only really works in a closed system that has constant regularities. But although history may, on occasion, rhyme, it does not repeat itself. Historical events—from the largest to the smallest—are unique. Human decision-making is free and unfolds in a novel way. In such a system, Bayesianism will only produce dross. At best, it will be backwards-looking to the extent that it will never produce novel predictions about the future. The moment the automobile becomes relatively widespread, the Bayesian will still be looking backwards and saying that the horse and cart are still the dominant modes of transport. At worst, it will try to specify models of historical and economic phenomena that are so complex that no one who spends their time fiddling with such models would have the capacity to even begin to think through what is going on as the present whizzes by his/her ears pushing him/her into the future.

This backwards-looking tendency also probably explains a rather interesting phenomenon among the contemporary economics profession. After the crisis of 2008, a whole host of models came out explaining what had happened after the fact. A test of being a good modeller became to show that you had adequately digested that rather a hard-to-swallow event. This became a sort of game in its own right. It was also a way for the mainstream of the profession to regain their collective self-esteem. During and immediately after the crisis, the profession had largely hidden away. There was, for a time, a collective sense of guilt. But then as the models that 'explained' the crisis (in various ways, all of them wrong) began to pour into the journals, the profession regained their posture. They had narrativised the crisis to themselves, and so they could once again pontificate on the present. The techniques were the same; the blind spots remained—the really deep blind spots, not the shallow pseudo-blind spots—but none of this mattered much. It then became clear to some non-mainstream economists what all this modelling business was about: it was a giant story that the profession told to themselves about their past. It was a sort of mythic narrative structure which they used to capture past events, pin them down and ensure that they were adequately narrativised.

When they had no story, they felt themselves floating in a vast ocean of uncertainty in a boat without a paddle. But when they had their own personal story—whatever it might be—they felt in control once again. Rather than stopping for a moment to truly contemplate how vast and powerful the ocean they were floating in was, they instead closed their eyes and once again told themselves that they were in control. The new models became the theoretical equivalent of slipping self-help tapes under one's pillow. 'You are in control; you do know what is going on; you have a grasp on this situation', they said to themselves in warm tones. In this new environment, Bayesianism became extraordinarily trendy in economics. The grasping nature of the methodological approach undoubtedly reflected the process of coming to terms with the past that many in the profession felt. If the marketers had run focus groups allowing economists to convey their feelings about Bayesian theory in these years, I have no doubt that these are the associations they would have found.

This led to more and more models that included Bayesian agents. To those who had long suspected that the agents economists included in their models were actually little egos—little representations of how the economists thought about themselves—this was nothing short of hilarious. The perfectly rational agent who could see everything coming before it happened—the economists' self-perception in an era of relative tranquillity—became a little groping Bayesian agent—the economists' self-perception in an era of reconstruction after a rather unexpected storm. The question that now needs to be asked is: how do these economists justify modelling all the agents in the economy as Bayesians?

A little self-reflection will show that you, dear reader, likely do not make all your day-to-day decisions based on updating a Bayes theorem of some form. (If you do indeed do this, I would warmly suggest consulting a mental health professional.) Even if we are experts on probability theory, it is very unlikely that we will do this. And if we do indeed do this, it is very likely that the outcomes will not be rational. So, if we ourselves do not do this, then why do we assume that everyone in the economy is doing this all the time?

What is more, it is very likely that only a fraction of a percentage of the population is familiar enough with the mathematics of Bayesianism to even try to undertake such a Herculean (clownish?) undertaking. Do we not need to assume that everyone within the economy must be aware of the Bayesian framework and familiar with its application in order to further assume that they are indeed applying this framework in their day-to-day decisions? And is this not rather easy to test? Ask the people around you the two following questions:

1. Are you familiar with Bayesian subjective probability theory?
2. Do you use this theory to make most of your day-to-day decisions, especially those in relation to your economics decisions?

After alienating most of your friends and family, and perhaps a few strangers at the bus stop, you will probably find rather quickly that people do not make decisions in this way. This should clear the matter up nicely. If you have a Bayesian friend who prefers mysticism to empiricism and claims that people may act in line with Bayesian probability without knowing the theory, point out that the burden of proof is on them for such an assumptive statement. If we are to take this highly mystical conception seriously, we must have extremely strong evidence showing its validity. Unfortunately, the evidence we do have—which won a Nobel Prize in economics and so is presumably accepted in mainstream economics—is that even when people are faced with situations in which they can form concrete probability estimates they do not act in line with these in what economists consider a 'rational, utility-maximising' manner (Kahneman and Tversky 1974).[21] One can only imagine what we would find if we examined human decision-making in circumstances when they cannot make concrete probability estimates. Of course in such a situation, we would ourselves have to construct the model to study this and in doing so would introduce an element of tautology into the game. Again, all the problems that we have raised above would quickly bubble to the surface, and we would be back to where we started.

If the reader is still concerned as to the validity of making such deductions based on evidence, it might be worth noting that a 2012 ruling in a British court of law seems to have ruled out the Bayesian method as one that is applicable in legal cases. The judge made his statement as follows:

> Sometimes the 'balance of probability' standard is expressed mathematically as '50+ % probability', but this can carry with it a danger of pseudo-mathematics, as the argument in this case demonstrated. When judging whether a case for believing that an event was caused in a particular way is stronger that the case for not so believing, the process is not scientific (although it may obviously include evaluation of scientific evidence) and to

> express the probability of some event having happened in percentage terms is illusory. (Lord Justice Toulston 2013)

The concept of probability discussed is properly Bayesian in that it is the idea that you can assign probabilities to an event that has already occurred. The judge in the case was perfectly correct in saying that this was illusory. If the courts were to take a Bayesian view, we would quickly enter a totalitarian nightmare world in which, if a statistician found that there was a 51 % chance that you had committed a murder, then you would be found guilty of the murder. It might only be one-step from here to courts that made decisions based on the supposed future probabilities of a person committing a crime. Under such a system if you fell into a group with a high probability of committing a crime, you might be prosecuted even though you are perfectly innocent of any crime. Instead, a non-totalitarian court system must find proof beyond a reasonable doubt to make a conviction. While this is somewhat vague, it is nevertheless quite functional and is a far more preferable manner of decision-making in courtrooms than some sort of probabilistic or Bayesian alternative. Of course, the decisions both economic agents make and economists themselves deal with are very similar to those made in a courtroom as the material being dealt with is very similar in all of these cases. The material that we deal with in the economic and social world is far, far more similar to the material dealt with in a courtroom than it is to the material dealt with in the hard sciences where probabilistic estimates are far less misleading due to their dealing with closed systems that we can subject to repeated experiment.

One might go so far as to say that systems of justice in a non-totalitarian society rely on the underlying idea that people have freedom of choice. The actions of people are not, as the marginalist economists think and the Bayesians presuppose, determined by some prior probability distribution or some pre-determined laws. In this case, it is questionable whether people could even be held responsible for their actions. After all, if their actions are pre-determined, then how can we lay blame upon them? In a non-totalitarian society, we must assume freedom of the will and freedom of choice. Those economists and social scientists who argue to the contrary are not only likely to get things wrong over and over again but they are also the unwitting propagandists for an inherently totalitarian ideology that could cause great damage were it ever allowed to seep into key social and political institutions.

The lasting impact of Bayesianism will be a vague belief among bad economists that the future can be predicted using backward-looking but responsive and updated probability theorems. This will produce a culture of economists building clanking, clumsy models and banging them against the data trying to convince themselves that they will eventually get a model that will tell them everything they need to know about the future. Meanwhile, working economists and people serious about the discipline will have to tarry with the newly created, the ever-generating novelty of history and the wind of the future blowing in their hair. And frankly, from this writer's perspective, that does not really sound like a bad thing at all.

Notes

1. Perpetual ruminating on uncertainty might thus be said to be part of certain neurotic disorders, particularly, anxiety disorders. We might also raise the sociological point that in a world where economic uncertainty becomes greater due to the breakdown of functioning economic institutions—that is, in a world where job security is diminished and access to sufficient income is more uncertain—we will likely find a greater outbreak of certain neurotic mental disorders. This might go a long way to explaining, for example, why suicide rates are well known to fluctuate with the business cycle; rising in recessions and falling during booms (Crosby et al. 2011).
2. This question was also taken up by Keynes in his philosophical-cum-mathematical *A Treatise on Probability*. See Keynes 1921, pp. 217–232; and Pilkington 2013f.
3. It should be noted that, while we can use the terms 'Keynesian uncertainty' and 'Knightian uncertainty' interchangeably for most purposes, there is a subtle philosophical difference between the two (Davidson 1996). Keynesian uncertainty deals with what we might call 'ontological uncertainty'. This is uncertainty that lies at the heart of how we actually experience the world around us. It is, as it were, built into our cognitive make-up and can never be overcome. Meanwhile, Knightian uncertainty deals with what we might call 'epistemological uncertainty'. This is uncertainty that we experience because our current state of knowledge does not permit us to gain access to the data needed to overcome it. While there is a gulf of philosophical difference between the two ideas, when we

discuss economic issues it really does not matter which we are referring to as they have identical effects. But readers will see a distinct difference of approach to this question in, for example, the popular work of Nassim Nicholas Taleb (2010) who deals with Knightian uncertainty versus the work of the Post-Keynesians who generally deal with Keynesian uncertainty (Dequech 2004). The present writer finds the latter to be a more promising philosophical account of the problem.

4. We will deal with the economic consequences of this event later in the chapter.
5. The reader might note an immediate overlap between this idea and the construction used by some economists known as 'long-run equilibrium'. The idea of a 'long-run equilibrium' is a strongly teleological conception.
6. Some economists refer to these models as 'comparative statics' models.
7. It should also be noted that different people approaching ISLM models with different interpretations of the world around them will come up with different results. For example, you may think that the LM-curve is currently flat, and I might think it vertical. You will say that fiscal policy will raise output without any price effects, and I will say that fiscal policy will raise prices without any output effect. The model is completely and totally subordinate to how we calibrate it. In this regard, it is unclear that the model actually says anything about the world at all. With this in mind, it is particularly amusing to watch certain economists tell us, with the perfect self-assuredness, that the rest of the profession is getting policy advice 'wrong' because they do not understand certain models. For example, Paul Krugman writes:

> That's why in early 2009, when the [Wall Street Journal], the Austrians, and the other usual suspects were screaming about soaring rates and runaway inflation, those who understood IS-LM were predicting that interest rates would stay low and that even a tripling of the monetary base would not be inflationary. (Krugman 2011)

Actually, I might 'understand' the ISLM perfectly well and come to the opposite conclusion by simply assuming that the parameters are different from the parameters that Krugman is assuming. Much of the profession seems to have a similarly difficult time understanding what models say and what they do not say. Malleable models like the ISLM (or the AS-AD) say absolutely nothing at all. Rather, they are made to speak by the person using them. The profession will only recognise this when they reflect deeply on what models actually say and do.

8. Other noteworthy dynamic models are the Cambridge growth model (Pasinetti 1974), the Kalecki model (Kalecki 1965) and John Hicks' business-cycle model (Hicks 1961).
9. Although for the sake of a simple thought experiment, we conceded to turn our model into a dynamic model proper by creating an investment function that was determined by profits, animal spirits and a liquidity preference theory of the interest rate. Of course, implicit in this formulation was the fact that most of these variables could never truly be known with any precision precisely because they are highly dependent on all those factors which make up what we have called 'the news'.
10. Keynes then adds, rather caustically:

> Any other way of applying our formal principles of thought (without which, however, we shall be lost in the wood) will lead us into error. It is a great fault of symbolic pseudo-mathematical methods of formalising a system of economic analysis, such as we shall set down in section vi of this chapter, that they expressly assume strict independence between the factors involved and lose all their cogency and authority if this hypothesis is disallowed; whereas, in ordinary discourse, where we are not blindly manipulating but know all the time what we are doing and what the words mean, we can keep "at the back of our heads" the necessary reserves and qualifications and the adjustments which we shall have to make later on, in a way in which we cannot keep complicated partial differentials "at the back" of several pages of algebra which assume that they all vanish. Too large a proportion of recent "mathematical" economics are mere concoctions, as imprecise as the initial assumptions they rest on, which allow the author to lose sight of the complexities and interdependencies of the real world in a maze of pretentious and unhelpful symbols. (Ibid.)

11. They also colloquially became known by Cambridge economists of the day as the 'mad monetarists' because of their uncompromising usage of empirically dubious economic policy. In the USA, a simi-

lar movement was credited with being 'voodoo economists' which perhaps reflected then President Reagan's tendency to also take policy advice from astrologers and soothsayers (Roberts 1988).

12. Godley made other very salient predictions too. For example, in a 1992 article in the *London Review of Books* entitled 'Maastricht and All That', he rightly predicted the problems that would eventually arise out of the design flaws in what would become the Eurozone currency union (Godley 1992).
13. He does lapse into this in the second half of the paper, and we shall critically examine this below when we discuss econometrics.
14. We have assumed knowledge of national accounts definitions here. If the reader is not familiar with them, there is extensive material available on this approach on the internet. A quick Google of 'sectoral balances' will turn up a whole host of relevant material.
15. It is worth pausing to reflect on this for a moment. The Iraq war and the ensuing budget deficits of that era were largely a response to the attacks on New York by Al-Qaeda on 11 September 2001. This was by far the most unpredictable event of the decade. Yet it had an enormous and lasting economic impact. This is an extremely nice example for the purposes of highlighting the nature of uncertainty because it paints a picture of just how fruitless it is to make very concrete long-term predictions about the future. It is so much better to focus on unsustainable processes plain and simple and leave the crystal-ball gazing to the mystics.
16. We can see that these forecasts were at least comparable to the real data because Godley's estimates of a 2.9 % government deficit and a 2.8 % trade deficit roughly cancel out, while the real data shows government and trade deficits that also basically cancel out. Godley's model, however, puts the unemployment rate extremely high at 9.6 % when in reality it peaked at the not so high number of around 6 %.
17. It should be noted that the present author by no means considers statistical collection to be dirty work. If the profession could reform itself to prestige large-scale data collection over misguided macroeconometric modelling, it would go a very long way towards fixing itself. The success of the French economist Thomas Piketty's book, *Capital in the Twenty-First Century*, at the time of writing seems to be a positive departure in this direction (Piketty 2014). Piketty

himself has said in an interview published at the time of writing, rather scathingly but quite correctly:

> I was only too aware of the fact that I knew nothing about the world's economic problems. To put it bluntly, the discipline of economics has to get over its childish passion for mathematics and for purely theoretical and often highly ideological speculation, at the expense of historical research and collaboration with the other social sciences. (Piketty in Cassidy 2014)

18. Brent oil price ($) is sourced from the Federal Reserve of St. Louis together with £/$ exchange-rate data to adjust the oil price. Scottish oil export data is sourced from the Scottish National Accounts Project (SNAP).
19. In fact, a good test to see if an economic policy pundit is talking nonsense is to stop and ask yourself whether his or her policy advice would tend to increase or decrease uncertainty. If it turns out to be the former, you are dealing with a zombie economist, and you would be best to steer clear, if it turns out to be the latter they might be worth listening to and engaging with.
20. When you descend into the jungle of statistics jargon, you are often encountered with monsters of various kinds. These scary creatures are mathematicians, statistical theorists and economists who are averse to philosophical argument but who nevertheless cloak half-baked philosophical arguments in statistics jargon. This is why the term 'objective' in statistics-speak is far cruder than the same term in philosophical-speak.
21. The reader who has actually confronted someone who holds fast to Bayesianism applied in this manner despite substantial evidence to the contrary might be interested in how one of these thinkers explained to themselves the persistence of belief in an obviously failed theory as such:

> I can explain it only by a weakness of the scholarly mind that I have often observed in myself. I call it theory-induced blindness: once you have accepted a theory and used it as a tool in your thinking, it is extraordinarily difficult to notice its flaws... You give the theory the benefit of the doubt, trusting the community of experts who have accepted it. (Kahneman 2011, pp. 276–277)

There is a great deal of truth in what Kahneman is saying here. He forgets to mention one key aspect though: certain types of theory attract certain types of people. Economic modelling that uses deterministic models of human beings, be they stochastic or otherwise, attracts people of a deterministic mind-set.
When both of these aspects are considered, it becomes obvious that you really cannot convince people who adhere to these theories that they might be wrong. So, the goal becomes rather to allow a space within economics for those that think they might be and see who, in the aggregate, produces more functionally useful work.

References

Cassidy, J. (2014, May 13). Rebellious economic students may have a point. *Rational Irrationality Blog*. New Yorker. http://www.newyorker.com/online/blogs/johncassidy/2014/05/rebellious-economics-students-have-a-point.html

Crosby, A., Florence, C., Luo, F., Ouyang, L., & Quispe-Agnoli, M. (2011). Impact of business cycles on US suicide rates, 1928–2007. *American Journal of Public Health, 101*(6), 1139–1146.

Davidson, P. (1996). Reality and economic theory. *Journal of Post Keynesian Economics, 18*(4), 479–508.

Dequech, D. (2004). Uncertainty: Individuals, institutions and technology. *Cambridge Journal of Economics, 28*, 365–378.

Garrone, G., & Marchionatti, R. (2004). Keynes on econometric method: A reassessment of his debate with tinbergen and other econometricians, 1938–1943. *Department of Economics "S. Cognetti de Martiis" Working Paper Series.* Working Paper No. 01/2004. http://www.cesmep.unito.it/WP/2004/1_WP_Cesmep.pdf

Godley, W. (1992). Maastricht and all that. *London Review of Books, 14*(19). http://www.lrb.co.uk/v14/n19/wynne-godley/maastricht-and-all-that

Godley, W. (1999). Seven unsustainable processes. *Levy Institute of Bard College*. Special Report. http://www.levyinstitute.org/pubs/sr/sevenproc.pdf

Godley, W., & Lavoie, M. (2006). *Monetary economics: An integrated approach to credit, money, income, production and wealth*. UK: Palgrave Macmillan.

Hicks, J. (1961). *A contribution to the theory of the trade cycle*. UK: Clarendon Press.

Hume, D. (1739). *A treatise on human nature: Being an attempt to introduce the experimental method of reasoning into moral subjects*. UK: Penguin Classics.

Kahneman, D. (2011). *Thinking fast and slow*. USA: Farrar, Strauss & Giroux.

Kahneman, D., & Tversky, A. (1974). Judgment under uncertainty: Heuristics and biases. *Science, 185*(4157), 1124–1131.

Kaldor, N. (1982). *The scourge of monetarism.* UK: Oxford University Press.

Kaldor, N. (1983). *The economic consequences of Mrs. Thatcher.* UK: Duckworth.

Kalecki, M. (1965). *Theory of economic dynamics: An essay on cyclical and long-run changes in capitalist economy.* USA: Monthly Review Press.

Keynes, J. M. (1921). *A treatise on probability.* USA: BN Publishing.

Keynes, J. M. (1924). Alfred Marshall 1842–1924. *The Economic Journal, 34*(135), 311–372.

Keynes, J. M. (1936a). *The general theory of employment, money and interest.* http://www.marxists.org/reference/subject/economics/keynes/general-theory/

Keynes, J. M. (1936b). *Preface to the German edition of the general theory of employment, money and interest.* http://gutenberg.net.au/ebooks03/0300071h/printall.html

Keynes, J. M. (1939). Professor Tinbergen's method. *The Economic Journal, 49*(195), 558–577.

Krugman, P. (2011, October 9). IS-LMentary. *The conscience of a liberal.* http://krugman.blogs.nytimes.com/2011/10/09/is-lmentary/

Maloney, J. (2012). The treasury and the new cambridge school in the 1970s. *Cambridge Journal of Economics, 36*, 995–1017.

Marx, K. (1852). *The eighteenth Brumaire of Louis Bonaparte.* http://www.marxists.org/archive/marx/works/1852/18th-brumaire/ch01.htm

McCoy, P. A. (2007). The moral hazard implications of deposit insurance: Theory and evidence. In *Seminar on current developments in monetary and financial law.* https://www.imf.org/external/np/seminars/eng/2006/mfl/pam.pdf

Lord Justice Toulston. (2013). Nulty & ors versus milton keynes burrough council. http://www.bailii.org/ew/cases/EWCA/Civ/2013/15.html

Pasinetti, L. (1974). *Growth and income distribution—Essays in economic theory.* UK: Cambridge University Press.

Piketty, T. (2014). *Capital in the 21st century.* USA: Harvard University Press.

Pilkington, P. (2013f, September 16). Keynes' philosophy: Induction, analogy and probability. *Fixing the Economists.* http://fixingtheeconomists.wordpress.com/2013/09/16/keynes-philosophy-induction-analogy-and-probability/

Pilkington, P. (2014c). A sustainable monetary framework for an independent scotland. *Levy Institute at Bard College.* Public Policy Brief No. 134. http://www.levyinstitute.org/publications/a-sustainable-monetary-framework-for-an-independent-scotland

Roberts, S. (1988, May 4). White house confirms reagans follow astrology, up to a point. *New York Times.* http://www.nytimes.com/1988/05/04/us/white-house-confirms-reagans-follow-astrology-up-to-a-point.html

Royal Economic Society. (2010). *RES Newsletter, July 2010*. No. 150. http://www.res.org.uk/SpringboardWebApp/userfiles/res/file/obituaries/godley.pdf

Shackle, G. L. S. (1965). *A scheme of economic theory*. UK: Cambridge University Press.

Shackle, G. L. S. (1966). *The nature of economic thought*. UK: Cambridge University Press.

Taleb, N. N. (2010). *The black swan: The impact of the highly improbable* (2nd ed.). US: Random House.

CHAPTER 11

Non-Dogmatic Approaches to the Economics of Trade

Only fools are certain and immovable.

—*Michel de Montaigne*

Never put all your eggs in a single basket. That is pretty good advice, no? But why do we counsel people not to walk around with a single basket full of all their precious eggs? Well, probably because if they drop the basket, an awful lot of their eggs will break. The key here is the element of uncertainty. We cannot be sure that we will not drop the basket and therefore we take measures to insulate ourselves against this potentiality: in this case, we keep our eggs in a variety of different locations. Investment professionals, in their more sober moments, get paid lots of money to tell you something similar. They say that you should diversify your investment portfolio. What they mean by that is that you should allocate your savings to a variety of different investment vehicles. That way, if one or two of these investments take a turn for the worst all will not be lost. The golden rule of safe investing is: never put your nest egg in a single investment basket.

Now imagine for a moment that you were sitting in the waiting room outside the office of your investment adviser. Their secretary has told you that they will see you in 20 minutes. As you sit and wait, you are accosted by an odd-looking man in a suit. Before he opens his mouth, you know that there is something funny about him; his eyes bulge ever so slightly; his hair is dishevelled; and you are not 100 % sure that he has showered

W.P. Pilkington, *The Reformation in Economics*,
DOI 10.1007/978-3-319-40757-9_11

in the last 24 hours. He begins to tell you that your investment adviser has been fooling you all this time. He has, the man insists, been selling you lies as truth and dismissing truth as lies. All this diversification nonsense, the strange man tells you, is only a means to keep you playing with the herd when really you could be playing with the champions. You are intrigued. Not so much because you believe what this man is saying but rather because you want to find out what his idea is. So you continue to hear him out.

He tells you that he has found a single investment or a few specific investments that will bring you far more prosperity than diversification. You ask him how he knows this. He removes a tissue from his pocket and begins sketching out a diagram on the back with a pencil he removes from behind his ear. His argument is simple and logically consistent on its own terms but you instinctively know that it is nonsense. The real world is a far more complex place than his little logical games lead him to believe. You remember hearing that a famous psychiatrist once said that the most intransigent and worrying delusions are the ones that are most internally consistent. As you politely dismiss him, he gets angry and starts ranting about how you are a fool who cannot grasp the truth of the matter. He tells you that you will always be a mediocrity and that you will never aspire to greatness. You wryly ask him whether he has yet made his fortune using his little logical construction to which he responds that he has not. 'One day', he says, 'I will prove all of you wrong. I will show you all that what I am saying is true and you will regret not listening to me!' After that he storms out of the room.

When economists make the case for free trade, they are often doing something quite similar. They may make their case in a more calm tone, they may be better at maintaining their personal hygiene, and they may lack the wild glint in their eye but their arguments are nevertheless very similar. They too have the characteristic of an unflinchingly held *idée fixe*—a fixed idea—that cannot be modified or criticised within the mind of the person that holds it. The truth of the idea is self-evident, and it need not be weighed against the real world or probed for veracity. Yes, this is characteristic of much mainstream economic thought. But for some reason, the idea of free trade is particularly poignant in this respect, bending even the more reasonable of the economists to its everlasting truth.

Comparative Advantage

The theory of comparative advantage goes all the way back to David Ricardo's writing at the beginning of the nineteenth century. Indeed, one of the reasons why Ricardo created his economic theories was to try to convince the British government to open the economy—and the economies of its colonies—to free trade. During the nineteenth century, this became an extremely popular doctrine and largely became the modus operandi of the British government. This especially so after the Great Irish Famine of 1845–1852 when the severity of the situation there and the reluctance of the British authorities to intervene directly gave a huge boost to the free trade dogma.

The argument itself is remarkably simple. Let us assume that we have two countries. One country, call it country A, is highly productive in the technology industry while the other country, call it country B, is highly productive in agriculture. Let us also assume that country A is not very productive in agriculture and country B is not very productive in technology. We must also assume that people in both countries want access to both agricultural goods and technological goods. Now, if we assume the existence of autarky—that is, the closure of both countries to external trade—then the production possibilities of the two countries will be as it is shown in Table 11.1.

If we allow, however, that each country simply focuses on what it does best then the total output of the two countries should increase. This is because together they can use the same resources to produce more goods. If we open the countries to free trade, the situation will be one that is shown in Table 11.2.

Table 11.1 Comparative advantage I

	Production	Consumption
Country A		
Agricultural Goods	500	500
Technological Goods	1000	1000
Country B		
Agricultural Goods	1000	1000
Technological Goods	500	500
World		
Agricultural Goods	1500	1500
Technological Goods	1500	1500

Table 11.2 Comparative advantage II

	Production	Consumption
Country A		
Agricultural Goods	0	750
Technological Goods	2000	1250
Country B		
Agricultural Goods	2000	1250
Technological Goods	0	750
World		
Agricultural Goods	2000	2000
Technological Goods	2000	2000

This is a shockingly simple idea. It basically amounts to saying: 'If you are better at fixing computers and I am better at gardening would it not be better if you fix my computer and I tend to your garden rather than me wasting my time fixing my own computer and you wasting your time tending to your garden? If we do it this way we will get the whole thing done an awful lot faster.' Sounds good, right? Well, not really. There are a number of hidden assumptions in this argument that render it questionable when we remove it from the abstract world of ideas and transport it into the real world of economic development.

First of all, the argument assumes that there is full employment of resources in both countries. If there are unemployed resources in either of the countries under discussion—as is so often the case in the real world—then these resources can be deployed cost-free to engage in production of any type. When free trade deals are made, they often lead to layoffs in the population that has adopted the new policies. In order to assume that the layoffs that are affected in one sector are matched by gains in a new export sector, a whole host of very special assumptions must be made. These are the same assumptions that mainstream theory makes to assume that the economy always tends to full employment. Once some of these assumptions are taken away—any of them, really—it becomes by no means clear that if a factory that was geared towards domestic production closes down in Detroit due to a free trade deal, it will be replaced with a new factory geared towards export production. A whole host of factors will have to come into play here to rebalance the economy from this shock and ensure that it reaches some sort of equilibrium; otherwise, the result will simply be unemployment and a serious downward pressure on wages in the higher wage country.

This is precisely what we have seen in the USA over the past 30 or so years. These deals can also undermine worker organisations through the unemployment they create, and this can give rise to a rebalancing of class forces that will ensure a more unequitable distribution of income. This, in turn, can give rise to a stagnation of effective demand in the face of rising productivity which can give the economy a serious bias towards debt accumulation and instability. Basically, the comparative advantage theory rests on the same ideas as the ideas that assume that market economies have a tendency to full employment equilibrium, that is, wage and price flexibility, perfect substitution effects and so on. It also abstracts away from institutional factors, like the existence of labour unions and their role in distributing income, and so cannot incorporate the roles that these institutions play in the structuring the economy.

The next problem with the theory is that it is entirely static. It completely ignores the effects that specialising in any one industry might have for the future trajectory of the economy. For example, is it really convincing to assume that countries that do not adopt high-tech industries early on get an advantage in the future? In fact, if we examine the future history of the case used by Ricardo over 200 years ago—that is, of England and Portugal—this is precisely the dynamic that played out over the course of the nineteenth century. Writing about the theory of comparative advantage from this angle Joan Robinson stated:

> The most misleading feature of the classical case for free trade (and the arguments based upon it in modern textbooks) is that it is purely static. It is set out in terms of a comparison of productivity of given resources (fully employed) with or without trade. Ricardo took the example of trade between England and Portugal. He argued that England, by allowing imports of wine from Portugal, would expand the production and export of cloth to pay for it. Ricardo, of course, was thinking of the English side of the exchange but the analysis is perfectly symmetrical; it implies that Portugal will gain from specialising on wine and importing cloth. In reality, the imposition of free trade on Portugal killed off a promising textile industry and left her with a slow-growing export market for wine, while for England, exports of cotton cloth led to accumulation, mechanisation and the whole spiraling growth of the industrial revolution. (Robinson 1979, p. 103)

This is precisely the case for some degree of protectionism made by the founding fathers of the USA, and it was this theory that drove (protectionist) US trade policy in the nineteenth century. In his seminal *Report on Manufactures*, founding father Alexander Hamilton wrote:

> The superiority antecedently enjoyed by nations who have preoccupied and perfected a branch of industry, constitutes a more formidable obstacle than either of those which have been mentioned, to the introduction of the same branch into a country in which it did not before exist. To maintain, between the recent establishments of one country, and the long-matured establishments of another country, a competition upon equal terms, both as to quality and price, is, in most cases, impracticable. The disparity, in the one, or in the other, or in both, must necessarily be so considerable, as to forbid a successful rivalship, without the extraordinary aid and protection of government. (Hamilton 1791, p. 8)

The subsequent history of the US economy, of course, shows that Hamilton might not have been altogether incorrect. The protectionist policies there did indeed give rise to companies that would eventually go on to dominate the global marketplace. When the US had become an economic hegemon in the wake of the Second World War, it too began to proselytise on the benefits of free trade. This is not to say that the effects of free trade deals have not damaged certain segments of the American population, but it does suggest that the elites of a country that has risen to the status of economic hegemon often seem to be the biggest proponents of free trade. At the very least, that bears some consideration.

The most damaging argument against free trade, however, we have already laid out earlier in this chapter. This is the idea that narrow specialisation will lead to prosperity. There are many problems with this notion. First of all, it leaves a country that has specialised too much in, say, an agricultural good open to swings in demand for this good and hence its prices. The classic case is that of Ghana which became heavily dependent on the cocoa market after the Second World War and whose economy collapsed when cocoa prices fell in the 1960s. On the supply side, a good contemporary case at the time of writing is that of Scotland which relies far too heavily on oil exports which, at some point in the future, will dry up. Diversification is a good thing in and of itself because it allows economies to insulate themselves against unforeseen swings in the supply and demand of certain goods. Again, we should always remember that it is not a good idea to put all one's eggs in one basket lest that basket fall to the ground.

Narrow specialisation also opens up the risk that an economy, especially a developing economy, will become overly dependent on a single good to the detriment of all others. Consider in this respect the examples of Saudi Arabia and Iran. Both countries are major oil producers but one is a backward monarchy and the other is emerging into a modern industrial democracy. Saudi Arabia depends almost completely on its oil revenues while Iran has undertaken substantial government intervention in its economy (a good deal of which are necessitated by the regular economic sanctions that are imposed on that country) in order to promote domestic industry and the advanced technical education needed to run this industry. The contrast could not be clearer. If the oil were to run out tomorrow, Saudi Arabia would collapse completely while Iran would, after a period of probably serious economic crisis, eventually prosper. Dependence on a single good can also give rise to toxic institutional dynamics within the country in question. It can give rise to massive accumulation of wealth at the top of the pyramid—as is the case in Saudi Arabia—which can, in turn, help to establish anti-democratic regimes that self-perpetuate this inequality.[1]

Ricardian Zealotry

This is not to say that free trade is always a bad thing. Rather, what needs to be stressed is that free trade is, like many things we encounter in economic life, a very complex issue. It is one that must be approached with a level head and an appreciation for institutional nuance. The best way to approach this is to look both at the immediate reality of the situation and the long-term sustainability. What changes will opening up an industry to free trade have in the countries in question? Is there reason to believe that the labour that loses employment will automatically find it elsewhere and will the jobs be of equal quality? Are we making a country too reliant on a single good when we open them up to free trade and enforce specialisation? What effects will the opening up of a country to free trade have on income distribution? And, I would say most importantly because free trade is an inherently political issue: what political forces within the countries in question are for the free trade policies and what political forces are against them?

For reasons that are not without historical interest, the issue of free trade has become the primary dogma in contemporary economics. Economists tend to disagree on almost everything, but on the idea of free trade there is generally consensus. This consensus has bred within the profession a sort of zealotry that is, on occasion, quite terrifying. The level of self-assuredness that an argument as lacking in nuance and sophistication as free trade generates is nothing short of shocking. One would be forgiven for thinking that it has, in recent times, become a sort of a pre-requisite for being a respectable member of the discipline. Yet from our discussion of the policy above, it should be clear to any remotely reasonable person that it is an extremely complex issue that cannot be reduced to the simple explanations that economists have a tendency to preach and proselytise.

The lengths to which those in the profession go to push their simplistic narrative are nothing short of exasperating. When reading some of the pronouncements and arguments put forward by proponents, you would be hard pushed not to think that you were looking at the words of cult members or conspirators. Consider the words uttered by Paul Krugman—often supposed to be a liberal or left-of-centre economist. Krugman is determined to tell his audience that those who argue that Ricardo's argument is not relevant to the real world simply do not understand it. He then equates rejection of Ricardo's theory with rejection of evolutionary theory and equates both with some sort of aversion to mathematics. He writes:

> At the deepest level, opposition to comparative advantage—like opposition to the theory of evolution—reflects the aversion of many intellectuals to an essentially mathematical way of understanding the world. Both comparative advantage and natural selection are ideas grounded, at base, in mathematical models—simple models that can be stated without actually writing down any equations, but mathematical models all the same. The hostility that both evolutionary theorists and economists encounter from humanists arises from the fact that both fields lie on the front line of the war between C.P. Snow's two cultures: territory that humanists feel is rightfully theirs, but which has been invaded by aliens armed with equations and computers. (Krugman 1996)

The patronising tone[2] is manifest here in that Krugman is implicitly invoking what we earlier called the 'limiting principle'. The naïve dupes who reject the economist's advice on free trade are the cultural theorists and the postmodernists. These are the intellectuals that spend more time reading books than they do undertaking the hard work of writing down equations and looking at statistics. Krugman's speech is dog whistle politics all the way—and we should stress that it is *politics* because free trade is a highly politicised issue that only economists think can be sanitised in such a crude fashion.

These economists become what Vladimir Lenin in the context of a rather different ideology called 'useful idiots'. That is, propagandists that are being used by others for motivations that they do not understand. In the 1990s, they were useful idiots for large corporations that wanted to scrap factories in the West and move them overseas. At the time of writing, they are useful idiots for corporations who want to protect intellectual property rights in the face of new technologies under the guise of the free trade ideology. Rather, hilariously dogmatic free traders today have also become the useful idiots of monopolistic forces who use public sector subsidies and technologies to produce products that they then sell to the public at exorbitantly high prices. When this price-gouging activity is threatened by overseas companies making generic knock-offs at a fraction of the cost, the corporations call in the free trade army to defend their so-called 'property rights'.

The forces at work behind dogmatic free trade arguments at any given moment in time will never be self-identical. In order to understand the agenda behind any trade policy at any given moment in time, you must examine it in critical detail. What the free trade dogma does is it tricks economists fooled by their own simplistic narratives into becoming propagandists for whatever the powers-that-be want to impose on various countries at any given moment in time. This is not an exaggeration either. In his talk, Krugman closes by laying out a series of propaganda tactics to preach the generally unpopular argument for dogmatic free trade to the general public and, most especially, the soppy 'cultural' intellectuals. He says:

> I cannot offer any grand strategy for dealing with the aversion of intellectuals to Ricardo's difficult idea. No matter what economists do, we can be sure that ten years from now the talk shows and the op-ed pages will still be full of men and women who regard themselves as experts on the global economy, but do not know or want to know about comparative advantage.[3] Still, the diagnosis I have offered here provides some tactical hints. (Ibid.)

In this book, I have tried to steer away from direct considerations of policy. But I have laid out a brief discussion about free trade not because I am advocating protectionism but because it is a prime case where we see what function abstract economic theory can play in politics and society. That much economic theory is based on ridiculously narrow assumptions and unrealistic *a priori* premises should, at this stage, be obvious. But it is worth being clear how the types of people that espouse this sort of thing can be used by political forces that they do not understand and cannot comprehend.

I have always been averse to the idea that economics as it is currently taught is some sort of organic outgrowth of the ideology of the ruling class. I do not find the Marxist story convincing that economics as it is currently taught is a mere reflection of the interests of the ruling class. Rather, I think that the explanation is much simpler: economists have cast such darkness over their own discipline that they can make themselves believe in basically anything that suits them at any given moment in time. All one has to do is feed them a very simple argument that seems internally consistent, and they will mistake this consistency for some Absolute Truth about the real world. Such people are very useful to the powers-that-be. They are the same people who were promoted to positions of power in the Medieval Church. It was not that what they were saying was so much a reflection of the interests of the elite so much as it was that what they were saying was a brilliant distraction from what was really going on. Contemporary mainstream economics is less the ideology of the ruling class than it is the opiate for establishment intellectuals who find that their little models and their ridiculously simplistic arguments get them invited to all the right parties.

Notes

1. Economists at MIT, presumably operating outside of the narrowing Ricardian comparative advantage framework, have begun to form what they call 'complexity measures'. They try to determine which sectors account for a countries exports and give 'complexity' scores to countries that display a high level of what we have called 'diversification' above. Typically, the countries that have low level of diversification are those that have focused their economies on natural resource extraction. See: http://atlas.media.mit.edu/. Work like this indicates that practical-minded economists interested in studying the real world without the blindness caused by narrow *a priori* presuppositions seem to be moving further and further away from the Ricardian dogma. With any luck, such work will drive the dogma

out of the textbooks and cause its adherents to think twice before they pontificate to the rest of us.

2. It should be noted that Krugman is playing to his audience's elitism in his rhetoric by calling Ricardo's idea 'difficult' as he does throughout his lecture (entitled 'Ricardo's Difficult Idea'). In fact, it is not a remotely difficult idea. Most teenagers understand it perfectly well when it is laid out in high school economics class. The more reflective ones, however, do not swallow it hook, line and sinker.
3. Krugman is being *very* disingenuous here. Because he surely must know that some of the most eminent economists of the generation prior to his own were sceptical of dogmatic free trade arguments (e.g. see Kaldor 1985). Indeed, Krugman must also surely have been aware that Keynes himself was sceptical even in the 1920s (Keynes 1926). Is Krugman really saying that these economists were ignorant of one of the most well-known arguments in economics? It seems unlikely. But one gets the sense that Krugman is more concerned with rhetoric and the invocation of the limiting principle in this talk than he is with rational argument or with historical accuracy.

References

Hamilton, A. (1791). *Report on the subject of manufacturing*. New York, NY: Cosimo Classics.

Kaldor, N. (1985). *Economics without equilibrium*. USA: M.E. Sharpe.

Keynes, J.M. (1926). The end of Laissez-Faire. http://www.panarchy.org/keynes/laissezfaire.1926.html

Krugman, P. (1996). Ricardo's difficult idea. http://web.mit.edu/krugman/www/ricardo.htm/

Robinson, J. (1979). *Aspects of development and underdevelopment*. Cambridge: Modern Cambridge Classics.

CHAPTER 12

Conclusion

In 1642, civil war broke out in England. The fight was between the 'Cavaliers' or 'Royalists', who sought to maintain the status quo of an absolute monarchy where the King was established through divine right, and the 'Roundheads' or 'Parliamentarians' who sought to give the English Parliament executive control over the land. The terms 'Roundheads' and 'Cavaliers' referred to the styles of dress popular to each group. The Cavaliers were seen to dress in the courtly fashion of the day, with long-flowing hair and decorated attire, while the Roundheads tended to wear their hair close-cropped and more humble clothes. Some Roundhead factions were indeed quite radical. The Diggers and the Levellers, for example, are well known today to be the agrarian progenitors of modern-day radical socialism.

Needless to say, the English Civil War constituted an entire shake-up of the social order of the day. Those who did not explicitly take sides were wont to find themselves extremely confused indeed. All the old pieties were being called into question by the Roundheads. A Crown that many thought until only months before to have, in some literal sense or other, descended from the Heavens was being called into question, and new ideas such as Parliamentary Democracy were being heard from the mouths of men. This was also the period in which the popular press began to grow up. In such turbulent times, it was only natural that the common man would seek out explanations for the social turmoil that he was

W.P. Pilkington, *The Reformation in Economics*,
DOI 10.1007/978-3-319-40757-9_12

experiencing. In the same year as the outbreak of the civil war, a publication called the *Marine Mercury*, which specialised in the accounts of amazing sea-beasts, had a headline that ran as such:

> A True Relation of the Strange Appearance of a Man-Fish about three miles within the River Thames, having a musket in one hand and a Petition in the other, credibly reported by Six Sailors who both saw and talked with the monster, whose names here following are inserted. (Hunt 1850, p. 113)

In retrospect, it is obvious for any historically informed person to see that the supposed appearance of the Man-Fish was not just nonsense plain and simple. The Man-Fish that the sailors reported carried a musket in one hand and a petition in the other. He was clearly a representation of the new, confusing political discourse that was spreading through England at the time, causing upheaval against the old political order. Why then, were these ideas personified in the figure of the monstrosity to people in that era? The French philosopher Michel Foucault, who did extensive archival work on material from the era, provides us with the answer when he writes:

> The monster ... plays a very precise role in [the general configuration of representation]. On the basis of continuum held by nature, the monster ensures the emergence of difference. This difference is without law and without any distinct structure ... Thus, against the background of the continuum, the monster provides an account, as though in caricature, of the genesis of difference. (Foucault 1970, p. 171)

Foucault found that in this era, when modern science was being born, monsters were beings that were classified as being outside of the system of representation. Thus we might find a perfect 'continuum' of creatures—a sort of crude evolutionism based on divine intervention—but every now and again a 'monster' would pop up that we did not understand. Whereas the continuum represented 'identity'—that is, a structure that made logical sense given the then contemporary mode of discourse—the monster represented 'difference'—that is, something that stood radically outside of the contemporary mode of discourse. It is not surprising then that, in the popular newspapers of the day, the new political ideas of the democrats were represented as a sort of monster.

The financial crisis that arose in 2008 was to the economists akin to the breakout of the English Civil War to the Royalists, and it came to be represented as something of a monster within the system of representation that these economists use, namely marginalist economics. It was an event that simply did not conform to the continuum of representation that economists and those that listened to them had built for themselves. They had based their representations on the idea that the economy tended towards a long-run market equilibrium position and that any external shocks—any monsters—that arose would quickly disappear as the economy marched on towards its inevitable teleological end point. The intellectual historian Philip Mirowski has noted that out of this crisis emerged a new type of publication: namely the 'crisis book'. The crisis book is an attempt by economists and economic policymakers to 'come to terms' with the crisis in some way or other. In order to be a serious person in the field, these days you need a crisis book. The function of the crisis book seems tied up with a strange phenomenon that Mirowski notes in a book that he wrote as a direct response to the outflow of crisis books from the profession: it seeks to reintegrate the crisis into the dominant narrative that came before; it seeks to slay the monster and reintegrate the terrifying prospect of historical change back into the market equilibrium framework; and in philosophical terms, the crisis book and those who write them seek to reduce the difference that emerged in 2008 back into the identity that it is their duty to assure us that events hold to (Mirowski 2013).

If we dig a little deeper, we find that something similar was going on in the pages of the *Marine Mercury* back in 1642. While the Man-Fish may have appeared to have been the representation of the new radical democratic ideas spreading through the English countryside at the time, he was made by the authors to speak in kind, reassuring words.

> According to the monster's own account of himself, he came on a friendly errand, and the paper he held in his hand contained an account of the plots of foreign princes against the country. He also offered his assistance as a courier to collect News, for which he was well adapted, seeing that his steeds were the rapid monsters of the deep. (Hunt 1850, p. 113)

The authors made the monster appear at first to be something threatening and potentially destabilising but then they quickly domesticated him and made him speak in reassuring tones. He was, despite his strange and unnerving appearance, here to help. He was here to spread news to the common people and defend the State against interference by foreign enemies. Since 2008, the outpouring of crisis books has sought to serve the same purpose. We are told that marginalist economics is not dead—indeed, how could it be, for it is science after all!—but rather that the crisis is a sort of Man-Fish or monster that, while it appears to be carrying with it new ideas, actually appears in order to confirm and prop up the status quo. The crisis was not, according to the writers of the crisis books, an inherent challenge to the dominant economic narrative. Rather it was a funny-looking creature that, although he appeared unfamiliar at first, a closer examination rendered him altogether familiar and harmless.

Marginalist economics is above all else the discourse of identity and social order that exists in our own time *par excellence*. It is a discourse of identity in form, structure, meaning and message. Agents within the discourse are self-identical; historical time is the eternal repetition of the same; and the economy always tends towards a selfsame end equilibrium point. Marginalist economics gives the contingencies of history a meaning and structure that conforms to very old notions of teleology that became popular in the Enlightenment period but which waned in other disciplines in the twentieth century. Although history may appear to simply be a series of somewhat contingent events, marginalist economics claims to find laws—laws of identity, of $x = x$ and $y = y$—beneath this clamour of difference.

In this book, we have presented a different way of thinking about economics. We have accepted history as it is: contingent, fickle and the eternal emergence of the ever new. We have accepted people as they are: creators of their own destiny whose existence plays out in an uncertain world and not selfsame robots that are 'rational', predictable and ultimately without agency. And we have accepted the economy for what it is: an unfolding of various contingent events played out against a political and cultural backdrop that cannot be ignored or fully reduced to equations and models. What we hope to have shown is that when we accept these premises we need not scatter what is left of economics to the winds. There is much that can be and need to be done by economists who recognise the economy for what it is and the study of economics for what it should be.

What we have not offered however is an ideology, a discourse that provides its adherents with reassurances and justifications for the world as they think that it is or, more properly, for the world as they think it should be. Throughout, we have argued that this is misleading and leads only to myopia and blindness. But this is a powerful idea and is always sought out by those who wish to justify the status quo and sweep under the rug the fact that man, to a very large extent, makes his own history. Such an idea is not specific to a given system of social organisation, and marginalism can be used to justify either the purest form of free market capitalism or a fully planned communist economy. The essence of marginalist economics is not, as some think that it is, an ideological defence of capitalism. Rather it is a brilliantly constructed ideological defence of whatever the status quo seems to be. And as Keynes said, 'we have no interest in the status quo as such'.

Some might interpret the above words as a call to revolution. This may be true, but they are not a call to social revolution. In this book, we have been clear that our intention is not to replace one dogma with another. We trust that people can form their own political opinions and do not need priests battering their ears with ideology clothed in mathematics to articulate how they think society should be organised. Rather the above words are a call to a revolution in how we think about the world around us and, more specifically, about the economy. It does not matter whether the reader thinks themselves left-wing or right-wing; what we are asking them to realise is that social and economic reality is contingent and ever-changing. Economies do not tend towards some long-run market equilibrium, and any attempt to justify whatever economic system you favour by claiming this is only so much hodgepodge that is based on a mode of discourse that is long out of date. Economists must become far more attuned to the contingencies of history than they are today; to the contingencies of human psychology and human decision; and to the fact that, ultimately, we make our own choices and we cannot fob off responsibility for these choices through an appeal to a ghostly self-equilibrating market that only exists in an imagination that has been made sick by learning nonsense.

There are rewards for those that follow this path. They will make much more able economic commentators than the previous generation. As we have seen, they are not without tools to make sense out of such a world. It is the identity thinkers, the marginalists terrified of historical contingency and difference that prance around today calling out crises where none emerge and preaching tranquillity just prior to collapse. Such people are useful to those in power—although one suspects they are becoming decreasingly so—but they are looking ever more like fools in the eyes of the public. This opens up a space where a completely new conception of economics can and must emerge. It is unlikely to emerge from the halls of academia. Marginalism still seethes in those corridors, stinking and rotten.

The profession over the past 50 or so years has structured itself in such a way that it only attracts identity thinkers, organisation men who fall in love with Eternal Truths and who hide their ignorance behind a typically haughty and arrogant attitude. Those with a taste for contingency and human complexity are incentivised to choose a different discipline soon after they enter into the marginalist Church. Thus what is contained in this book will likely be completely incomprehensible to those within the profession, but this gives us some advantage as the discourses they spin are perhaps more transparent to us than they are to themselves and this puts them firmly on the back foot. New approaches and ideas will emerge from a new generation, a generation that has seen first-hand the need for a Reformation in economic thought. The present author only hopes that the pages the reader has just read help them to clarify exactly what is wrong, what needs to be changed and what provides at least a basic framework that can be worked off in order to make these all-too-necessary changes.

References

Foucault, M. (1970). *The order of things: An archaeology of the human sciences.* USA: Routledge Classics.

Hunt, F. K. (1850). *The fourth estate: Contributions towards a history of newspapers, and of the liberty of the press.* UK: David Bogue. https://archive.org/details/fourthestatecon02huntgoog

Mirowski, P. (2013). *Never let a serious crisis go to waste: How neoliberalism survived the financial meltdown.* USA: Verso Books.

Philosophical and Psychological Appendices

Determinism and Free Will in Economics

Most people do not really want freedom, because freedom involves responsibility, and most people are frightened of responsibility.

—*Sigmund Freud*

Most of the really fundamental debates in economics today are very old debates indeed. But economists—and not just the economists of the post-war period—have been scrupulous in avoiding many of them. Other social sciences do not suffer the same defect, and one wonders why this might be the case in economics. The key philosophical difference between the view of economics put forward by the marginalists and the one championed in this book is that the former believe that all human action is pre-determined while the author of the present book believes in a large amount of freedom in human affair.

This debate is as old as philosophy itself. But it took its modern form, not coincidentally given the title of this book, around the time of the Christian Reformation. The two men involved, Desiderius Erasmus and Martin Luther, were both reformers although they had differing views about how the Reformation should proceed. Erasmus favoured salvaging church institutions intact. He argued that reformers should focus on learning and scholarship, and this would undermine the dogmatic structures of religion that existed at that time from within. Luther was more radical. He wanted to tear down the religious institutions and hand every Christian a

W.P. Pilkington, *The Reformation in Economics*,
DOI 10.1007/978-3-319-40757-9

Bible that they could read and interpret themselves. For Erasmus, society needed a structure of authority but for Luther the only authority that counted was God and this authority was reflected in God's word that we receive from the Bible.

As we shall see in what follows, Luther was, in spirit, a marginalist to the bitter end. His insistence that only the individual's direct relationship with God counted was identical to the marginalist claim that only the individual's direct relationship with the market counts today. Like the marginalists too, Luther required that human beings had no free will for his theology to work. This was because, if we took his advice to tear down religious institutions seriously, then the result would be anarchy unless we assumed that Man operated like a wind-up toy that was ultimately wound up by God Himself in his infinite Goodness and Grace.

Erasmus, coming from the humanist tradition, argued that we should keep religious structures intact because Man actually possessed free will. Man, Erasmus argued, could make his own destiny, and he needed institutions to guide him on the path to Salvation lest he fall into Sin. In this regard, Erasmus was arguing far more in line with the view put forward in the present book. In his *The Freedom of the Will*, Erasmus defined free will as such:

> By "free will" here we understand a power of the human will by which man may be able to direct himself towards or turn away from what leads to eternal salvation. (Erasmus in Miller ed. 2012, p. 6)

As the reader can probably already appreciate, the debate, like the one surrounding marginalist economics, was never value neutral. It was deeply tied up with questions of Good and evil. Luther attacked Erasmus for being inconsistent because the latter admitted that if Man falls into Sin, he may indeed be controlled by it and lose his free will. In his *The Bondage of the Will*, Luther wrote:

> But away with these verbal monstrosities. For who can put up with such misuse of language as to say that a person has free will, while asserting at one and the same time that he has lost freedom and is forced into slavery to sin and cannot will anything good? Such statements fly in the face of common sense and make language totally useless. (Luther in Miller ed. 2012, p. 62)

Thus, in Erasmus, free will was tied up with the notion of the good. If Man chooses a righteous path, he will be endowed with the Grace of God and will lead a happy and free existence. If he turns his back on the righteous path, he will quickly become enslaved to Sinful ways and will lead a miserable and unfree life. While, for Luther, people are effectively the puppets of God who will always work to try to give to Man eternal salvation. Without God's direct intervention, Man falls straight into Sin. But this also means that Man needs no religious instruction as God is already standing by ready and waiting to guide him to Salvation.

Marginalist economists, as we have said, implicitly follow Luther. In postulating that Man is guided by some ineffable force that guides him inevitably towards the Good—that is, utility maximisation—the marginalists are saying that Man is a puppet of this underlying, unseen force. The image of maximum satiation that the marginalists hand to their readers and listeners is structurally identical to the inevitability of 'eternal salvation' that Luther puts forward. Indeed, if one recalls that Adam Smith (a devout Protestant) explicitly posits his 'hidden hand' as the hand of God, it quickly becomes obvious that Pareto-efficient market equilibrium is the direct descendent of Luther's inevitable tendency towards eternal salvation (Denis 2005).

For Erasmus, life was far more difficult. Eternal salvation is not a given. Man is not a puppet of forces that drag him towards this inevitable happy 'equilibrium' point. Rather he has to make a variety of correct decisions if he wants to lead the Good Life, free and happy. As we shall see, this is precisely the vision that Keynes and those who followed him put forward. They did not appeal to ineffable forces but rather to the facts of experience as we live them. It does indeed seem that we have the freedom to make decisions, and so it is on this basis that we must start any analysis of Man or of his social, political and economic institutions. Keynes' vision, as we have stressed throughout the current book, also opened up an enormous space of freedom for Man to design his social, political and economic institutions to obtain better outcomes than just sitting idly by, apathetic to the issues of the day.

While the Reformation of yesteryear arose out of Luther's deterministic vision, it seems that today's must come from Erasmus' non-deterministic vision. In this vision, Man must take responsibility for his own actions and must not try to fob this responsibility off onto some inevitable Utopia that will be reached if people are just left to themselves. By not *choosing* the righteous path, Man will fall into Sin and be confronted with the fruits of this Sin in the form of an economic world that has spiralled out of control to the point where he feels trapped, unfree and alone.

In 1943, the philosophy of decision-making under free will reached its pinnacle when the French philosopher Jean-Paul Sartre published his magnum opus *Being and Nothingness*. The great work arose out the phenomenological philosophical movement of the early twentieth century and launched what would become mid-century Existentialism. The 122 pages in the book collected under the chapter heading 'Being and Doing: Freedom' remain the finest philosophical-cum-psychological account of what it means to make a decision when we suppose that we have free will to do so. The following quote can summarise the argument laid out in the chapter rather well:

> Thus at the outset we can see what is lacking in those tedious discussions between the determinist and the proponents of free will. The latter are concerned to find cases of decision for which there exists no prior cause, or deliberations concerning two opposed acts which are equally possible and possess causes (and motives) of exactly the same weight. To which the determinists may easily reply that there is no action without a cause and that the most insignificant gesture (raising the right hand rather than the left hand etc.) refers to causes and motives which confer its meaning upon it. Indeed the case could not be otherwise since every action must be intentional; each action must, in fact, have an end and the end in turn is referred to a cause … *It is in fact impossible to find an act without a motive but this does not means that we must conclude that the motive causes the act; the motive is an integral part of the act.* For as the resolute project toward a change is not distinct from the act, *the motive, the act and the end are all constituted in a single upsurge. Each of these three structures claims the two others as its meaning.* But the organized totality of the three is no longer explained by any particular structure, and its upsurge as the pure temporalizing nihilation of the in-itself is one with freedom. It is the act which decides its ends and its motives, and the act is the expression of freedom. (Sartre 1957, pp. 458–460—my emphasis)

What Sartre recognised is that we cannot really get a God's-eye view of how our motivations and actions unfold. They unfold through time, and to retroactively explain an action by some supposedly prior motivation is misleading. Rather, we have to recognise that these things come into existence, in a sense, all at once. The act and the motive cannot be untangled from one another. Even if the motive is posited at an earlier point in time—for example, if I plan to attend a concert next week—in some sense, I have already undertaken that action in my own imaginings of the future. The decision to attend the concert does not 'cause' the attendance; rather, they are one and the same process unfolding at different moments in time.[1] The source of what Sartre aptly calls this 'upsurge' is the seat of consciousness as we experience it every moment we live our lives. Consciousness *creates* these motive-acts as it moves through time, and this is why we say that we have the freedom of decision. We cannot view consciousness like we do a standard causal chain where one event causes another event which causes another event and so on. Rather, consciousness intervenes directly in the causal chain through the creation or 'upsurge' of motive-acts that are at the heart of decision-making proper.

We find something very similar in Keynes' work although it is not properly articulated. The roots of this viewpoint can probably be traced back to his earlier mentor, the philosopher G.E. Moore. This is very hard for economists today to appreciate. Economists today instinctively sign on to a sort of vulgar Newtonian view of the world. That is, they instinctively think in terms of a space in which a variety of forces play themselves out—often, in the case of the marginalists, at a given instant of time. But this sort of philosophy was long dead in the humanities at the time Keynes was writing. Rather, the philosophies of Moore and Keynes start from the seat of consciousness. We do not start from the vulgar assumption that reality 'is' in some sense a space with deterministic forces playing themselves out. This schema, thought construction or model is fully recognised in Keynes to be something cooked up by consciousness.

This, I think, accounts for why many economists find Keynes' writings so obscure. It also accounts for why those with training in philosophy or psychology will find them far more accessible than those with training in mainstream economics, physics or engineering. Keynes' works are written from the point-of-view of the reasoning subject. This is the natural starting point for Keynes. Consciousness comes first; models and metaphors are adopted later. That is why in Keynes' work we are from time to time put in the shoes of the investor trying to make decisions about the future. In mainstream economics, agents making investment and consumption decisions are reduced to little objects that reason in a pre-determined manner. In Keynes, by contrast, economic agents making investment and consumption decisions are full subjects endowed with a consciousness that is identically structured to the one that we ourselves possess. Thus in order to understand the choices made by these agents, we do not simply reduce them to little puppets that behave how we assume them to behave but rather we must try to get 'inside their heads'.

It is clear that in Keynes the economic agent also makes contingent choices. As we discussed earlier in this book, there is no assumption of a teleological end point in Keynes' expectations equilibrium. People are not pre-determined; they are not little puppets that act in a manner which we can predict *a priori*; rather they have to make *choices* and *decisions* in the face of an uncertain future. This accounts for why, for example, savings decisions and investment decisions might not converge with one another. If all the savers at a given moment in time are deciding to save a lot of money while all the investors at that same moment of time are deciding only to invest a very small amount, we will find ourselves with an unemployment equilibrium driven by divergent expectations. It is the fact that people must make decisions without knowing exactly what the decisions of other people will be or exactly what the outcome of their own decisions will be that provides the true backbone of Keynes' economics. He says so explicitly when he writes:

> We are merely reminding ourselves that human decisions affecting the future, whether personal or political or economic, cannot depend on strict mathematical expectation, since the basis for making such calculations does not exist; and that it is our innate urge to activity which makes the wheels go round, our rational selves choosing between the alternatives as best we are able, calculating where we can, but often falling back for our motive on whim or sentiment or chance. (Keynes 1936a, Chapter 12)

The fact that people make decisions also implies that they have free will. They are not, as they are in marginalist economics, assumed to follow a pre-determined path. What is more, as we have shown in a previous chapter, they do not have access to sufficient information that would allow them to make 'objective' decisions about the future based on the calculations of probabilities which would effectively make their actions pre-determined anyway. In order to gain insight into how people make investment and savings decisions, the best experiment we can do is a thought experiment: how do we ourselves make such decisions? Do we know the exact outcomes of these decisions? If we do not can, we assign the possible outcomes' probability estimates and then calculate these to form our decision? If we can indeed put probability estimates on these possible outcomes, do we actually do this when we make these decisions? Some reflection will soon show the reader that when we make such decisions we have extremely limited information about their possible effects and we cannot and do not make them based on probability estimates.

Because Keynes' understanding of decisions implies that we have free will and because Keynes' work always begins from the seat of human consciousness rather than from naïve, vulgar God's-eye/Newtonian physicist view of the world, the manner in which he describes these decisions is very close to what Sartre's own discussion of decision-making. This is particularly so in the case of what Keynes calls the 'marginal efficiency of capital' about which he writes:

> The reader should note that the marginal efficiency of capital is here defined in terms of the *expectation* of yield and of the *current* supply price of the capital-asset. It depends on the rate of return expected to be obtainable on money if it were invested in a *newly* produced asset; not on the historical result of what an investment has yielded on its original cost if we look back on its record after its life is over. (Ibid., Chapter 11—emphasis in original)

Here the act of decision-making is eminently Sartrean. The investor carries out a decision based on an imagined future—a future created through the act of decision—and this decision then opens up a variety of possibilities that may or may not come into existence. Just as if I decide to go to a concert next week this opens up a multitude of possibilities—the concert may be cancelled, it may be better than I thought it would be, I may meet someone who I have not seen for a long time at the concert and so on—the decision to undertake an investment in the face of an uncertain future based on a back-of-the-envelope calculation of its *expected* yield or profit opens up a multitude of potential future possibilities. It is the freedom to imagine and come up with this expected yield or profit that allows the investor to make a purely *free* decision with regard to the future. But this freedom comes with a price: because our decisions are not pre-determined and cannot be said to produce what we might consider the best economic outcome, there is no guarantee that individuals making decisions alone will act in such a way as to bring about the future, their desired future.[2] This also entails that decisions that do not line up with desired outcomes can be self-perpetuating. In this regard Keynes writes:

> This means, unfortunately, not only that slumps and depressions are exaggerated in degree, but that economic prosperity is excessively dependent on a political and social atmosphere which is congenial to the average business man. If the fear of a Labour Government or a New Deal depresses

> enterprise, this need not be the result either of a reasonable calculation or of a plot with political intent;—it is the mere consequence of upsetting the delicate balance of spontaneous optimism. In estimating the prospects of investment, we must have regard, therefore, to the nerves and hysteria and even the digestions and reactions to the weather of those upon whose spontaneous activity it largely depends. (Ibid., Chapter 12)

Thus, for example, the intentions of a government may be thwarted by the effects that the election of this government has on the decisions made by businessmen. Again, this is not a necessary relationship, and a government could take steps to counteract it but it does provide a clear picture of the contingent world full of free decision-makers that Keynes is painting for us. This is not a world in which everything tends towards a certain Utopian end point. Rather it is a world in which people make choices, and these choices, often being divergent from one another, have an impact on the imagined end points that the decision-makers had originally hoped for. This is a vision of an extremely complex world that cannot ever be reduced to a sort of mechanical system or a series of simultaneous equations. Again, this does not mean that we cannot tease out necessary relationships in such a world—if this were the case, then economics would be an impossible discipline, and I would not have written this book—but we must recognise that the forces causing the relationships to come into being (e.g. the magnitude of savings or investment at any given moment in time) cannot be understood to be determined within the system. Rather they arise from decisions made by agents within the economy that are undertaken freely, are thus not pre-determined and cannot be modelled or predicted in any meaningful sense.

Such a vision will undoubtedly disturb some souls who have ventured into the field of economics out of a desire to obtain comforting stories about how the world works. These people, who currently dominate the profession, have typically entered it for the same reason that in times past people entered into institutions of religious instruction. They are told that the future can be predicted, that people act in a certain way and that, ultimately, there is a benign force pulling society towards a Utopian outcome. Given this supposed knowledge, they can then go into the world preaching as to what people and governments should do and how they should behave. We offer no such vision here. As Freud noted long ago, such a vision is only taken up by those who fear the dimension of individual responsibility. In the face of human freedom, the question of responsibility is one of the first that arises. But if the future is pre-determined, then there is no need for responsibility proper. Those who are frightened by human freedom and responsibility have no place in doing an economics that is remotely worthwhile. One can only hope that institutionalised religion undergoes a revival in the near future to ensure that such people can find a position in the world that does not interfere with the profession of economics any longer. Behind an altar such people are relatively harmless and everyone can see what they are doing clearly; given power over government and influence on economic policy, they are dangerous men and women indeed.

Between Personal Responsibility and Poor Theory

Economics is a science of thinking in terms of models joined to the art of choosing models which are relevant to the contemporary world. It is compelled to be this, because, unlike the typical natural science, the material to which it is applied is, in too many respects, not homogeneous through time ... Good economists are scarce because the gift for using "vigilant observation" to choose good models, although it does not require a highly specialised intellectual technique, appears to be a very rare one.

—*J.M. Keynes*

There is an interesting argument that surfaces quite frequently amongst mainstream economists. They claim that the problem with economics is not economics at all, but rather economists. They argue that there are a whole variety of models using the marginalist framework and that the problem is that there are too few 'good' economists to choose between these models. It even appears, from the quote above, that Keynes adhered to this view. Yet we must remember historical context: he was writing in a particular time in history when applied economic technique was very little developed; he was also, in the same letter, saying that models are just 'tools for thinking' and should generally not be applied to data directly.

This defence of marginalist economics is an interesting one. For one thing, as a general proposition, it has some truth to it, as we shall discuss in a moment. But it also highlights the contentious nature of the discipline. Contemporary economics is plagued with disagreement on matters of the highest importance. Some mainstream economists advocate strong interventionist measure while others are very 'free market' in their outlook. This is often commented upon and is highlighted in the well-known joke that if you ask five economists their opinions on a certain matter, they will give you six mutually exclusive replies. The mainstream economics profession seems to only maintain coherence through reference to a common broad research programme (marginalism), certain methodological precepts (do not ask questions), a tendency to favour certain modes of empirical enquiry (model fitting) and the exclusion of outsiders that disagree strongly with any of the above. Without this epistemological coherence, the profession would undoubtedly descend into political squabbling, as it is extraordinarily obvious that marginalist economists tend to push policies that line up with their personal political proclivities.

Now it is true that, in order to engage in applied economics properly, we must learn to choose our model. In order to show why we consider neo-Austrians and monetary theories, the neo-Austrians constantly try to apply the same conception of a crude quantity theory of money married to an assumption of full capacity utilisation to absolutely every situation (Pilkington 2013g). In doing so, they seem to constantly claim that there is impending hyperinflation—or at least, very high inflation. But the hyperinflation never ever materialises. The US-Austrian economist Bob Murphy wrote the following at the beginning of 2009:

> It would not surprise me at all if the national unemployment rate and the annualized rate of consumer price inflation both broke through into double digits by the end of 2009. Moreover, regardless of when it actually starts, I predict that things will get much worse before they get better, and that the United States will be mired in a malfunctioning economy for at least a decade, with price inflation in the double-digits (possibly higher) the entire time. We can call this condition "hyper-depression."

The economy, as we now know, was in a deflationary recession—not an inflationary depression—and began a sluggish recovery of both output and prices towards the end of 2009; this was followed by a period of very meagre price inflation that policymakers tried unsuccessfully to boost through monetary interventions. Clearly, Murphy was completely and utterly wrong. He quite literally could not have come up with a worse set of predictions. Meanwhile, many mainstream economists in central banks were assuming something like a deflationary recession and were attempting to intervene accordingly. They got it largely correct. But Murphy was reasoning based on his mentor Murray Rothbard's ideas about the economy. Murphy saw that as the financial crisis of 2008 set in the US government moved to stimulate the economy and the Federal Reserve tried to generate inflation. These conditions, according to Rothbard, would generate hyperinflation. Rothbard writes:

> Hyperinflation occurs when the public realizes that the government is bent on inflation, and decides to evade the inflationary tax on its resources by spending money as fast as possible while it still retains its value. (Rothbard 1963, pp. 81–82)[3]

Although we can hardly call Rothbard's assertions a 'model', it is nevertheless a process of economic reasoning that can be applied to empirical data. It was because of the faulty reasoning that Murphy relied upon that he arrived at false conclusions.

But this is not enough to verify the claim that mainstream economics is perfectly healthy and that the problem is that there are so few good economists. Consider briefly that many economists in the wake of 2008 used as their tool of reference the old ISLM model that we have explored in detail in the previous passages. Many of these economists would claim that after 2008 we found ourselves in a 'liquidity trap'—that is, a situation in which monetary policy becomes ineffective and fiscal policy must be used. Yet the model itself does not tell us this. Two economists could both be using an ISLM model to analyse the post-crisis economic landscape and could come to completely different conclusions because one might think that we are in a liquidity trap and the other might not. The model really tells us very little; indeed, it is just a framework for thinking through problems.

The fact of the matter is that it is not the models that economists use that dictate how they think; rather, it is the paradigm that they are part of. Mainstream economists are by no means politically homogenous—some are interventionists, some are free marketeers—but they are homogenous in the way that they view a capitalist economy. They all think in terms of long-term full employment equilibria; they all largely ignore money and finance as a side issue; they assume that balance of payments issues are impermanent and fleeting; and they all assume that capitalism is naturally pretty stable. These are not so much models as *a priori* conceptions. These are the *a priori* conceptions that drive their models, and it is these that matter. Mainstream economists may disagree on many things amongst themselves but they are all thinking in the same framework—and it is, from our perspective, this framework that is the problem; it is this framework that stifles thought. True consensus is generated by the *a priori* conceptions, and it is the *a priori* conceptions that ultimately rule the minds of men. What is more, when this is consciously recognised, it seems to have the interesting effect that greater consensus is reached in the realm of policy.

What is so fascinating about Post-Keynesian economics is that, although it is far more diverse in terms of models and approaches than the mainstream—there are Kaleckian models, Kaldorian models, Sraffian models, Minskyian models and so on—there is actually a pretty decent convergence on practical and empirical issues. The disagreements that these different approaches tend to generate within Post-Keynesian circles seem more about emphasis than actual concrete processes driving the capitalist economy. For example, a Kaldorian might claim that the balance of payments is the most important aspect to consider in terms of macroeconomic dynamics while a Minskyian will insist on financial instability. Yet in the wake of a recession, both the Kaldorian and the Minskyian will probably draw the same conclusions as to policy. Why? Because both of their *a priori* conceptions about capitalist economies are largely the same. They both believe in unemployment equilibria in both the short- and long-run; they both believe that money and finance are inherently important; they both believe that balance of payments disequilibria can be structural; and they both believe that capitalism is chronically unstable.

What is more, there is a lot of weight in Post-Keynesian circles placed on laying out these implicit agreements. It is because of this, I would argue, that, in spite of its diversity, Post-Keynesian economics is a far more unified field than mainstream marginalist economics. This in turn has to do with the Post-Keynesian focus on realism. Post-Keynesian spend a lot of time talking amongst themselves about their assumptions. There is a healthy and consistent probing of assumptions. This maintains consensus while keeping everyone on their toes and ensures that they do not slip too far into methodologically lazy and empirically dubious obscurantism. In the mainstream, no such safeguards are in place, and so the discipline becomes fractious, incoherent, and obscurantist and is shot through with squabbles about the most basic policy issues. Faced with this cacophony, the mainstream only maintains coherence by repressing any attempts at self-reflection and banishing anyone who does not toe the line vis-à-vis the implicit *a priori* conceptions underlying the paradigm.

The roots of the problems of mainstream economics are not to be found in the quality of the economists themselves. That is an argument made by a mainstream economist caught in a rivalrous battle with a colleague from across the political spectrum. The roots of the problems lay buried in the unspoken, unquestioned and rigidly dogmatic *a priori* conceptions underlying the mainstream economics paradigm. These are like a bad smell amongst the mainstream that everyone tries to ignore. Because they know that, if they do not, the whole consensus will deteriorate, and the feigned coherence of the profession will slip into oblivion. And so instead, rivalries in mainstream economics play out like theatre, and at the end of the day, everyone goes home feeling satisfied and included. Nothing changes; nothing moves forward; and everyone remains trapped in his/her own personal political prison. But it is a happy incarceration; it is peaceful at least.[4]

Economic Modelling: A Psychologistic Explanation

Can anything be imagined so ridiculous, that this miserable and wretched creature, who is not so much as master of himself, but subject to the injuries of all things, should call himself master and emperor of the world, of which he has not power to know the least part, much less to command the whole?

—*Michel de Montaigne*

Throughout this book, we have been rather harsh on economists. We have accused them of engaging in all sorts of silly behaviour, of constructing irrelevant theories and of being a key force darkening the doorway of knowledge and spreading ideology. But so far we have not really sought out motivation. Are we to assume that most economists working today are nefarious crooks and scoundrels? I should think not. Most economists working today are well-meaning people who genuinely want to make the world a better place. They are men and women who truly believe that they are constructing useful knowledge that will help humanity progress as a species in the future. That they typically make the world a worse place and cloud the judgements of people is not altogether their fault.

What is it then that drives these people to Bedlam and back? This is something that the present writer has thought about quite a lot. I have come to this conclusion: these men and women are chasing after a Holy Grail, one that has been sought since time immemorial. At first it was sought in the sphere of religion, but after this it was sought in the field of philosophy and, finally, science. Today the sphere in which this Holy Grail is most aggressively sought is in the field of economics. What then characterises this Holy Grail? Well, it is the Holy Grail of perfect knowledge. It is the drive that exists in many intellectually minded men and women to find a sort of perfection, a total and pristine knowledge that would make them, in a very real sense, omnipotent or, at least, omniscient. This Holy Grail was first formulated in the modern age by the French mathematician and astronomer Pierre-Simon Laplace when he wrote:

> We ought then to regard the present state of the universe as the effect of its anterior state and the cause of the one which is to follow. Given for one instant an intelligence which could comprehend all the forces by which nature is animated and the respective situation of the beings who compose it—an intelligence sufficiently vast to submit this data to analysis—it would embrace in the same formula the movements of the greatest bodies of the universe and those of the lightest atom; for it, nothing would be uncertain and the future, as the past, would be present in its eyes. (Laplace 1902, p. 4)

For some rather odd reason, this thought experiment has become known as 'Laplace's Demon' today. In fact, readers of older philosophers will recognise that this is identical to how many philosophers conceived of an image of God. For many writers, God is an omniscient being that has total knowledge of all causes and effects and has a sort of 'single formula' in His immediate consciousness that explains everything across time and space. He is, in this conception, outside of time and space and thus merely observes everything happening at once in the form of this timeless, perfect formula.

When economists try to build totalising models, they are doing something similar. They are trying to figure out all the mechanisms—the causes and effects—that pertain in the economy at all times, and then they are trying to reduce these to a single model. If they could ever find their Holy Grail, they would then, in the words of Laplace, have 'the future, as the past, present in their eyes'. They are reaching for perfection. In a strange psychological sense, they are seeking to become like the old conceptions of God that many philosophers and theologians held. Again, they are not the only ones that do this. Many physicists reach for the same Holy Grail and try to generate 'theories of everything'. But it is in economics, which is not only a far more inexact discipline but also a far more ambitious one, that this fantasy has done the most damage.

The psychological roots of this tendency are inherently narcissistic. By that, I do not mean that economists are all pathologically narcissistic. No, psychologists have long recognised that all of us have narcissistic tendencies buried within our minds. They are absolutely necessary for us to form a coherent sense of self. Somewhere buried within our minds, we all have an image of perfection that haunts us. This can manifest in any number of different ways. One person's image of perfection might be a certain celebrity, and so this person might try to either emulate this celebrity. Another person's image of perfection might be some sort of perfect gym-body that he/she will always try to reach for. On occasion, such a narcissistic image can become an obsession and do serious psychological and physical damage to a person. One only need to think of the unfortunate figure of the anorexic or bulimic person who tries to reach a fantasy, 'perfect' body image, but who, in process, destroys himself/herself and his/her health. Such an image of perfection that we carry around can be a force for good or evil. It can be highly motivational in that it can be a force causing us to try to get better at whatever we do. But it can also be a force for evil if we do not recognise that the idea of perfection is not an idea that is actually attainable. There is no such thing as true perfection just as there is no such thing as a unified theory of how the economy works that will be valid across time and space. These are fantasies and illusions that, if we do not understand them to be illusions, can lead us down wayward paths.

We have argued throughout the book that economics today is predominantly ideology. But just as certain forms of religious discourses were the key ideologies of the past, economics too activates these deep psychological structures within its practitioners to ensure that they remain stuck on a treadmill, chasing ghosts rather than engaging with the real world. Certain religious discourses offered its adherents a sort of union with God if they studied the sacred texts hard enough. This kept these conduits of ideology away from the real world and ensured that they engaged in largely useless activity in their fruitless search for omniscience by connecting with God. Economics today does something similar in that it encourages its adherents to build models that are supposed to be true across time and space. The adherents are then encouraged to test these models against data using highly problematic econometric techniques, after which the whole discipline starts to ruminate if they stop yielding accurate results.

The result is a stagnant discipline. Every few years, economic theory will go into crisis as some real world event calls into question the predominant models. Economists will then go back and reconstruct the doctrines in light of recent events only to have them fall apart once more when something changes in the economic world. It is a bit like watching an unfortunate though well-meaning man build and rebuild his house along an earthquake fault line always insisting that this time the house will survive. Or a cult devotee that continuously says that the end of the world is coming on a given date only to push this date back every time the end of the world does not arrive.

It is in the tendency to model itself—which has deep psychological roots—that leads economics down this dead end and makes it a sort of clown science. If economists would just drop the silly image of timeless truths and recognise that in economics we deal with contingent historical events, we would all be better off. But this cannot happen unless the economics profession as a whole reorients its narcissistic image away from trying to search out Holy Grails and towards trying to manage as best they can in a highly complex and changing world. If this were ever achieved the manner in which argument and debate take place within the discipline would completely and utterly change. This would be wonderful but it would also mean that economics would have to stop being an ideology. This would, in turn, mean that economists would have to stop projecting the image that they hold crystal balls and can see the future. That might not only be a blow to their egos but it might, in a strong sense, also diminish the standing that they hold as ideologues in the political and social arena. Whether economics can ever exist as a non-ideology is an open question. Personally, I believe that it can. But, given that I do not pretend to have a crystal ball, only posterity can pass absolute judgement on the matter.

Notes

1. Even if the concert is cancelled, this does not really affect the argument. In such an instance, the cancellation of the concert will have effects of its own. For example, it might lead to disappointment on my part. But this potential for disappointment is already 'built into' the possibilities that I opened up by forming my decision to attend the concert. The disappointment that might occur if the concert is cancelled or the joy that might occur if it turns out to be better than I expected are already potentialities built into the initial decision. Thus, they are not in any coherent sense 'caused' by the initial decision rather they are part of this decision. To understand the process in a mechanical, causal way is to misunderstand how, in a very real sense, human consciousness is structured.

We are, as we shall shortly see, dealing with a remarkably similar process when we study the investment decisions of individuals. The instant that the expected profit rate is estimated by an investor and the investment placed all the possibilities of the future actual profit rate are set in stone. Again, this is not to say the future itself is set in stone—it is not—but all the possibilities for that particular investor are opened up. The act of investing at a given expected profit rate is part and parcel of what the eventual outcome will be. This is precisely how the undertaking of an investment decision is actually experienced in real time.

2. Note that we take the example of savings and investment here because it is the most obvious. But we can extend these insights to all economic relationships. For example, a trade union may try to raise their wages but by doing so they may unwittingly cause firms to raise their prices. Thus while the trade union may have intended to raise their real wages—that is, the amount of purchasing power they commanded—they may not be able to do so due to *unintended consequences* that their actions had on the decisions of other economic agents.
3. In actual fact, this is not why hyperinflation generally occurs, and Rothbard provides no evidence for his statements. Historically, hyperinflations have generally been due to supply shocks as a result of war or natural disasters or they have been due to a currency collapsing on the foreign exchange market due to a country being overburdened with foreign currency denominated loan repayments. See Montier 2013a, b.
4. I really cannot lay too much emphasis on how violent this repression is. I have personally spoken to highly respected Nobel Prize winners in economics who will privately question key methodological assumptions but will then tell you never to quote them on anything they have said. There is a genuine fear in the profession amongst more critical members of disturbing the wrath of the gods. It is really quite a fascinating primitive tribal feature to observe at close proximity.

   I am not fully clear on how it is enforced. But it appears from reading some of the literature that a strong royal 'We' is regularly invoked that seems to bear the spectre of anyone falling outside of this 'We' risking some sort of excommunication. Consider

Krugman's argument against an argument that many Post-Keynesians hold to be correct:

It just seems fundamentally implausible that over stretches of decades balance of payments could be preventing long-term growth ... *We all know* that the difference in growth rates among countries are primarily determined by difference in the rate of growth of total factor productivity, not differences in the rate of growth of employment. (Krugman 1988, p. 12—my emphasis)

Now many Post-Keynesian economists hold that differences in the rate of growth of employment can play a large role in growth divergences. What is more, at the time of writing, Krugman almost certainly knew this as he had co-authored with one of them ten years earlier on trade (Krugman and Taylor 1978). So, the royal 'We' here seems to be something resembling a means of enforcing 'correct' opinions.

References

Denis, A. (2005). The invisible hand of god in Adam Smith. *Research in the History of Economic Thought and Methodology, 23*(1), 1–32.

Keynes, J.M. (1936a). *The general theory of employment, money and interest.* http://www.marxists.org/reference/subject/economics/keynes/general-theory/

Krugman, P. (1988). Differences in income elasticities and trends in real exchange rates. *NBER Working Paper Series No. 2761.*

Krugman, P., & Taylor, L. (1978). Contractionary effects of devaluation. *Journal of International Economics, 8*, 445–456.

Laplace, P. S. (1902). *A philosophical essay on probabilities.* USA: John Wiley & Sons.

Miller, C. (Ed.). (2012). *Erasmus and Luther: The battle over free will.* Indianapolis, IN: Hackett Publishing.

Montier, J. (2013a). Hyperinflation, hysteria and false memories. *GMO White Paper.* http://s3.amazonaws.com/presspublisher-do/upload/567/JM_Hyperinflations_213-1.pdf

Montier, J. (2013b). Hyperinflations, hysteria, and false memories. *GMO White Paper.*

Murphy, B. (2009, March 25). The threat of hyper-depression. *Lew Rockwell.*

Pilkington, P. (2013g, March 6). Hyperinflation! The libertarian fantasy that never occurs. *Naked Capitalism.*

Rothbard, M. (1963). *What has the government done to our money?* Auburn, AL: Mises Institute.

Sartre, J. P. (1957). *Being and nothingness.* USA: Routledge.

Index

W.P. Pilkington, *The Reformation in Economics*,
DOI 10.1007/978-3-319-40757-9

Printed by Printforce, the Netherlands